THE U.S.A. SINCE
1945

S

THE U.S.A. SINCE 1945

AFTER HIROSHIMA

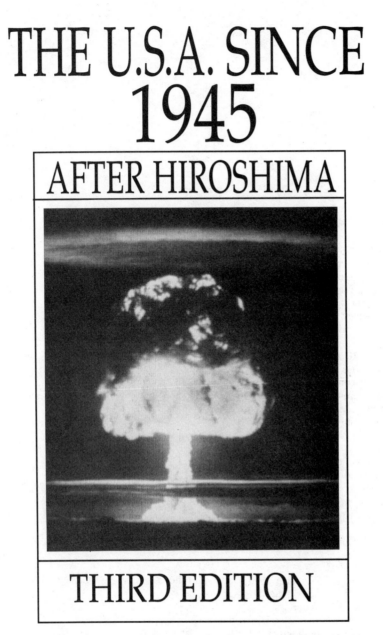

THIRD EDITION

GANLEY/LYONS/ SEWALL

Longman
New York & London

The U.S.A. Since 1945: After Hiroshima

Longman, 10 Bank Street, White Plains, N.Y. 10606

Associated companies:
Longman Group Ltd., London
Longman Cheshire Pty., Melbourne
Longman Paul Pty., Auckland
Copp Clark Pitman, Toronto

Executive editor: Lyn McLean
Production editor: Linda Witzling
Cover design: Kevin C. Kall
Text art: Anne Pompeo
Production supervisor: Richard Bretan

Library of Congress Cataloging-in-Publication Data

Ganley, Albert C.
     The U.S.A. since 1945 : after Hiroshima / Albert C. Ganley, Thomas
T. Lyons, Gilbert T. Sewall.—3rd ed.
        p.   cm.
     Rev. ed. of: After Hiroshima. 1979.
     Includes bibliographical references and index.
     ISBN 0-8013-0934-4
     1. United States—History—1945– I. Lyons, Thomas T.
II. Sewall, Gilbert T. III. Ganley, Albert C. After Hiroshima.
IV. Title.
E741.G38 1992
973.92—dc20   OCT 2 2 1997   92-7161
                                 CIP

5 6 7 8 9 10 -ML- 99 98 97 96

CONTENTS

Preface   *vii*

1 The Cold War in Europe, 1945–1961   1

2 Conflicts in East Asia, 1945–1961   27

3 The United States and the Developing Nations, 1945–1981   51

4 The Vietnam War   86

5 From Détente to Renewal of Cold War   118

6 Adjusting to a Changing International Scene   152

7 Prosperity and Its Limits   179

8 The Supreme Court, Individual Liberty, and Equality   210

9 The Struggle for Racial Justice   249

10 The Presidency: Politics and Power   283

Suggested Reading   *343*

Index   *359*

Illustrations

MAPS

United States Collective Defense Arrangements, 1947–1960   14–15
The Korean War   44
The Caribbean Area   54
The Middle East in 1978   77
Southern Africa in 1980   83
Southeast Asia   93
The Persian Gulf Region   138
Election of 1948   292
Election of 1960   299
Election of 1968   305
Election of 1976   317

TABLES AND GRAPHS

Distribution of U.S. Economic and Technical Aid   52
U.S. Grants and Credits to Developing Nations   53
U.S. Economic Aid To Latin America, Fiscal Years 1949–1974   61
U.S. Aid to Israel and Egypt, 1946–1976   75
U.S. Economic Aid to South Vietnam, Fiscal Years 1954–1965   97
U.S. Commitment to Vietnam, 1960–1972   110
Comparative Military Expenditures   123
Changes in U.S./Soviet Strategic Levels, 1966–1980   125
National Defense Expenditures, 1981–1987   126
U.S. Military Exports to Foreign Nations, 1982–1987   132
Statistics on African Americans and White Americans   278–282
Party Identification, 1937–1991   284
Percentage Change, Annual Rate of Inflation, 1974–1991   322
Annual Unemployment Rate, 1974–1991   323
U.S. Budget Deficits, 1977–1991   323
Interest Rates—Annual Averages, 1974–1991   324
Gross National Product, 1970–1991   324

PREFACE

This third edition of *The U.S.A. Since 1945: After Hiroshima* became a necessity with the dramatic end of the cold war. Whether one cites the U.S.–Soviet INF Treaty of 1987, the destruction of the Berlin Wall in 1989, or the demise of the Soviet Union and the Soviet Communist party in 1991, the authors in January 1990 felt the need to bring the book up to date. This new edition represents a two-year effort. By editing, rewriting, deleting, and adding new material, the authors have brought the post–World War II history of the United States up to the present without adding significantly to the book's length.

The new edition continues to provide students with a narrative history of the United States in the decades following 1945. Rather than a detailed, all-inclusive account of the years from 1945 to 1992, we have written 10 focused, self-contained essays on foreign relations and domestic events. In foreign affairs the narrative tells how the cold war began, developed, ended, and asks, "What now?" The book traces the development of U.S. efforts to secure U.S. interests in a dangerous world of nuclear weapons, ideological conflict, national tensions, and power struggles. The first six chapters describe the evolution of post-1945 U.S. policies in Europe, East Asia, Latin America, the Middle East, Africa, and Southeast Asia. At home the last four chapters focus on economic ups and downs and their social consequences, the Supreme Court's initiatives and retreats in securing individual liberties and promoting equality under law, the long struggle of African Americans and other minorities and women to gain equal rights, and a summary chapter on presidential power and politics.

There is no attempt to get into historiographical debate. We have not adopted any historical school of interpretation or busied ourselves or the readers with a particular theory of history. We recognize our limited time perspective, the elusiveness of objectivity, particularly in writing about such recent events, and the fragmentary documentary record available at this time.

The chapters represent 10 narratives, rich in historical detail, concrete events, and influential personalities. We have made a conscious effort to define terms explicitly and to write clearly. We have tried to avoid vague generalizations and personal biases.

This book is not simplistic. The student will learn not only the meaning, but also the application of concepts such as national security, monetary policy, and affirmative action. Statistics are used to document statements and to provoke reader analysis. The authors believe that the book fills a void left by textbooks, specialized monographs, and journalistic essays.

CHAPTER 1

The Cold War in Europe, 1945–1961

"I believe that it must be the policy of the United States to support free peoples who are resisting attempted subjugation by armed minorities or by outside pressures."

Harry S. Truman, 1947

"For us to think that what the central struggle is about is just Berlin would be a great mistake. They're fighting for New York and Paris when they struggle over Berlin. Therefore, I think we would have to make it cold—and mean it—that we would fight."

John F. Kennedy, 1959

ORIGINS OF THE COLD WAR

Nine days after a B-29 dropped an atomic bomb on Hiroshima a somber Emperor Hirohito in his first radio address to the Japanese people announced the end of World War II. He explained, "Should we continue to fight, it would not only result in an ultimate collapse and obliteration of the Japanese nation, but also it would lead to the total extinction of human civilization." An elated President Harry S. Truman then told the American people that "this is the day when fascism and police government cease in the world."

Neither the despair in Japan nor the optimism in the United States would long endure. Postwar Japan devoted its energies and resources to recovery from the war's devastation, and within three decades became a major world economic power. The United States found itself facing serious disagreements with its wartime ally the Soviet Union. This discord threatened international peace for more than four decades and involved U.S. forces in localized combat in East Asia, Latin America, and the Middle East.

The Disintegration of the Grand Alliance

The wartime marriage of convenience lacked the deep faith and mutual admiration necessary to sustain an enduring close relationship. Sharp disagreements over basic principles had so poisoned the association that only deep changes in attitudes could prevent a disastrous quarrel. Such different values and aspirations

1

divided the United States and the Soviet Union that only exceptional patience and willingness to compromise could maintain good will and cooperation.

Badly mangled by the war, the Soviet Union had suffered 15 million dead, 9 percent of its prewar population, and sustained heavy losses in its European industrial plant and agricultural resources. Soviet national interest demanded guaranteed military protection against any repetition of invasion from Western Europe. Centuries old dreams—control of the Turkish Straits, the outlet for the Black Sea, and the union of all Slavs under Russian leadership—likewise remained prime objectives of the Kremlin. In addition, the rebuilding of a wartorn country demanded immediate attention, and as early as January 1945 prompted the Soviets to ask the United States for a $6 billion loan for postwar reconstruction. In pursuing these national interests, Stalin and his associates intended to act according to Marxist–Leninist principles while keeping the leadership of the communist world in Moscow. Communists believed that elimination of economic classes and establishment of a society of social equals were more important than expansion of the liberty of the individual. The good of the society, according to Communists, took precedence over individual freedom to acquire property, to have free speech, and to vote for one's own candidate. According to Marx, capitalism would inevitably fail, and communism would triumph.

By contrast, the United States had lost 400,000 dead, or less than .03 percent of its population, and its great industrial and agricultural productivity was undamaged by the war. U.S. leaders saw the national interest best served by a restoration of a free Europe as it existed before Hitler, with fascism eradicated, democracy installed, and no one power dominant. Some hard-learned lessons of the past seemed obvious. The Munich error of appeasing the aggressor, who threatened to use force, must be avoided whatever the cost. World trade, on which U.S. prosperity and security depended, must be restored by rebuilding disrupted capitalist economies of Europe and Asia. Contrary to Communists, Americans valued human liberty above economic security and equality. Individual freedom to acquire and use property had first priority, even if it led to inequality of living conditions. Communist denial of the existence of God and of the right to private property, Stalin's bloody purges of rivals and dissidents, his 1939 nonaggression pact with Hitler followed by Soviet seizure of Polish territory, an aggressive war against Finland, and the annexation of Latvia, Estonia, and Lithuania had convinced most Americans of the wickedness of the Soviet system.

Americans looked at the Soviet Union through a lens blurred by two images—one, an aggressive nation state suppressing human freedom while expanding its power—the other, an international communist conspiracy, with headquarters in Moscow, spreading revolutionary doctrine throughout the world. Predictably, confusion about the appropriate response to these threats divided

Americans. A few assumed that concern for security against attack justified Soviet expansion into Eastern Europe. Viewing the United States' atomic monopoly as inciting the Soviet Union to a "defensive aggressiveness," holders of this position opposed any use of the bomb as a bargaining weapon. Some even believed it would be wise to offer the Soviet Union full partnership in atomic development because scientists had warned that only a short time would elapse before the Soviets built a bomb of their own. Strongly opposed to any deal whatsoever with the Communists, a small minority even toyed with the idea of preventive war while the United States still held the atomic monopoly. But, in general, Americans desired peace without making any concessions to the Soviets. Suspicious of schemes for international control of atomic energy without foolproof safeguards and worried about Soviet expansion, most Americans wanted their government to maintain a firm anticommunist stance.

In this inauspicious climate regular meetings of the foreign ministers of the big powers became bogged down. The U.S. monopoly of the atom bomb failed to give James F. Byrnes, the new secretary of state, the leverage in negotiations so confidently expected. In November U.S. Ambassador to the Soviet Union W. Averell Harriman wrote to Byrnes warning that as a result of the bomb "the Russian people have been aroused to feel that they must again face an antagonistic world; American imperialism is included as a threat to Russia." Publicly stating that the bomb would frighten only the "weakwilled," Stalin manifested little interest in a U.S. plan for international control of atomic energy. Failure of Byrnes to obtain acceptable agreements at the Moscow meeting of foreign ministers in December 1945 increased the pressures on Truman "to get tough with Russia." A disappointed president concluded that "unless Russia is faced with an iron fist and strong language another war is in the making. Only one language do they understand—how many divisions have you?" On this low note the president said to Byrnes, "I'm tired of babying the Soviets." In December 1945, to insure that the nation's military forces functioned most effectively, Truman asked Congress to unite the services into a single defense department.

The Iranian Crisis, 1946

As the split in Europe widened, a new trouble spot—Iran—enlivened the first meeting of the United Nations General Assembly and Security Council in London in January 1946. The Soviet Union had failed to withdraw its 30,000 troops from Iran after the war as promised. According to Iran, these Soviet forces, originally sent to protect Lend–Lease supply lines, were aiding a communist-inspired separatist movement in the province of Azerbaijan. The Iranian government, backed by the United States and Great Britain, lodged a complaint against the "interference of the Soviet Union . . . in the internal affairs of Iran." Functioning as a world forum, the United Nations so publicized Soviet misconduct toward Iran that the Soviet Union evacuated all Red Army troops by May. The lesson seemed clear—take a strong stand, marshall world opinion, and the Soviets will back down.

The Iron Curtain

In Germany the problem defied such a simple solution. The first winter after the war revealed disastrous consequences of the division of Germany into four zones. Suffering from a food shortage in their zones, the British and Americans had to import food, an expense that an insolvent Britain could hardly afford. Interested only in reparations from the western zone, the Soviets refused to export any surplus food produced in their zone. To make matters even worse, the western zones would lose machinery and tools necessary to develop self-sufficiency if they allowed the Soviets to obtain reparations demanded.

Winston Churchill visited the United States in early March 1946 as a private citizen, and in a speech made in Fulton, Missouri, he described a disturbing scene:

> From Stettin in the Baltic to Trieste in the Adriatic an iron curtain has descended across the Continent. . . . The Communist parties, which were very small in all these eastern states of Europe, have been raised to preeminence and power far beyond their numbers and are seeking everywhere to obtain totalitarian control.

The phrase "Iron Curtain" immediately crept into the vocabulary of the West, amidst growing public disillusionment with the effort to negotiate with the Soviet Union. A Gallup poll in March revealed that 60 percent felt that the United States was being "too soft" in its policy toward the Soviets. A majority of Americans also believed that the Soviet Union was engaged in hostilities as threatening as armed conflict. Although no fighting had taken place, a deadly cold war had shattered dreams of a world without international tensions.

In the early spring of 1946 Moscow's flat rejection of Byrnes's proposed 25-year Big Four Treaty to keep Germany disarmed, a remarkable departure from traditional U.S. policy of nonentangling alliances, brought into sharp focus the deep disagreement over Germany. When the Soviets showed no inclination to move toward economic integration, Washington began discussions with London that culminated in December with an agreement to combine their zones for economic administration.

Demobilization

Despite the danger signals emanating from Europe, the American public continued to demand a return to the conveniences and bounty of peacetime. A "bring the boys home" refrain reached a climax during 1946 that no candidate for national office could ignore. That the Soviets continued to keep over 5 million men under arms mattered less to most Americans than the prompt return of their men to private life once World War II ended. By the end of 1946 the U.S. military force in Europe was reduced from over 3 million men to just under 400,000.

Bipartisanship

But no serious domestic challenge to the administration's foreign policy developed. When Henry A. Wallace, Truman's predecessor as vice-president and now a holdover from Roosevelt's cabinet as secretary of commerce, attacked the "get tough with the Soviets" approach, the president fired him. Truman also carefully emulated Franklin D. Roosevelt's tactic of blunting partisanship by involving key Republicans, notably Senator Arthur H. Vandenberg (R., Mich.) and foreign affairs expert John Foster Dulles, in the formulation and execution of policy. Such practical political expedients helped to stop politics "at the water's edge" on several occasions, and avoided the tragic error made by President Wilson in failing to consult opposition leaders about the Treaty of Versailles. Labeled "bipartisan" by the press, this nonpartisan policy attracted wide approval.

However, some prominent Republicans, notably Senator Robert A. Taft of Ohio, refused to endorse the concept of a bipartisan foreign policy, especially because they disagreed with its premise that foreign policy was above politics. Claiming the responsibility of the party out of power to alert the public to policy decisions that might jeopardize the nation's interests, Taft insisted on retaining his freedom to criticize administration policy when he disagreed with it. He warned that the limitation of dissent in foreign policy could promote tyranny at home and abroad.

DEVELOPMENT OF CONTAINMENT POLICY

The Truman Doctrine, 1947

Soon after the end of the war, the Soviets began to exert heavy pressure on the Turks to place the Dardanelles and Bosporous under joint Turkish–Soviet defense. Late in 1946 Edwin G. Wilson, U.S. ambassador to Turkey, reported that "Turkey will not be able to maintain indefinitely a defensive posture against the Soviet Union."

Simultaneously, a serious situation developed in Greece. British efforts to establish political stability and to promote economic recovery were undermined by intense hostility between conservative royalists in power and communist-dominated groups, who waged guerrilla war from bases in the northern hills. Finding it increasingly difficult to maintain a garrison of 40,000 men in Greece, the British sounded out U.S. officials about furnishing help to the Greek government.

In February 1947 the U.S. ambassador to Greece alerted the State Department to rumors that Britain was considering withdrawal of its forces because of its own precarious financial condition. Shortly thereafter, the U.S. representative on a United Nations Commission of Investigation in Greece advanced the concept, subsequently called the "domino theory," when he asked: "(1) If Greece goes through our default, have we released forces in Azerbaijan and Turkey? (2) If that force is released, where does it stop?" When the British government officially notified the United States that it would have to pull out of Greece by April 1, 1947, a committee of experts under the leadership of General George C. Marshall, the new secretary of state, recommended immediate aid to Greece and Turkey to prevent the entire region from falling under Soviet control.

Effective action by the Truman administration required the support of an unfriendly, Republican controlled Congress. True to campaign promises, the Republicans proposed both deep cuts in the budget to bring it into balance and more conservative fiscal policies so that taxes could be cut 20 percent. Sharp disagreements with the president over these domestic programs threatened to affect foreign policies.

Banking on the appeal of nonpartisanship in foreign policy, Truman invited a group of congressional leaders of both parties to the White House for a briefing on the Greek crisis. After hearing Under Secretary of State Dean Acheson's convincing description of the threat, Vandenberg exclaimed: "Mr. President, if you say that to Congress and the country, I will support you and, I believe that most of its members will do the same." The Michigan senator understood full well the American people's intolerance of ambiguity. Before making sacrifices, they needed to see themselves arrayed against a wicked enemy.

Two weeks later on March 12, 1947, Truman addressed Congress in a speech described as "the opening gun in a campaign to bring people up to the realization that the war isn't over by any means." Taking Vandenberg's advice, the president painted a scene designed, according to one aide, "to scare hell out of the country." Carefully refraining from direct charges against the Soviet Union, Truman said, "Greece must have assistance if it is to become a self-supporting and self-respecting democracy. . . . As in the case of Greece, if Turkey is to have the assistance it needs, the United States must supply it." Then describing a much bigger, worldwide struggle, he warned, "We shall not realize our objectives, however, unless we are willing to help free peoples to maintain their free institutions and their national integrity against aggressive movements that seek to impose upon them totalitarian regimes." Employing the "domino theory" as his basic premise, the president concluded, "If Greece should fall under the control of an armed minority, the effect upon its neighbor Turkey would be immediate and serious. Confusion and disorder might well spread throughout the entire Middle East."

Truman asked Congress to appropriate $400 million through June 1948 to assist Greece and Turkey in their hour of need. His proposal, soon labeled the Truman Doctrine, assumed that communism, always seeking to expand, fed on despair and discord, and that economic and military aid could enable a regime, resisting communist penetration, to satisfy the needs and desires of its people.

Not all Americans agreed. Some critics denounced Truman for bypassing the United Nations, whereas others protested that the president's request was imperialistic and would inevitably involve the United States in a war. A few disliked the idea of bolstering corrupt and undemocratic regimes in Greece and Turkey. And some thought that "there was a little too much flamboyant anti-communism in the speech."

But Truman had another ace to play. To further dramatize the case against the communist danger, later in March the president issued a loyalty order to root out of government jobs all security risks. Public opinion swung behind the president, and within two months, Congress, by large margins, appropriated funds to aid Greece and Turkey.

The Truman Doctrine marked both a beginning and an end in U.S. foreign policy. While abandoning the nation's historic policy of noninvolvement in Europe's internal affairs, the doctrine initiated an unprecedented commitment of U.S. resources to aid other nations to resist communism. Having taken this first plunge, the United States would find it difficult to resist requests for similar ventures.

The Marshall Plan

During the debate over the Truman Doctrine, an economic crisis in Western Europe worried U.S. leaders. Economic activity was slowed by inflation, acute shortages of food, fuel, and raw materials, as well as by strikes. French opposition to increased German industrialization and to centralized administration of German economic enterprise frustrated British and U.S. efforts to restore normal economic activity. Without German production of industrial goods for export, the economic recovery of Europe faced long delays. A State Department group under George F. Kennan worked all spring to develop a program satisfactory to the United States, while requiring vigorous efforts by the Europeans themselves. Such a design, it was hoped, would avoid a storm of protest against an "American give-away."

At Harvard's commencement on June 5, 1947, Secretary of State Marshall, in soft, almost inaudible tones, outlined what Europe and the United States might do together to save the former from economic collapse. He explained:

> The truth of the matter is that Europe's requirements for the next three or four years of foreign food and other essential products—principally from America—are so much greater than her present ability to pay that she must have substantial help or face economic, social and political deterioration of a very grave character. . . .
> Our policy is directed not against any country or doctrine but against hunger, poverty, desperation and chaos. . . . The initiative, I think must come from Europe.

If further division of Europe occurred, Marshall contended, the Soviets would have to bear the responsibility, for he offered the Kremlin the opportunity to become an integral part of the European economic community. Almost immediately a favorable press identified the new U.S. proposal as the Marshall Plan.

Within two weeks the British and French foreign ministers met with Molotov to discuss how Europeans might cooperate in a recovery plan. Although the Soviet foreign minister urged the British and French to reject the U.S. proposal as interference in their internal affairs, the latter invited 22 European nations, including the Communist bloc, to a July meeting. When Czechoslovakia accepted, Moscow pressured the Czechs to withdraw. But by September 16 European nations had set up a Committee for European Economic Cooperation (CEEC) that requested $590 million in aid from the United States for the next six months.

· After consultation with leaders of both parties, Truman called Congress into special session and asked for that amount of emergency foreign aid through March 1948 to help Europeans survive the coming winter. Although the *New York Daily Mirror* called economic aid to Europe "the greatest fool's gamble ever proposed with a straight face to an intelligent nation," the U.S. press generally portrayed a disturbing picture of the communist threat and supported the Marshall Plan.

On September 27, 1947, the very day when the CEEC sent to Washington its report on the Marshall Plan, representatives of communist parties meeting in Poland founded the Cominform (Communist Information Bureau) "to meet the aggressive and frankly expansionist course to which American imperialism had committed itself since the end of World War II." Ironically, these Soviet words and actions helped to push an interim foreign aid bill through Congress by the end of the year.

The Mr. X Article

In the midst of the debate over the Marshall Plan, an article in *Foreign Affairs* directed wide attention to the assumptions underlying U.S. policy. Published in July over the signature "Mr. X," George Kennan's essay gave birth to the concept of "containment" as the cardinal principle of U.S. foreign policy. Kennan argued that

> it will be clearly seen that the Soviet pressure against the free institutions of the western world is something that can be contained by the alert and vigilant application of counter-force at a series of constantly shifting geographical and political points, corresponding to the shifts and maneuvers of Soviet policy.

Although Kennan later protested that he did not mean an inflexible policy of military resistance either to Soviet expansion or to seizure of power by national communist parties, his widely praised essay was so interpreted by many U.S. political and military leaders.

Reorganization of National Defense

Heightened national concern over international developments persuaded Congress to respond to Truman's request, first made in October 1945, to modernize the nation's defense establishment by passing a National Security Act in July 1947. This law set up a single Department of Defense and established the Joint Chiefs of Staff (JCS) and a National Security Council (NSC) to advise the president. In addition, it created a Central Intelligence Agency (CIA) under a director appointed by the president. This consolidation of defense and intelligence gathering under the executive branch had many unforeseen consequences.

The Debate over Foreign Aid

Despite the economic implications of containment, Truman was eager to maintain the balanced budget deemed vital in the fight against inflation. Accordingly he set an arbitrary ceiling for fiscal 1948–1949 on arms expenditures well below that advocated by the Defense Department. Yet at the same time he asked Congress for $17 billion in foreign aid over four years, including $6.8 billion to cover the first 15 months (to June 30, 1949) of the European Recovery Program (ERP). Each proposal was unpopular in certain quarters, but the foreign aid program attracted the sharpest attack.

A strange array of opponents condemned the $17 billion request. On the Left, Henry Wallace and pro-Soviet sympathizers denounced the Marshall Plan and ERP as a blatant scheme to extend U.S. economic domination over Europe. On the Right, Senator Taft criticized ERP as "a global W.P.A. . . . . pouring money down a rat-hole." Economy-minded members of Congress pointed out that already in the first two years of peace the United States had funneled about $11 billion into the reconstruction of Europe. Could the nation afford, they asked, to give much more aid without causing bankruptcy, higher taxes, and inflation?

The size of the request astonished even the administration's strongest supporters. According to Sam Rayburn (D., Tex.), House minority leader, "It will bust the country," but Truman was soon able to win him over. Diverse economic groups, such as important farm and labor organizations and the National Association of Manufacturers, lined up in support of the Marshall Plan. The shock of a communist minority seizing control of the democratic government in Czechoslovakia in February 1948 helped to sway both Houses of Congress in March 1948 into a approval of an authorization of $5.3 billion for the first 12 months.

Although a minority led by Taft attempted each year to cut the ERP grant, between April 3, 1948, and June 30, 1952, Congress appropriated $13 billion in foreign aid, none of it of a military nature prior to June 1950. By helping the West Europeans, Americans also helped themselves. The dramatic European recovery process stimulated the U.S. economy and benefited worker, farmer, and investor. The Marshall Plan appeared to be a master stroke.

The Berlin Crisis of 1948–1949

The cold war's division of Europe into East and West caused greatest tension in Germany and Austria where families, as well as nation and capital city, were cut in two. Berlin, over 100 miles inside the Soviet zone of Germany, and Vienna, 45 miles inside the Soviet zone of Austria, presented difficult military and economic problems for the Western powers. With strong military forces close at hand, the Soviets could easily sever access and take over either city or both at any time. Berlin served as a gap in the Iron Curtain through which East Germans could see the attractions of a free society and escape into it, so the temptation to the Kremlin to close that breach was great.

Late in March 1948 the Soviets withdrew their representative from the Allied Control Council in Berlin, and began to delay train and truck convoys to West Berlin at border points with allegations that they did not conform to agreed on regulations. At the same time the Communists procrastinated in establishing a uniform German currency, desired by the United States to curb inflation caused by currency printed in the Soviet zone. General Lucius Clay, commander of U.S. forces in Europe, described the atmosphere as "exceedingly grave." When Moscow demanded more direct control of U.S. military train service through the Soviet zone into Berlin, Clay ordered soldier guards on the trains "to prevent Soviet military from entering U. S. passenger trains but not to shoot unless fired upon." A concerned Marshall warned, "If we mean . . . to hold Europe against communism, we must not budge."

Throughout the spring, tension over Berlin mounted. On June 1, the three Western powers announced plans to convene a constituent assembly, elected by

Germans, before September 1, 1948 to draft a federal democratic constitution for Germany. A Soviet warning that the policy of the West was "pregnant with such consequences as can suit only all kinds of instigators of a new war" was ignored. On June 18 Clay informed Moscow of the introduction of a new currency for the western zones of occupation, excluding Berlin, to take effect in two days.

Denouncing the "illegal new western currency," the Soviets suspended all interzonal passenger traffic and incoming traffic on all roads, including pedestrian entry into the Soviet zone. Interdiction of land traffic into Berlin left western officials with a difficult decision that would test their firmness and patience. In a letter to his daughter, Truman said, "We are faced with exactly the same situation with which Britain and France were faced in 1938–39 with Hitler." U.S. officials emphasized that they were in Berlin by right and intended to stay. There would be no "Munich appeasement."

As the crisis worsened, the administration found an ingenious solution—go by air until the land routes were reopened. Clay quickly organized air lifts to ferry necessary supplies into Berlin. After sending a sharp warning to Moscow by dispatching to Britain and Germany two squadrons of B-29 bombers, the only aircraft capable of delivering an atomic bomb, Truman confided in his diary, "I do not pass the buck, nor do I alibi out of any decision I make." If the Soviets played tough, the United States could more than match them.

A July Gallup poll indicated that 80 percent of those interviewed agreed that the United States and its allies should stay in Berlin even if it meant war. Facing a difficult uphill political campaign for re-election, the president had correctly gauged public opinion. The Soviet blockade of Berlin made it very difficult for Republicans to wage an all-out attack on the containment policy without appearing disloyal.

For 321 days a great battle of wills continued as the Soviets blockaded Berlin via land, while on an around-the-clock schedule the United States airlifted the supplies necessary for sustaining life in the German capital. U.S. and British planes made over 270,000 flights and carried nearly 2.5 million tons of cargo. In Truman's words, "Berlin had become a symbol of America's—and the West's—dedication to the cause of freedom."

Complicating the Kremlin's task in the Berlin crisis was the appearance of internal dissension in the communist camp—the defiance of Marshall Tito, communist leader of Yugoslavia. Tito's refusal to sacrifice his nation's independence to the interests of the Soviet Union caused a break between the two nations in June 1948 at the beginning of the Berlin showdown. Although this crack in the monolithic image that the Soviets wished to present to the outside world opened infinite possibilities for exploitation by the West, few Western leaders understood that a nation with a communist government could act independently or as a neutral in the East–West struggle. This lack of perception would plague U.S. policy-making for two decades.

Clearly losing the propaganda war and failing to dislodge the West from Berlin, the Kremlin opened secret negotiations that resulted in the lifting of the blockade in May 1949. Steadfast determination had produced success for the United States without a "hot war." Again the lesson seemed clear—firm resistance would foil aggressors.

THE DEFENSE OF WESTERN EUROPE

Early in 1948 Britain, France, and the Benelux nations took preliminary steps toward a united defense in Western Europe by signing the Brussels Pact, a 50-year treaty pledging unprecedented economic and military cooperation for their collective defense. Truman responded, "I am sure that the determination of the free countries of Europe to protect themselves will be matched by an equal determination on our part to help them do so."

The Vandenberg Resolution

Conditions favored the administration. Any faith in the effectiveness of the United Nations in promoting peace and justice had been seriously weakened by the Soviet Union's frequent use of the veto to paralyze the security council. Consolidation of communist power in Czechoslovakia and the ominous rumblings in Berlin prompted scare headlines in the U.S. press that nourished strong anti-Soviet feelings. Truman's request in March 1948 for $3 billion in addition to the $11 billion military budget already proposed for the next fiscal year spotlighted the need for U.S. strength in a hostile world. A Gallup poll in the spring of 1948, showing 65 percent of the U.S. people in favor of a Western alliance, indicated public readiness for action by Washington.

In this setting Vandenberg introduced in the Senate in May 1948 a resolution advising the president, in accordance with Article 51 of the Charter of the United Nations, to seek the "association of the United States by constitutional process with such regional and other collective arrangements as are based on continuous and effective self-help and mutual aid, and as affect its national security." By including the phrase "by constitutional process," a reference to the power of Congress to declare war, Vandenberg blunted the opposition of foes of an alliance requiring the nation to fight in support of an ally. On June 11, 1948, the eve of the Berlin blockade, after only eight hours of debate the Senate approved the Vandenberg Resolution, 64 to 6. But further action on a collective security treaty was delayed until after the 1948 election.

The North Atlantic Treaty

After winning the 1948 presidential election and sweeping in a Democratic Congress, Truman pledged in his inaugural address "to strengthen freedom-loving nations against the dangers of aggression" by negotiating "a joint agreement designed to strengthen the security of the North Atlantic area." To give teeth to this pact he offered "military advice and equipment to free nations which will cooperate with us in the maintenance of peace and security." Writing the precise language of a North Atlantic Treaty became the task of Truman's new secretary of state, Dean Acheson, who replaced the ill Marshall. Acheson, long convinced that it was futile to negotiate with the Soviets, believed in making the West so unified, strong, and prosperous that Moscow would have no choice but to cease its aggressive actions. The pact creating the North Atlantic Treaty Organization (NATO) was ready for the 12 participating nations early in April 1949. The powers pledged that they "by means of continuous and effective self-help and mutual aid, will maintain and develop their individual and collective capacity to resist armed attack." In addition, they agreed "that an armed attack against one or more of them in Europe or North America shall be considered an attack against them all."

Although public opinion polls throughout the spring of 1949 indicated strong public support for ratification of the North Atlantic Treaty, critics rushed to the attack. Henry Wallace asked, "Supposing the Soviets had military bases on the Mexican border? The Canadian border? On Cuba? Could a treaty which put guns in our faces be called a pact of peace?" And in 10 days of Senate debate in July, diehard opponents of the treaty focused on the military obligations of the United States as well as the treaty's possible dangerous impact on the Soviet Union. Taft deplored the U.S. tendency "to assume that we are a kind of demigod and Santa Claus to solve the problems of the world." He defended his intention to vote against the treaty on the ground that "the pact carries with it an obligation to assist in arming at our expense, the nations of western Europe, because with that obligation . . . it will promote war in the world rather than peace."

The Ohio senator attracted few adherents in either party, as senators tended to be more impressed by the polls, and by such arguments as that of Senator Tom Connally (D., Tex.): "The Atlantic Pact is but the logical extension of the principle of the Monroe Doctrine." After voting down an amendment barring arms aid, the Senate ratified the treaty by 82 to 13, 11 of the negative votes being Republican. On July 25, 1949, Truman signed the North Atlantic Treaty, the first military pact between the United States and a European nation since the 1778 alliance with France came to an end in 1800.

Proponents of the pact proclaimed that the United States and its allies now had "the shield" to make it less likely that the United States would ever have to

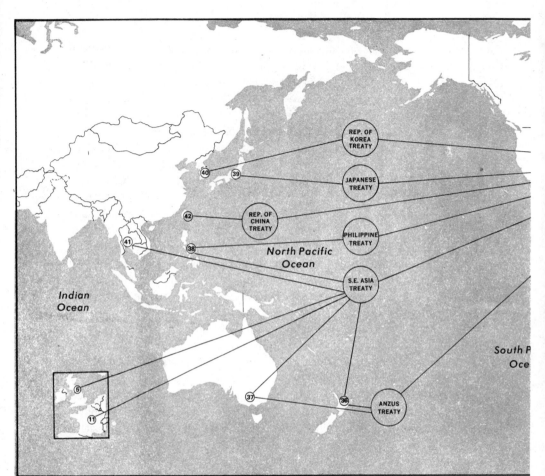

NORTH ATLANTIC TREATY (15 NATIONS)

A treaty signed April 4, 1949, by which "the Parties agree that an armed attack against one or more of them in Europe or North America shall be considered an attack against them all; and . . . each of them . . . will assist the . . . attacked by taking forthwith, individually and in concert with the other Parties, such action as it deems necessary, including the use of armed force . . ."

1 UNITED STATES	9 LUXEMBOURG
2 CANADA	10 PORTUGAL
3 ICELAND	11 FRANCE
4 NORWAY	12 ITALY
5 UNITED KINGDOM	13 GREECE
6 NETHERLANDS	14 TURKEY
7 DENMARK	15 FEDERAL REPUBLIC OF GERMANY
8 BELGIUM	

ANZUS (Australia — New Zealand—United States) TREATY (3 NATIONS)

A treaty signed September 1, 1951, whereby each of the parties "recognizes that an armed attack in the Pacific Area on any of the Parties would be dangerous to its own peace and safety and declares that it would act to meet the common danger in accordance with its constitutional processes."

1 UNITED STATES
36 NEW ZEALAND
37 AUSTRALIA

PHILIPPINE TREATY (BILATERAL)

A treaty signed August 30, 1951, by which the parties recognize "that an armed attack in the Pacific Area on either of the Parties would be dangerous to its own peace and safety" and each party agrees that it will act "to meet the common dangers in accordance with its constitutional processes."

1 UNITED STATES
38 PHILIPPINES

SOUTHEAST ASIA TREATY (7 NATIONS)

A treaty signed September 8, 1954, whereby each party "recognizes that aggression by means of armed attack in the treaty area against any of the Parties . . . would endanger its own peace and safety" and each will "in that event act to meet the common danger in accordance with its constitutional processes."

1 UNITED STATES
5 UNITED KINGDOM
11 FRANCE
36 NEW ZEALAND
37 AUSTRALIA
38 PHILIPPINES
41 THAILAND

United States Collective Defense Arrangements, 1947–1960

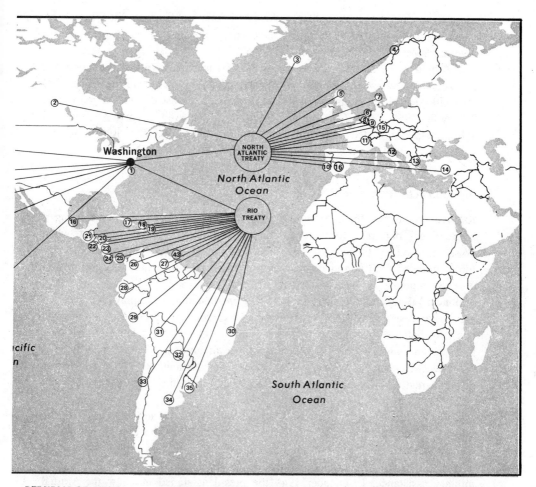

Washington

NORTH ATLANTIC TREATY

North Atlantic Ocean

RIO TREATY

South Atlantic Ocean

Pacific

REPUBLIC OF CHINA TREATY (BILATERAL)

A treaty signed December 2, 1954, whereby each of the parties "recognizes that an armed attack in the West Pacific Area directed against the territories of either of the Parties would be dangerous to its own peace and safety . . ." and that each "would act to meet the common danger in accordance with its constitutional processes." The territory of the Republic of China is defined as "Taiwan (Formosa) and the Pescadores."

1 UNITED STATES
42 REPUBLIC OF CHINA (FORMOSA)

JAPANESE TREATY (BILATERAL)

A treaty signed January 19, 1960, whereby each party "recognizes that an armed attack against either Party in the territories under the administration of Japan would be dangerous to its own peace and safety and declares that it would act to meet the common danger in accordance with its constitutional provisions and processes." The treaty replaced the security treaty signed September 8, 1951.

1 UNITED STATES
39 JAPAN

REPUBLIC OF KOREA TREATY (BILATERAL)

A treaty signed October 1, 1953, whereby each party "recognizes that an armed attack in the Pacific area on either of the Parties . . . would be dangerous to its own peace and safety" and that each Party "would act to meet the common danger in accordance with its constitutional processes."

1 UNITED STATES
40 REPUBLIC OF KOREA

RIO TREATY (22 NATIONS)

A treaty signed September 2, 1947, which provides that an armed attack against any American State "shall be considered as an attack against all the American States and . . . each one . . . undertakes to assist in meeting the attack . . ."

1 UNITED STATES	26 COLOMBIA
16 MEXICO	27 VENEZUELA
17 CUBA	28 ECUADOR
18 HAITI	29 PERU
19 DOMINICAN REPUBLIC	30 BRAZIL
20 HONDURAS	31 BOLIVIA
21 GUATEMALA	32 PARAGUAY
22 EL SALVADOR	33 CHILE
23 NICARAGUA	34 ARGENTINA
24 COSTA RICA	35 URUGUAY
25 PANAMA	43 TRINIDAD AND TOBAGO

use "its sword"—the atom bomb. An indifferent public took little notice. A national poll taken two years later showed only one third of the people able to give a reasonably correct description of NATO.

Although the North Atlantic Treaty had no termination date, it contained a provision for review at the end of 10 years and an option permitting withdrawal after 20 years. Three non-Atlantic nations were admitted later—Greece and Turkey in 1952, West Germany in 1955—and one Atlantic nation—Spain in 1982. Despite repeated communist efforts to weaken NATO, it long remained the keystone of U.S. policy in Europe. (See Map, pp. 14–15.)

A Deterrent Force in Europe

Ratification of the North Atlantic Treaty was only the first step in creating a conventional deterrent force to discourage aggression in Europe. But when Washington turned to the next step—the building of a strong European military force equipped with non-nuclear weapons—it became clear that a large infusion of U.S. military aid was necessary. Truman's request in mid-1949 for $1.45 billion in military aid to strengthen NATO encountered stiff opposition in Congress. For fiscal 1949–1950 Congress had exceeded the president's budget request for defense by appropriating $15.9 billion, the largest defense budget ever in peacetime, and by providing for 70 combat air groups, 15 more than Truman requested. But giving the president money for arming other nations was a different matter, and opponents fought for a new measure with less money and with limits on the president's authority.

Once again events outside the United States aided the administration. In the midst of the debate Truman dropped a bombshell with the cryptic announcement: "We have evidence that within recent weeks an atomic explosion occurred in the U.S.S.R." The House responded by accepting the Senate version of military assistance. In October 1949 the president signed into law the Mutual Defense Assistance Act authorizing $1.13 billion in aid to NATO nations. The latter soon agreed on a strategy based on a "balanced force" to which each power would contribute its share "in the light of its geographic position, economic capability, and population." As the U.S. share, Truman assigned two U.S. divisions in Europe to NATO—hostages, in effect, to prove the nation's good will.

NSC No. 68

The Soviet Union's development of an atom bomb prompted Truman late in 1949 to order the National Security Council (NSC), created two years earlier to advise the president, to devise a plan for guaranteeing the security of the United States. The secret NSC-68 claimed that "the Soviet Union is developing the military capacity to support its design for world domination." Assuming that U.S. goals could not be achieved by negotiating with the Soviets, NSC-68 recommended a "bold and massive program of rebuilding the West's defensive potential to surpass that of the Soviet world, and of meeting each fresh challenge promptly and unequivocally." This comprehensive statement of strategy, emphasizing that "security must henceforth become the dominant element in the national budget" would long influence U.S. policies. For decades the nation would confront each communist threat with the counterthreat of military force.

Nuclear Superiority

The loss of nuclear monopoly rekindled the debate about whether to initiate, early in 1950, a crash program to build a super weapon—a hydrogen bomb—to regain nuclear superiority. Every scientist on the Advisory Committee to the Atomic Energy Commission counseled that such a project "might weaken rather than strengthen the position of the United States" by encouraging an unlimited race in the development of nuclear weapons of mass destruction. Advocates of this view pointed out that every congressional increase in spending for arms merely resulted in a Soviet response to match or exceed it. This cycle offered no pleasant ending—bankruptcy or annihilation.

Proponents of the hydrogen bomb weighed in with strong counterarguments. The Pentagon told Truman that the Soviets, unless deterred by greater U.S. destructive power, might employ their nuclear capability to achieve their objectives. Acheson, hawkish as usual, warned that "we are in a situation where we could lose without firing a shot." The American people, 81 percent of whom believed, according to a 1950 Gallup poll, that the Soviet Union was trying to become the ruling power of the world, demanded a "military posture" second to no one.

Small wonder then that Truman gave a green light to the project that in November 1952 resulted in the detonation of the first hydrogen bomb. About 700 times more powerful than the atom bomb dropped on Hiroshima, the H-bomb weighed about 65 tons, too heavy for any plane to carry. As the nation applauded, an awed president wrote to his daughter: "So powerful was the explosion that an entire island was blown away and a large crater left in the coral."

McCarthyism

In the 1950 congressional election campaigns political considerations loomed large in the debate over foreign policy. With Senator Vandenberg silenced by illness, new Republican voices revealed restiveness with bipartisanship. They viewed the communist triumph in China, the outbreak of war in Korea (see

Chapter 2) in June, and the perjury conviction of Alger Hiss (see p. 36) as evidence of the incompetence of Democratic party leaders. In February 1950 Senator Joseph McCarthy (R., Wis.) claimed to have a list of 205 names "made known to the Secretary of State as being members of the Communist Party and who nevertheless are still working and shaping policy in the State Department." Although a special Senate subcommittee headed by Senator Millard Tydings (D., Md.) accused McCarthy of "a fraud and a hoax," not a single Republican voted for the subcommittee's final report. Congress responded to the growing turmoil generated by McCarthy and his supporters by enacting over Truman's veto the McCarran Internal Security Act in September. It required communist organizations and their members to register with the attorney-general, allowed the deportation of aliens who had been Communists, and barred members of communist organizations from holding federal appointive office.

The Great Debate

Some Republican leaders, bolstered by impressive gains in the 1950 elections, criticized not only the abandonment of traditional noninvolvement in Europe but also the "unconstitutional extension of Presidential power in military and economic aid programs." Seventy-six-year-old ex-President Hoover denounced the sending of "another man or another dollar" to nations of Western Europe until they themselves had "organized and equipped combat divisions of such large numbers as would erect a sure dam against the red flood." Basing his faith in a "Fortress America," Hoover urged overwhelming U.S. air and sea power "to preserve for the world this Western Hemisphere Gibraltar of civilization." Taft, hopeful of winning the Republican presidential nomination in 1952, seized the chance to argue that it was ill-conceived to fight communism "on the vast land areas of the continent of Europe or on the continent of Asia, where we are at the greatest possible disadvantage."

In defense of the administration's position, Acheson ascribed the threat to Western Europe as "singularly like that which Islam had posed centuries before, with its combination of ideological zeal and fighting power." He also upheld Truman's constitutional right to deploy U.S. troops as he thought necessary for national security. To administration officials the Hoover–Taft position appeared dangerously akin to the foolish isolationism of the 1920s and 1930s.

The public backed the administration. A Gallup poll taken in the midst of the "great debate" indicated that almost half of the people were even "willing to risk their lives to keep the Russians from taking over Western Europe." And despite efforts by Republican spokespersons to direct attention to Asia, Americans believed that it was more important for the United States to stop the Soviet Union in Europe. In April 1952 the Senate approved the dispatch of the four divisions to Europe, while implying no more without congressional approval.

Thereby the Truman–Acheson grand design of collective security in Europe was completed, except for the establishment of a European Defense Community that included a rearmed West German Republic. Truman's decision not to seek another term left that task to a new president.

A New Look

In an article in *Life* published before the 1952 Republican national convention, John Foster Dulles called for a "New Look" in foreign policy to deal with any communist military threat. He proposed that the free world "develop the will and organize the means to retaliate instantly against open aggression by Red Armies, so that if it occurred anywhere, we could and would strike back where it hurts by means of our own choosing." At the convention Dulles fashioned his party's foreign policy plank that distinguished "Republican principles" from disastrous Democratic policies, namely, "the negative, futile and immoral policy of 'Containment' which abandons countless human beings to a depotism and godless terrorism," and proclaimed that "the policies we espouse will revive the contagious, liberating influences which are inherent in freedom." In other words, there would be no negotiation or accommodation with the devil, that is, any communist leader

While echoing the conventional view that the Soviet Union sought "the economic containment and gradual strangulation of America," presidential candidate Dwight D. Eisenhower took a hard line against the Soviets. In a campaign speech to the American Legion, he hinted at the replacement of containment by liberation when he declared that "until the enslaved nations of the world have in the fullness of freedom the right to choose their own path, that then, and then only, can we say that there is a possible way of living peacefully and permanently with Communism in the world."

With vice-presidential candidate Richard M. Nixon leading the way, Republicans exploited national frustration over the failure of U.S. nuclear and economic dominance to produce victories over communism. Nixon denounced "the Dean Acheson College for Cowardly Containment of Communism," and party stalwarts charged Democrats with "Communism, Corruption, and Korea." They blasted Truman's "soft" reaction to communist aggression as willingness "to live with it, presumably forever." Accusations against the loyalty of Alger Hiss and State Department officials in recent Democratic administrations trumpeted incessantly by Senator McCarthy drowned out voices of moderation and nurtured an anticommunist hysteria (see p. 36). McCarthy gave his blessing to the "New Look" by ridiculing containment "as a big word which grew out of the Groton vocabulary of the Hiss–Acheson gang." The election outcome was never in doubt, especially after Eisenhower's dramatic announcement that if elected he would go to Korea in an effort to end the war.

The new Eisenhower administration had an opportunity to apply the Dulles liberation concept in June 1953 when rioting broke out in East Berlin against Soviet labor policies and quickly spread to other East German cities. But beyond claiming that these convulsions behind the Iron Curtain were at least the indirect result of the administration's pronouncements, Washington made no move. Critics quickly pointed out that the heralded new look bore an amazing resemblance to the old.

Continuity of Truman policy characterized the new administration's effort to secure a European Defense Community Treaty. Although Dulles pressured the French by implying that their failure to ratify EDC "would compel an agonizing reappraisal of basic United States policy," in August 1954 the French Assembly rejected the treaty. But France did join Britain and the United States in an agreement to end the military occupation of Germany. Eventually, in May 1955 West Germany was admitted to full membership in NATO. Shortly thereafter the Soviet Union reacted by forming the Warsaw Pact, a mutual security treaty with its East European allies. Two armed camps divided Europe.

The Soviet announcement on August 8, 1953, that the United States had no monopoly on the hydrogen bomb, followed in four days by a powerful nuclear blast in Soviet Central Asia, worried Washington and spurred interest in an international agreement on atomic energy before a nuclear holocaust. In a speech to the United Nations in December, Eisenhower attempted to break the deadlock by proposing "atoms for peace." Inviting the two governments to "begin now and continue to make joint contributions from their stockpile of normal uranium and fissionable materials to an International Atomic Energy Agency," Eisenhower challenged the Soviet Union to show its peaceful intentions. No favorable response came from the Kremlin.

Early in 1954 Dulles suggested that the modern way for a nation to "get maximum protection at bearable cost" was "to place more reliance on deterrent power and less on local defensive power." Such a policy, Dulles repeated, would "depend primarily upon a great capacity to retaliate, instantly, by means and at places of our choosing." As viewed by administration officials, this "New Look" assumed that only a surprise nuclear attack could knock out the United States, and the Korean War had taught an unpleasant lesson against fighting brushfire wars with conventional weapons on other continents. Merely brandishing a nuclear deterrent, according to this view, would convince an enemy not to risk annihilation. Equipped with atomic weapons, the U.S. Strategic Air Command (SAC) would be more efficient and less costly than an army to match the 175 Soviet divisions in Europe. In defense of the "New Look," Eisenhower explained in his *Memoirs* that: "I refused to turn the United States into an armed camp. . . . I saw no sense in wasting manpower in costly small wars that could not achieve decisive results under the political and military circumstances then existing." In effect, by installing nuclear weapons on the soil of its allies in

Western Europe, the United States assumed the right of first use—that is, to fire nuclear weapons in response to a Soviet attack on Western Europe, even though the Soviets had not used nuclear weapons.

Labeled "massive retaliation" by critics and ridiculed as a plan designed primarily to produce "a bigger bang for the buck," the "New Look" generated an uproar at home and abroad. Some charged that domestic political considerations, namely a balanced budget to appease conservative Republicans, was the motivating force. Opposition came from the navy and army who saw the air force winning the lion's share of resources, and from members of Congress worried about economic consequences of a projected cut of $4 billion in the 1954–1955 budget. Paradoxically, the administration drew fire from those who feared it might start a nuclear war, as well as from those who believed that it was bluffing because it would never use such weapons. Both Eisenhower and Dulles found it necessary to reassure the world of the United States' peaceful intentions and to acknowledge that no radical change in U.S. policy had occurred. "Massive retaliation" soon joined "liberation" in the limbo populated by campaign hyperbole of the past.

PEACEFUL COEXISTENCE?

Soviet Overtures

Stalin's death in March 1953, a few weeks after Eisenhower's inauguration, encouraged hopes of reversing the course of the cold war. New leaders in the Kremlin began to soften Soviet language toward the West. Georgi Malenkov, the new Soviet premier, suggested "peaceful coexistence" and "competition between the capitalist and socialist systems." Dulles remained skeptical. He interpreted this new Soviet line as the result of internal weakness and outside pressures, so he advised Eisenhower "to keep up those pressures right now."

The Decline of McCarthyism

In truth, the Eisenhower administration was the prisoner of public opinion molded by years of anticommunist rhetoric by U.S. leaders and the press. To accede to specific Soviet proposals, however promising, would challenge the McCarthy interpretation that previous deals with and sellouts to the Communists had cost the nation so much. As long as McCarthy's following appeared numerous and strong, the individual who crossed him risked humiliation and defeat at the polls. Few public officials were so brave.

Television, now in most U.S. homes, rescued the administration. In the spring of 1954 millions of Americans watched the hearings conducted by McCarthy's Special Senate Committee investigating charges of communism in the U.S. Army. What they saw was so disturbing that McCarthy's influence waned rapidly, and by the end of the year his Senate colleagues dared to censure him for contempt of a Senate subcommittee.

Geneva Conference, 1955

With McCarthy muffled, it became possible to consider a relaxation of tension with the Communist bloc. When the Soviet Union announced its intention early in 1955 to sign a peace treaty with Austria, it appeared that the post-Stalin generation of Soviet leaders really wanted a thaw in the cold war. Although Dulles feared that a summit conference, proposed by the Soviets, might "be nothing but a spectacle and promote a false euphoria," a skeptical Eisenhower was encouraged by others to agree to meet with the heads of state of Britain, France, and the Soviet Union at Geneva, Switzerland in July 1955.

On the fourth day of the conference, Eisenhower, looking directly at the Soviet delegation, declared that "the United States will never take part in an aggressive war." Then the president made a dramatic "open skies" proposal that would allow each side unrestricted aerial surveillance of the other's territory to inspect for surprise military moves. By such an exchange of military blueprints another Pearl Harbor could be avoided. But Nikita Khrushchev, the new Soviet leader, dismissed the idea as "nothing more than a bald espionage plot against the U.S.S.R."

The generally cordial atmosphere, however, and agreement on measures to increase friendship between peoples of the West and the Soviet Union raised hopes that "the spirit of Geneva" promised a reduction in the intensity of the cold war. Not even two serious crises in October 1956—one in the Middle East (p. 55), the other in Hungary—escalated the cold war. Hungarian "freedom fighters" elicited many admiring words from Americans, but no liberating weapons. Washington had no intentions of risking war to aid the oppressed peoples of Europe.

Nuclear Arms Race

The post-Geneva calm was shaken by an astonishing Soviet feat in October 1957—the launching of Sputnik into orbit 560 miles above the earth. Any lingering doubts about the ability of the Soviets to deploy an intercontinental ballistic missile (ICBM) vanished. Alarm spread that the Soviet Union might be ahead in the cold war and might be tempted to use its ICBM superiority to destroy a vulnerable United States. Such fears increased after a special government appointed committee of private citizens testified in November 1957 to the ability of the Soviet Union within two years to launch 100 ICBMs with megaton nuclear warheads against the United States. Washington rushed to equip NATO bases with short-range missiles capable of hitting Soviet targets. Many saw civilization teetering on a "delicate balance of terror."

A confident Nikita Khrushchev, having gained the premiership after a bitter internal struggle, now moved to exploit the leverage of the Soviet Union's new nuclear capability. But throughout the spring of 1958, Eisenhower, wary of Soviet efforts to dismantle NATO and to stop nuclear testing after their own successful tests, parried the Kremlin's overtures for another summit meeting.

Berlin Crisis, 1958–1959

Then in November 1958 Khrushchev initiated a new crisis. Turning over the administration of East Berlin to Moscow's East German satellite, the German Democratic Republic, the Soviet premier set a six-month deadline for withdrawal of all troops from Berlin and the transfer of authority over the West's access to Berlin to East Germany. In December, Moscow warned that after it turned over control to East Germany "any attempt to force a way into Berlin" would lead to a "military conflict" involving "the most modern means of annihilation." By rattling his nuclear sabre, Khrushchev hoped to pry loose from NATO the more vulnerable nations. But fortunately Khrushchev was not Stalin. Confining his aggressiveness to threatening language, the new Red leader allowed Allied convoys to move through the Soviet zone to West Berlin. Only desperate East Germans, attempting to flee to freedom, encountered gunfire.

Eisenhower was not intimidated by threats. Standing fast by U.S. rights in the German capital, as had Truman a decade earlier, the president held the Soviet government "directly responsible for the discharge of its obligations undertaken with respect to Berlin under existing agreements."

Confronted by such U.S. firmness, Khrushchev, in Eisenhower's words, "executed a remarkable diplomatic retreat." In March 1959 the Red leader called for a new summit conference and downgraded the six-month "ultimatum" to a negotiable deadline. In May the Big Four foreign ministers met in Geneva to resolve the deadlock over Berlin and nuclear testing. In August, Khrushchev and Eisenhower agreed to exchange visits. In September, Khrushchev in Washington said that "we and all peoples should live in peace and friendship." And by the end of his tour of the United States from Disneyland to an Iowa farm and a Pittsburgh steel mill, the Soviet leader had convinced many Americans that peaceful coexistence was here to stay. A surprising 20 percent of people surveyed in a Gallup poll even believed that he was "sincere in wanting to work out an effective disarmament plan." But most Americans regarded Khrushchev's overtures as temporary tactics to gain an advantage, not as a fixed goal.

The U-2 Incident, 1960

Eisenhower never returned the visit. In early May 1960 the Soviets shot down a U-2, a U.S. photo-reconnaissance plane, some 1,300 miles inside the Soviet Union. Khrushchev waited until the State Department attempted to disguise the ill-fated U-2 flight as a weather-gathering mission that had wandered off course due to mechanical failure. He then paraded the captured pilot and displayed fragments of the U-2 as evidence of U.S. espionage and dishonesty. At a news conference Eisenhower admitted to the U-2 flights, initiated in 1956, as a "distasteful but vital necessity" to obtain accurate intelligence in the absence of agreements on disarmament and cessation of nuclear testing. In fact, there occurred in the 1950s over 30 incidents involving attacks by Soviet MIG fighter planes against U.S. planes engaged in "ferreting" the borders of the Soviet Union to pick up emissions of air defense radar, ground communications, and microwave signals for analysis by the National Security Agency.

Although the president stopped further flights, he refused Khrushchev's demand that those responsible for U-2 missions be punished. An angry Khrushchev scuttled the summit conference in Paris on its first day, and Eisenhower's subsequent trip to Moscow was postponed indefinitely. On this sour note, progress toward relaxation of East–West tension ended as the nation entered the 1960 election campaign.

The Berlin Crisis of 1961

In his campaign for the presidency John F. Kennedy took a hard anticommunist line and criticized the Eisenhower administration for allowing a missile gap to develop. Assuming that the Communists prepared for peace only if the United States prepared for war, Kennedy stressed the need to "strengthen our conventional forces" and then "move ahead full time on our missile production." In this fashion the United States would possess what Kennedy called a "flexible response." Missing from his campaign speeches was a commitment to negotiate with the Soviets to strengthen peaceful coexistence. Although Kennedy's tough talk may have garnered votes, it failed to faze Soviet leaders. Evidence suggests that Khrushchev regarded the youthful U.S. president as inexperienced and likely to back down if pushed to the brink.

At the very outset of his term Kennedy faced a new Soviet engineered crisis over Berlin, where the United States, according to a campaign statement, had "a commitment that we have to meet if we're going to protect the security of Western Europe." Early in January Khrushchev issued a six-month ultimatum requiring the end of allied occupation of West Berlin and recognition of it as a demilitarized city. If the West did not agree, then the Soviet Union would sign its own peace treaty with East Germany thereby terminating the agreement for the Western presence in Berlin.

With the firm Berlin stands of Truman and Eisenhower as precedents, Kennedy could ill afford any sign of indecision. In his State of the Union Message on January 30, 1961, he warned that the country faced "an hour of national peril," and "the tide of events has been running out and time has not been our friend." But Kennedy's willingness, early in his term, to accept a humiliating defeat in the abortive Bay of Pigs venture (p. 59) rather than risk war apparently encouraged the Kremlin to believe that Kennedy's boldness was confined to words.

Exhilarated by the achievement in April 1961 that sent a Soviet cosmonaut on the first manned space flight, a confident Khrushchev proposed a meeting with Kennedy. But the Soviet leader had misjudged his opponent. Suspecting that the Soviets were testing the U.S. will to resist and his own toughness, Kennedy refused to abandon West Berlin. Before leaving for the Vienna meeting with Khrushchev he asked Congress for a massive arms buildup and increased defense expenditures of almost $3 billion. Kennedy warned that "the Free World's security can be endangered not only by a nuclear attack, but also by being slowly nibbled away at the periphery, regardless of our strategic power."

At the two-day Vienna meeting in June, the Soviet premier, eager to halt the embarrassing flow of 4,000 refugees each week from East Germany into West Berlin and freedom, held fast to his deadline. Kennedy painted a somber picture in his report on the talks in Vienna. Claiming that "the adversaries of freedom plan to consolidate their territory," he found the nation facing "a contest of will and purpose as well as force and violence—a battle for minds and souls as well as lives and territory. And in that context, [he said] we cannot stand aside." Vienna had settled nothing.

Khrushchev kept up the pressure with a July announcement of a one-third increase in Soviet military spending and a suspension of the partial demobilization of the Red Army. In this deadly game of nuclear poker, each round of increases led to another round with no end in sight. Presidential adviser Arthur M. Schlesinger, Jr., deplored the tendency to define the issue as: "Are you chicken or not?" Failure to retaliate in kind should not be construed, according to Schlesinger, as being "soft, idealistic, mushy."

Yet Kennedy knew there could be no negotiations under the threat of an ultimatum. He told the nation on July 25: "We cannot and will not permit the Communists to drive us out of Berlin, either gradually or by force." After announcing that he was asking Congress for $3.25 billion more for defense, he said that he was calling up certain reserve and National Guard units. After reviewing the steps being taken for civil defense, the president assured the nation: "In the coming months, I hope to let every citizen know what steps he can take without delay to protect his family in case of attack." Despite such alarmist talk, Kennedy claimed that "we are willing to consider any arrangement or treaty in Germany consistent with the maintenance of peace and freedom, and with the legitimate security interests of all nations."

Throughout the summer of 1961 tension over Berlin mounted as 30,000 refugees fled to West Berlin in July alone. On August 13, East German troops began to install roadblocks and barbed wire barricades along the line dividing East and West Berlin. Four days later the Communists began construction of a concrete wall along the line. Eventually the wall wound its way through more than one hundred miles of Berlin streets and alleys. Resisting pressure from the "hawks," who as usual advocated retaliating with bombs, Kennedy avoided war while insisting on U.S. rights in Berlin. He ordered 1,500 combat troops to move from West Germany to Berlin, and he sent Vice-President Lyndon B. Johnson to reassure the German people of U.S. commitment.

By the end of August the administration's firm stand had persuaded the Soviets to begin negotiations. Again it appeared that holding fast to an established position against threats was the wisest approach in dealing with the communists. Although the talks on Berlin dragged on sporadically for a decade, a compromise agreement upholding Western rights was reached in 1973. But long before this satisfactory conclusion of the crisis in Europe, developments in other parts of the world had heated up the cold war.

CHAPTER 2

Conflicts in East Asia, 1945–1961

"The unfortunate but inescapable fact is that the ominous result of the civil war in China was beyond the control of the government of the United States."

General Omar Bradley, 1951

Dean Acheson, 1949

"This strategy would involve us in the wrong war, at the wrong time, and with the wrong enemy."

General Omar Bradley, 1951

THE UNITED STATES AND THE CHINESE CIVIL WAR

The Failure to Achieve Wartime Unity in China

A few hours before Harry Truman swore the oath as president of the United States on April 12, 1945, a C-54 of the Air Transport Command landed in Washington, D.C. Aboard was a career officer in the State Department, John S. Service, whose activities in China soon embroiled the Truman administration in sharp controversy. Eleven days earlier Service had held official conversations in Yenan, China, with communist leaders at the residence of Mao Zedong (Mao-Tse-Tung), leader of the Chinese Communist party. Now, although Service did not know it, he had been recalled to Washington at the insistence of U.S. ambassador to China, Patrick J. Hurley. Eight months earlier, President Roosevelt had sent Hurley to China as his personal envoy to try to settle the 20-year internal conflict between the governing Nationalist party, the Guo Mindang (Kuomintang, KMT) under the leadership of 57-year-old Jiang Jieshi (Chiang Kai-shek), and the Communists. Hurley had returned to Washington in February to urge vigorous support of the Nationalists only.

Truman soon discovered that the Hurley–Service disagreement dramatized a sharp division over U.S. policy toward the civil conflict in China. On one side, steadfast supporters of Generalissimo Jiang, such as Hurley, believed that his inspiring leadership would bring victory over the Communists and Japan if Washington furnished adequate support. Taking a very different position, some

27

officials concluded that flagrant corruption, incompetence, and hostility to basic reforms weakened the Chinese war effort against Japan and doomed Jiang and the KMT to ultimate defeat by Mao. Several foreign service officers, including John Service, had sent a message in March to the State Department proposing that

> the President inform the Generalissimo in definite terms that we supply and cooperate with the Communists and other suitable groups who can assist the war against Japan . . . and that we are taking direct steps to accomplish this end. . . . we can point out the advantage of having the Communists helped by us rather than seeking Russian aid or intervention.

But Truman had serious concerns about Moscow's intentions in China, even though at Yalta Stalin had agreed "to conclude with the National government of China a pact of friendship and alliance." So the president instructed Harry Hopkins on his special mission to Moscow in late May to promote a formal agreement between Jiang and Stalin to forestall new troubles in Asia. Hopkins did obtain from the Soviet dictator a pledge to "do everything he can to promote unification under the leadership of Chiang-Kai-shek." In Washington, hopes revived for a coalition government dominated by the Nationalists.

A long summer of negotiations between Chonqing and Moscow produced on August 14, 1945, the day of the Japanese surrender, a treaty of friendship and alliance. But real agreement between the Nationalists and the Chinese Reds failed to materialize. As the war ended the immediate task of disarming the Japanese generated friction between the two Chinese parties. The generalissimo, reassured by the treaty with the Soviet Union as well as by the steady flow of aid from the United States, would not overrule his generals and Nationalist officials who opposed any sharing of power with the Communists. Chinese Red leaders, disappointed by Moscow's treaty with Jiang, hoped that direct involvement of the Soviet Union in disarming the Japanese in Manchuria would improve their own position.

Unsuccessful Efforts to Avert Civil War in China

Truman sent Hurley to attempt to resolve the crisis by bringing Mao and Jiang together in Chonqing for talks early in September, but the two adversaries could not reach an agreement. Complicating Hurley's task, the Soviets, despite Stalin's pledge at Potsdam, allowed the Chinese Communists to take possession of Japanese arms in Manchuria and refused to allow Nationalist troops to land at Dairen, southern Manchuria's major port.

Washington faced a tough decision. General Albert C. Wedemeyer, Army Secretary Robert P. Patterson, and Navy Secretary James V. Forrestal favored all-out military aid to Jiang. Truman and his closest advisers, however, believed that to guarantee a Nationalist victory would require U.S. intervention on a scale matching the military effort against Nazi Germany. Given the mood of the American people, who wanted the return of members of the armed services now that World War II had ended, such a step was unthinkable. U.S. Marines and Air Force personnel, therefore, received instructions to assist only in the transfer of Nationalist forces to North China.

Emotionally and physically exhausted, Hurley returned to Washington late in September 1945 as fighting broke out in North China. Stung by press and congressional criticism of his diplomacy and incensed by the recent appointment of his old adversary, John Service, to the Far Eastern Commission under General MacArthur, Hurley concluded that the Chinese Affairs Division of the State Department was trying to thwart his efforts to carry out, as he put it, "Roosevelt's Asian policy based on the Atlantic Charter." A scathing condemnation of Hurley's "blank check" support of Jiang by Congressman Hugh DeLacy (D., Wash.) so infuriated Hurley that, without first informing the president, he gave the press his blistering letter of resignation charging that "a considerable section of our State Department is endeavoring to support Communism generally as well as in China."

Hurley's tirade against a Democratic State Department whipped into action congressional Republicans impatient with Truman's China policies and eager to find a winning issue. Senator Styles Bridges (R., N.H.), who had repeatedly condemned the administration's "softness" toward communism and its tolerance of disloyal career men in the State Department, urged Hurley to "shoot the works" by disclosing the secret Yalta agreement.

Bipartisanship had never been the rule in U.S. Asian policy. Republican leaders, proud of their party's institution of the Open Door policy early in the century, protested that they had not been consulted when basic decisions about China had been made at Big Three Conferences. Having had no voice in making policy that, in their eyes, left Nationalist China in jeopardy, many Republicans clamored for a greater U.S. effort to save China from communism. Although a Senate investigation in December dismissed Hurley's charges as unfounded, they poisoned the dialogue.

Moving quickly to counter the uproar instigated by Hurley, an angry president asked retired General Marshall to succeed the ambassador. Truman feared that civil war in China would enable the Soviets to extend their control because of the weakness of the Nationalist government. Hurley's failure to bring the two sides together did not mean that the idea was unsound. Therefore, to nudge the generalissimo toward democratic reforms and unity, Truman authorized Marshall to announce "that a China disunited and torn by civil strife could not be considered realistically as a proper place for American assistance." But the United States had no real alternative other than to continue to back the Nationalists.

A superhuman task confronted Marshall. A confident Jiang counted on

U.S. aid, which amounted to over $700 million in Lend–Lease alone after V-J Day, to assure ultimate victory. He viewed any coalition with the Communists as not only undesirable but as unnecessary. The Communists, outnumbered two-and-a-half to one, without U.S. aid and confined to the northern provinces, favored U.S. mediation to establish a coalition government in which they would occupy a legitimate place. Playing for time to gain position, Red leaders visualized a broadening of their base in the North and an expansion of their appeal. They counted on Nationalist blunders and resistance to reforms to shrink Jiang's support until the overwhelming majority of Chinese people turned to the Communists to take over control of China. The construction of such different plots in the minds of the principal actors foreshadowed frustration for any director attempting to blend the two into one scenario.

Marshall's prestige and skill did produce a cease-fire in North China and Manchuria on January 25, 1946, and adoption of procedures for negotiations. But meetings in Chonqing to work out details of a coalition government stalled when Jiang refused to participate in joint truce teams to supervise a cease-fire in Manchuria. A disappointed Marshall explained to Truman that Jiang was "in an extremely difficult position struggling with the ultra conservative and determined wing of each group [the army and KMT], many if not most of whom will lose position and income, all or in part by the changes proposed." The precarious truce collapsed soon after Marshall's return to Washington in mid-March for consultations. When the Soviets finally began to withdraw from Manchuria in early April 1946, Jiang ignored military advice of U.S. officers, including Wedemeyer, and sent troops into Manchuria to destroy the Red Chinese forces.

On his return to China in April, Marshall blamed both sides for the fighting. He chided Nationalist General Yu Daway (Yu Ta-wei), "I do not know who the Generalissimo's advisers are but whoever they may be, they are very poor ones. Instead of constructive action they got the government into trouble." In a message to Truman, Marshall criticized the Communists for violating the cease-fire agreement by resisting the government's efforts to establish sovereignty in Manchuria.

Neither side was happy with U.S. mediation efforts. Chinese communist officials condemned U.S. policy that professed to be neutral and committed to peace, but continued to furnish extensive military and economic aid to the Nationalists. Red leaders refused to accept Jiang's terms that threatened the very existence of their own party. On the other side, the generalissimo saw no reason to make concessions to an enemy seeking to destroy him. Convinced that extension of territorial control spelled military success, Jiang marched on. Unable to defeat communist forces who avoided battle, Nationalist officials complained that Marshall's policies held them back from total victory. Caught in the middle, General Marshall labored to prevent the full-scale conflict that appeared imminent.

Growing polarization in the United States paralleled this division in China. An influential group, the so-called "China Lobby," funded by wealthy Chinese and U.S. businesspeople propagandized the cause of the Nationalists. On May 15, 1946, 65 prominent Americans, including representatives Walter Judd (R., Minn.), a former medical missionary in China, and Clare Booth Luce (R., Conn.), wife of the publisher of *Time* and *Life,* condemned the Yalta agreement for pledging "to deliver the promised concessions in Manchuria and Mongolia to Soviet Russia whether the Chinese government agreed or not." This charge that the United States had sold out China at Yalta attracted Roosevelt haters and those convinced that Asia was more important than Europe to the United States.

Arrayed against the China Lobby stood diehard opponents of more aid to the "decadent Nationalists." They found a new argument in a June 1946 United Press story charging that "there was solid evidence that a clique of officials in the Guomindang, the Generalissimo's party, under the inspiration of German Nazi advisers, were opposed to peace with the Communists under any conditions." Subsequent news articles supported the contention that the obstacle to unification of China was a Nazi-influenced group in the Guo Mindang. On June 30 the United States officially protested the Chinese government's removal of 400 persons from a list of "dangerous and objectionable Nazis to be shipped to Germany." Apparently these Germans had bribed Nationalist officials with sums ranging from $15,000 to $75,000 in order to remain in China. Understandably many Americans felt bewildered as they tried to identify the "good guys" in China.

As government forces, meanwhile, advanced in sharp fighting in Shandong (Shantung) province, Chinese Communist attitude toward the United States turned bitter. Red propagandists accused the Nationalists of using Marshall's mediation as a cover for expanded military operations. Not even Marshall was spared the invective of communist radio broadcasts and newspaper stories accusing him of deliberately promoting civil war in China in behalf of "imperialist circles" in the United States, Mao ridiculed the "so-called mediation as a smokescreen for strengthening Chiang Kai-shek in every way."

Marshall's warning of impending financial collapse failed to deter the Nationalists from military expenditures consuming about 70 percent of their budget and promoting ruinous inflation. Discouraged by the continued irresponsibility of Jiang's government, Truman, at Marshall's request, imposed in August a temporary embargo on further shipment of military supplies to China as a means of forcing reforms. Administration leaders thought that the Nationalists could not win a military victory and that their only hope of retaining power was to make a political settlement with Mao. Late in 1946 Marshall sadly advised Truman to terminate U.S. participation in the mediation effort and to withdraw the 10,000 Marines still in China. Blaming both sides for the civil war, a disenchanted Marshall left China for the last time early in January 1947 and flew back to Washington to replace James F. Byrnes as secretary of state.

The Wedemeyer Mission and the Debate over U.S. Policy in China

Each Nationalist reverse in the early weeks of 1947 built up pressures in the new Republican-controlled Congress to resume aid to Jiang. In House hearings on Truman's proposal to aid Greece and Turkey, Judd asked why the administration did not show the same concern for the Chinese resisting communism. Secretaries Patterson and Forrestal, supported by the Joint Chiefs of Staff, argued for the removal of the embargo on munitions as necessary to prevent a communist triumph. Signs of a major debacle for Nationalist forces in Manchuria amidst new reports of student strikes for peace in many Nationalist cities, persuaded Marshall to lift the 10-month-old embargo in May.

Washington, however, had no desire to become more deeply involved in China. Marshall later admitted that "the thing that concerned me was that the Chinese [Nationalists] have long been intent on the United States going to war with the Soviet Union with the expectation that the United States would drag the Chinese government out of its difficulties." Truman also feared that partisan debate over China might jeopardize the European Recovery Program. He decided, therefore, to send General Albert C. Wedemeyer to China on a fact-finding mission. The president saw in Wedemeyer, highly regarded by the generalissimo, an opportunity to quiet discordant notes arising from Republican ranks in Congress and from the pro-Nationalist press. Wedemeyer was instructed to tell Chinese officials that the United States "can consider assistance in a program of rehabilitation only if the Chinese Government presents satisfactory evidence of effective measures looking toward Chinese recovery."

A grim picture confronted the U.S. general, who reported soon after his arrival in China that the Nationalists "do not understand why they should die or make any sacrifices. They have lost confidence in their leaders, political and military, and they foresee complete collapse. Those in positions of responsibility are therefore corruptly striving to obtain as much as they can before the collapse." Conditions were so bad that Wedemeyer warned Nationalist leaders that "the Central Government cannot defeat the Chinese Communists by the employment of force, but can win the loyal, enthusiastic and realistic support of the masses of the people by improving the political and economic situation immediately."

Despite these misgivings, in his September report to Truman Wedemeyer argued that criticism of the Nationalist government "should be tempered by a recognition of handicaps imposed on China by eight years of war, the burden of her opposition to Communism, and her sacrifices for the Allied cause." The general recommended "moral, advisory, and material support to China and that Manchuria be placed under a Five-Power Guardianship or under a United Nations Trusteeship." In an explicit criticism of recent U.S. policy in China, he declared that "it may be said that the American mediation effort has been to the advantage of the Chinese Communists and conversely to the disadvantage of the Nationalist Government."

Wedemeyer's report did not sit well with the administration. Marshall contended that the proposals for Manchuria might offend the Nationalists and perhaps encourage the Soviet Union to urge a similar trusteeship for Greece, thereby jeopardizing the Truman Doctrine. The secretary of state advised Truman: "It seems to be mandatory that we treat Wedemeyer's report strictly top secret." Wedemeyer was left, as he later complained, "to twiddle my thumbs" while his report was buried in "foggy bottom," the critics' term for the Department of State.

But the China Lobby did not observe a respectful silence. Judd and Bridges charged that the administration suppressed Wedemeyer's report because the report favored Jiang. They implied that the Truman administration was abandoning China to the Communists at a time when additional aid, modest in comparison to the billions allotted to Europe, could save China. Judd revealed that the generalissimo had asked him "why the U.S. took a different view of Communism in the East than in the West. . . . was it a racial matter, that the United States cared for white people but not for yellow?"

"Three Cheers" for the Nationalists

In February 1948 President Truman, bending to Republican pressure, asked Congress for $570 million in economic aid for 15 months to assist "in retarding the current economic deterioration and thus give the Chinese government a further opportunity to initiate the measures necessary to the establishment of more stable economic conditions." Testifying in support of this request, Marshall claimed that in order to reduce the Communists to a negligible force in China the United States "would have to be prepared virtually to take over the Chinese Government and administer its economic, military, and governmental affairs." Such a step, the secretary argued, "would inevitably play into the hands of the Russians." Marshall made it clear that the administration had no intention of falling into the abyss of a land war in China.

In March a National Security Council report supported the administration's position with the conclusion that any economic and military assistance program in China "should be regarded as subordinate to the efforts to stabilize conditions in areas of more strategic importance." Although Wedemeyer still contended that limited military aid could be effective, a majority of Congress would support only a token gesture. Senator Vandenberg candidly admitted: "I think it is perfectly obvious that this is essentially three cheers for the Nationalist government in hope that it can get somewhere in the face of Communist opposition." Congress at length passed a bill that appropriated only $338 million for economic support to China for one year and, a meager $125 million for military supplies.

William C. Bullitt, a former ambassador to Russia, sent to China by *Life* for an on-the-spot study in the spring of 1948, undercut the administration by telling KMT leaders that Marshall blocked more aid for China. Bullitt suggested that "if the Chinese can only manage to hold on until after the coming Presidential elections they can count on the fuller measure of assistance which they require because Mr. Truman will not be elected." But Truman did not waver in his China policy. In fact, implementation of military aid to China under the 1948 act proceeded so slowly that by the end of September only about $3 million of military supplies had been sent.

Throughout the summer and early fall, Ambassador J. Leighton Stuart's communications from China matched the gloom of public opinion polls on Truman's chances for reelection. On August 10 Stuart reported, "The Communists continue to win the civil war. They have retained the initiative with all the advantage given by the offensive and government troops just do not seem to have the will or ability to fight." A major Red drive launched in September resulted in the taking of important cities in Manchuria and in the capture of thousands of Nationalist soldiers and an estimated 75 percent of their U.S. equipment. Forrestal's attempt to obtain reconsideration of all-out aid drew the State Department's warning that such a step would be "a course of action of huge, indefinite and hazardous proportions." Even Vandenberg conceded that "there are limits to our resources and boundaries to our miracles."

Rejection of Last Ditch Efforts to Save Nationalist China

Truman's unexpected reelection meant that the United States was not going to bail out Nationalist China. Frantic requests for more aid by Jiang, and a desperate end-of-year visit to Washington by Madam Jiang to make an emotional appeal for help elicited only expressions of sympathy. More influential was the analysis of Major General David Barr, director of the U.S. Military Advisory Group to the Government of China. In mid-December he reported: "Only a policy of immediate employment of United States Armed Forces, which I emphatically do not recommend, would enable the Nationalist Government to maintain a foothold in Southern China against a determined Communist advance." At year's end the State Department issued formal warnings to Americans to leave North China while normal transportation facilities remained available. Abandoning hope for miracles, thousands of Chinese refugees streamed to Formosa carrying large amounts of U.S. currency and gold, while the generalissimo and his dwindling forces remained to carry on a forlorn cause.

In January 1949 the National Security Council emphasized the folly of any major effort to save Nationalist China and recommended that the United States should regard "efforts with respect to China as of lower priority than efforts in other areas where the benefits to U.S. security are more immediately commensurate with the expenditure of U.S. resources." A few weeks later the NSC suggested that "it is even questionable whether we have anything to gain from political support of any of the remaining anticommunist public figures in China. They are likely to prove only slightly less impotent than Yugoslav royalists."

Although U.S. aid totaling more than $1.5 billion since V-J day had been ineffective—much of it falling into the hands of the Communists—a last-ditch effort was made in the new Democratic controlled Congress in 1949 to save Nationalist China. Employing the rhetoric of the China Lobby, a young member of Congress, John F. Kennedy (D., Mass.), complained that "what our young men have saved, our diplomats and our President have frittered away." Twenty-five Republicans joined 25 Democratic senators in sponsoring a bill providing Nationalist China with $1.5 billion in credits for economic and military aid.

But the administration opposed this futile gesture to a terminally ill patient. Dean Acheson, the new secretary of state, pointed out that such a huge loan "would embark this government on an undertaking the eventual cost of which would almost surely be catastrophic." He claimed that "the Chinese government forces have lost no battles during the past year because of lack of ammunition and equipment, while the Chinese Communists have captured the major portion of military supplies, exclusive of ammunition, furnished the Chinese Government by the United States since V-J day."

In a sharp counterattack Senator William Knowland (R., Calif.) charged that Acheson "had pulled the rug out from under" the Chinese Nationalists. A less temperate Senator Styles Bridges (R., N.H.) accused the secretary of actions that "might be called sabotage of the valiant" Nationalists. The self-confident Acheson, aristocratic in appearance and manner, represented a tempting target to politicians eager to impress the folks back home.

The issue of additional aid to Jiang was overtaken by events in the spring of 1949. Mao's armies crossed the Yangzi and took Shanghai in May. The victorious Reds formed "People's Governments" for liberated areas preliminary to proclaiming formally on October 1, 1949, the People's Republic of China. The Soviet Union and its satellites immediately recognized the new government of China, but the United States refused to do so. At year's end, the Nationalists, driven from Canton and threatened in Chonqing, fled to Taiwan (Formosa).

When the new secretary of defense, Louis Johnson, raised the question of the defense of Formosa, Knowland, Taft, and former President Herbert Hoover promptly advocated U.S. naval protection for the island. Speaking for those disillusioned with Nationalist China, Senator Tom Connally (D., Tex.), head of the Foreign Relations Committee, ridiculed Knowland's plea for aid to Formosa with the withering retort: "The Senator wants to pour money down this rat hole . . . and there at the bottom of the rat hole you'll find old Chiang, the Generalissimo who never generalissimos." Truman, unwilling to be pushed into a policy that might involve direct conflict with Red China, asserted that the United States had no "intention of utilizing its armed forces to interfere in the present situation." The president was supported by the Joint Chiefs and the NSC, which had reaffirmed in August 1949 that "the strategic importance of Formosa does not justify overt military action."

The Hiss Case

Although the domestic scare over internal communist subversion had helped the Truman administration gain support for its European policies, just the opposite happened in regard to its Asian policies. Two events early in 1949 furnished ammunition to those contending that traitors inside the government had betrayed U.S. secrets to the Communists. In March, 28-year-old Judith Coplon, a Justice Department employee, was arrested and charged with being a spy for the Soviet Union. At the same time the perjury trial of Alger Hiss, a former State Department adviser who attended the Yalta Conference, enthralled the nation.

Testimony by Whittaker Chambers, an ex-writer for *Time,* before the House Committee on Un-American Activities combined with the relentless pursuit of evidence by freshman member of Congress Richard M. Nixon (R., Calif.) had led to the indictment of Hiss in December 1948. Hiss was charged with lying when he testified that he had not given copies of classified documents from the State Department in 1938 to Chambers, who confessed that he was a Communist at the time. Like Acheson, Hiss, with an aristocratic bearing and Ivy League education, irritated men of less privileged background. But many prominent people, including John Foster Dulles, issued statements in support of Hiss. Truman denounced the congressional investigations as a "red herring." Although this first trial of Hiss ended in a hung jury, the case played into the hands of the administration's political opponents.

In this acrimonious climate of the summer of 1949 the administration's publication of a defense of its policies in a "White Paper" on China, including Wedemeyer's report, attracted hostile comments from critics contending that a more vigorous program of U.S. aid would have saved Nationalist China. A Gallup poll of September showed that 53 percent of the American people disapproved of the way the government handled the China situation, whereas only 26 percent thought the United States "did the best it could under the circumstances."

The partisan assault on administration policies quickened in the early weeks of 1950. In a Senate speech in January, Taft alleged that the State Department had "been guided by a left-wing group who obviously wanted to get rid of Chiang and were willing to turn China over to the Communists for that purpose." Proclaiming that Acheson had lost the confidence of the American people, Senator Knowland demanded the secretary's resignation. When a second trial convicted Hiss of perjury, on January 21, 1950, Acheson, who had known

Hiss from earlier State Department days, invited a torrent of verbal abuse by saying: "I do not intend to turn my back on Alger Hiss."

The communist victory in China following so soon after the communist advances in Eastern Europe had made rational discussion of U.S. foreign policy almost impossible. The American people were unprepared to accept anything but their ideal of China—a democratic, united ally maintaining postwar stability in Asia. The Coplon and Hiss cases fueled simplistic conclusions that Americans, either sympathetic to or in collusion with the Reds, had caused the loss of China. The stage was set for Senator Joseph McCarthy to whip up national hysteria with sweeping accusations of treason and communism in high places (see p. 18). Discord, suspicion, and fear stalked the land as events in another Asian country drew the United States into a new crisis.

THE KOREAN WAR

The Temporary Division of Korea Becomes Permanent

Lights burned throughout the night of August 10, 1945 in the Pentagon office of John J. McCloy, assistant secretary of war, where the State, War, and Navy Department's Coordinating Committee (SWNCC) studied a pressing problem. A day earlier the dropping of the second atom bomb, this time on Nagasaki, had made imminent the end of the war in the Pacific. Assigned the task of drafting plans for accepting the surrender of Japanese forces throughout the Pacific area, SWNCC found few guidelines for Korea, ruled by Japan since 1910. In the Cairo Declaration of 1943 Roosevelt, Churchill, and Jiang Jieshi had promised Korea its independence "in due course." At Teheran a few days later Stalin agreed. In February 1945 at Yalta the Big Three approved general terms for a temporary international trusteeship over Korea, but made no specific plans for the liberation of Korea.

That evening the committee (SWNCC) debated between military and political points of view. War Department officials pointed out that the United States, with its nearest available troops located in Okinawa, 600 miles from Pusan, the largest port on Korea's southern coast, would be hard pressed to achieve the State Department's goal that U.S. forces receive the Japanese surrender throughout the major part of Korea. McCloy finally asked Colonel C. H. Bonesteel of the War Department's general staff and Dean Rusk, assistant secretary of state for Far Eastern affairs, to frame a proposal that would harmonize political desires and military capabilities. By morning the two men produced a plan making the United States responsible for liberating Korea south of the 38th parallel, where almost two thirds of the Korean population lived, with the

Soviets responsible for the area north of that latitude line. Approved by the Joint Chiefs and accepted by Moscow, this plan was sent to General Douglas MacArthur, commander of U.S. forces in the Pacific theatre, for implementation.

As in Europe, geography worked against the United States. Sharing a common border with Korea for about 50 miles, the Soviet Union had a major naval base at Vladivostok, only 100 miles from two large seaports in North Korea. The Soviets exploited this advantage of proximity and made amphibious landings in Korea on August 10, only two days after declaring war against Japan. Soviet troops, accompanied by two Korean divisions trained in Siberia, advanced rapidly to reach the 38th parallel within two weeks. Not until September 9 did U.S. forces accept the surrender of Japanese forces south of the 38th parallel.

The fact that Koreans disagreed about future political organization of their country caused immediate problems. A large, vocal group of older, better educated, and well-to-do Koreans in Seoul had strong attachments to a provisional government in exile in China. Headed by 70-year-old, Princeton-educated Dr. Syngman Rhee, this Korean faction stood for an independent, united Korea. Professing commitment to democratic principles, Rhee's supporters urged U.S. officials to expedite his return to Korea. An opposition group led by "radicals," who had already organized a People's Republic in the South, complicated matters by establishing ties with Communists in North Korea. In this internal struggle for power, the United States found it impossible to remain neutral. Before year's end Rhee was allowed to return. He promptly formed a democratic council, and demanded withdrawal of all occupying forces and an independent Korea.

In the North the Soviets placed Korean Communists in positions of authority and began training and equipping a People's Army that grew to 125,000 men by early 1948. Kim Il-Sung, a young Korean Communist, formed a government that immediately undertook a program of distributing farm land to landless tenants. Whereas the United States intended to restore Korea to complete independence in it's own democratic image, the Soviet Union aimed to create another communist nation that would strengthen Soviet power and influence in Asia.

Confident that democratic groups in South Korea could organize an acceptable government and unite the nation with popular support, MacArthur counseled abandonment of the trusteeship idea and withdrawal of U.S. and Soviet forces. But Harriman advised the president that "far from insuring Soviet paramountcy, a trusteeship would probably mean [the] U.S.S.R. having but one of three or four equal votes." Truman agreed and supported trusteeship as the most practical way to unite Korea. Efforts of a Joint Soviet-U.S. commission in the spring of 1946, however, failed because each side maneuvered to set up a Korean government friendly to its interests.

The JCS assured the administration that "from the standpoint of military security, the U.S. has little strategic interest in maintaining the present troops and bases in Korea." In September 1947 Washington referred the Korean problem to the United Nations. The latter responded by calling for the withdrawal of all military forces as soon as practical. But when the General Assembly voted 40 to 6 in November to establish a nine-nation UN Commission in Korea to supervise election of representatives to a Korean National Assembly, the Soviets denied it permission to enter North Korea.

Moscow and Washington proceeded to establish separate Korean governments. In May 1948 UN supervised elections in the South chose a national assembly that adopted a constitution in July for the Republic of Korea. On the third anniversary of V-J day, August 15, U.S. military authorities turned over the government of South Korea to Syngman Rhee, president of the new Republic of Korea. Meanwhile, North Korean Communists under Soviet supervision adopted a constitution for the People's Democratic Republic of Korea and claimed jurisdiction over all Korea. The fate of postwar Germany, rigid division of the nation, now befell Korea.

The U.S. Defense Perimeter in the Pacific

Inside the Truman administration a top secret NSC report in April 1948 warned: "The United States should not become so irrevocably involved in the Korea situation that an action taken by any faction in Korea or by any other power in Korea could be considered a casus belli [act of war] for the United States." When the Soviets evacuated the last of their 45,000 soldiers from North Korea in December 1948, the United States responded by reducing its military garrison to 16,000 at the end of the year.

Washington continued to assign highest priority to Europe. With Congress absorbed in debates over foreign aid, the North Atlantic Treaty, and China, the executive branch tried to avoid domestic controversy over its Korean policy. Help came from General MacArthur, who reported to the NSC in March 1949 that "complete withdrawal of U.S. troops from Korea was justified and would not adversely affect our position in Korea." A few days later Truman ordered withdrawal by June 30, 1949, of the remaining U.S. soldiers in Korea, except for a regimental combat team of about 500 men—left to help train the Korean army. Late in the year the NSC confirmed the desirability of such action with the assertion: "It is essential that a successful strategic defense in the 'East' be assured with a minimum expenditure of military manpower and material in order that the major effort may be expended in the West." Under these circumstances Truman found Congress reluctant to appropriate funds to aid South Korea. When he asked for $60 million in the 1950–1951 budget, Republicans combined with renegade Democrats in the House to reject the request by one vote. Only after Acheson agreed to spend $10.5 million in aid to Formosa did Congress agree to a comparable appropriation for Korea.

Still ambiguous was America's responsibility to South Korea in the event of an attack from the North. Encouraged by positions taken privately by MacArthur and the NSC, in a January 1950 speech Acheson indicated that the U.S. defense line in the Pacific, extending from the Philippines through Japan, excluded both Formosa and Korea. Responsibility for areas beyond that line rested with the United Nations. Since the end of World War II, U.S. strategy in the Pacific had emphasized the importance of keeping Russia out of Japan. An industrialized and technologically advanced Japan appeared vital to peace and stability in the Pacific, whereas the smaller and less developed Formosa and Korea seemed relatively unimportant to U.S. interests. In early May 1950 Senator Tom Connally admitted that Korea was not "very greatly important" in the defense strategy of the United States and surmised that the Communists were going to overrun Korea when they got ready just as they "probably will overrun Formosa."

Republican critics, however, castigated Acheson and the administration for writing off Taiwan, although they expressed little concern about Korea. Senator Knowland resurrected a popular analogy by charging that "Munich certainly should have taught us that appeasement of aggression, then as now, is but surrender on the installment plan." As the verbal assault droned on, the administration was bolstered by a June 19, 1950, secret CIA memorandum suggesting that "the USSR would be restrained from using its troops by the fear of general war; and its suspected desire to restrict and control Chinese influence in northern Korea would militate against sanctioning the use of regular Chinese Communist units in Korea."

The Outbreak of War and UN Intervention

In the drizzly predawn darkness of Sunday, June 25, 1950, seven North Korean divisions and their support units illuminated the sky with an artillery bombardment along the 38th parallel. Although shooting skirmishes had become an expected part of life for South Korean military units on the border, the sustained ferocity of this assault surprised the four divisions in the area. With many of their ablest officers on a training mission in Japan, the outnumbered and inadequately equipped South Koreans offered ineffective resistance.

Shortly after 10:00 P.M. (Central time) on Saturday, June 24, a telephone call interrupted President Truman, relaxing at his home in Independence, Missouri. A tense Dean Acheson relayed the disquieting news of the North Korean attack. After a few minutes conversation the two men agreed to ask the UN Security Council to hold a special meeting to deal with the crisis.

On Sunday's return flight to Washington Truman reflected about other occasions when the strong had attacked the weak and "how each time that the democracies failed to act it has encouraged the aggressors to keep going ahead." The president mused that "if the Communists were permitted to force their way into the Republic of Korea without opposition from the free world, no small nation would have the courage to resist threats and aggression by stronger Communist neighbors." Dismissing the possibility that the conflict was a civil war, Truman assumed that the Soviet Union had sanctioned the attack and was "trying to get Korea by default." Many years later Khrushchev's *Memoirs* revealed that Stalin only reluctantly consented to Kim Il Sung's plan, which predicted a quick victory before the United States could respond.

On Sunday, June 25, the Security Council adopted a U.S. resolution branding the North Korean action "a breach of the peace." The resolution also called for North Korea to withdraw its armed forces to the 38th parallel, and asked "all Members to render every assistance to the United Nations" to bring about the end of hostilities. Having boycotted the Security Council since early in the year in protest against a vote rejecting Red China's application for admission to the United Nations, the Soviet Union had no representative present to veto the resolution. Truman responded by authorizing General MacArthur in Japan to give the South Koreans whatever military supplies he could spare as an interim measure.

After North Korea failed to reply to a request to cease hostilities, the Security Council adopted a resolution on June 27 recommending that "members of the United Nations furnish such assistance to the Republic of Korea as may be necessary to repel the armed attack and to restore international peace and security in the area." On the same day, Truman announced that he had "ordered United States air and sea forces to give the Korean Government troops cover and support" and that he had "ordered the Seventh Fleet to prevent any attack on Formosa."

The Decision to Send American Troops

North Korean units smashed through weak South Korean defenses. MacArthur reported on June 28 that "the United States would have to commit ground troops if the thirty-eighth parallel were to be restored." Following a personal inspection of the Korean front, the general informed the president he could "hold Korea with two American divisions." After consulting with advisers and congressional leaders, Truman on June 30 authorized the air force "to conduct missions on specific military targets in Northern Korea, wherever militarily necessary." In addition, he ordered a naval blockade of the Korean coast and approved MacArthur's use of "certain supporting ground units." Although the immediate response to the UN call was disappointing, eventually 15 nations did contribute supplies or troops before the war ended.

Through a simple exercise of presidential power, U.S. policy in Asia was reversed almost overnight. Truman, without seeking formal congressional approval, extended the nation's defense perimeter in the Pacific to include territory that had been excluded so calculatedly only months earlier, and committed U.S. soldiers to defend it. The rapid movement of events had exposed the limitations of the U.S. system of separation of powers and checks and balances when emergencies required decisive action.

Even though many Republican members of Congress had pressed for a U.S. guarantee of Taiwan's security ever since Jiang fled to that island, several were unhappy about Truman's ordering U.S. forces into action in Korea without a congressional resolution. In a partisan attack, Senator William Jenner (R., Ind.) charged that "the Korean debacle also reminds us that the same sellout-to Stalin statesmen, who turned Russia loose, are still in the saddle, riding herd on the American people." A more dignified Taft questioned the constitutionality of the president's executive order and blamed the administration for the trouble in Korea. He endorsed the proposal of Representative H. Alexander Smith (R., N.J.) that the White House seek a congressional resolution approving the president's action. But Congress had taken its normal July 4th recess, and Truman was unwilling to call it back into session and wait for it to act. He justified his orders to MacArthur on his constitutional authority as commander-in-chief of the armed forces and cited "precedents" dating back to Washington and Jefferson.

Crossing the 38th Parallel

After initial reverses forced U.S. troops back to a defense perimeter around the port of Pusan, MacArthur made an amphibious landing at Inchon, west of enemy-controlled Seoul (map, p. 44) to cut North Korean lines of communication and force their retreat. Within two weeks U.S. soldiers recaptured Seoul, and by the end of September South Korean units had advanced north to the 38th parallel. A serious dilemma now faced the UN forces. Were they authorized to cross the parallel, and, if so, for what purpose?

With the Soviet delegate again in his seat in the UN Security Council, the United States turned to the General Assembly for a resolution of the problem. On October 7 the latter established a commission for the unification of Korea under a democratic government and authorized UN forces to cross the 38th parallel to assist in this program. Truman then gave MacArthur permission to advance on the condition that "there had been no entry into North Korea by major Soviet or Chinese communist forces, no announcement of intended entry, nor a threat to counter our operations militarily in Korea." Zhou Enlai's warning on October 2 that China would enter the war if U.S. forces advanced north of the 38th parallel was ignored. When the U.S. First Cavalry Division crossed into North Korea on October 7, 1950, the goals of the United States and the

United Nations had changed from merely driving the aggressor back across the 38th parallel to unifying Korea under a democratic government.

The MacArthur–Truman Controversy

Buoyed by the popular support for destroying North Korea's ability to attack South Korea again, but also worried about a possible expansion of the war, in mid-October Truman flew to Wake Island to confer with MacArthur. The commanding general of the United Nations forces advised the president that there was little chance of either Chinese or Soviet intervention and confidently predicted that all communist resistance in Korea would end by Thanksgiving.

When UN units advanced northward toward the Yalu River in late October, however, Chinese "volunteers" suddenly attacked U.S. Marines and South Korean troops some 50 miles south of the Chinese border. MacArthur assured Washington that full-scale Chinese intervention appeared unlikely and heavy casualties had forced the Chinese to withdraw after their first attack. He continued his drive to the Yalu in what he believed would be the "final offensive" leading to victory. But in less than a month his offensive was stopped and reversed by an army of 300,000 Chinese soldiers. Outnumbered and outfought, UN troops had to make a costly 275-mile retreat back to the 38th parallel. Early in the new year the United States and its allies pushed through the General Assembly a resolution condemning Communist China as an aggressor, but there was no rush to aid the United Nations cause with soldiers.

The unexpected setback in Korea eroded public support for the administration, and the midterm November 1950 elections sharply cut the Democrats' majority in both Houses of Congress. A late December Gallup Poll revealed that only 38 percent of the people thought that the government was doing a good or fair job in Asia. The war in Korea became, in the eyes of the president's opponents, "Mr. Truman's War."

The 71-year-old MacArthur, highly critical of official policy that "tied his hands," proposed air attacks on the "enemy's privileged sanctuaries" in China, a blockade of China, and the use of Chinese Nationalist troops in a diversionary attack on the mainland. He contended that such action would destroy Red China's military potential. Taking a very different view of the situation, the JCS advised Truman to reject MacArthur's plan as dangerously expanding the war in Asia and exposing Western Europe to a communist attack.

Although the president adopted a JCS recommendation to seek an end to the war by reestablishing the 38th parallel as the boundary between North and South Korea, MacArthur continued to speak out for his proposals. He disregarded directives ordering all public officials in the war zone to clear with Washington statements about U.S. war policies. In a series of interviews granted to U.S. and foreign correspondents, MacArthur implied that the administration's

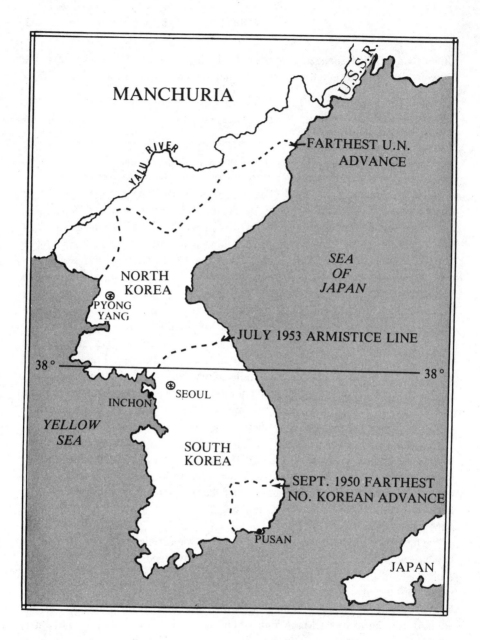

The Korean War

policies were preventing him from achieving a triumph over communism in Asia. In March 1951 he wrote to Joseph Martin (R., Mass.), minority leader of the House:

> It seems strangely difficult for some to realize that here in Asia is where the Communist conspirators have elected to make their play for global conquest,

and that we have joined the issue thus raised on the battlefield; that here we fight Europe's war with arms, while the diplomats there still fight it with words; that if we lose this war to Communism in Asia, the fall of Europe is inevitable; win it and Europe most probably would avoid war and yet preserve freedom. As you pointed out, we must win. There is no substitute for victory.

After Martin read the letter in the House of Representatives in early April, Truman, supported by the Joint Chiefs, removed MacArthur from all of his commands for insubordination. The president believed that MacArthur had challenged his constitutional authority as commander-in-chief and that control of the military by elected civilian officials was in jeopardy. In his *Memoirs* Truman claimed that "even before he [MacArthur] started his ill-fated offensive of November 24, he still talked as if he had the answer to all questions. But when it turned out that it was not so, he let all the world know that he would have won except for the fact that we would not let him have his way."

An hysterical popular reaction followed the announcement of the firing of MacArthur. A flood of telegrams to Congress ran 10 to 1 against Truman. House Republicans urged that MacArthur be called to testify, and Martin hinted that impeachments might be sought. Senator Jenner exclaimed that "this country today is in the hands of a secret inner coterie which is directed by agents of the Soviet Union. . . . Our only choice is to impeach President Truman and find out who is the secret invisible government." McCarthy used the occasion to call the President a "sonofabitch" who must have made his decision while he was "drunk on bourbon and benedictine."

Frustrated with the unending war in Korea and the "general foreign mess," the masses turned to MacArthur for clear, easy answers. The general, who had spent the last 14 years in the Orient, was welcomed home as a hero by enthusiastic crowds in San Francisco, Washington, and New York. An audience of millions listened to or watched on television his emotional address to a Joint Session of Congress.

Senate hearings on the government's policy in East Asia, however, revealed that the nation's military experts had opposed MacArthur's recommendations and that his analysis had focused on Asia only. After a renewed offensive in Korea under General Matthew Ridgway recovered territory back to the 38th parallel and stabilized the front, the clamor against the administration lessened.

Although Truman's popularity continued to decline to a low of only 24 percent approval and 61 percent disapproval, polls indicated that the public strongly believed that stopping communism in Europe was more important than stopping it in Asia. When a Gallup poll in July 1951 showed a majority approving a truce at the 38th parallel, it was clear that MacArthur, despite his great personal prestige, had not proved his case.

Ending the Korean War

As the uproar over the firing of MacArthur subsided, private discussions with the Soviets at the United Nations led in July 1951 to cease-fire negotiations between Ridgway and the Chinese Communists. The talks stalled over China's demand that all foreigners leave Korea and that Formosa be returned to the People's Republic of China. When the Reds abandoned these demands late in the year it was agreed that the demarcation line in Korea would be the battle line on the date of the armistice. But a new snag arose over the repatriation of prisoners of war (POWs). After discovering that many of the 170,000 prisoners captured by UN forces did not want to return to North Korea or China, the Americans refused forced repatriation as demanded by the Communists. Truman declared: "We will not buy an armistice by turning over human beings for slaughter or slavery." Vigorous communist protests against the U.S. position blocked progress in negotiations in the spring of 1952 as the American people geared up for the presidential election.

The Korean War, with U.S. casualties (dead, wounded, and missing) climbing over the 100,000 mark, became a major issue even before the nomination of candidates and Truman's withdrawal from the race. Eisenhower's pledge to go to Korea caught the public fancy, and in December, as president-elect, he fulfilled this commitment by journeying to Korea for a firsthand look. His appraisal of the military situation convinced him that the United States "could not stand forever on a static front and continue to accept the casualties without any visible results." If satisfactory terms ending the war could not be obtained, Eisenhower believed that the United States would have to take off the wraps and use the weapons necessary for a military victory.

Once in office, Eisenhower discovered that Mao expected better peace terms because of Republican campaign promises to end the war. Although the new president rejected pressure from the military to use tactical nuclear weapons to break the deadlock, he did encourage Dulles to drop a hint that "in the absence of satisfactory progress, the United States would no longer be responsible for confining hostilities to the Korean peninsula." At a National Security Council meeting the secretary of state suggested that while "in the present state of the world opinion, we could not use an A-bomb, we should make every effort to dissipate this feeling."

Early in February 1953 the adminstration removed the Seventh Fleet from the Formosa Straits in a gesture of "unleashing" Jiang Jieshi. At the end of the month the Communists abandoned their long-held position on forced return of all prisoners and expressed a willingness to repatriate seriously sick and wounded prisoners of war at once, and to negotiate other issues. Eisenhower accepted, talks resumed, and the Communists agreed to repatriation of prisoners of war willing to return. On July 27, 1953, an armistice ended more than three years of fighting.

CONTAINMENT IN ASIA

Southeast Asia Treaty Organization

In his first State of the Union Message, Eisenhower proclaimed that "the freedom we cherish and defend in Europe and in the Americas is no different from the freedom that is imperiled in Asia." As its first step, the Eisenhower administration drafted a mutual defense treaty with South Korea in January 1954. To strengthen this new ally the United States began to provide financial support to the Rhee government that would soon amount to 75 percent of the latter's military budget and about half of its civil budget.

The Manila Conference in September 1954 produced the next part of the administration's Pacific plan—the Southeast Asia Treaty Organization (SEATO)—advocated by Dulles during the crisis that preceded the French defeat in Vietnam (pp. 89–94). By this pact the United States agreed with Britain, France, the Philippines, Australia, New Zealand, Pakistan, and Thailand that

> aggression by means of armed attack in the treaty area against any of the Parties or against any State or territory which the Parties by unanimous agreement may hereafter designate, would endanger its own peace and safety, and agree that it will in that event act to meet the common danger in accordance with its constitutional processes.

An accompanying protocol designated Cambodia, Laos, and the free territory under the jurisdiction of the state of Vietnam as being included in the treaty area to be defended. While emphasizing the deterrent objective, Dulles carefully pointed out that SEATO was not a replica of NATO because it had no supporting military force. Formosa, China's offshore islands, and Hong Kong, geographically the most vulnerable to Chinese communist aggression, were not included in the area explicitly defended by SEATO. Skeptics quickly pointed out that only Pakistan and Thailand of the signatories were really Asian nations and that their defense was hardly vital to the United States.

Mutual Defense Treaty with Nationalist China

To coincide with the arrival of Dulles in the Philippines to complete the negotiations for SEATO, Mao Zedong initiated heavy artillery bombardment of the offshore island of Quemoy occupied by nearly 50,000 nationalist soldiers. "A horrible dilemma," according to Dulles, confronted the U.S. government. Defense of the offshore islands would involve the United States directly in China's civil war, whereas failure to act might be interpreted by the Communists as a signal that an attack on Formosa would not provoke a forceful U.S. reaction.

The Joint Chiefs, except for General Ridgway, favored defending the islands and aiding the Nationalists in attacking the mainland. Although Eisenhower believed that "concessions were no answer," he resisted the advice of the military on the grounds that "We're not talking now about a limited brushfire war. We're talking about going to the threshold of World War III."

The Formosa Straits crisis led to the final step in the grand plan for containing communism in Asia. In December 1954 the United States and Nationalist China signed a Mutual Defense Treaty. The two nations agreed that an armed attack on either would be considered a threat to the other. Although the treaty included the Pescadore Islands, it left optional the defense of the offshore islands. A week after signing the treaty, in a secret agreement Jiang pledged not to attack the mainland without prior agreement of the United States. In Eisenhower's words this security treaty with Nationalist China "rounded out the far Pacific security chain." Whereas Acheson's defense perimeter of 1950 had been drawn in the water so that the United States could hold it with superior sea and air power, Dulles extended the line to land masses of the Asian continent, the defense of which would require massive U.S. land forces or the use of nuclear weapons. Proponents rejoiced that communism would now be contained in Asia as in Europe. Critics warned that the Asian policy, confusing quantity for quality in the number of U.S. allies, had acquired for the United States "severe liabilities and few assets." Largely ignored was the irony that the Eisenhower administration not only had endorsed containment but had expanded it.

Brinkmanship

When the Chinese Communists probed U.S. intentions by launching attacks early in 1955 on offshore Tachen Island, Eisenhower turned to Congress for authority to use armed forces for "protecting Formosa and the Pescadores against armed attack," and "related positions . . . now in friendly hands." The president alone would judge whether an attack on the off-shore islands was preliminary to an assault on Formosa. Congress approved the request with only six dissenting votes. Senator Hubert Humphrey (D., Minn.) pointed out that rejection "would be to undermine the president's authority completely and totally." He failed to point out that Congress was establishing a precedent in acquiescing to a broad grant of power to the President to conduct foreign affairs and use military force without a congressional declaration of war.

Washington deliberately kept the Formosa Resolution, as it came to be called, ambiguous in order to keep the Chinese Communists in the dark as to what the United States would do in the event of an attack on Quemoy or Matsu. In response to questions about U.S. intent, Dulles hedged, "It cannot be assumed that the defense would be static and confined to Taiwan itself or that the aggressor would enjoy immunity." Privately he told the president: "If we defend

Quemoy and Matsu, we'll have to use atomic weapons. They alone will be effective against the mainland airfields." At a press conference a few days later, Eisenhower appeared to sanction the use of nuclear weapons as "a bullet against strictly military targets for strictly military purposes." Such statements playing on the ambiguity in the Formosa Resolution distressed many Americans and prompted Churchill to advise Eisenhower that the United States should give Jiang "its shield but not the use of its sword."

A new storm developed when Dulles, according to an interview published in *Life* in January 1956, revealed that his skillful diplomacy in averting war in the Formosa Straits was the third such occasion on which he had saved the day. The author of the article claimed that Dulles had used the nuclear threat to persuade the Chinese Reds to agree to an armistice in Korea in 1953, and that he had threatened U.S. military action if the Chinese Communists intervened in the Indochina War in 1954. The secretary was quoted as saying: "The ability to get to the verge without getting into the war is the necessary art. If you cannot master it, you inevitably get into the war. If you try to run away from it, if you are scared to go to the brink, you are lost." Howls of indignation arose at home and abroad. Adlai Stevenson, Eisenhower's opponent in 1952 and again in 1956, exclaimed that he was "shocked that the Secretary of State is willing to play Russian roulette with the life of the nation." Several members of Congress demanded that Dulles resign because of his irresponsible and tactless words. A new word, "brinkmanship," heated the political atmosphere and captioned cartoon and editorial.

Rejection of Rapprochement with Communist China

In the weeks prior to this furor over "brinkmanship," Eisenhower and his advisers had to assess conciliatory gestures made by Beijing, whose relations with the Soviet Union had deteriorated. In mid-summer 1955 Mao initiated limited diplomatic contacts with the United States in Geneva. But Washington, having bombarded the public for years with admonitions of the wickedness of the Chinese Reds, could hardly afford to soften its opposition to any deals with them without risking the loss of political support at home. Dulles as usual took the high moral position and closed the door to Chinese overtures with the statement that "under present conditions, neither recognition, nor trade, nor cultural relations, nor all three together would favorably influence the evolution of affairs in China." In April 1958 the United States suspended the occasional diplomatic talks with the Chinese Communists in Geneva. Its task done, the China Lobby relaxed.

Defending its policy of nonrecognition of Red China, the State Department released in August 1958 a memorandum declaring that "the Soviet bloc, of which Communist China is an important part, is engaged in a long-range struggle to destroy the way of life of the free countries of the world and bring about the global dominion of Communism." Official assumptions had not changed. Monolithic communism remained the enemy. Between 1957 and 1961 the percentage of Americans, according to Gallup polls, who thought that Communist China should be admitted to the United Nations never climbed higher than 20 percent. In 1958 Chinese communist bombardment of offshore islands still occupied by nationalist Chinese strengthened U.S. suspicions that leaders of the People's Republic of China intended to expand its domain.

As the Eisenhower administration came to an end, U.S. policy in Asia continued to function in the context of the U.S.–Soviet cold war. Primary attention continued to be centered on Western Europe. Although some signs of a rift between China and the Soviet Union had appeared, Americans continued to regard Mao's China as part of the international conspiracy headquartered in Moscow. Developments in Africa, Latin America, and Asia tended to reinforce such beliefs that precluded any lifting of the bamboo curtain that isolated China until 1972.

CHAPTER 3

The United States and the Developing Nations, 1945–1981

"We have a natural sympathy with those everywhere who would follow our example."

John Foster Dulles, 1954

"We must strengthen the cause of freedom throughout all Latin America, creating an atmosphere where liberty will flourish, and where Cuban Communism will be resisted, isolated, and left to die on the vine."

John F. Kennedy, 1960

"The division of the planet between rich and poor could become as grim as the darkest days of the cold war."

Henry Kissinger, 1975

THE DEVELOPING NATIONS AND THE COLD WAR

The Third World

South of the industrialized nations of North America, Europe, and Asia, over one hundred countries occupy slightly more than half of the world's land surface and contain almost half of the world's population. Three-fourths of these countries, with mostly nonwhite populations, were once colonies of Western nations who exported Christianity, white supremacy, and industrial products while extracting valuable raw materials. A lack of modern technology and heavy reliance on agriculture contribute to keeping these countries underdeveloped economically. A high birthrate and widespread illiteracy also retard progress. Millions live in primitive conditions where inadequate diet, poverty, and disease reduce life expectancy to about half that of developed countries.

Except for the nations of Latin America, older and more advanced in general because of longer Western influence, the developing nations tended to remain unaligned or neutral in the cold war. The French label, "Tiers Monde," or Third World, defined the whole area as outside the arena in Europe and Asia where East and West jostled for domination immediately after World War II. The United States had economic as well as strategic interests in many Third World nations. Not only did the latter furnish important products such as petroleum, tin, bauxite, and tungsten, but they served as a market for U.S. goods and services as well as a place for profitable investment of U.S. capital.

51

By 1978 Americans had invested over $40 billion in less developed nations—almost one-quarter of the nation's total foreign investment. Moreover, the United States consistently enjoyed a favorable balance of trade with less developed nations, who in 1977 purchased 35 percent of all U.S. exports.

Although attracted by the principles of the Declaration of Independence and delighted with the promises of the Atlantic Charter, many Third World peoples had ambivalent feelings about the United States. They praised its postwar stance in granting independence to the Philippines and in encouraging the British to withdraw from India. But racism in the United States and U.S. reluctance to pressure its allies to relinquish Asian and African colonies tarnished the U.S. image. In addition, costly struggles by native leaders to free their peoples from tenacious Western control built up resentment against the West. Some Third World reformers, seeking to end the ownership of their nation's land and resources by a small privileged class, viewed the economic activities of Americans as supporting the exploitation of the people by the upper class.

Seeking to capitalize on widespread discontent and disaffection with the West in the developing nations, the Soviet Union exported Marxist propaganda against "the imperialists" and recruited native leaders to organize national communist movements. In 1955, Khrushchev initiated Soviet military aid programs to several developing countries. Thus, within a decade of the end of World War II, the cold war had spilled over into Latin America, the Middle East, Africa, and Southeast Asia.

U.S. Assistance to the Developing Nations

In his Inaugural Address on January 20, 1949, President Harry Truman recommended as the fourth point in his foreign policy "a bold new program for making the benefits of our scientific advances and industrial progress available for the improvement and growth of underdeveloped areas." Point Four assumed that communism flows from poverty and discontent, and that technical aid

Distribution of U.S. Economic and Technical Aid

Years	Average annual amount ($ billions)	% to Europe	% to Third World
1949–1952	3.4	86	14
1953–1957	1.8	25	75
1958–1961	1.85	6	94
1962–1966	2.3	0	100
1967–1971	2.2	0	100
1972–1976	3.37	0	100

SOURCE: Agency for International Development (AID)

U.S. Grants and Credits to Developing Nations ($ millions)

Region	1946–1955	1956–1965	1966–1975
Middle East	2,110	6,161	8,438
S. Asia	593	8,384	7,002
East & SE Asia	9,678	16,119	34,778
Africa	147	2,272	3,610
Latin America	1,248	5,181	6,816

SOURCE: U.S. Department of Commerce.

would promote economic development and an improvement in living standards that would make communism unattractive. Although Truman asked for a modest $45 million in the first year of Point Four aid, Congress reluctantly appropriated only $27 million. To coordinate and administer assistance programs to Third World nations, Congress in 1950 passed the Act for International Development (AID). As its focus switched from Europe following the outbreak of the Korean War, Washington funneled more and more aid to the Third World as the preceding tables illustrate.

THE UNITED STATES AND LATIN AMERICA IN THE COLD WAR, 1945–1981

Different Needs and Goals

With almost $3 billion of private U.S. capital invested, U.S. consumers the main market for Latin American goods, and U.S. industry the principal supplier of imports, the United States dominated the Latin American economy at the end of World War II. More important to the United States than economic interests, Latin America's geographic location involved it intimately with the security of the United States. The Caribbean area, where Cuba at one point is separated from Florida by less than 100 miles of water and where dozens of islands lie in the traffic lanes of ships using the Panama Canal, had special strategic importance for the United States.

. Following World War II, differing priorities led to misunderstandings and friction between the United States and Latin America. Responding to its assessment of the needs of the domestic economy, the Truman administration allowed special wartime purchase arrangements with Latin American nations to lapse and reduced orders for their products. Although hemispheric defense appeared secure against outside threats, Latin American economic problems and political instability remained. Some Americans stressed the need to furnish direct economic aid

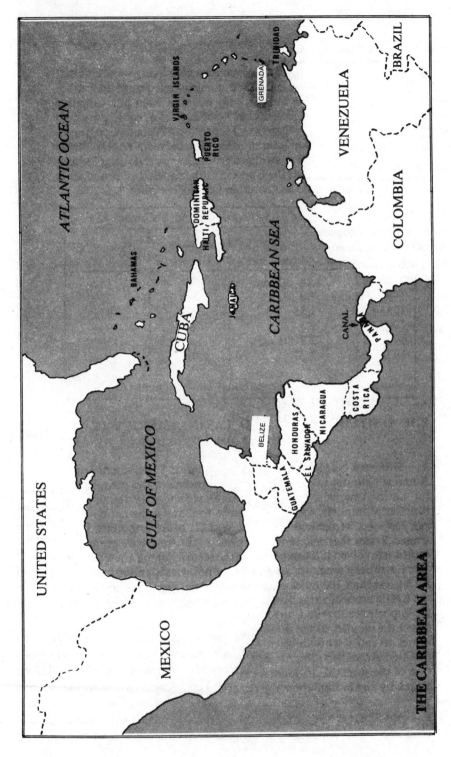

THE CARIBBEAN AREA

UNITED STATES

MEXICO

GULF OF MEXICO

ATLANTIC OCEAN

BAHAMAS

CUBA

JAMAICA

HAITI

DOMINICAN REPUBLIC

PUERTO RICO

VIRGIN ISLANDS

CARIBBEAN SEA

BELIZE

GUATEMALA

EL SALVADOR

HONDURAS

NICARAGUA

COSTA RICA

PANAMA

CANAL

GRENADA

TRINIDAD

VENEZUELA

COLOMBIA

BRAZIL

54

to prevent such conditions from attracting revolutionary ideology and communist infiltration. The prevailing U.S. view, however, held that if Latin Americans practiced Yankee virtues of hard work, self-reliance, and frugality, they would solve their problems. Washington answered requests for direct assistance with lectures about the need for proper management of their resources and for being hospitable to the investment of private capital. U.S. business and government appeared indifferent, if not hostile, to large-scale industrialization.

Having expanded production of raw materials to meet wartime demand, Latin Americans resented the abrupt decline in orders, reduction in credit, and much higher prices for U.S. goods. As unemployment increased and inflation accelerated, discontent and anti-American nationalism blossomed. Latin American spokespersons wanted a long-term commitment of U.S. economic aid and the freedom to use that aid as they saw fit.

The Rio Pact, 1947

As the cold war evolved, the United States moved to safeguard the Western Hemisphere through an autonomous regional security system as projected in the wartime Act of Chapultepec and in Articles 51 and 52 of the UN charter. In September 1947 an Inter-American Conference in Brazil produced the Rio Pact, whereby each contracting nation reaffirmed "that an armed attack by any State against an American State shall be considered an attack against all the American states." In addition, the treaty provided that if the territory or political independence of any American State should be threatened "by an aggression which is not an armed attack, or by any extra-continental or intra-continental conflict, or by any other fact or situation" the parties agreed to "meet immediately in order to agree on measures which must be taken." Championed by Vandenberg in the Senate, the Rio Pact, ratified with only one dissenting vote, became the first peacetime military pact of the United States and the model for NATO.

The Organization of American States

Three months later at Bogotá, Colombia, the Ninth Pan-American Conference drafted the charter of the Organization of American States (OAS) establishing machinery for dealing with aggression against any American nation. The United States delegation also pushed through a resolution that condemned "international communism or any other totalitarian doctrine" as being "incompatible with the concept of American freedom."

But only a trickle of U.S. foreign aid, about $160 million per year, or less than 3 percent of its total for all nations, reached Latin America between 1946 and 1952 (see p. 61). At the Bogotá Conference Marshall admitted that there would be no Marshall Plan for Latin America. "It is beyond the capacity of the

United States government itself," he said, "to finance more than a small portion of the vast development needed." Private capital, fearful that Latin American regimes might nationalize industrial and commercial enterprises, likewise dribbled southward very sluggishly, except for investment in Venezuelan oil.

The Eisenhower–Dulles Policy

Although the bombast of the 1952 election campaign, featuring charges of neglect of Latin America, promised otherwise, the Republican triumph did not usher in major changes in the nation's Latin American policy. Economic aid was increased modestly, but the major concern remained the security of the Western Hemisphere against any communist penetration. To guarantee such security, Eisenhower and Dulles became deeply involved in the internal affairs of two Latin American states in the Caribbean area—Guatemala and Cuba.

Intervention in Guatemala, 1954

On May 15, 1954, a Swedish cargo ship outbound from Stettin, Poland docked at Puerto Barrios, Guatemala laden with 1,900 tons listed in the manifest as "hardware and optical goods." Unloaded at night in great secrecy, the cargo actually consisted of 15,000 cases of rifles, machine guns, and other military equipment manufactured in Czechoslovakia and consigned to the Guatemalan government.

The arms had been purchased by the administration of Colonel Jacobo Arbenz Guzmán, elected president in November 1951 on a platform pledging major land reforms in a nation where 2 percent of the 3 million people owned 70 percent of the land. Guatemala's economy had long been dominated by the U.S.-owned United Fruit Company whose banana plantations furnished an important part of the nation's foreign exchange. Early in 1953 Arbenz expropriated over 200,000 acres of uncultivated land owned by United Fruit and began a program of land distribution among the landless peasants. He offered to compensate United Fruit by paying $600,000 in government bonds, the assessed value of the land for tax purposes, but the company demanded $15 million.

In late 1953 the new U.S. ambassador, John Peurifoy, reported that "unless the Communist influences in Guatemala were counteracted, Guatemala would within six months fall completely under Communist ,control." Although no known Communists held cabinet posts in the government, Arbenz openly accepted the Communists as a legitimate national party (estimated 3,000 members) and used communist leaders to administer educational and agrarian reforms.

The CIA arranged covert "Operation El Diablo" to overthrow the Arbenz government. With the help of United Fruit Company executives, the CIA enlisted exiled Colonel Carlos Castillo Armas to lead a coup. Secret headquarters were established in Honduras, with a training center on an island off the Nicaraguan coast. Early in 1954, Arbenz accused the United States of intervention in internal affairs of Guatemala and opened negotiations with the Soviet Union for arms.

Washington moved promptly to isolate the Arbenz government. At the Tenth Inter-American Conference in Caracas in March 1954, extreme U.S. pressure forced adoption of an OAS resolution proclaiming that "the domination or control of the political institutions of any American state by the international Communist movement . . . would constitute a threat to the sovereignty and political independence of the American states, endangering the peace of America."

The arrival of the arms from Czechoslovakia in May drew a sharp protest and compensatory U.S. arms shipments to Nicaragua and Honduras. CIA agents speeded up plans for overthrowing Arbenz. On June 18, 1954, about 150 armed men led by Castillo Armas crossed the Guatemalan border from Honduras and were joined by some 500 supporters. Aided by an air cover of four old World War II P-47 Thunderbolts, supplied by the United States and flown by U.S. pilots employed by the CIA, the invaders advanced into Guatemala meeting little resistance. The most stirring battle took place in the United Nations in New York as a result of Guatemala's demand for Security Council action. While the United States parried the thrust by Guatemala and the Soviet Union in the United Nations by claiming OAS jurisdiction, Guatemala's regular army defected and joined the rebels. By June 27 the government had collapsed, and Arbenz had fled.

Three days later John Foster Dulles proclaimed that "the people of the United States and the other American Republics can feel tonight that at least one great danger has been averted." The secretary of state announced that "the ambitious and unscrupulous will be less prone to feel that Communism is the wave of their future." Guatemala's dictatorship speedily disfranchised 70 percent of the population, suspended all constitutional liberties, and returned confiscated land to the United Fruit Company. It had all been so easy and inexpensive— covert aid to a native group committed to overthrow a regime deemed unfriendly to U.S. interests. This successful venture served as a precedent for subsequent Latin American activities by the United States.

The Anti-Nixon Demonstrations

The overthrow of a legitimately elected government by a coup clandestinely engineered by the United States did not sit well with many Latin Americans. Anti-Americanism smoldered from Mexico to Argentina. Increased economic and modest military aid during the next three years (see p. 61) failed to appease those critical of both U.S. obsession with fighting communism and U.S. failure to do much to solve Latin America's serious problems. This hostility erupted during Vice-President Nixon's Latin American "good will" trip in May 1958. Protesters in Lima, Peru and in Bogotá, Colombia stoned, booed, and spat on the vice-president's motorcade. In Caracas, Venezuela an angry mob threatened to overturn the automobile in which Nixon was riding. Blaming the demonstrations on Communists, Nixon reported to Eisenhower that "the threat of Communism in Latin America is greater than ever before." Subsequent events in Cuba soon made more Americans concerned about that threat.

Friction with Castro's Cuba, 1959–1960

On January 1, 1959, followers of Fidel Castro's 26th of July Movement took over the streets of Havana, Cuba, following the sudden flight of Fulgencio Batista, the military dictator of Cuba since 1933. One week later the 32-year-old leader of the victorious revolutionaries, after more than five years of guerrilla warfare, entered the capital city to a tumultuous welcome. Within a few weeks he committed himself to a radical social revolution designed to terminate the domination of Cuba by the United States.

Castro and his followers had many reasons for feeling unfriendly toward the United States. Until 1958 the United States sold arms to Batista and maintained a military training mission in Cuba. Following Batista's downfall, his supporters had found a hospitable haven in the United States, and thousands of refugees fled to Florida. Americans had invested over $1 billion in Batista's Cuba, supplied Cuba with three-fourths of its imports, and purchased about 60 percent of Cuba's exports. Cuba's revolutionary leaders resolved to change all that. In May 1959 an Agrarian Reform Law expropriated large land holdings and divided them among landless peasants.

U.S. investors and businesspeople were outraged, even though Castro promised compensation in Cuban bonds, and called on their government to act. Reflecting the feeling of U.S. investors in Cuba, the *Wall Street Journal* observed that "this revolution may be like a watermelon. The more they slice it, the redder it gets." When Castro visited the United States at the invitation of the American Society of Newpaper Editors in April 1959, Eisenhower refused to meet with him and rejected his request for arms. Castro then turned to the Soviet Union and obtained a credit of $100 million. Denouncing the Rio Pact, he made speech after speech condemning "Yankee imperialism."

Worried about Cuba's drift toward communism, Eisenhower made a fateful decision early in 1960. He secretly ordered Allen W. Dulles, head of the CIA, to direct the funding, training, and equipping of a military force of Cubans-in-exile to liberate Cuba from Castro. Over the next several months at secret bases in friendly Guatemala, the CIA prepared several hundred Cubans for an invasion of their homeland.

In late June 1960 Castro seized U.S. oil refineries in Cuba without offering compensation. When Eisenhower retaliated by suspending the balance of Cuba's 1960 quota of sugar imported by the United States, Castro nationalized without compensation all 36 sugar mills owned by Americans and additional property valued at about $750 million. Vice-President Nixon called Castro "either incredibly naive about Communism or under Communist discipline." In October the administration imposed an embargo on exports to Cuba, covering everything except food and medicine.

The Bay of Pigs Disaster, 1961

By the time the CIA, shortly after the election, had briefed President-elect Kennedy on the invasion plan, relations with Cuba had deteriorated to the breaking point. A joint Soviet–Cuban communique in mid-December 1960 expressing socialist solidarity convinced leaders of both political parties that Castro was pro-Communist and a serious threat to U.S. interests. Seventeen days before the inauguration of Kennedy, Eisenhower broke diplomatic relations with Cuba.

With Pentagon approval, Allen Dulles pressured the new president to proceed with the invasion. Dulles reminded Kennedy that he (Dulles) had stood there in front of Eisenhower's desk in 1954 and told him that he was certain of the success of the CIA-supervised Guatemalan revolution against Arbenz. Now, argued Dulles, "the prospects for this plan are even better than they were for that one." It appeared to Kennedy that, if he failed to act, Castro might become "a much greater danger than he is today." Moreover, a veto of an attempt to depose the Cuban leader might furnish ammunition to Kennedy's political opponents at home while encouraging the Soviets to regard it as a sign of weakness.

Although Senator J. William Fulbright (D., Ark.) warned the president that "to give this activity even covert support is of a piece with the hypocrisy and cynicism for which the United States is constantly denouncing the Soviet Union in the United Nations and elsewhere," Kennedy gave the go-ahead. To reassure anxious allies and a public confused by rumors, the president pledged on April 12 that "there will not be, under any conditions, any intervention in Cuba by United States armed forces."

Just before midnight on April 17, a flotilla of small ships approached the southern coast of Cuba, east of the Bay of Pigs. The 1,400 CIA-trained Cubans on board included just 150 professional soldiers. Crammed into 14-foot fiberglass boats, the advance group floundered on coral reefs and lost equipment and supplies in the darkness. The first "liberator" did not land until 4:00 A.M. Until ammunition ran out four days later, the invaders inflicted heavy casualties on Castro's forces. But as befits an ill-conceived plan, everything went wrong. The underground uprising did not occur, Castro's planes sank or drove away supply ships, and a supporting air strike was canceled by Kennedy, who feared it would put the United States in an untenable position before the bar of world opinion. By April 21 Castro's men were rounding up the survivors, and Kennedy was accepting responsibility for the fiasco. Not only had the operation failed to pave the way for the overthrow of Castro, but it had also given him and other U.S. opponents the opportunity to point a morally accusing finger at the United States.

The Alliance for Progress

Kennedy decided that a different policy was needed to encourage economic and social progress in Latin America as a barrier against the spread of Castroism. In his campaign Kennedy had referred to a new "Alliance for Progress" with Latin America to demonstrate "that man's unsatisfied aspiration for economic progress and social justice can best be achieved by free men working within a framework of democratic institutions." At Punte del Este, Uruguay, in August 1961, 20 American republics, with only Cuba abstaining, drafted a charter for an Alliance for Progress. It pledged "to improve and strengthen democratic institutions . . . to accelerate economic and social development . . . to encourage programs of comprehensive agrarian reform." For its part the United States offered to provide $20 billion over the next 20 years. Latin America seemed finally to have its version of the Marshall Plan.

Operation Mongoose

The sense of humiliation following the Bay of Pigs disaster increased the appeal of eliminating Castro himself. To this end Operation Mongoose was devised and placed under the direct supervision of Attorney-General Robert Kennedy. According to William Moyers, later an adviser to President Johnson, the CIA assumed that the goal made permissible the covert plan initiated in the Eisenhower administration to assassinate the Cuban leader. In September 1961 the Cuban press reported that several Cubans, alleged agents of the CIA, had been arrested for an attempt on Castro's life. No confirming evidence has been made public to date.

When Castro declared himself a Marxist–Leninist in December 1961, the rift with the United States appeared beyond repair. At a second Inter-American Conference at Punta del Este early in 1962 strong U.S. pressure prompted the expulsion of Cuba from the OAS by a 14 to 6 vote. The Kennedy administration thereby isolated Cuba in the Western Hemisphere, but Cuba had drawn ever closer to the Soviet Union. For three decades Castro would be a thorn in the side of the United States.

Millions
of dollars

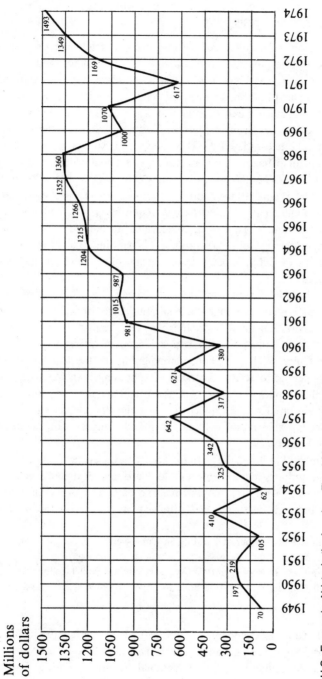

U.S. Economic Aid to Latin America, Fiscal Years 1949–1974

SOURCE: Agency for International Development (AID)

61

The Cuban Missile Crisis, 1962

On Monday, October 22, 1962 Americans tuned in television or radio sets to hear an address by the president. Since late summer the news media had carried alarming reports of a Soviet missiles and arms build-up in Cuba, and the nation sensed a crisis at hand. Kennedy revealed that the Soviet Union was installing missiles in Cuba capable of carrying nuclear warheads to Washington, D.C., the Panama Canal, and other prime targets in North and South America. Somberly he explained that he had ordered the U.S. Navy and Air Force to impose a strict "quarantine" on all offensive military equipment under shipment to Cuba. He pledged that it would be the nation's policy "to regard any nuclear missiles launched from Cuba against any nation in the Western Hemisphere as an attack by the Soviet Union on the United States, requiring a full retaliatory response upon the Soviet Union." The United States also introduced a resolution in the Security Council calling for "the prompt dismantling and withdrawal of all offensive weapons in Cuba, under the supervision of U.N. observers, before the quarantine can be lifted."

The crisis had developed with dramatic speed. Late in August, two U.S. U-2 reconnaissance planes photographed in Cuba sites for surface-to-air missiles that military experts regarded as defensive. On August 31 Senator Kenneth Keating (R., N.Y.) claimed that he had evidence of Soviet troops and rocket installations in Cuba. Richard Nixon, campaigning for the California governorship, used the opening to accuse Kennedy of appeasing both Castro and Khrushchev. Fearful that Soviet activities in Cuba might be the forerunner of a new move on West Berlin, Kennedy hoped to downplay the Cuban situation. But in order to protect his own political flank, he asked Congress for authorization to call up 150,000 reservists.

On September 11, Tass, the official Soviet news agency, claimed that "the armaments and military equipment sent to Cuba are designed exclusively for defensive purposes." At a press conference two days later, Kennedy underscored the difference between defensive and offensive missiles with the warning that

> if at any time the Communist build-up in Cuba were to endanger or interfere with our security in any way . . . or if Cuba should ever . . . become an offensive military base of significant capacity for the Soviet Union, then this country will do whatever must be done to protect its own security and that of its allies.

Not until Sunday, October 14, did a U-2 photograph evidence of the construction of Soviet medium-range missile bases. Two days later Kennedy met with an Executive Committee of the National Security Council (ExCom) and decided to proceed in strictest secrecy until both the facts and the U.S. response could be announced. ExCom held round-the-clock meetings for the next four days. Additional U-2 photos revealed a total of six 1,000 mile range missile sites and excavations for three 2,200 mile range missiles. Suggestions of direct private negotiations with Castro, as well as a proposal to turn the matter over to the United Nations, were quickly dismissed by the ExCom as totally unacceptable. Ambassador to the United Nations Adlai Stevenson's suggestion of a deal agreeing to withdraw U.S. missiles from Turkey in exchange for the withdrawal of the Soviet missiles from Cuba was ridiculed by the hard-liners. Finally, after rejecting both a "surgical" air strike to knock out the missiles and a full-scale military intervention proposed by the Joint Chiefs, the ExCom decided on a blockade as a "more limited, low-key military action than the airstrike." According to presidential adviser Ted Sorensen, Kennedy "liked the idea of leaving Khrushchev a way out, of beginning at a low level that could then be stepped up." From OAS members, European allies, and congressional leaders of both parties, the administration received overwhelming support.

For five days following the president's speech, the world marked time waiting for deliverance from a threatened holocaust. U.S. armed forces were placed on war alert. Polaris nuclear submarines took up positions at sea within range of targets inside the the Soviet Union, while the Strategic Air Command kept fleets of long-range bombers, loaded with nuclear weapons, in the air round the clock.

At sea 26 ships of a U.S. naval force established a blockade line 500 miles east of Cuba. The fleet had orders to "disable but not sink" any Soviet ship that attempted to continue on course toward Cuba. But on Wednesday morning, October 24, the navy informed Washington that the Soviet ships nearest Cuba had apparently stopped or altered course.

Tension continued, however, because the danger of the missiles still remained. New U-2 photos revealed work on the sites going ahead at full speed and indicated that all of the medium-range missiles would be operational within a few days. Kennedy massed in Florida the largest invasion force since World War II and readied plans for a bombing strike. Then, at the height of the crisis a letter from Premier Khrushchev expressed a willingness to negotiate the removal of the missiles in return for lifting the quarantine and a U.S. pledge not to invade Cuba. A second Khrushchev letter, more belligerent in tone, added a demand for the removal of U.S. Jupiter missiles from Turkey.

In his reply Kennedy concentrated on the terms suggested in the first letter. He agreed that in return for "cessation of work on missile sites in Cuba and measures to render such weapons inoperable, under effective international guarantees," the United States would lift the quarantine and give assurances against an invasion of Cuba. On Sunday, October 28, Khrushchev, accepting Kennedy's terms, agreed to remove the missiles. Nuclear war had been averted. As Secretary of State Dean Rusk put it, we were "eyeball to eyeball, and they blinked first." Critics later contended that the United States had so humiliated the

Soviets in the Cuban Missile Crisis that the Kremlin embarked on an all-out effort to gain nuclear equality.

The 1963 Test Ban Treaty and a Thaw in the Cold War

Three crises in 24 months—Berlin, Cuba, and Laos (p. 98)—appeared to induce Moscow to reappraise its policies. Late in November 1962 Khrushchev responded favorably to a Kennedy proposal for a test-ban treaty, and the way was prepared for discussions. In early June 1963 in a commencement address at American University, Kennedy described peace as "the necessary rational end of rational men" and appealed to Soviet leaders to take steps necessary to relax international tensions. In July 1963, after months of negotiations, a treaty to cease atmospheric testing of nuclear weapons was signed. Later that summer a special teletype circuit linking Moscow and Washington, "the hot line," was installed to provide instant communications in the event of a grave crisis. To many Americans these developments signaled a warming trend in the cold war.

Continuing Problems in Latin America

Serious problems, however, continued to beset U.S. relations with Latin America. Although Washington poured in aid and private capital (see graph, p. 41), the Alliance for Progress floundered. Projected economic growth rates were not achieved, in large measure due to failures by the Latin Americans themselves. Most Latin American countries still had unfavorable balances of trade, and political instability remained widespread. Inefficiency, injustice, and corruption invited revolutionary activity. The Cuban "solution" appeared contagious and difficult to contain. Continuing efforts to get rid of Castro failed. For example, on the day that President Kennedy was assassinated, the CIA delivered to an agent in Cuba a hypodermic needle and high-grade poison to be used to kill the Cuban leader.

Intervention in the Dominican Republic, 1965

About 50 miles east of Cuba in the Caribbean Sea lies the island of Hispaniola divided into two nations—Haiti and the Dominican Republic. When Washington received word on April 25, 1965, of growing disorder inspired by opponents of the government of President Cabral, President Lyndon Johnson ordered a naval task force, including a marine battalion, to sail to the vicinity of the Dominican Republic. On the next day, the U.S. chargé d'affaires, William Connett, cabled that rebels supporting the return of former president Juan Bosch had seized the presidential palace. Connett warned Washington that the political philosophy of groups supporting Bosch foreshadowed danger of a communist government, and that a U.S. "show of force" might be useful. On April 28 Ambassador W. Tapley Bennett wired Washington that the situation was "deteriorating rapidly" and that "American lives are in danger." He urged "armed intervention . . . to prevent another Cuba."

Stressing the need to protect and evacuate U.S. civilians, Johnson, on April 28, without first consulting the OAS, authorized the landing of 500 marines, the first U.S. combat-ready troops to enter a Latin American country since 1925. Later that day an urgent message from Ambassador Bennett warned: "All indications point to the fact that if present efforts of forces loyal to the government fail, power will be assumed by groups clearly identified with the Communist party." Johnson ordered the landing of an additional 1,500 marines and the sending of paratroops from the 82nd Airborne Divison. Within a week the United States had 23,000 troops on the island as the OAS attempted to arrange a cease-fire.

When pressed by reporters for evidence of the communist role, the State Department supplied a list of 58 alleged Communists said to be active in the revolt. Later investigations by reporters disclosed 3 names appeared on the list twice, while some of the 55 were out of the country or in jail. In a nationwide radio and TV address on May 2, 1965, Johnson defended his action by contending that "what had begun as a popular democratic revolution, committed to democracy and social justice, very shortly moved and was taken over and really seized and placed into the hands of a band of Communist conspirators." Many Americans, however, remained skeptical. For instance, the *New York Times* complained that "little awareness has been shown by the United States that the Dominican people—not just a handful of Communists—were fighting and dying for social justice and constitutionalism." Few were aware that 28 Americans died in the course of securing the island.

The June 1, 1966, elections resulted in victory for Joaquin Balaguer, who ruled with an iron hand in Trujillo fashion until his defeat in the 1978 election. U.S. intervention had neither saved the people of the Dominican Republic from oppressive rule, nor had it won the plaudits of sister republics in Latin America. But Lyndon Johnson made sure that no political rival could accuse him of lacking the will to meet the Communists head-on. He also strengthened his own confidence in the efficacy of military force to smash communist threats—a faith later tested severely in Vietnam.

Intervention in Chile, 1964–1973

At a June 1970 meeting of the top secret "Forty Committee," a special inter-agency group that controlled covert operations of the federal government, Henry Kissinger said, "I don't see why we need to stand by and watch a country go Communist due to irresponsibility of its own people." President Nixon's national security adviser was referring to the September presidential election in Chile where Salvador Allende, a 61-year-old Socialist, was the candidate of left-wing parties in a three-man race.

Disturbed by Allende's support from communist groups and by his platform calling for seizure of property owned by such U.S. corporations as International Telephone and Telegraph, Anaconda Copper, and Kennecott, both the Eisenhower administration in 1958 and the Johnson administration in 1964 aided Allende's more conservative opponents. In the 1964 campaign, according to Director William Colby, the CIA spent $3 million to defeat Allende. Kissinger's appeal in 1970 produced an allocation of $500,000 by the Forty Committee for an anti-Allende operation.

Despite the best efforts of U.S. intrigue and money, Allende received about 40,000 more votes than his nearest competitor in 1970, but only 36 percent of the total vote. He, however, would not become president unless elected in October by the Chilean Congress. According to Kissinger, on September 15 President Nixon told CIA Director Richard Helms: "If there were one chance in ten of getting rid of Allende we should try it; if Helms needed $10 million he would approve it. Aid programs to Chile should be cut; its economy should be squeezed until it 'screamed.' " So U.S. efforts to prevent Allende's election continued. An internal ITT memorandum on September 18, 1970, indicated that U.S. ambassador to Chile, Edward Korry, had received from Washington "maximum authority to do all possible—short of a Dominican Republic-type action—to keep Allende from taking power." According to Congressman Michael Harrington (D., Mass.) the Forty Committee authorized $350,000 "to bribe the Chilean Congress." But the latter followed tradition and elected the highest vote getter—Allende. He thereby became the first avowed Marxist to win election to the highest office in a Western Hemisphere nation.

The Nixon administration, however, was unwilling to accept the result, especially after Allende nationalized the $1 billion holdings of U.S. copper mining companies and offered "inadequate" compensation. Nixon secretly ordered the CIA to "get rougher" to undermine Allende. According to a 1975 report of a Senate Select Committee on Intelligence Activities, the U.S. government "remained in intelligence contact with the Chilean military, including officers who were participating in coup plotting." Under Kissinger's direction, the Forty Committee furnished $5 million for a "destabilization" program that included strikes, demonstrations, sabotage, and antigovernment propaganda in the Chilean press. Military aid to the Chilean armed services jumped from less than $1 million in 1970 to over $12 million in 1972. In the autumn of 1973 Chilean army officers staged a coup that resulted in the murder of Allende and the installation of a new, conservative dictatorship. Congenial to U.S. corporate investment in Chile, the new government gained immediate recognition by the United States.

Critics of covert U.S. participation in the overthrow of the legitimate government of Chile pointed to a disturbing pattern. Washington assisted Guatemala, the Dominican Republic, and Chile in putting into power authoritarian regimes willing to subordinate immediate aspirations of their own people to the interests of the United States. Many Latin Americans saw the United States as their oppressor rather than as a partner in democracy and rising expectations.

The Panama Canal Treaties, 1978

The 1903 Treaty that gave the United States "in perpetuity, the use, occupation and control" of the 10-mile-wide Panama Canal Zone became a long-standing source of friction between the United States and Latin America. Panamanians resented the relatively small economic return to Panama, the total U.S. control of all activities in the Zone, and the contrast between the luxurious American standard of living there and the poverty in Panama itself.

A crisis erupted in January 1964 when rioting broke out after a group of U.S. students at Balboa High School in the Canal Zone raised a U.S. flag in front of the school contrary to a 1962 agreement. Four U.S. soldiers and 20 Panamanian rioters died. After breaking relations with the United States, Panama brought its case to the United Nations and to the OAS. With broad bipartisan support, President Johnson committed the United States to negotiate a new treaty. But in 1970, General Torrijos, Panama's new leader, rejected as inadequate treaties drafted in 1967 that would have abrogated the 1903 Treaty and provided for eventual Panamanian sovereignty in the Zone and ownership of the canal.

Supported by sister Latin American republics, Panama brought its cause before a special UN Security Council meeting in Panama City in the spring of 1973. After the United States vetoed a Security Council resolution calling for the two nations to negotiate a "just and equitable treaty," Secretary of State Kissinger explained that the United States wished to deal with Panama bilaterally, without outside pressure. In early 1974 the two nations agreed on general principles ending the concept of perpetuity, transferring jurisdiction in the Canal Zone to Panama, and continuing U.S. responsibility for defense of the canal.

Three years of hard negotiations ensued, amidst a rising clamor from U.S. opponents of any "Panama Canal giveaway," before specific phrasing of two treaties was agreed on in August 1977. The first treaty gave Panama immediate territorial jurisdiction over the Canal Zone but the United States retained responsibility for operating and defending the canal until the year 2000. The second treaty guaranteed the permanent neutrality of the canal after control passed to Panama.

A torrent of well-organized protest flowed from those who agreed with former California governor Ronald Reagan's pronouncement: "We bought it, we paid for it, and they can't have it." Public opinion polls throughout 1977 and early 1978 indicated that a majority of citizens disapproved of the treaties. Opponents stressed the danger of a communist takeover of the canal and the threat to the nation's security.

The Carter administration, nevertheless, worked vigorously and effectively to convince enough senators to muster the necessary two-thirds vote. Supporters worried that, if the United States failed to ratify the treaties, acts of violence and sabotage might close the canal. In April 1978 the Senate approved the Panama Canal Treaties with one vote to spare. An elated President Carter noted:

> This is a day of which Americans can always feel proud. . . . These treaties can mark the beginning of a new era in our relations not only with Panama but with all the rest of the world. They symbolize our determination to deal with the developing nations of the world, the small nations of the world, on the basis of mutual respect and partnership.

An important step had been taken to counter the imperialist image and the "colossus of the North" reputation that had long plagued the relations of the United States and Latin America. But many Americans continued to deplore the "give-away" of the canal.

THE UNITED STATES AND THE MIDDLE EAST

The First Israeli–Arab War, 1948–1949

Eleven minutes after Israel proclaimed its independence on May 14, 1948, the United States extended de facto recognition to the new nation. Truman made this decision despite the opposition of Secretary of State Marshall and many other close advisers who favored a UN trusteeship for Palestine and believed that immediate recognition of Israel would be seen as a response to domestic political considerations in an election year. Before the day ended, five Arab nations—Egypt, Lebanon, Syria, Iraq, and Jordan—attacked Israel with the intent to destroy the Jewish state. The ancient confiict between Arab and Jew in Palestine placed the United States in a very difficult situation. Sympathetic with the Jewish desire for a national state, especially after the horror of Nazi extermination policies, yet understanding legitimate Arab nationalism after a long domination by Western colonialism, Americans faced a dilemma. No clear choice between right and wrong existed.

In the turbulent Middle East the United States desired stable political conditions that curbed expansionist nationalism and communist penetration while preserving national independence and territorial boundaries. It was important to maintain ready access to Mideast oil, about 60 percent of the proven oil reserves in the world. The Arab–Israeli conflict threatened these U.S. objectives, especially because the Soviet Union supported Israel by a prompt shipment of arms from Czechoslovakia.

Complicating the problem for the United States was its "special relationship" with Israel. Many elected officials had a large constituency with strong personal interests in and emotional attachments to the new Jewish state. Washington felt a steady pressure to give special consideration to Israel's well being. No Arab nation had a similar lobby. In his 1948 campaign, Truman responded to this political reality by successfully stalling until after the election a UN Security Council vote to apply sanctions against Israel, if the latter did not give up all territory gained in the Negev as a result of the war.

Dispute over this territory delayed a cease-fire until early January 1949. The UN plan for the partition of Palestine was one of the victims of the war. Even more ominous, the war had rendered homeless almost one million Palestine Arabs. In an effort to stabilize conditions pending a permanent solution, in 1950 the United States joined Great Britain and France in a Tripartite Declaration. The three nations agreed to provide arms to Israel and the Arab states for internal security and self-defense only, and to oppose "the use of force between any of the states in that area." But U.S. support of Israel continued, and at year's end the Export–Import Bank granted Israel a new loan of $35 million.

The Iranian Crisis, 1951–1953

As the uneasy truce between Israel and the Arab states held, events in Iran, a non-Arab nation, enabled the United States to strengthen its Middle East position. In 1951 Mohammed Mossadeq led a nationalist movement that reduced the Shah, Iran's monarch, to a figurehead role and nationalized the Anglo-Iranian Oil Company owned by British investors. Efforts by the Truman administration to resolve differences between Iran and Britain failed. When Prime Minister Mossadeq in the spring of 1953 appealed to the United States for economic aid and increased purchases of Iranian oil, Eisenhower replied that Americans would oppose such actions while the Anglo-Iranian dispute remained unsettled. Concerned that "Iran's downhill course toward Communist-supported dictatorship was picking up momentum," Eisenhower approved a CIA covert operation, led by a grandson of Theodore Roosevelt, that toppled the Mossadeq government. The United States secretly provided guns and military equipment to the Shah's forces. Not only did the coup install Iranian leadership friendly to U.S. interests in the Middle East, but it also opened the door to an agreement to set up a new oil consortium in which five major U.S. oil companies acquired a 40 percent interest.

The Baghdad Pact, 1955

Obsessed by fear of communist expansion, Secretary of State John Foster Dulles envisioned a defense pact to do for the Middle East what NATO had done for Western Europe. Despite relative Soviet inaction in the area and peaceful coexistence gestures, in 1954 Dulles promoted an anti-Soviet security agreement between Turkey and Pakistan. A year later his treaty expanded into the Baghdad Pact with Britain, Iran, and Iraq joining.

This action, carrying out the British concept of a "northern tier defense line," antagonized the new Egyptian president, Gamal Abdel Nasser, who desired to lead the region into a Pan-Arab, nonaligned bloc. Haunted by the humiliating defeat in the 1948 war, Nasser saw the need to overcome internal weaknesses and to build Arab military strength. Disagreeing with Dulles, Nasser saw neutrality in the cold war as essential to Arab goals.

Arms Buildup, 1954–1956

In 1954 Nasser approached the United States for arms. When Washington priced the Egyptian leader's list of defense requirements at $27 million in cash, he turned to the Soviets. Dismissing a Soviet offer to Nasser as pure bluff, Dulles refused to modify the U.S. position. Nasser's opposition to the Baghdad Pact irked the secretary of state, who viewed neutralism as immoral and a transitional stage leading to communist control.

Nasser had become the champion of Arab nationalism by imposing a blockade on Israeli shipping through the Suez Canal and on all goods destined for Israel. He also began to restrict Israeli commerce in the Straits of Tiran to prevent use of Israel's key port—Elath at the head of the Gulf of Aqaba (map, p. 77). Circumventing the 1950 Tripartite Agreement, Nasser in October 1955 concluded a deal with Czechoslovakia—bartering cotton for arms. Israel at once sought arms to balance Communist bloc aid to Egypt. Rebuffed by the United States, who stood by the 1950 Agreement, Israel negotiated a $50 million purchase of French jet planes and tanks.

The Suez Crisis, 1954–1956

Although the arms buildup created a dilemma for Eisenhower, Nasser's ambitions offered an opportunity to direct Egypt's energies to peaceful pursuits. The Egyptian leader sounded out Washington about assisting in financing the Aswan Dam, a gigantic power and irrigation project on the Upper Nile with a price tag of $1.3 billion. Sensing an opportunity to link economic aid to Egypt with a final solution to the explosive Arab-Israeli conflict, Dulles convinced Eisenhower to join the British and the World Bank in financing the dam. Dubious about the sincerity of a Soviet offer to finance construction of Aswan, the administration tentatively agreed in December 1955 to a cash grant of $56 million and a loan of $200 million from the World Bank with the possibility of additional grants.

By the spring of 1956 Washington began to have second thoughts about aiding Nasser. Strong criticism came from southern cotton interests, supporters of Israel, and the conservative Right opposed to all foreign aid. Nasser hurt his own cause by recognizing Red China and negotiating with the Soviets for increased trade and economic aid. When Israel and Egypt rejected a secret proposal in which the United States offered economic aid and a formal guarantee of fixed boundaries for a peace agreement and settlement of the refugee problem, the administration's interest in helping Nasser, increasingly viewed as the real villain in the Middle East, weakened. Although warned by Eugene Black, president of the World Bank, that "Hell might break loose" if the United States withdrew its offer of aid, Dulles on July 19 told the Egyptian ambassador that the offer was withdrawn. Eisenhower later explained that Nasser "gave the impression of a man who was convinced that he could play off East against West by blackmailing both."

One week after the U.S. snub, Nasser shocked the West by nationalizing the Suez Canal. British Prime Minister Anthony Eden immediately cabled Eisenhower that his government believed it "must be ready, in the last resort, to use force to bring Nasser to his senses." The president cautioned "as to the unwisdom even of contemplating the use of military force at this moment." In September the British and French grudgingly accepted a U.S. proposal to create an international Suez Canal Users' Association to supervise canal traffic. Nasser would have none of it, so the crisis continued. The American people, however, did not view the situation as warranting strong action against Nasser. A Gallup poll taken in late September revealed that 55 percent opposed the sending of U.S. troops even if England and France did.

Although Dulles insisted that the Suez issue be treated separately from the Arab–Israeli conflict, the British, French, and Israelis did not agree. Without informing the United States, they proceeded with plans to drive Nasser from power and regain control of the canal. Late in October, eight days before the U.S. presidential election, Israel initiated a surprise attack on Egypt. Routing Nasser's forces, the Israeli quickly advanced to the canal. Two days later the British and French, claiming the need to intervene to safeguard the canal and separate the combatants, began to bomb Egyptian air bases and parachuted troops to capture Port Said. An irate Eisenhower, already concerned about the crisis in Hungary (p. 22), instructed Dulles—"All right, Foster, you tell 'em that, goddamn it, we're going to apply sanctions, we're going to the United Nations, we're going to do everything that there is so we can stop this thing."

On October 31 the president said he believed that the Israeli, British, and

French actions were "taken in error." He promised that "there will be no United States involvement in these present hostilities." The administration's resolution in the Security Council demanding that Israeli forces withdraw to their own territory was vetoed by Britain and France. With Communist bloc support the General Assembly adopted a U.S. resolution condemning the action of the three powers, demanding an immediate cease-fire, and proposing a UN truce team to maintain peace in the area. Within a week a cease-fire was in effect, hastened no doubt by a U.S. move that cut off Britain's and France's supply of oil from Latin America and by Soviet threats against the two powers. United Nations forces took over British and French positions in Egypt, and the Israelis withdrew.

Although the United States had won the appreciation of the Arab world, the anomaly of acting in conjunction with the Soviet Union against Britain, France, and Israel distressed most Americans. Shaken by the Suez War, which shattered Britain's stabilizing presence while strengthening Nasser's position and Soviet influence in the Arab world, Eisenhower and Dulles resolved to develop a stronger policy in the Middle East.

The Eisenhower Doctrine, 1957

Two days after his triumphant re-election, Eisenhower asserted that the United States had to be "ready to take any kind of action . . . that will exclude from the area (Middle East) Soviet influence." The president believed that "the Soviet objective was, in plain fact, power politics: to seize the oil, to cut the canal and pipelines of the Middle East, and thus seriously to weaken western civilization."

Early in January 1957 Eisenhower asked Congress to authorize the executive branch to employ "the armed forces of the United States to secure and protect the territorial integrity and political independence of such nations, requesting such aid, against overt armed aggression from any nation controlled by International Communism." He did not intend to get trapped in a situation, as Truman had in Korea, without advanced congressional authorization to respond with force to communist aggression. The president also requested $200 million for military and economic aid for the Middle East. Although Senator Fulbright questioned giving a "blank check" to an executive branch that included "a current Secretary of State who greets the dawn with a boast about his triumphs, and meets the dusk with scare words of panic, saying that the Nation will be ruined unless it unites to ratify the mistakes he made during the day," Congress complied with Eisenhower's request.

Dubbed the Eisenhower Doctrine by the press, this corollary to the Truman Doctrine attracted a mixed reception in the Middle East. The Arab response ranged from open hostility by Egypt, Syria, and Saudi Arabia to warm endorsement by Lebanon and the northern tier of states—members of the Baghdad

Pact. To convince the Arab world of the fairness and desirability of the Eisenhower Doctrine, Washington pressured Israel to comply with a UN resolution requiring withdrawal of her forces to pre-October 1956 lines. Fearing UN sanctions, Israel gave in after the United States announced it would support a UN Emergency Force in the Gaza Strip to prevent Egyptian attacks and would work to assure free passage through the Gulf of Aqaba. But the Arabs remained skeptical. The Eisenhower Doctrine appeared to support a status quo in the Middle East, whereas Arab leaders were committed to change—the elimination of Israel and promotion of Pan-Arabism.

Aid to Jordan, 1957

In April 1957 when riots in Jordan, allegedly stirred up by Nasser, threatened King Hussein's rule, Eisenhower sent the Sixth Fleet to the Eastern Mediterranean and extended $30 million in aid to the beleaguered Jordanian government. The State Department explained the president's actions as necessary "because of the threat to . . . Jordan by international Communism, as King Hussein himself stated." Critics quickly charged that this first application of the Eisenhower Doctrine overlooked the fact that the real issue was not communist interference, but Nasser's effort to unite the Arab world.

Intervention in Lebanon, 1958

A year later, concern that President Chamoun of Lebanon might circumvent the six year constitutional limitation on his term precipitated street violence and protests in Beirut. Chamoun, a Christian, was regarded as an obstacle to Arab unity by the United Arab Republic (UAR), the newly formed union of Egypt and Syria. The UAR aided the Lebanese Arab insurrectionists who formed a United National Opposition Front. As a counter to the UAR, the State Department encouraged King Faisal of Iraq and Hussein of Jordan to join their countries in a federal state, the Arab Union. When on May 13, 1958, Chamoun asked the United States what it would do if he requested military help, Washington replied that the United States would honor such a request if conditions warranted it. Eisenhower later explained that "behind everything was our deep-seated conviction that the Communists were primarily responsible for the trouble, and that President Chamoun was motivated only by a strong feeling of patriotism."

A pro-Nasser unit of the Iraqi army assassinated King Faisal on July 14 and overthrew the government. Chamoun immediately asked the United States for assistance against possible threats to his regime. Sniffing a communist plot behind the Iraqi coup, Eisenhower, after consulting with congressional leaders, ordered Marines to Lebanon to protect 2,500 Americans living there. He wanted to dispel any sentiment in the Middle East "that Americans were capable only of words, that we were afraid of Soviet reaction if we attempted military action."

Greeted by the curious stares of "sunbathers and Coca-Cola vendors," a combat-ready Marine contingent waded ashore at high tide on Red Beach, south of Beirut, in midafternoon on July 15. As the Marines landed Eisenhower told the nation that "what we now see in the Middle East" is "the same pattern of conquest with which we became familiar during the period of 1945 to 1950." In the president's mind "the question was whether it would be better to incur the deep resentment of nearly all of the Arab world (and some of the Free World) and in doing so risk general war with the Soviet Union or to do something worse—which was nothing."

Within three days, three Marine battalions with tanks and armored amphibians had landed in Lebanon. On July 19 an army battle group arrived from Europe. At the end of the month over 15,000 U.S. troops were in Lebanon in a show of force designed to impress the Soviet Union. The latter condemned the U.S. landing as "a direct act of war and piracy," but made no military moves. A crisis-hardened U.S. public appeared somewhat skeptical about the situation according to a Gallup Poll that showed only 42 percent approving the sending of troops into Lebanon.

In Lebanon, Chamoun bowed out of the presidential race, preparing the way for a new government. By the end of October all U.S. forces had been removed as demanded by a General Assembly resolution. Not a single casualty was suffered, and apparently not a single shot had been fired at an enemy, but the Soviets had learned that the Eisenhower Doctrine was no paper tiger.

A fragile truce prevailed in the Middle East for a decade as Nasser reaffirmed his neutral position in the cold war and worked for Arab unity under Egyptian leadership. The Communist bloc saw the Arab cause as their own because they viewed the elimination of Israel as the elimination of the West from the Middle East. U.S. leaders committed the nation to maintain an arms balance so that Israel could defend itself.

The Six Day War, June 1967

A telephone awakened the president in his White House bedroom at 4:35 A.M. on June 5, 1967. Lyndon Johnson heard the grave voice of Walt Rostow, his national security adviser, saying that war had broken out in the Middle East with a surprise Israeli attack against Egypt. A few minutes before 8:00 A.M. Johnson received on that telephone a message heard for the first time by a U.S. president. Secretary of Defense Robert McNamara said, "Mr. President, the hot line is up." Johnson hastened to the Situation Room where he took a message from Aleksei Kosygin, chairperson of the Council of Ministers of the Soviet Union, explaining Soviet intent to work for a cease-fire and urging the United States to exert influence on Israel. Johnson replied that "we would use all our influence to bring hostilities to an end." To stop the fighting before Israel's victory reached proportions that might tempt Soviet leaders to intervene to save their Arab friends became the major concern. In six days Israeli forces occupied all of Palestine including the old city of Jerusalem, the entire Sinai Peninsula to the banks of the Suez Canal, and the Golan Heights of Syria. The magnitude of the Israeli victory was at once humiliating to the Arabs and embarrassing to the Soviets.

On June 10 Kosygin informed Johnson on the hot line that unless Israel halted all military operations within the next few hours, the Soviet Union would take "necessary actions, including military." In his *Memoirs,* Johnson noted, "The room was deathly still as we carefully studied this grave communication." Deciding that he had to warn the Kremlin that "the United States was prepared to resist Soviet intrusion in the Middle East," the president issued orders to the Sixth Fleet to move within 50 miles of the coast of Syria. As in the Dominican Republic incident, Lyndon Johnson was determined to stand up to the Communists. But he carefully assured Kosygin that he "had been pressing Israel to make the ceasefire completely effective and had received assurances that this would be done." A tenuous armistice soon reduced fighting without stopping it. Later in the month, Kosygin, on a visit to the United Nations in New York, met with Johnson at Glassboro, New Jersey. Unable to agree on any substantive matters, the two leaders did reaffirm the need for a prompt and durable cease-fire in the Middle East and the right of every nation to live in peace.

The Six Day War of June 1967 convinced Washington that keeping Israel strong enough to hold off any Arab coalition reduced the risk of a Middle East war that might necessitate U.S. involvement. Aid to Israel was increased in 1968, and before leaving office the Johnson administration approved the sale of 50 F-4 Phantom jet fighters to Israel. Although supportive of UN efforts to achieve an accord, Washington refused to pressure Israel to withdraw from occupied territory, including the Golan Heights, the West Bank of the Jordan, and the Sinai Desert.

U.S. Aid To Israel & Egypt, 1946–1976 ($ millions)

	1946–1952	1953–1961	1962–1967	1968–1972	1973–1976
Israel					
Economic	86.5	507.2	262.8	289.6	1,228.8
Military	0	0.9	136.4	985.0	4,590.2
Egypt					
Economic	12.3	302.3	580.5	1.5	856.5
Military	0	0	0	0	0

SOURCE: Agency for International Development (AID)

The Yom Kippur War, October 1973

A week after his inauguration, Richard Nixon said of the Middle East: "I consider it a powder keg, very explosive. It needs to be defused." In midsummer 1970 Secretary of State William P. Rogers persuaded the Arabs and Israelis to accept a total cessation of military actions. But high expectations for a U.S.-sponsored peace agreement collapsed when Israel balked at Arab terms. Earlier in the year Nasser, under pressure from ardent Nationalists, had turned to Moscow for help. He received not only surface-to-air missiles (SAMs), tanks, and late model supersonic MIGs, but also thousands of Soviet "technicians and military advisers."

Nixon responded by delivering the Phantom jets promised under Johnson and by approving an additional $500 million in aid to Israel. By the end of its first term the Nixon administration had furnished to Israel more military and economic aid than had all previous administrations combined. Instead of being defused, the powder keg was refilled.

On 6 October 1973, the day of Yom Kippur, the most solemn Jewish holiday, the explosion occurred. Egyptian infantry launched a surprise attack on Israeli fortifications in the Sinai and drove forward. Simultaneously three Syrian armored divisions attacked the Israeli lines on the Golan Heights.

Preoccupied with accumulating Watergate revelations and perhaps lulled by progress in détente with the Soviet Union, Washington was completely surprised. The Nixon administration may also have misread the fact that Anwar al-Sadat, elevated to the presidency by Nasser's death in September 1970, had ordered the Soviet technicians and advisers out of Egypt in 1972 and had even approached the United States to exert influence on Israel. But, having lost hope of achieving his goal of Israeli withdrawal to pre-1967 boundaries and under heavy domestic pressure, Sadat turned to a military solution.

When Israel sustained heavy losses before gaining the initiative in the October war, Nixon ordered an all-out airlift of military supplies to Israel from the United States as well as from NATO bases. The president also asked Congress for an emergency $2.2 billion in military aid for the hard-pressed Israelis. In retaliation the Arab-dominated OPEC (Organization of Petroleum Exporting Countries) imposed an oil embargo. An acute shortage of petroleum soon threatened the economies of Western Europe and Japan, who now demonstrated that their interests in the Middle East were economic by expressions of sympathy for the Arabs and criticisms of U.S. policies. But the uproar from its allies seemed mild in comparison to the storm of protest from angry Americans who faced long lines at filling stations, reduced fuel oil deliveries during a cold winter, and lay-offs because of plant shutdowns.

Eager to end the fighting before Israel could mount an effective offensive, Leonid Brezhnev, the Soviet leader, approached Washington to cooperate in bringing about a cease-fire. On Brezhnev's invitation Kissinger flew to Moscow

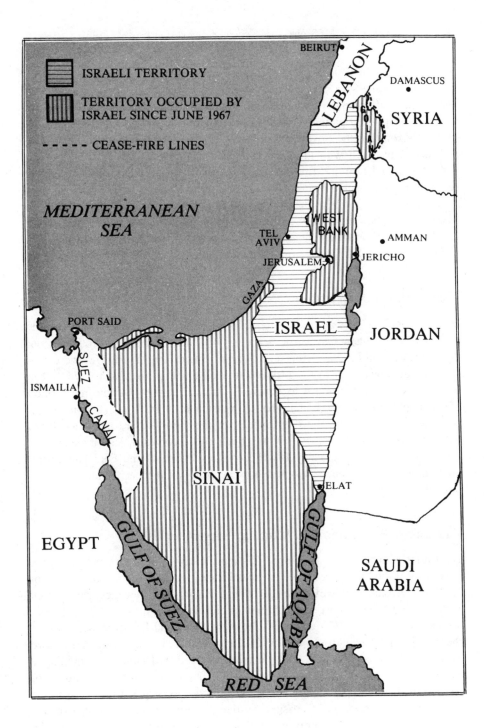

The Middle East in 1978

on October 20. In two days the two men worked out a cease-fire formula and provisions for the start of negotiations. But when the cease-fire failed to hold, both Sadat and Brezhnev proposed the immediate sending of U.S. and Soviet troops to stop the fighting. After Washington rejected this idea, Brezhnev informed Nixon that the Soviet Union might find it necessary to take "appropriate" action by itself with the "gravest consequences" for Israel.

In the midst of a "firestorm" over the firing of the special Watergate prosecutor, Nixon put U.S. forces, including nuclear strike units, on global alert as evidence of U.S. determination to prevent unilateral Soviet action. The crisis passed when the belligerents agreed on October 25 to the sending of a UN peacekeeping force. Israel consented only after Nixon and Kissinger warned they would suspend deliveries of arms if Israel continued its military drive.

The Kissinger Step-by-Step Peace Effort

In the months following the October War, Kissinger embarked on "shuttle diplomacy" to obtain permanent peace in the Middle East. He brought about disengagement on the Suez front in January 1974, as well as an effective cease-fire. His diplomacy led to the lifting of the oil embargo in March 1974 and to increased U.S. economic aid to Israel, Egypt, and Jordan. Despite the turmoil of the impeachment proceedings that culminated in Nixon's resignation in August 1974, Kissinger produced in September the Sinai Accord by which Israel withdrew from the western part of the Sinai and accepted a demilitarized zone occupied by a UN Emergency Force. For the duration of the Ford administration, Kissinger continued his step-by-step plan without achieving a breakthrough.

The Camp David Summit Meeting, September 1978

The Carter administration abandoned Kissinger's step-by-step personal mediation in favor of a total package settlement of all issues. A precedent-breaking visit of Sadat to Jerusalem in November 1977 and face-to-face meetings with Israeli leaders eased Middle East tensions and offered hope for peace. After negotiations stalled, President Carter invited President Sadat and Prime Minister Menachem Begin of Israel to a meeting at Camp David in September 1978. Two weeks of discussions ended with the signing of two documents providing a comprehensive settlement of the issues and "a framework for the conclusion of a peace treaty between Israel and Egypt." A promising step toward peace in the Middle East had been made possible by the good offices of the United States. But some regarded it as unfortunate that a law, pushed by Kissinger in the Nixon administration, forbade any contact with the Palestine Liberation Organization (PLO) until it recognized Israel and disavowed terrorism.

The Mideast Peace Agreement, 1979

When an impasse developed between Israel and Egypt over "linkage" of a peace treaty with an overall peace plan resolving the status of Palestinians on the West Bank of the Jordan and in the Gaza Strip, President Carter again mediated. He flew to Egypt and to Israel in March 1979 and negotiated the agreement of President Sadat and Prime Minister Begin to sign a peace treaty as the first step. The opposition of most of the Arab World to the Egypt–Israel Treaty raised the spectres of possible Soviet involvement and a revival of an anti-Western oil policy by the Arab nations. But in the interest of stability and peace between the ancient enemies, Carter took these risks and agreed to furnish extensive military aid to both Israel and Egypt. In Washington's eyes a balance of power between nations friendly to the United States and those armed and backed by the Soviet Union seemed to offer the best guarantee of long range peace in the Middle East.

Iranian Revolution, 1979

The sense of relief following the Egypt–Israel Treaty was tempered by disastrous developments in another Middle Eastern nation—Iran. Simmering discontent with the regime of Shah Mohammed Reza Pahlavi, who had been returned to power in 1953 with covert U.S. assistance (p. 69), erupted into violence in the summer of 1978. Riots and demonstrations against the government by both leftist and rightist groups became a regular occurrence in Iranian cities. U.S. support of the Shah, and official pronouncements that Iran was "the island of stability in one of the more troubled areas of the world," rested on an inaccurate assessment of the depth and breadth of opposition to the Shah's policies. When the embattled Shah finally fled in mid-January 1979, the United States announced support of the caretaker government appointed by the Shah. Within a month that regime was toppled by the backers of the 78-year-old Ayatollah Khomeini who was committed to the establishment of an Islamic Republic in Iran. Violent anti-U.S. demonstrations, including a storming of the U.S. Embassy in Teheran, forced the evacuation of Americans from Iran and temporarily shut down production of Iranian oil. In protest of the admission of the deposed Shah into the United States for medical treatment, Iranian militants on November 4, 1979, seized the U.S. embassy in Teheran and held as hostages 52 Americans.

During the next 14 months diplomatic efforts, economic pressure, and a commando rescue mission all failed to free the hostages. Frustration and anger felt by many Americans caused a sharp decline in support of the Carter administration in an election year. After Ronald Reagan's defeat of Carter in the November election, Iran, with Algeria having served as mediator, agreed on January 19, 1981, to release the hostages in return for $7.9 billion in Iranian assets frozen in the United States by Carter. Technicalities, perhaps deliberately devised by Iranians in order to deprive Carter of a last minute success, delayed the flight of the released hostages from Teheran until Reagan had been sworn in as president on January 20, 1981. Subsequent allegations that William J. Casey, chairman of the Reagan presidential campaign, made a deal with Iranians promising arms if Iran delayed release of the 52 hostages until after the U.S. presidential election prompted demands for a congressional investigation in 1991. Shipment of U.S. arms to Iran via Israel began only a few days after Reagan's inauguration, evidence, claims Bani-Sadr, president of Iran at the time, that Reagan intermediaries had made a deal to prevent an "October Surprise"—that is, a release of the hostages—that would aid Carter in the last days before the presidential election.

THE UNITED STATES AND AFRICA

Relative Neglect, 1945–1960

Although over 10 percent of its own population claimed African ancestry, the United States had little interest in Africa. With only four independent nations in 1945, Africa remained the province of Europe. U.S. trade and investment remained relatively small, and strategic concerns even smaller. In the early stages of the cold war, U.S. leaders, fearing that premature independence might open the door to communism, favored European interests in Africa over those of the Africans. In the words of Assistant Secretary of State George McGhee in 1950, Africa was a place "where in the broadest sense—no crisis exists . . . in which no significant inroads have been made by Communism." Washington intended to keep it that way.

The strong nationalism that infected other Third World areas and led to East–West involvement arrived late in Africa. Fragmented by over two thousand different languages or dialects, Africa had no national states when imperialists took over in the nineteenth century. When Eisenhower became president there existed only five free nations in Africa, and the United States had fewer foreign service officers in all of Africa than in West Germany alone. Washington remained more concerned about nationalist revolutions creating a power vacuum that the Soviets might exploit than about legitimate aspirations of the people of Africa.

But under the pressure of African developments U.S. policy began to change during the second Eisenhower term. When Kwame Nkrumah led Ghana to independence in 1957 Black Africa was reborn. By the end of 1960 22 nations, including 16 in September and October, had gained independence since the end of World War II. U.S. leaders recognized the need to soften warnings about premature independence and to acknowledge that colonialism was ending. Washington established a new Bureau of African Affairs and increased loans and grants to Africa. Yet the administration could not turn its back on European allies still holding territory in Africa. Its ambivalence appeared in a May 1959 statement by Joseph Satterthwaite, assistant secretary of state for African affairs: "We support African political aspirations where they are moderate, nonviolent and constructive and take into account their obligations to and interdependence with the world community. We also support the principle of continued African ties with Western Europe." This desire to have it both ways was soon put to the test in Congo.

The Congo Civil War, 1960–1964

Within two weeks after gaining its independence from Belgium in late June 1960, the Republic of the Congo faced tribal civil war. Moise Tshombe refused to accept the jurisdiction of the central government and declared the secession of Katanga Province. Belgian business interests immediately convinced their government to aid Katangan rebels with paratroopers. Tshombe also hired white soldiers from Rhodesia and South Africa. When asked by President Joseph Kasavubu of Congo to intervene, Eisenhower suggested referral of the problem to the United Nations. The Security Council responded to Congo's request with a call for the withdrawal of Belgian troops and by approving a peacekeeping force that would not take sides in the civil conflict.

In support of the United Nations, the United States agreed to supply the airlift, food, and equipment needed to preserve order. Eisenhower and his advisers believed that the new Congo Republic would be unable to support itself and would be susceptible to communist penetration if it lost Katanga—its richest province with 60 percent of the world's cobalt and 10 percent of its copper and tin. Significantly the United States obtained nearly 75 percent of its cobalt and about 80 percent of its industrial diamonds from Congo. Complicating the problem was the defection of Premier Patrice Lumumba who broke with Kasavubu, established a separate government in Stanleyville, and turned to Khrushchev for aid to drive from Katanga the Belgians and their "white mercenaries." Eisenhower viewed Lumumba as "radical and unstable" and "a Communist sympathizer if not a member of the Party."

Although campaign rhetoric had promised otherwise, Kennedy's African policy, in adviser Theodore Sorensen's words, "was largely an extension of the Eisenhower policy" aimed at keeping the Soviets out of an independent and united Congo. Three weeks after his inauguration, Kennedy received news that Lumumba had been killed, allegedly as he tried to escape from the custody of Tshombe's soldiers. A new crisis loomed when the Soviet Union after recognizing Antoine Gizenga, Lumumba's vice premier, as head of Congo, introduced a resolution calling for the withdrawal of all UN troops from Congo. Determined to avoid another Laos or Cuba, Kennedy immediately pledged support for continued UN presence in Congo and for the government of Kasavubu. Washington sent military advisers along with military equipment to Colonel Joseph Mobutu, chief of the Congolese Army. The State Department explained the U.S. policy as one of "sanitary intervention" to contain radicalism in central Africa. A secret panel set up by Kennedy to study the interests of the United States in Africa concluded that "we see Africa as probably the greatest open field of maneuver in the worldwide competition between the Communist bloc and the non-Communist world."

The administration's support of the UN peacekeeping force and its refusal to back Katanga drew the fire of Republican Senator Barry Goldwater who accused his government of "condoning aggression by international machinery and paving the way for a Communist takeover in the Congo." The American Committee for Aid to Katanga Freedom Fighters, promoted by a Belgian public relations expert, lobbied hard against Kennedy's policy.

Although the Katanga secession ended in February 1963, Gizenga continued the conflict against the central government. When the UN forces withdrew in 1964, the Johnson administration sent both a military mission to train Congolese soldiers and military equipment. The CIA furnished Cuban Bay of Pigs veterans as pilots and paratroopers to aid the government now directed by its new premier, Moise Tshombe. Much of Africa viewed the U.S. action as imperialist intervention to aid Tshombe and his white mercenaries.

In late December 1964, the General Assembly passed a resolution calling for a cease-fire and an end to outside intervention in Congo's domestic affairs. The United States had spent $400 million to preserve Congo unity and to keep communism out. The cost in Third World good will was not so easily measured.

When Mobutu seized power in 1965 he renamed his country Zaire and continued close military and economic ties with the United States. That Mobutu became a corrupt dictator, while the masses of his nation suffered from poverty and a lack of basic rights, mattered little to U.S. policymakers. In Africa, as elsewhere, the exclusion of native Marxists seemed more important than the promotion of human rights.

The Rhodesian Problem

Engrossed in the Vietnam War abroad and in the Great Society at home, the Johnson administration assigned a low priority to Africa following the cease-fire in Congo. But Africa would not go away. In English-speaking South Africa growing opposition to racism joined nationalism on center stage and demanded U.S. attention.

In November 1965 white leaders of Southern Rhodesia declared indepen-

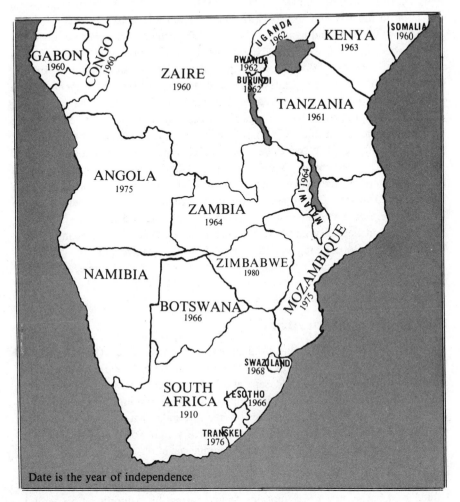

Southern Africa in 1980

dence of Great Britain and set up a government totally controlled by the white minority representing only 4 percent of the population. Black nationalists reacted by organizing to fight for a black nation—Zimbabwe. In the midst of a campaign to obtain equal rights for U.S. African Americans, the Johnson administration could hardly support white supremacy in Africa. But Washington faced strong pressure to keep open the supply of strategic minerals, especially chrome ore, from Rhodesia. Taking a middle road, the government endorsed a UN sponsored arms embargo and denounced racism in any form in any place while continuing limited trade with Rhodesia. When the Security Council voted a total trade embargo in 1968, important U.S. industries expressed concern. Making an exception to the UN embargo on grounds of national security, in 1971 Congress passed the Byrd amendment to permit the importation of strategic materials from Rhodesia. Later both the Nixon and Ford administrations called for its repeal, but Congress did not comply until the Carter administration in 1978.

Although the United States continued to support the movement for an independent Zimbabwe and served as "an honest broker among the contending parties," little progress toward a peaceful settlement was made. When the State Department warned in mid-1978 that "Soviet and Cuban intervention is a strong possibility if the conflict continues" neither Congress nor the public clamored for direct U.S. intervention. A token effort at establishing an integrated government, initiated by the white leadership in Rhodesia in 1978, attracted little enthusiasm from the Carter administration. Eventually in December 1979 the British government worked out a blueprint for a cease-fire that paved the way for elections in February and independence in April 1980. The African National Union party of Robert Mugabe, an avowed Marxist, won 63 percent of the vote in a national election and proceeded to set Zimbabwe on a moderate, nonaligned course.

Problems in Southern Africa

Meanwhile in South Africa and in Namibia, its mandate since 1920, the United States faced an even more difficult balancing act. There the ruling white minority maintained a policy of rigid separation of the races known as apartheid. In 1958 the Eisenhower administration supported a UN resolution expressing "regret and concern" about apartheid on the grounds that it violated the UN Charter, but U.S. capital continued to flow freely into South Africa. The Kennedy administration in 1961 opposed economic sanctions against South Africa, but a year later Kennedy banned the sale of arms to South Africa.

Although Richard Nixon visited 31 different countries as president of the United States, he never set foot in Africa during his administration, and he seemed little interested in the emerging nations there or in their people. During his presidency a secret "Tar Baby" policy relaxed the standing embargo on arms sales to South Africa and to Portugal trying to hold on to its African colonies. Dozens of U.S. corporations continued to invest in South African subsidiaries, while large banks extended loans to the South African government despite the efforts of students at a score of U.S. schools and colleges to discourage the practice. By 1976, $1.5 billion, about 40 percent of American capital in Africa, was invested in South Africa. The pursuit of profits remained more important than the promotion of democracy and justice.

The sudden collapse of Portuguese rule in Angola and Mozambique in 1974 complicated U.S. problems in southern Africa. The granting of independence by Portugal led almost immediately to civil war in Angola between a Marxist group, Popular Movement for the Liberation of Angola (MPLA), supported by the Soviet Union, and anti-Marxist groups, notably the National Front for the Liberation of Angola (FNLA) and the National Union for the Total Independence of Angola (UNITA) led by Jonas Savimbi. In early 1975 the Ford administration began to carry out a CIA plan of covert military aid to the anti-Marxists. Fidel Castro, responding to the requests of the Marxists, sent 12,000 Cuban soldiers by the end of the year. Angola became a base for guerrillas seeking to dismember Zaire and to topple the oppressive white regimes in Rhodesia and South Africa. The spreading conflict attracted white soldiers from the Republic of South Africa, Portuguese mercenaries, and about three hundred Americans recruited by the CIA to fight against the Communists.

A worried Congress reacted early in 1976 by passing the Clark Amendment prohibiting U.S. military assistance to any Angolan group without congressional authorization. Decisive victories by government forces in the spring of 1976 brought an end to the fighting with the Marxists firmly in control. With Cuban troops remaining in Angola, the Ford administration proclaimed a policy of nonrecognition of Angola—a policy continued by Carter. However, the United Nations recognized Angola as did 51 members of the Organization of Africa Unity.

The situation in Angola complicated the Namibian issue. Carter's espousal of human rights, his condemnation of apartheid, and his pressure on South Africa to expedite peaceful change under UN supervision failed to advance the cause of independence for Namibia. In 1978 Carter became the first U.S. president in office to visit sub-Saharan Africa. His trip to Liberia and Nigeria aimed at setting up a broad-based foreign aid program. Other demands on U.S. funds unfortunately doomed this effort.

The Continuing Challenge: How to Reconcile Geopolitical Interests and a Concern for Human Rights

At stake, in addition to the strategic resources of Southern Africa and U.S. investments there, was the sea passage around the southern tip (Cape of Good Hope), the route for more than 60 percent of Western Europe's oil from the Persian Gulf. If the Communists gained control of that route and the Horn of Africa overlooking the Red Sea and the entrances to the Suez Canal, U.S. NATO allies would be weakened seriously. On the other hand, if Washington attempted to maintain stability by supporting white regimes or native governments subservient to white interests, it risked its moral leadership in the cause for human rights. As in Asia and Latin America, the strategic and economic interests of the United States made it tempting to pursue policies in Africa unsupportive of the aspirations of native peoples for basic human rights.

CHAPTER 4

The Vietnam War

"The wicked are wicked, no doubt, and they go astray and they fall, and they come by their deserts; but who can tell the mischief which the very virtuous do?"

William Makepeace Thackeray, 1855

"Once on the tiger's back we cannot be sure of picking the place to dismount."

George W. Ball, 1964

A FATEFUL STEP

Nine senators and seven representatives, the congressional leadership of both parties, hastened to the White House in response to an emergency summons from the president of the United States. The heat and humidity of the early August day had moderated only slightly as the eight Democrats and eight Republicans assembled in the cabinet room. Forgotten for the moment was the presidential election campaign just getting under way. After perfunctory greetings, Secretary of Defense Robert S. McNamara, businesslike as usual, described in detail North Vietnamese torpedo boat attacks earlier in the day on two U.S. destroyers in the Gulf of Tonkin. Although no Americans were injured and no U.S. ships damaged, the secretary said that the United States must respond or face further violations of its rights. He then outlined the government's plan for immediate retaliatory air strikes against North Vietnamese naval bases.

A grave President Lyndon B. Johnson, who had come directly from a meeting of the National Security Council, next read a statement that he planned to deliver later that evening to the American people. He asked the 16 leaders to back a congressional resolution of support for the administration's entire position in Southeast Asia. Admitting that the nation "might be forced into further action," the president said, "I do not want to go in unless Congress goes in with me." After reminding his listeners that Congress had supported President Eisenhower in this way in both the Lebanon and Formosan crises, Johnson asked each person for a "frank opinion." The 15 men and 1 woman expressed "wholehearted endorsement of both the government's course of action and of the proposed resolution." Later that evening of August 4, 1964, after U.S. aircraft carriers had launched the first of 64 bombing strikes in reprisal, the president appeared on television to inform the nation of the crisis and of the "limited and fitting" U.S. response. The next day Johnson defended his action with the words: "The world remembers, the world must never forget that aggression unchallenged is aggression unleashed. . . . There can be no peace by aggression and no immunity from reply."

In an election year, rare is the member of Congress who opposes presidential foreign policy measures widely regarded as in the national interest. On August 7, 1964, only two members of Congress warned against the executive's use of his power as commander-in-chief to carry on a war when the Constitution delegated the power to declare war to the legislature. A passive House of Representatives by a unanimous 416 to 0 vote and the Senate by an 88 to 2 vote approved the "Gulf of Tonkin Resolution." The astute Johnson had prevailed on the highly respected J. William Fulbright (D., Ark.), chairman of the Senate Foreign Relations Committee, to steer the resolution through the Senate. Only senators Wayne Morse (D., Oreg.) and Ernest Gruening (D., Alaska) voted in the negative.

Morse suspected that the PT boat attacks were provoked by the shelling of North Vietnamese islands by South Vietnamese naval vessels on Friday, July 31, and by a shooting encounter between the U.S. destroyer Maddox and North Vietnamese ships two days later. Doubts about the legality, necessity, or desirability of U.S. reprisal raids also appeared in the UN Security Council, where only Nationalist China and Britain supported the United States.

The congressional resolution authorized the president "to take all necessary measures to repel any armed attack against the forces of the United States and to prevent further aggression." In addition, the resolution stated that "the United States is . . . prepared, as the President determines, to take all necessary steps, including the use of armed force, to assist any member or protocol state of the Southeast Asia Collective Defense Treaty requesting assistance in defense of its freedom." Upon signing the resolution on August 10, Johnson announced, "To any armed attack upon our forces, we shall reply. To any in Southeast Asia who ask our help in defending their freedom, we shall give it." In his memoir published in 1971 Johnson explained that he "hoped this strong congressional endorsement would help influence North Vietnam to refrain from accelerating aggression." Unfortunately, the president and his advisers had made a serious miscalculation. A new phase in the long Vietnam War was about to begin.

DEEP ROOTS AND MANY BRANCHES: ORIGINS OF THE VIETNAM WAR

Creation of Democratic Republic of Vietnam, 1945

By 1964 28 million Vietnamese had endured military strife for almost two decades. In the latter stages of World War II nationalist Vietnamese, the Viet Minh, had carried on a guerrilla struggle against the Japanese who occupied Indochina (the states of Laos, Cambodia, and Vietnam). Leader of the Viet Minh, the 55-year-old Ho Chi Minh, as a young man in exile in Paris in the 1920s became a Leninist, helped to found the French Communist party, and served as a Comintern agent in Europe for 15 years before the outbreak of World War II. He then returned to Vietnam to liberate his native land from foreign aggressors.

As World War II drew to a close the United States left to France the decision about the future of Indochina. But in Hanoi on V-J Day, September 2, 1945, Ho Chi Minh, having liberated North Vietnam from the Japanese, declared the independence of the Democratic Republic of Vietnam in a document paraphrasing parts of the U.S. Declaration of Independence.

U.S. Dilemma in Indochina

French determination to reestablish control over Indochina, despite strong opposition of Vietnamese nationalists, placed the United States in a difficult position. Practical considerations conflicted with idealistic principles. After fighting broke out between the returning French forces and the Viet Minh, the State Department in October 1945 tried to resolve the dilemma by declaring that "it is not the policy of this government to assist the French to re-establish their control over Indochina by force."

Nor would it be U.S. policy to assist the Viet Minh. When Ho asked in 1946 for U.S. support at the United Nations for a resolution guaranteeing Vietnam the same free status recently granted the Philippines, he received no answer. Repeated requests for U.S. economic and technical aid to help rebuild Vietnam's shattered economy attracted the same stony silence. The United States could hardly subordinate its interests in Europe to an idealistic stance in an area of the world that appeared relatively insignificant to U.S. interests. But while reassuring the sensitive French that the United States did not question their sovereignty over Indochina, Washington did not bestow a blank check. In October 1945 the State Department warned that "the willingness of the United States to see French control reestablished assumes that French claim to have the support of the population of Indochina is borne out by future events."

Under Secretary of State Dean Acheson admitted the nation's lack of options in December 1946 instructions to the U.S. diplomatic representative in Hanoi: "Keep in mind Ho's clear record as [an] agent [of] international Communism, [the] absence [of] recantation, [his] Moscow affiliations. . . . Least desirable eventuality would be establishment [of] Communist-dominated Moscow-oriented state [in] Indochina." Two months later Secretary of State Marshall reminded the U.S. embassy in Paris that "we do not lose sight of the fact that Ho Chi Minh had direct Communist connections and it should be obvious that we are not interested in seeing colonial empire administrations supplanted by philosophy and political organization emanating from and controlled by [the] Kremlin."

An obsessive fear of communism dominated U.S. Southeast Asian policy, even though in midsummer 1948 the State Department acknowledged that it had "no evidence of a direct link between Ho and Moscow but assumes it exists." The Truman administration would not take a chance that Ho might be acting independently of the Soviet Union. The success of the Chinese communists in 1948 and early 1949 made Washington more jittery about Indochina. A June 1949 NSC study concluded that "colonial-nationalist conflict provides a fertile field for subversive Communist activities, and it is now clear that Southeast Asia is the target of a co-ordinated offensive directed by the Kremlin." If Indochina fell, the other dominoes, namely the rest of Southeast Asia, and eventually the Middle East, and Australia, would follow according to the assumptions often expressed by NSC members in the next three administrations.

Failing to win a decisive military settlement against Ho, the French turned to a political solution. Somewhat reluctantly, Paris sponsored a nationalist movement under Bao Dai, a former playboy emperor who spent much of his time on the French Riviera. In January 1950 France recognized the independence of Bao Dai's Vietnam and identified Laos and Cambodia as Associated States, all within the French Union. Ho Chi Minh immediately denied the legitimacy of the new Vietnam state, while the Soviet Union and People's Republic of China promptly extended recognition to Ho's Democratic Republic of Vietnam as the "only legal government of the Vietnam people."

Condemning the "surprise" recognition by the Soviet Union, Secretary of State Acheson asserted that "the Soviet acknowledgment of this movement should remove any illusions as to the 'nationalist' nature of Ho Chi Minh's aims and reveals Ho in his true colors as the mortal enemy of native independence in Indochina." In early February 1950 Washington recognized the Bao Dai government. The cold war had come to Vietnam.

The First Step: U.S. Aid to France in Indochina

When France in mid-February 1950 requested military and economic aid in prosecuting the Indochina war, Secretary of Defense Louis Johnson advised Truman that, "the choice confronting the United States is to support the legal governments in Indochina or to face the extension of Communism over the remainder of the continental area of Southeast Asia and possibly westward." A National Security Council report at the end of February pointed out that "there is already evidence of movement of arms" from Communist China to Ho Chi Minh's forces." The State Department endorsed aid to the French, and the JCS recommended immediate allocation of $15 million. Truman and his key advisers continued to assume it necessary to bolster France in Asia in order to have a strong France in Europe. On May 9, 1950, Truman approved $10 million in military aid for Indochina. A little more than two weeks later the State Department announced the intent to establish an economic aid mission to Cambodia, Laos, and Vietnam and recommended a "modest" appropriation of $60 million. The crucial first step of involvement in Vietnam's war was taken.

The outbreak of the Korean War in June 1950 gave a new urgency to developments in Vietnam. Even though it had become clear that Bao Dai was little more than a figurehead for the French, Truman announced on June 27 that he had "directed acceleration in the furnishing of military assistance to the forces of France and the Associated States in Indochina and the dispatch of a military mission to provide close working relations with those forces."

When Communist China entered the Korean War (p. 43) U.S. leaders feared that the Chinese might intervene in Indochina, especially in view of the large number of Chinese troops on the border of Vietnam and the substantial aid being furnished to Ho Chi Minh. The National Security Council drafted a plan for the "resolute defense" of Indochina in case of a massive Red Chinese intervention. To assist the French, the Truman administration budgeted almost $600 million in military aid for the French in Indochina in the fiscal years 1950–1953.

In effect, the Truman administration had little room for maneuvering in its Southeast Asian policy. The United States could exert little pressure on France because of concern that Paris might reject the European Defense Community Treaty (p. 20). Moreover, given the political climate in the United States, Washington could not push for a negotiated settlement with communists. For, as the frustrations of the Korean War mounted, administration leaders felt the stings of Senator McCarthy and his cohorts who accused the Democrats of being "the party of treason" and "soft on communism." (p. 18).

A Second Step: U.S. Military Technicians in Vietnam

Republican oratory in the successful presidential campaign of 1952 promised a more vigorous effort to contain communism in Asia. From the beginning of his administration Eisenhower and his closest advisers assumed that Indochina "had probably the top priority in foreign policy, being in some ways more important than Korea because the consequences of loss there could not be localized, but would spread throughout Asia and Europe." But the same factors that limited

Truman's options in Southeast Asia still applied. For instance, whereas a June 1953 Gallup poll indicated that twice as many Americans favored as opposed sending war materials to help the French in Indochina, 85 percent in a September poll opposed sending U.S. soldiers to Vietnam.

Administration leaders sensed that the French were fighting only to keep Vietnam in the French Union, whereas the Vietnamese wanted complete independence. At a NSC meeting in February 1954 CIA Director Allen Dulles reported that "the most disheartening feature of the news from Indochina was the evidence that the majority of people in Vietnam supported the Vietminh rebels." Yet, the belief developed in Washington that most Vietnamese, if promised complete independence, would fight against the Vietminh after adequate training—something that the French had not provided.

Eisenhower proceeded with caution. The National Security Council proposed aid to France and the Associated States in "an aggressive military, political, psychological program, including covert operations to eliminate organized Viet Minh forces by mid-1955," and would have the United States take "necessary military action" if Red China intervened. But Eisenhower limited his action to proposals for increased military aid for Indochina in his fiscal 1954 budget. The president also agreed to send 200 uniformed U.S. Air Force mechanics to Vietnam, provided they were stationed at a safe distance from combat areas.

A Step Almost Taken, 1954

A Big Four agreement to discuss the Indochina question at a forthcoming international conference scheduled to convene in Geneva in late April 1954 disturbed U.S. officials, who felt that negotiations would end in capitulation unless the French first won a substantial military victory. The JCS warned early in March that "a settlement based upon free elections would be attended by almost certain loss of the Associated States to Communist control." Admiral Radford, chairman of the JCS, suggested that "the United States must be prepared to act promptly, and in force possibly, to a frantic and belated request by the French for United States intervention."

As the news from the front became grim, Washington worked to keep France from negotiating with Ho Chi Minh and withdrawing from the war. But a disaster was in the making—15,000 of France's best troops were under siege at Dien Bien Phu in northern Vietnam more than 200 miles behind enemy lines. The administration hastened efforts to secure allied agreement to a Southeast Asia collective defense pact corresponding to NATO (p. 47). In a letter to Prime Minister Winston Churchill, Eisenhower argued the lesson of history:

> We failed to halt Hirohito, Mussolini and Hitler by not acting in unit and in time. That marked the beginning of many years of stark tragedy and desperate peril. May it not be that our nations have learned something from that lesson?

On April 3, 1954, eight congressional leaders received a surprise phone call from the secretary of state to come to an extremely important meeting. After detailing the critical status of French forces at Dien Bien Phu, Dulles indicated that the administration wanted Congress to pass a joint resolution that would permit the president to use air and naval power in Indochina. Admiral Radford supported the secretary and proposed a single massive air strike. But under close questioning from senators Earle Clements (D., Ky.) and Lyndon B. Johnson (D., Tex.), Radford acknowledged that no other member of the JCS agreed with him; Dulles admitted that he had not consulted America's allies. The three Republican and five Democratic members of Congress, therefore, concurred that Dulles should first find out whether he had British and French support.

Meanwhile, Douglas Dillon, U.S. ambassador to France, sent word that the French Government claimed that "immediate armed intervention of U.S. carrier aircraft at Dien Bien Phu is now necessary to save the situation." At the same time the President's Special Committee on Southeast Asia recommended that the United States be ready for active participation "and without French support should that be necessary." But the meeting between Dulles and congressional leaders had convinced Eisenhower that any U.S. military involvement in Indochina would require a coalition with allies to pursue "united action," as well as congressional approval and France's commitment to speed up the independence of the Associated States.

When Senator John F. Kennedy (D., Mass.) questioned whether any amount of U.S. military aid in Indochina could defeat the Viet Minh, Eisenhower defended his policies in a press conference with an explanation of the "falling domino" principle.

> You have a row of dominoes set up, you knock over the first one, and what
> will happen to the last one is the certainty that it will go over very quickly.
> So you could have a beginning of a disintegration that would have the most
> profound influences.

Having originated in the Truman administration, the domino theory had strong adherents in the Democratic party, as Eisenhower well knew.

Washington, however, failed to convince the British that the domino theory applied to Southeast Asia. London opposed any united action before the Geneva Conference in April 1954. When British leaders refused to agree to a U.S. air strike to save the French at Dien Bien Phu, Dulles informed the French that the United States could not intervene without congressional approval and without "united action." Two days later the Geneva Conference convened.

The Geneva Conference, 1954

Pessimistic from the outset about the Geneva Conference, the Eisenhower administration found little satisfaction in the course of the deliberations. A JCS recommendation that a satisfactory political settlement precede any cease-fire

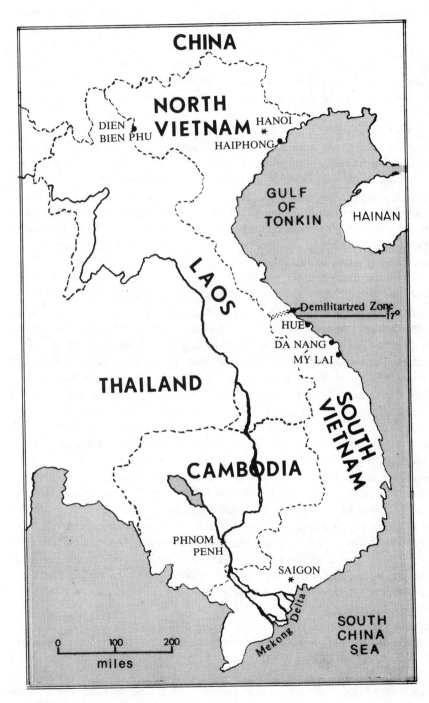

CHINA

NORTH
VIETNAM
DIEN
BIEN PHU
HANOI
HAIPHONG

GULF
OF
TONKIN
HAINAN

LAOS

Demilitarized Zone
17°
HUE
DA NANG
MY LAI

THAILAND

SOUTH
VIETNAM

CAMBODIA

PHNOM
PENH

SAIGON

Mekong Delta

SOUTH
CHINA
SEA

0   100   200
miles

Southeast Asia in 1954

guided administration officials, who tried in vain to convince the French to avoid concessions merely to end hostilities. A discouraged Dulles left Geneva on May 4, four days before the conference even began discussion of Indochina, and the U.S. delegation was downgraded to an "observer mission." Washington had no intention of fueling domestic criticism by taking a prominent part in negotiations almost certain to result in placing millions of Vietnamese under communist rule.

After the French surrender at Dien Bien Phu on May 7 foreshadowed a communist diplomatic triumph at Geneva, Dulles advised that the United States would not approve any ceasefire, armistice, or other settlement . . . subverting the existing lawful governments of the three aforementioned states [Laos, Cambodia, Vietnam] or of placing in jeopardy the forces of the French Union in Indochina." At the height of the Geneva Conference almost 75 percent of those polled by Gallup expressed opposition to sending troops to Indochina, while only 18 percent believed that the United States would stop the spread of communism by fighting in Indochina.

The final declaration of the Geneva Conference, signed on July 21, 1954, established a truce between North Vietnam and France by dividing Vietnam temporarily at the 17th parallel with a demilitarized zone separating North and South Vietnam. Ho agreed to withdraw his troops north of that line, and France was to move its forces south and remain until requested to withdraw by the Vietnam parties. General elections supervised by an international commission were to be held in Vietnam within two years, and in Laos and Cambodia in 1955. The Geneva Accords also prohibited any military alliances and the establishment of any foreign military base in either zone of Vietnam.

Refusing to join in the declaration of the conference, the United States issued a unilateral declaration affirming that it would "refrain from the threat or the use of force to disturb them (the agreements)" and that "it would view any renewal of the aggression in violation of the aforesaid agreements with grave concern." The U.S. statement also noted that "in the case of nations now divided against their will, we shall continue to seek to achieve unity through free elections supervised by the United Nations to insure that they are conducted fairly." As Dulles explained to the British and French, "The memories of Yalta in the United States are very fresh. The United States government cannot be associated with a settlement which would be portrayed in the United States as a second Yalta." According to this widely held view, to participate with Communists in an agreement that would appear to guarantee them the fruits of their aggression would invite public criticism and political defeat.

Nor did the new South Vietnamese state, granted independence by France on June 4, 1954, after 70 years of French rule, sign the Accords. South Vietnamese delegates opposed the partition of Vietnam as "deeply wounding the national sentiment of the Vietnamese people." Poorly understood at the time, the

Geneva Accords contain fatal flaws—U.S. disassociation, opposition of South Vietnamese leaders, and reliance on a weakened France to carry out the agreements.

The Next Step: U.S. Support of the Diem Regime

An ardent Nationalist, Ngo Dinh Diem (Ning-ow Ze-yuh Zee-emm), arrived in Saigon in late June 1954. Diem had lived in self-imposed exile since 1933 to protest French rule and belonged to Vietnam's feudal aristocracy. A Roman Catholic in a predominantly Buddhist country, he returned home after living for the past four years at Maryknoll seminaries in New York and New Jersey.

Appointed premier by Bao Dai, Diem moved at once to consolidate his control of the power structure and to get rid of the hated French. He repudiated the Geneva agreements as signed by a foreign military command "in contempt of Vietnamese national interests" and not binding on his government. He refused to consult with the North Vietnamese and even rejected economic relations and postal exchanges with Ho's government. The 17th parallel became a rigid line dividing Vietnam into two hostile countries.

Diem gained solid backing in Washington. On August 17, 1954, Eisenhower directed that aid to Indochina henceforth be given directly to the Associated States rather than through the French. After approving a NSC recommendation that the United States assume the burden of defending South Vietnam, in a letter to Diem in October the president offered U.S. aid to assist "in developing a strong, viable state, capable of resisting attempted subversion or aggression through military means." In return, Diem was expected to undertake needed political and economic reforms. U.S. officials, meanwhile, continued to refuse to have any dealings with Ho Chi Minh, even though there was some speculation in the press that he might become an Asian Tito, independent of control by either Moscow or Beijing.

Problems developed almost immediately for Diem and the United States. Over 800,000 refugees from the North, a majority of them Catholic, crowded into the South. Diem's authoritarianism and nepotism aroused serious opposition in the army and among municipal leaders. Popular support from the masses for Diem did not develop. Diem's outspoken criticism of the Geneva Accords coupled with his repeated refusals to prepare for elections that would lead to the unification of Vietnam angered a French government obligated to carry out those agreements. French leaders urged Washington to help in replacing the "irresponsible" Diem. But Eisenhower had no enthusiasm for elections according to the Geneva formula. In his *Memoirs* he confessed:

> I have never talked or corresponded with a person knowledgeable in Indochinese Affairs who did not agree that had elections been held as of the time

of the fighting, possibly 80 percent of the population would have voted for the Communist Ho Chi Minh as their leader.

With the backing of congressional leaders and the JCS, Dulles told the French that "Diem is the only means US sees to save South Vietnam and counteract revolutionary movement underway in Vietnam. . . . Whatever US view has been in past, US must support Diem whole-heartedly." The secretary's arguments convinced the reluctant French to keep their Expeditionary Corps in South Vietnam until a national assembly could be elected and a strong Vietnamese state established.

French Withdrawal

Buoyed by almost unqualified U.S. support, Diem moved against his opposition. He arrested and imprisoned without due process thousands of known and suspected Communists. He centralized administration by eliminating the autonomy of South Vietnam's 2,500 villages. After winning 98.2 percent of the vote against Bao Dai in a "rigged" referendum in October 1955, Diem proclaimed the establishment of the Republic of Vietnam with himself as president.

Diem's policies made the French position untenable, and in 1956 they began to evacuate the last of their troops. Into the vacuum rushed the United States to safeguard a defenseless South Vietnam against any communist threat. In May the administration added 350 men to its Military Advisory Group that worked to equip and train a South Vietnamese army of 150,000 men. Washington also assumed full cost of the military training, that averaged $85 million in each of the next five years. In 1956 the NSC instructed U.S. agencies to "assist Free Vietnam to assert an increasingly attractive contrast to conditions in the present Communist zone."

A NEW WAR AND ESCALATING U.S. INVOLVEMENT, 1955–1964

Viet Cong Insurgency

The July 1956 Geneva deadline for elections throughout Vietnam passed without any move to enforce the agreement. But Vietnam did not loom large among international concerns through most of the second Eisenhower term. More pressing problems in Europe, Latin America, and the Middle East after 1955 crowded Vietnam almost out of any mention in Eisenhower's *Memoirs*. Peaceful coexistence also appeared to have encouraged a measure of complacency. Public opinion polls between 1955 and 1961 showed a steady increase in the percent-

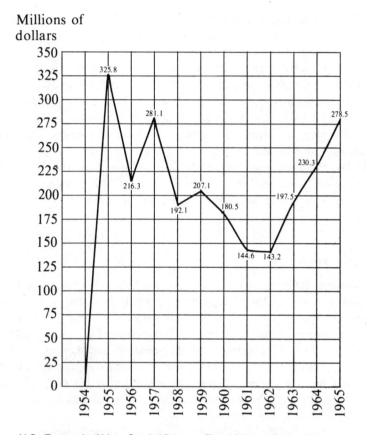

Millions of
dollars

U.S. Economic Aid to South Vietnam; Fiscal Years 1954–1965

SOURCE: Statistical Abstract of the United States

age of Americans who believed that the United States and Soviet Union could live peacefully together.

Dispatches from U.S. officials in Vietnam, however, expressed concern about Diem's failure to win broad popular support. They also criticized the fact that after five years of alleged land reform, 15 percent of the population still owned 75 percent of the land. Yet Washington remained reluctant to pressure Diem as long as no threat appeared to undermine Vietnam's security. The Eisenhower administration continued to support Diem with substantial economic aid (see graph above), three-fourths of which went for military expenditures.

No change in U.S. policy occurred even when dissident South Vietnamese, the Viet Cong, began in 1957 to rebel against the government of Diem. An increase in assassinations, kidnappings, and acts of terrorism by the Viet Cong prompted the United States Military Assistance Advisory Group to report in July 1957 that "the Communists have been forming front organizations to influence portions of anti-government minorities." By 1959 the Viet Cong had evolved from a secret political movement to overthrow Diem into an open military operation to defeat the Republic of Vietnam.

Large-scale infiltration of troops and supplies from the North finally per-suaded the Joint Chiefs to propose a counterinsurgency plan in March 1960. But State Department officials resisted. Believing that Diem's authoritarianism caused the insurgency, they favored pressuring him to make reforms. The De-fense Department, however, contended that military weakness caused Diem's problems and that a buildup of military force against communist subversion was needed. The Pentagon won the debate, and in June 1960 the U.S. Advisory Group was more than doubled to a total of 685 men. But in its remaining weeks in office the Eisenhower administration did not implement a counterinsurgency plan.

Trouble in Laos

Before leaving office Eisenhower told President-elect Kennedy that the "Laos mess" was so bad that "you might have to go in there and fight it out." An anticommunist, pro-American faction in Laos backed by over 300 U.S. military advisers was losing to a Soviet Union backed faction of Communists, the Pathet Lao, and neutralists. U.S. officials on the scene advised that only U.S. troops could save the pro-U.S. faction from defeat. Kennedy went through the motions of preparing for war by moving the Seventh Fleet to the Gulf of Siam and flying 500 Marines into Thailand to convince the Communists of the desirability of a peaceful settlement.

Early in May 1961 a ceasefire was arranged. Fighting erupted again during prolonged negotiations to set up a government. Finally in October 1961 the parties agreed in principle to a coalition government under neutralist Souvanna Phouma. Ironically, a similar neutralist coalition had been toppled with CIA assistance in 1958 when the pro-U.S. government, now being abandoned in 1961, was put into power. U.S. intervention in Laos had cost over $300 million and left that nation with a very shaky peace and a devastated countryside. Throughout the rest of the Kennedy administration the threat of a communist takeover in Laos haunted U.S. leaders.

The Counterinsurgency Program in Vietnam

The situation in Vietnam did not look much brighter to the new administration. In December 1960 the newly created National Liberation Front of South Viet-nam (NLF) backed by North Vietnam stepped up guerrilla activity against the Diem regime. Although the NLF hinted a willingness to negotiate a settlement, Kennedy scorned the overtures. For a president elected by a very narrow margin, any deal with Communists that expanded their influence was politically unthinkable.

In April 1961 a Pentagon task force recommended an increase in the Military Assistance Advisory Group and deployment of 3,600 additional U.S. troops to Vietnam to train two new divisions of the Army of the Republic of Vietnam (ARVN). In May, Kennedy sent Vice-President Lyndon Johnson on a fact-finding tour with instructions to reassure Asian leaders that the United States could be counted on to support them. After Laos and the Bay of Pigs (p. 59) the administration needed a demonstration of will and strength. Impressed by Diem, whom he proclaimed "the Winston Churchill of Southeast Asia," Johnson reported to Kennedy that local leaders "do not want American troops involved in Southeast Asia other than on training missions." But the vice-president added, "We must decide whether to help these countries to the best of our ability or throw in the towel in the area and pull back our defenses to San Francisco and [a] 'Fortress America' concept."

Even before receiving Johnson's report, Kennedy decided to go ahead with a counterinsurgency program. Intrigued by the idea of employing guerrilla tactics against guerrillas, the president authorized the sending of 400 Special Forces troops, the Green Berets, to Vietnam. These troops had instructions to "infiltrate teams under light civilian cover to southeast Laos to locate and attack Vietnamese Communist bases and lines of communication. In North Vietnam, using the foundation established by intelligence operations, form networks of resistance, covert bases and teams for sabotage and light harassment."

When increased guerrilla attacks by the Viet Cong in early fall 1961 gained them control of most of the southern delta, pressures mounted within the administration to send U.S. ground forces. To look into the "feasibility" of such a move, in October Kennedy sent to Vietnam General Maxwell Taylor, army chief of staff, and Walt W. Rostow, White House aide. In a report combining optimism with urgency, Taylor and Rostow recommended that the United States "put in a task force consisting largely of logistical troops . . . a U.S. military presence in Vietnam capable of assuring Diem of our readiness to join him in a military showdown with the Viet Cong or Viet Minh."

Defense Secretary Robert McNamara and Secretary of State Dean Rusk countered that a decision on the introduction of combat forces could be deferred and that Diem should be pressured to "mobilize" all his resources and "overhaul" his military command structure in return for additional U.S. support forces such as helicopters and communication systems. The president embraced this proposal.

Actually Kennedy had increased U.S. military involvement to the extent that by the end of 1961 the size of the U.S. military force in Vietnam had tripled since inauguration day. By his actions Kennedy moved the United States from an adviser relationship to a limited partnership with South Vietnam. And for the first time members of the U.S. armed services lost their lives in the Vietnam War—a total of 11 in 1961.

The Strategic Hamlet Program

Early in 1962 Washington came up with a new twist to counterinsurgency—the Strategic Hamlet Program to "pacify" rural Vietnam and develop support among the peasants for the central government. This operation involved clearing Viet Cong insurgents from an area and resettling the population in villages to be defended by ARVN troops. Confidence in the eventual success of this program encouraged, in July 1962, secret adoption of a plan for phased withdrawal of U.S. forces from Vietnam over a period of three years and a reduction in military aid.

But the optimism that launched the Strategic Hamlet Program evaporated as peasants resisted resettlement while Diem exploited it to extend his control. In June 1963 belief in the possibility of cooperation with Diem went up in flames on the streets of Saigon. A Buddhist monk, protesting Diem's oppressive measures, set himself afire before a horrified crowd as cameras recorded the event for the next day's television in the United States. After Diem declared martial law and ordered attacks on Buddhist pagodas, Washington concluded that it could no longer tolerate Diem's continuation in power. "To sink or swim with Ngo Dinh Diem" as one correspondent put it, was not in U.S. interest.

Overthrow of Diem Government

With the full knowledge and even encouragement of U.S. authorities, a group of South Vietnamese generals plotted the overthrow of Diem. Kennedy's new ambassador to Vietnam, Henry Cabot Lodge, cabled Rusk late in August: "We are launched on a course from which there is no respectable turning back, the overthrow of the Diem government." On November 2, 1963, conspirators murdered Diem and his brother Nhu, who had supervised the attacks on the Buddhists. Shocked by the killings, Washington was reviewing its Vietnam policy when 20 days later in Dallas an assassin's bullet snuffed out the life of President John F. Kennedy.

Johnson's Hesitant Steps

The new president, Lyndon B. Johnson, pledged to "keep our commitments from South Vietnam to West Berlin" and to carry out all of the late president's policies. A few days after taking the oath of office, Johnson informed Lodge: "I am not going to lose Vietnam. I am not going to be the president who saw Southeast Asia go the way China went."

Relatively inexperienced in foreign affairs despite his long service in Congress, Johnson solicited advice from "wise experts of established reputation." Defense Secretary McNamara returned in December 1963 from a hurried trip to Vietnam with the gloomy report that "current trends, unless reversed in the next 2–3 months, will lead to neutralization at best and more likely to a Communist-controlled state." A pessimistic Senator Mike Mansfield (D., Mont.), advised withdrawal of U.S. advisory forces from Vietnam and acceptance of a division of the country similar to that in Korea. On the other hand, a CIA report that admitted "a serious and steadily deteriorating" situation, implied that more military involvement might save the day.

Gradually a hesitant president inched away from a political solution toward a military one. A McNamara–Taylor mission to Saigon in March 1964 confirmed that the military situation "has unquestionably been growing worse" and that Hanoi's involvement in the insurgency, "always significant, has been increasing." They urged that the United States "reiterate that it will provide all the assistance and advice required to do the job regardless of how long it takes." Late in March Johnson signed a top secret National Security Advisory Memorandum instructing U.S. forces "to be in a position on 72 hours notice to initiate . . . 'Retaliatory Actions' against North Vietnam, and to be in a position on 30 days' notice to initiate the program of 'Graduated Overt Military Pressure' against North Vietnam." What had been regarded as an internal struggle in South Vietnam had become, in the administration's eyes, a war between "free" South Vietnam and a communist aggressor, North Vietnam. The Vietnam conflict, in McNamara's words, was "a test case of U.S. capacity to help a nation meet a Communist war of liberation."

But in a presidential election year and with Great Society programs such as civil rights and antipoverty legislation to enact, Johnson did not want to go beyond beefing up the pacification program with more economic aid and advisory troops. Temporarily deferring phased withdrawal, the president in May 1964 increased the U.S. military force in Vietnam to over 17,000 men. In June he appointed General William C. Westmoreland as commander of U.S. forces in Vietnam. But U.S. troops were still not authorized to engage in combat against the North Vietnamese enemy. Washington sent more advisory troops in July, and expanded naval patrols in off-shore waters of North Vietnam. The Gulf of Tonkin incident in August came as no great surprise to the Pentagon or the White House.

Holding His Fire

Five days after the adoption of the Gulf of Tonkin Resolution, President Johnson, with one eye on the U.S. electorate and a sideward glance at Hanoi, projected an image of firmness with restraint. He told the American Bar Association: "No one should think for a moment that we will be worn down, nor will we be driven out, and we will not be provoked into rashness."

Unknown to the general public, the Defense Department and CIA in September drew up plans "to respond as appropriate against North Vietnam in case of an attack on U.S. units or of any 'special' North Vietnamese-Viet Cong action against South Vietnam." The Pentagon assumed that bombing strikes against North Vietnam "would be required at some proximate future date" to discourage Hanoi's underwriting the insurgency. Convinced by the unanimous endorsement of his advisers, Johnson approved the plans.

When the Viet Cong attacked a U.S. base north of Saigon just two days before the 1964 November election, Johnson followed the advice of civilian advisers and refused to authorize an "eye for an eye" air strike advocated by the JCS and the new U.S. ambassador to Vietnam, General Maxwell Taylor. Nor did the newly reelected president retaliate when on Christmas Eve another Viet Cong raid killed 2 and wounded 50 Americans. But even Johnson's civilian aides began to counsel that "calculated doses of force" would be needed to bring Hanoi to the bargaining table.

In his January 1965 State of the Union Message President Johnson reviewed the reasons for the U.S. presence in Vietnam as "first, because a friendly nation has asked us for help against Communist aggression. Ten years ago we pledged our help. Three Presidents have supported that pledge. We will not break it. Second, our own security is tied to the peace of Asia." For the next four years Lyndon Johnson stuck by that argument.

ESCALATION OF THE VIETNAM WAR, 1965–1968

Operation Rolling Thunder

Disturbed by the political instability and military ineffectiveness of South Vietnam, Ambassador Taylor reported early in January: "We are presently on a losing track and must risk a change. . . . To take no positive action now is to accept defeat in the fairly near future." John McCone, CIA director, advised the bombing of targets in North Vietnam.

Johnson was on the spot. The intelligence community had furnished evidence of large-scale infiltration of military units from North Vietnam. U.S. officials in Saigon did not think that the South Vietnamese government could prevent a communist takeover without direct participation by U.S. military forces. The American people were becoming restless and unhappy about Viet Cong killings of U.S. troops unable to fight back. A public opinion poll in late January 1965 revealed that 50 percent thought that the United States should use its military forces to stop such attacks, whereas only 28 percent opposed such action. Reluctantly the president authorized use of U.S. planes against the Viet Cong, but only in support of Vietnamese troops when Westmoreland considered it absolutely necessary.

Another Viet Cong attack on a U.S. base on February 6 killed 8 Americans and wounded 60. This incident convinced National Security Adviser McGeorge Bundy, in Saigon on a fact-finding mission, that the United States must respond. With a solid consensus supporting him, Johnson decided to hit back with an air strike against North Vietnam to "convince the leaders in Hanoi that we were serious in our purpose and also that the North could not count on continued immunity if they persisted in aggression in the South."

On February 7, 49 U.S. Navy jets bombed North Vietnamese barracks and staging areas 40 miles north of the 17th parallel. The next day Johnson decided to carry out "continuing action" against North Vietnam until its leaders stopped their aggression. "We have kept our guns over the mantel," said the president, "and our shells in the cupboard for a long time now. And what was the result? They are killing our men while they sleep in the night. I can't ask our American soldiers out there to continue to fight with one hand tied behind their backs." After more than 10 years of only military aid and advice to South Vietnam, the United States committed its air power to the war against North Vietnam. Johnson explained, "I saw our bombs as my political resources for negotiating a peace."

U.S. involvement in the war increased throughout the spring without much public awareness. Early in March Johnson approved the use of napalm to make the bombing attacks more effective, and he participated directly in hours of discussion to choose each target to be bombed. After repeated requests from Westmoreland, two Marine Battalion Landing Teams of 1,500 men, the first regular U.S. combat troops to be sent to Vietnam, arrived in March 1965 to protect the U.S. air base near Danang. But Johnson resisted the proposal of the JCS to send two U.S. divisions and one South Korean division for combat action against the Viet Cong in South Vietnam.

The Final Step: Commitment of U.S. Ground Forces

To the dismay of the administration, the bombing seemed to increase rather than decrease the attacks on U.S. installations. The Communists, ironically, not the United States, controlled the escalation of the war. After the Viet Cong blew up the U.S. embassy in Saigon, killing 20 persons, Johnson secretly authorized on April 2, 1965, participation of Marines in combat to protect nearby South Vietnamese units if necessary. He also decided to add 20,000 men to support U.S. forces already in South Vietnam. With the Gulf of Tonkin Resolution on his desk, the president believed he had no need to consult Congress nor explain his actions openly to the public.

Johnson still hoped to avoid that last step leading to ground fighting and U.S. casualties. In a speech on April 7, 1965, he signaled Hanoi that the United States "remains ready . . . for unconditional discussions" and that he would seek $1 billion in reconstruction funds for all of Vietnam immediately after peace was established. The North Vietnamese ignored the overture and refused to discuss or negotiate until all U.S. troops had been withdrawn from Indochina—a condition unacceptable to Washington.

By midsummer 1965 U.S. policymakers realized that bombing North Vietnam would not do the job by itself. The flow of men and supplies from North Vietnam to the insurgents in the South had to be cut off on the ground if Viet Cong attacks were to be stopped. Although Johnson secretly approved the sending of an additional 100,000 U.S. troops to Vietnam by the end of the year, he announced at a July press conference an increase of 50,000 and stated that this did "not imply any change in policy whatsoever." Without fanfare U.S. troops began to engage in combat against Viet Cong guerrillas. Westmoreland embarked on "search and destroy" missions that relied on helicopters to bring devastating fire power to hit the enemy. In his judgment, such tactics stood "a good chance of achieving an acceptable outcome within a reasonable time in Vietnam."

The Song of Doves

As U.S. involvement escalated throughout 1965 a different voice, faint and uncoordinated at first, echoed across the United States. A one-day moratorium to protest the war, at the University of Michigan in March 1965, set an example that spread to dozens of college campuses that spring. In May a National Teach-In to protest the war took place in the nation's capital. In October citizens in towns and villages across the nation held peace demonstrations. Later in the fall over 30,000 persons joined in a peace march in Washington.

Within the administration Under Secretary of State George Ball made dovish noises. Questioning the effectiveness of bombing, he said, "I have great apprehensions that we can't win under these conditions." Ball even argued that Vietnam was not vital to the security of the United States, and he suggested that the nation "cut its losses" by withdrawing. Doubts also infected upper echelons in the Defense Department. During another pause in the bombing between Christmas Eve 1965 and the end of January 1966 Assistant Secretary of Defense John McNaughton wrote a secret memo warning that "we have in Vietnam the ingredients of an enormous miscalculation. . . . We are in an escalating stalemate." Retreating from his early hard-line position, McNamara advised the president in 1966 that "even with the recommended deployments, we will be faced early in 1967 with a military standoff at a much higher level."

Dissenting voices were also heard in Congress. Senator Mansfield warned of a larger war involving Red China if the United States continued to expand its commitment. And Senator Fulbright, having second thoughts about the wisdom of the Gulf of Tonkin Resolution, said in June 1965 that "it is clear to all reasonable Americans that a complete military victory in Vietnam, though theoretically attainable, can in fact be attained only at a cost far exceeding the requirements of our interest and our honor." Seven months later, the Senate Foreign Relations Committee, chaired by Fulbright, held public hearings on the Vietnam War. Several senators challenged the administration's argument pushed by Secretary of State Dean Rusk that the United States was obligated according to the SEATO treaty (p. 47) to come to the aid of South Vietnam.

The Whir of Hawks

The pro-war faction, led by the Joint Chiefs and National Security Adviser Walt W. Rostow, answered the doves with statistics demonstrating military progress and with arguments for an expansion of U.S. military pressure to force North Vietnam to the bargaining table. Ambassador Maxwell Taylor testified before the Fulbright Committee hearings early in 1966: "We are not being licked. . . . we are looking for these people and destroying them at the greatest rate that has ever taken place in the history of the struggle." Administration spokespersons relied heavily on the "body count" of enemy dead to document the success of U.S. arms.

The hawks had strong allies in a Congress that continued to pass military appropriation bills requested by the administration. To vote against supplying necessary resources to U.S. combat soldiers was unthinkable to most members of Congress, even to those troubled about the war. And to back down under communist pressure was un-American and disloyal, as Richard Nixon argued. In a letter to the *New York Times* in October 1965 he suggested that "victory for the Vietcong . . . would mean ultimately the destruction of freedom of speech for all men for all time not only in Asia but the United States as well."

Although the tide of opposition to the war was clearly rising, a majority of the American people tended to believe their political and military leaders. Public opinion polls consistently showed throughout 1965 and 1966 that a clear majority supported the administration, even in bombing North Vietnam. Such backing encouraged officials to send more ground troops, to increase draft calls, and to continue the bombing. Johnson regarded his action as a reasonable middle course. By fighting a limited war in Vietnam, he believed that the United States could avoid World War III, bring about a negotiated peace, and have both "guns and butter." Opponents of the war he dismissed contemptuously as "Nervous Nellies" unwilling to see a tough job through to the end. But his policy, unless it produced measurable gains, risked antagonizing both those who thought the United States should pull out and those who believed in total victory. A spate of optimistic slogans emanated from Washington—Rostow saw a "light at the end of the tunnel"; Westmoreland claimed "the enemy's hopes are bankrupt"; and Taylor held "the cause in Vietnam is being won." In 1982 CBS aired revelations by former CIA officers that efforts to report an increase in enemy strength in 1966 and 1967 were blocked within the U.S. military bureaucracy to keep intelligence evaluations within totals that the command in Vietnam "could live with."

To Escalate or Not to Escalate?

But more bombings, an increase in the "body count" of enemy dead, and more property destroyed did not appear to weaken the Viet Cong. Nor did the bombing of North Vietnam's oil-storage facilities in July and August 1966 "bring the enemy to the conference table" or "cause the insurgency to wither," as so confidently predicted by the military. In fact, a secret Defense Department study by 47 scientists reported to McNamara in September that Operation Rolling Thunder, the heavy bombing of North Vietnam, "had no measurable direct effect" on North Vietnam's capability to make war. McNamara counseled the president to stop the bombing and negotiate a political settlement. In November 1966 he told Johnson that there is "no evidence" that additional troops, as requested by Westmoreland, "would substantially change the situation." Six months later a top secret CIA study for McNamara noted that "the outlook for marked success in achieving the current objectives of U.S. bombing programs is not bright. . . . The longer the war lasts, the more intractable our problem will become."

As the war dragged on with expanded bombing attacks and ground fighting, Westmoreland as usual requested more troops—this time a whopping 200,000. In addition, the Joint Chiefs pressured for the mobilization of reserves and "an extension of the war" into Laos and Cambodia. But Johnson, perhaps persuaded by Bundy's argument against ground escalation in 1967 and 1968 before a presidential election, authorized only a modest increase. Bundy may also have struck a sensitive chord with his suggestion that "what we must plan to offer as a defense of administration policy is not victory over Hanoi, but growing success—and self-reliance—in the south."

The Antiwar Movement in High Gear

In May 1967 a discouraged McNaughton confided to his chief, Secretary McNamara, that "a feeling is widely and strongly held that 'the Establishment' is out of its mind." McNaughton sensed a change in public attitude toward the war and a growing polarization of the nation. Television brought into U.S. homes nightly the horrors of modern war in vivid detail. The killing of innocent civilians, including women and children, and the devastation of the countryside distressed even many who had supported the war. So did mounting U.S. casualties that in 1967 reached 100,000 dead, wounded, or missing. (See table p. 110.) Public opinion polls, which in January 1965 had shown only 28 percent believing that the United States had made a mistake in sending troops to Vietnam, revealed in July 1967 that 41 percent thought so. For the first time, less than half of those polled thought that the United States should continue the bombing.

The protest movement accelerated throughout the spring and summer of 1967. In April more than 125,000 persons demonstrated in New York for an end to the war, while 30,000 marched in San Francisco. Muhammed Ali was stripped of his heavyweight boxing crown and imprisoned for refusing to be drafted. Hundreds of young men fled to Canada, Sweden, and other foreign havens to escape induction. Others defied the law and outraged supporters of the war by burning their draft cards and even the U.S. flag. Thousands of young persons, male and female, participated in Vietnam Summer of 1967 organizing teach-ins, sit-ins, and demonstrations against the war. An October citizens march on the Pentagon emphasized the intensity of the peace movement. Chanting, "Hey, hey, LBJ, how many kids have you killed today?" antiwar demonstrators paraded in front of the White House where the president remained a virtual prisoner. For months Johnson avoided public appearances except at military bases where a safe, friendly reception was assured. Efforts by supporters of the war to rally people behind the flag seemed to attract less attention and enthusiasm. The nation had become badly divided, and so had the national government.

Secretary of Defense McNamara's doubts reflected the division. He confessed to McNaughton that "the picture of the world's greatest superpower killing or seriously injuring 1000 noncombatants a week while trying to pound a tiny, backward nation into submission on an issue whose merits are hotly disputed, is not a pretty one." In November 1967 he submitted his resignation without recriminations, and early in the new year joined the growing ranks of former members of the Johnson administration.

The Shock of the Tet Offensive

The failure of U.S. military and political leaders to diagnose the realities in Vietnam was exposed early in 1968 when the Viet Cong violated the customary cease-fire marking the Tet, Vietnam's Lunar New Year holiday. On January 31, 1968, the first day of Tet, Viet Cong units launched a coordinated offensive against 36 major cities, scores of towns and villages, and a dozen U.S. bases, including even the U.S. embassy in Saigon.

Two days after the Tet offensive began, at a press conference Johnson claimed that the enemy attack had been "anticipated, prepared for and met," and that the enemy had suffered militarily "a complete failure." General Westmoreland, who had vainly attempted to stir the South Vietnamese to prepare for a major enemy offensive, believed that the enemy had decided "to go for broke" in hopes of fostering "American disenchantment with the war." He claimed that the Viet Cong had suffered "a catastrophic military defeat."

But the Tet offensive shocked the American people. Pictures of American corpses in the garden of the U.S. embassy in Saigon and nightly television pictures of hard fighting in and bombing of South Vietnamese cities over several weeks to dislodge the Viet Cong punctured optimistic official statements and cast doubt on the credibility of the nation's leaders. Opponents of the war found new strength. In their eyes a U.S. military officer unwittingly dramatized the futility of the war when he explained the destructive artillery and air attacks on Ben Tre, a small South Vietnamese city, with the remark, "It became necessary to destroy the town to save it."

Nevertheless, strong voices argued against abandoning the war. Richard Nixon, gearing up for another run for the presidency, contended, a few days after the Tet offensive began, that "the only effective way" to bring Hanoi to the peace table was to "prosecute the war more effectively." Administration leaders cautioned that defeatism at home played into the hands of the enemy. The chorus of opposition to the war was nurtured, according to Johnson, by "emotional and exaggerated reporting of the Tet offensive in our press and on television." An optimistic Westmoreland reported that enemy losses in the Tet attack provided "an opportunity to seize the initiative and materially shorten the war."

Many viewed Westmoreland's request for 200,000 more men as evidence of the desperate nature of the U.S. military position, rather than as a logical move to expand operations against a weakened enemy. Johnson turned down the request because it would necessitate calling up the inactive reserves—a step that would increase domestic opposition to the war and make it more difficult to open negotiations with Hanoi. Westmoreland was learning, as MacArthur had in Korea, that a U.S. military victory "in the classic sense," ending in the surrender of the enemy, had become impossible because the American people were unwilling to pay the heavy price of all-out war.

Public opinion polls also showed a sharp decline in the president's standing. The 40 percent that in late January approved Johnson's handling of the war dwindled by early March to only 26 percent. On March 31, just two months after the start of the Tet Offensive, the president announced on national television that he would halt the bombing north of the 20th parallel and that he would not be a candidate for reelection.

Peace Talks in Paris

Within a few days Hanoi responded favorably to Johnson's initiative, and peace talks began in Paris in May. But little progress was made during spring and summer sessions. The North Vietnamese insisted on the unconditional cessation of all bombing and "other acts of war" by the United States. U.S. officials replied that they could not comply until North Vietnam ceased its military operations against South Vietnam. Some observers suspected that Hanoi was stalling until after the U.S. election in hopes of a change in the U.S. position. But, 10 days before the U.S. presidential election, North Vietnam agreed to include South Vietnam in the talks, and Johnson responded by ordering a halt in all bombardment of the North and set November 6, the day after the election for commencement of peace talks in Paris. However, the Nixon campaign team had secretly encouraged the South Vietnamese to delay peace negotiations with the North Vietnamese until after the U.S. election. As a result, President Thieu announced three days before the election that he would not send a South Vietnamese delegation to the November 6 talks. Once again domestic politics controlled U.S. foreign policy.

VIETNAMIZATION OF THE WAR

Revival of an Old Approach

Nixon, like his immediate predecessors in the White House, opposed any peace settlement that left the Communists in control of all of Vietnam. He, too, did not intend to become the first president to lose a war. A separate, free South Vietnam had to be preserved. But Nixon realized, as he confided to aides during the campaign, "that there's no way to win the war." So the problem remained— "how to end the war without losing it."

To achieve that goal the new chief executive and his national security adviser, Henry Kissinger, a former Harvard professor, proposed to "Vietnamize" the war by the slow withdrawal of U.S. troops and their simultaneous replacement with U.S. equipped and directed South Vietnamese forces. During the transition period the United States could renew the bombing if Hanoi tried to take advantage of the withdrawal. After a "decent interval" the responsibility for fighting the Communists and defending the territory of South Vietnam from aggression would be shouldered by the South Vietnamese themselves.

Remarkably similar to Kennedy's "phased withdrawal," the Nixon–Kissinger plan appeared neat, tidy, and politically astute. Domestic opponents of the war would be quieted as U.S. soldiers returned home, casualties declined,

Troop Levels (as of Dec. 31)	Aid to South Vietnam (in millions)		
	Economic		Military
1960 — 900	1960 — $180.5		
1961 — 3,200	1961 — 144.6		
1962 — 11,300	1962 — 143.2		
1963 — 16,300	1963 — 197.5		
1964 — 23,300	1964 — 230.3		
1965 — 184,300	1965 — 278.5	—	297.0
1966 — 385,300	1966 — 337.0	—	862.0
1967 — 485,000	1967 — 568.0	—	1,204.0
1968 — 536,100	1968 — 537.0	—	1,055.0
1969 — 475,200	1969 — 414.0	—	1,608.0
1970 — 334,600	1970 — 477.0	—	1,693.0
1971 — 156,800	1971 — 576.0	—	1,883.0
1972 — 24,200	1972 — 455.0	—	2,383.0
	1973 — 502.0	—	3,349.0
	1974 — 654.0	—	941.9

Source: *Statistical Abstract of The United States*

U.S. Casualties			The Draft
Killed	Wounded		
1961 — 11	—	3	1955 — 215,000
1962 — 31	—	78	1960 — 90,000
1963 — 78	—	411	1963 — 74,000
1964 — 147	—	1,039	1964 — 151,000
1965 — 1,369	—	6,114	1965 — 103,000
1966 — 5,008	—	30,093	1966 — 340,000
1967 — 9,378	—	62,025	1967 — 299,000
1968 — 14,582	—	92,820	1968 — 340,000
1969 — 9,414	—	70,216	1969 — 265,000
1970 — 4,221	—	30,643	1970 — 207,000
1971 — 1,381	—	8,936	1971 — 156,000
1972 — 300	—	1,221	1972 — 27,000
1973 — 237	—	60	

Source: *Statistical Abstract of The United States*

and the draft ended. Avid hawks would be reassured by the commitment to stay in Vietnam until the government of South Vietnam was strong enough to stand on its own. And a solid base at home could be constructed from the so-called *silent majority*—the average, middle-class, white, patriotic, law-abiding citizens who detested the "hippies," draft-dodgers, and war protesters. This grand scheme would enable the United States to honor its commitments, deny the Communists victory in Vietnam, save the "dominoes," halt the decline of U.S. power and prestige, and guarantee Nixon's reelection in 1972. But first Nixon acted "to move the Paris negotiations off dead center" and to reduce heavy U.S. casualties, averaging over 350 killed each week in February and early March. On March 17 the new president ordered the secret bombing of communist sanctuaries inside the border of Cambodia, a neutral nation. When the *New York Times* on May 9 disclosed the secret bombing, the antiwar forces had new ammunition. And when National Security Adviser Henry Kissinger had wiretaps placed on four aides who might have leaked the information, he planted seeds for a bitter harvest.

The Nixon Doctrine

In early June 1969 Nixon announced "the immediate redeployment from Vietnam of a division equivalent of approximately 25,000 men." A month later during a trip to Southeast Asia the president embellished his strategy by announcing "the Nixon Doctrine," namely that hereafter problems of internal security and military defense "will be handled by, and the responsibility for it taken by, the Asian nations themselves." No longer would the United States bear almost single-handedly the burden of containing communism in Asia.

Neither Vietnamization nor the peace talks proceeded smoothly. The Paris negotiations remained deadlocked. The Viet Cong continued hit-and-run attacks in South Vietnam to which the administration felt obligated to respond with counterblows, or in the words of a Pentagon spokesperson, "protective reactions" by U.S. bombers. Equally discouraging were manifestations that U.S. programs, instead of strengthening South Vietnam's will and capability, had weakened both. General Thieu's government relied more and more on U.S. aid and less on Vietnamese resources.

Nixon's policies also led to angry confrontations with opponents of the war. Critics contended that Vietnamization merely "changed the color of the corpses." A huge antiwar demonstration in Washington in October 1969 elicited from the president the warning: "If a vocal minority, however fervent its cause, prevails over reason and the will of the majority, this nation has no future as a free society." He denounced demands by antiwar leaders for an arbitrary cut-off date for withdrawal of all troops as "defeatist." As the emotional rhetoric intensified, the polarization of U.S. society hardened.

My Lai Massacre

To make matters worse for Washington, revelations in November 1969 that U.S. soldiers in March 1968 in the aftermath of Tet had massacred over three hundred civilians, mainly women and children, in the village of My Lai set off a wave of horror and shame. So disturbing was the incident that a poll taken in St. Louis indicated that only 12 percent of those who had heard the story about My Lai believed it true. But demands for an investigation and for punishment of those responsible kept the issue before the nation for months and caused further division over the war.

More Troop Withdrawals

Nixon held fast to his contention that total withdrawal before South Vietnam could defend itself would mean defeat. In April he announced the projected withdrawal of 150,000 troops in addition to the 50,000 already withdrawn to date in 1970. It would be possible to pull out that large a number within the next 12 months, the president said, because "we finally have in sight the just peace we are seeking." Having heard such optimistic statements from high officials so many times, skeptics shook their heads in disbelief.

Invasion of Cambodia

In the meantime, the administration put into operation a new tactic that expanded the war and renewed the turmoil at home. In a move that caught the U.S. people by surprise, U.S. and South Vietnamese forces crossed the border into Cambodia (map, p. 93) at the end of April 1970 to destroy Viet Cong supplies and sanctuaries through which military supplies and troop reinforcements funneled into South Vietnam. In a national television address, President Nixon explained that "this is not an invasion of Cambodia. . . . Once enemy forces are driven out of these sanctuaries and once their military supplies are destroyed, we will withdraw." Appealing for popular support of this action, he said, "If, when the chips are down, the world's most powerful nation, the United States of America, acts like a pitiful, helpless giant, the forces of totalitarianism and anarchy will threaten free nations and free institutions throughout the world." On the next day U.S. planes carried out the heaviest bombing attacks on North Vietnam since Johnson announced a cessation on November 1, 1968. Unfortunately the U.S. invasion of Cambodia drove the North Vietnamese forces farther toward the populated center of Cambodia and led to more than two decades of conflict in that nation.

Denouncing this escalation of the war by the so-called "incursion" into neutral Cambodia, students on campuses of hundreds of colleges and schools demonstrated against the war and against the president. The national protest spread to Washington where 100,000 marched in opposition to the war. Hundreds were arrested by municipal police and National Guards. An angry president dismissed the young demonstrators as "bums . . . blowing up the campuses," while he praised "the kids" fighting in Vietnam as "the greatest." Such language fed the storm. On May 4, members of the National Guards, called out to maintain order on the campus of Kent State University in Ohio, shot to death four students and wounded eight.

Stirred to action by the national uproar over the "incursion" into Cambodia and the killing of the students, senators George McGovern, (D., S. Dak.) and Mark Hatfield (R., Oreg.) pushed for an "end-to-the-war" amendment to a regular appropriations bill, banning expenditure of funds for war in Vietnam unless Congress declared war. Even though Nixon claimed on June 3 that "the great triumph" in Cambodia had "eliminated an immediate danger to the security of the remaining Americans in Vietnam" and enabled him to speed up troop withdrawal, congressional opposition to his policies did not subside. The Senate, concerned about excessive executive power, voted to terminate the Gulf of Tonkin Resolution of 1964 that had given the chief executive "carte blanche" to deploy U.S. combat forces in Southeast Asia. But when Nixon pulled U.S. troops out of Cambodia at the end of June and announced a speed up of troop withdrawals from Vietnam for the rest of the year, emotions cooled. Conveniently overlooked was the fact that communist forces increased their control to more than half of Cambodia and had the Cambodian pro-Western government under heavy siege.

Throughout the summer and fall of 1970 efforts to secure North Vietnam's agreement to a cease-fire and peace terms failed, as Hanoi still insisted on the preliminary withdrawal of all U.S. forces. Instead of negotiating a truce, the North Vietnamese continued to move men and supplies into the South. When military intelligence estimated in mid-October that North Vietnamese infiltrations had exceeded U.S. withdrawals, Nixon ordered renewed large-scale bombing of the North.

PEACE WITHOUT VICTORY

Continuation of Vietnamization and Bombing

Renewed secret talks in Paris in late summer 1971 made no progress, as the issue of exchange of prisoners of war became a new, highly emotional obstacle. When the North Vietnamese stepped up infiltration into the South, in December Nixon resumed heavy bombardment of the North. But, having set in motion the "Vietnamization" of the war, the president found it politically necessary in an election year to maintain schedules of troop withdrawals. Early in January 1972 he announced that troop ceilings would be reduced to 69,000 men.

The failure of South Vietnam's army to contain heavy North Vietnamese attacks across the borders led to massive bombing of the North by American B-52s. In mid-April 1972 Nixon ordered the bombing of Hanoi and its port of Haiphong for the first time to pressure the North Vietnamese to cease military operations and to negotiate in good faith.

The apparent endless cycle of North Vietnamese infiltration, Viet Cong attacks, ineffective South Vietnamese resistance, and U.S. bombing frustrated large numbers of Americans who longed for peace. Nixon's decision to mine Haiphong harbor, through which flowed supplies from communist allies, triggered new antiwar demonstrations and protests. Senator Mansfield warned: "We are courting danger here that could extend the war, increase the number of war prisoners, and make peace more difficult to achieve." Senator George McGovern, emerging as the front-runner to capture the Democratic presidential nomination, charged that "the only purpose of this dangerous course is to keep General Thieu in power a little longer."

The administration took comfort in a Harris poll showing that 59 percent of those polled supported the mining of Haiphong. Moreover, when the Soviet Union failed to call off the summit meeting in Moscow, it appeared that Nixon's bold move rested on a sound analysis of the situation.

In May, in a televised address to the American people Nixon announced his terms for lifting what amounted to a blockade of North Vietnam. He said that "all American prisoners of war must be returned" and "there must be an internationally supervised cease-fire throughout Indochina." In a significant departure from past statements, the president made no mention of a required withdrawal of North Vietnamese forces from the South. This subtle signal of omission was aimed at Moscow and Hanoi.

At the Moscow Summit in May 1972, President Nikolai Podgorny of the Soviet Union agreed to go to Hanoi to urge a negotiated settlement of the Vietnam War on the basis of secret U.S. proposals. Washington would accept a tripartite electoral commission, which included the Viet Cong, to organize and administer the election of a government of South Vietnam. Nixon visualized "peace with honor" before November's elections.

Difficulties with South Vietnam

Kissinger immediately followed up this initiative with energetic efforts to achieve a cease-fire. After much shuttling between capitals, he eventually obtained Hanoi's agreement to sign a truce by October 31 to be followed by the withdrawal of the remaining U.S. troops and the establishment of the tripartite commission. But Kissinger failed to budge President Thieu of South Vietnam to accept the deal, so the United States could not sign the agreement without repudiating its ally. Nevertheless, both Kissinger and Nixon continued to indicate that "a significant breakthrough in the negotiations" made peace imminent.

Buoyed by the magnitude of his reelection triumph, Nixon pushed for the settlement of the war. Having established "Operation Enhance" to build up South Vietnam's military strength before the expected truce, Washington used threats of reduction in this aid to pressure Thieu to accept the agreement. Nixon also advised Thieu in a secret letter that in return for his cooperation, he had Nixon's assurance that the United States "will respond with full force should the settlement be violated by North Vietnam."

The Christmas Bombings

Postelection discussions with the North Vietnamese to obtain a new cease-fire agreement did not go well. When the chief North Vietnamese negotiator at Paris announced on December 14 that he was returning to Hanoi for several weeks to study the situation, Nixon felt betrayed by North Vietnam's "perfidy." Four days later, the president ordered a round-the-clock bombing of Hanoi, Haiphong, and other targets in the North to force the Communists into "serious negotiations." In the next 12 days U.S. planes dumped over 36,000 tons of explosives on North Vietnam—an amount equal to 10 times the total tonnage between 1969 and 1971. The "Christmas bombings" aroused bitter international and domestic protests, especially after the destruction of the largest hospital in Hanoi. Some charged that Nixon was trying to "bomb North Vietnam back into the Stone Age," as Air Force General Curtis LeMay had once suggested.

A Peace Agreement, January 1973

When on December 29, 1972, Hanoi expressed a willingness to resume negotiations on the "highest level," Nixon called off the bombing. Discussions produced a ceasefire on January 27, 1973, in Vietnam. The United States pledged to end all its military activities against North Vietnam and agreed not to continue "its military involvement or intervene in the internal affairs of South Vietnam." In addition, Washington promised to withdraw all its military forces within 60 days and close down its bases. Prisoners of war were to be released by both sides within the 60-day period. The agreement also provided that "the reunification of Vietnam shall be carried out step by step through peaceful means on the basis of discussion and agreement between North and South." Thus Nixon extricated the United States from the war without turning South Vietnam directly over to the Communists and without abandoning U.S. prisoners of war. The truce terms satisfied his definition of "peace with honor."

But the ink was barely dry on the peace documents when the two sides began to maneuver for advantage. Thieu had no intention of cooperating with Hanoi as long as he could count on U.S. economic aid, and as long as the Communists were intent on unifying Vietnam under their control. By late 1973 bloody fighting had broken out in South Vietnam.

Moreover, the January truce did not apply to Cambodia where the United States continued to bomb communist bases and supply lines. After Nixon vetoed a congressional bill that prohibited the use of funds for further war in Cambodia, a compromise was worked out that finally terminated the bombing in August 1973. Within two years Pol Pot's Khmer Rouge Communists toppled the pro-Western Cambodian government.

As the Nixon administration became paralyzed by the Watergate investigations (p. 308) it became difficult to persuade Congress to furnish funds to South Vietnam. But U.S. civilian advisers remained in Saigon, and Congress reluctantly voted economic aid to a beleaguered former ally. After Nixon's resignation in August 1974, the new president, Gerald Ford, tried to bolster the tottering South Vietnamese with more last minute aid. Congress and the American people, however, had had enough, and South Vietnam was left to go it alone. To many Americans the lesson was clear—never again get involved in the Vietnam quagmire, nor in a civil war in Asia.

In March and April 1975, as South Vietnamese resistance collapsed, Americans remaining in Vietnam and thousands of Vietnamese fled in undignified haste by air and sea. On April 29, 1975, the victorious Communists entered Saigon. The Vietnam War, the longest of all U.S. wars, had ended. The United States had expended human and material resources on a lavish scale (p. 110) without achieving victory. Loss of faith in the ability of the nation's armed forces to achieve national goals in international conflicts (the so-called Vietnam syndrome) would trouble many Americans and their leaders for the next decade and a half.

The Dominoes Do Not Fall

In the aftermath of the tragedy in Vietnam, the so-called "dominoes" in Southeast Asia (Thailand, Malaysia, Singapore, Indonesia, and the Philippines), which, according to a generation of U.S. leaders, would fall to communism if the United States abandoned South Vietnam, not only remained stable but grew stronger. By 1977 each of these nations enjoyed an economic growth rate of better than 6 percent and a prosperous trade with the United States. That the domino theory never had applied to Southeast Asia appeared clear and logical to a new generation.

A Crumbled Monolith

Ironically, the communist nations (China, Vietnam, and Cambodia), began to quarrel among themselves. Within five years of the U.S. withdrawal from Vietnam, the latter's invasion of Cambodia shattered the illusion that commitment to an international ideology took precedence over national interest and advantage. The spectacle of Communist Vietnam, supported by the Soviet Union, invading Communist Cambodia, supported by the People's Republic of China shattered the assumption that Moscow directed and totally controlled a unified international communist conspiracy. During his February 1979 visit to the United States, Vice Premier Deng Xiaoping (Teng Hsiao-ping) of Red China verified the deep antagonism between the two communist powers by warning the U.S. people of the threat of the Soviet Union's hegemony aspirations. When the People's Republic of China invaded Vietnam "to punish" the country for the invasion of Cambodia, the free world watched in fascination and concern. But this dramatic disintegration of what was once regarded as monolithic communism did not terminate international tensions.

CHAPTER 5

From Détente to Renewal
of Cold War

"In an era of strategic nuclear balance—when both sides have the capacity to destroy civilized life—there is no alternative to co-existence."
Henry Kissinger, 1975

"As long as I am president, the government of the United States will continue throughout the world, to enhance human rights. No force on earth can separate us from the commitment."
Jimmy Carter, 1978

"We have gone on piling weapon upon weapon, missile upon missile . . . helplessly, almost involuntarily, like the victims of some sort of hypnosis, like men in a dream, like lemmings headed for the sea."
George F. Kennan, 1981

"While they [the Soviets] preach the supremacy of the state, declare its omnipotence over individual man, and predict its eventual domination of all the peoples of the earth—they are the focus of evil in the modern world."
Ronald Reagan, 1983

DÉTENTE: THE CONCEPT AND ITS EARLY STAGES

The tragedy of the Vietnam War convinced many Americans that to mobilize and fight against the expansion of communism wherever it appeared, especially if in popular uprisings against privileged holders of power, did not always serve the national interest. Henry Kissinger, a great admirer of the balance of power concept developed in the nineteenth century by European statesmen after the defeat of Napoleon, envisioned understandings with the two largest communist powers, China and the Soviet Union, as the essential ingredient of long-term international stability and security. He believed that "the challenge of our time is to reconcile the reality of competition with the imperative of coexistence." In his view, a peaceful international order could not exist "unless both the Soviet Union and United States conduct themselves with restraint and unless they use their enormous power for the benefit of mankind." This meant that the two powers should pursue détente, defined by Kissinger as a continuing "process consisting of the following elements: an elaboration of principles; political discussions to solve outstanding issues and to reach cooperative agreements; economic relations; and arms control negotiations, particularly those concerning strategic arms." In effect, détente meant the continued containment of communism, but by peaceful, nonconfrontational, and less costly means.

Opening Relations with Communist China

In 1967 Richard Nixon wrote an article published in *Foreign Affairs* advocating normalization of relations with Red China as a crucial step toward peace in Vietnam. His anticommunist credentials, dating back to his earliest campaigns for public office, made it possible for Nixon, probably alone of all national leaders, to seek understandings with major communist powers. No one could accuse him of being "soft on Communism." His previous hard line against recognition of Red China or admitting it to the United Nations, and his vigorous attacks on those who had "lost China," had contributed to the isolation of the People's Republic of China. But more than two decades of turbulence and change had created a very different world. Nixon prided himself on his pragmatism—flexibility in adapting to new situations. The assumption that monolithic communism threatened to overrun the free world had been shattered by the clear split between Moscow and Beijing, a reality that made it tempting to U.S. leaders to play off one against the other.

Preparing the American people for a dramatic change in the nation's relations with its communist adversaries necessitated a careful step-by-step procedure. Secret contacts with the Chinese, beginning in Warsaw late in 1968 and continuing with Pakistani and Romanian assistance in 1969 and 1970, paved the way for a secret trip by adviser Henry Kissinger to Beijing in July 1971 and a resulting invitation from Chairman Mao to President Nixon to visit China early in 1972. In a dramatic public announcement of his forthcoming visit Nixon explained, "I have taken this action because of my profound conviction that all nations will gain from a reduction of tension and a better relationship between the United States and the People's Republic of China." The response of the American people was overwhelmingly enthusiastic, although the old China Lobby cried "betrayal and sell-out" of a reliable ally, Taiwan.

A carefully staged spectacle telecast throughout the Western world, Nixon's trip to China in February 1972 produced the Shanghai communiqué clarifying U.S. and Chinese positions on a wide range of divisive issues concerning East Asia. The two nations agreed to broaden contacts in "people-to-people" exchanges and to improve trade relations. Although carefully avoiding any abandonment of the Republic of China (Taiwan), the United States terminated its ostracism of the People's Republic of China by agreeing to "concrete consultations to further the normalization of relations." Nixon's initiative fostered the optimistic belief that the United States would not again blunder into a war to save East Asia from communism.

Peaceful Coexistence with the Soviet Union

Simultaneously with the quest for better relations with Communist China, Washington sought to improve relations with the Soviet Union. Nixon assumed that the Soviet desire for U.S. technology and agricultural products would encourage Kremlin leaders to agree to a relaxation of tensions. Initiated in Helsinki late in 1969, the first Strategic Arms Limitation Talks (SALT I) focused on establishing ceilings on the numbers of both defensive and offensive ballistic missiles. Months of secret discussions between Kissinger and Anatoly Dobrynin, Soviet ambassador to the United States, produced agreement on general principles in May 1971 to guide the Strategic Arms Limitation Talks.

Moscow Summit and SALT I

In May 1972 Nixon became the first president since Franklin Roosevelt to meet the leaders of the Soviet Union on their home soil. Two and a half years of difficult negotiations had finally produced a limited Strategic Arms Limitation Treaty (SALT I) for the leader of each nation to sign. The treaty of unlimited duration restricted both the Soviets and the Americans to 100 launchers and 100 antiballistic interceptor missiles (ABMs), froze for five years offensive intercontinental ballistic missiles (ICBM) at existing numbers, limited the number of ballistic missile launchers on submarines, and limited the tests of defensive missiles. To monitor compliance, the two nations agreed to establish a standing consultative committee. Supporters of détente heralded this first small step toward curbing the arms race, but inflexible anti-Communists in the United States charged that the treaty contained no adequate safeguards against Soviet violation.

Limited Progress in Détente during the Ford Administration

Post-Watergate and post-Vietnam trauma encouraged the Ford administration's commitment to détente. Secretary of State Kissinger continued to direct Washington's pursuit of a balance of power with the communist nations—a policy of live and let live rather than a crusade to overwhelm an evil, immoral foe. Ford journeyed to Vladivostok in November 1974 to meet with Brezhnev in an effort to establish guidelines for further reductions in strategic weapons in SALT II. The following July, in a dramatic demonstration of détente, the erstwhile enemies agreed to the linking together of the U.S. spaceship Apollo and the Soviet spacecraft Soyuz 140 miles above Earth.

The same cooperative spirit prevailed at the Helsinki Conference on Security and Cooperation in Europe (CSCE) in midsummer 1975. Officials of the two powers signed accords affirming the permanence of borders in Europe, pledging respect for human rights and fundamental freedoms, and agreeing to participate in periodic reviews of their human rights performance. U.S. allies, responding to the new realities in East–West relations, in Europe and in Asia, formally dissolved SEATO in 1975 after the end of the Vietnam War.

As an additional gesture of good will the Ford administration extended a helping hand to the Soviet Union when it faced a poor grain harvest. The United States allowed the Soviets to continue to make limited purchases of U.S. wheat and corn. When the administration also sought legislation to extend trade and grant loans for Soviet economic development, Congress in 1975 passed the Jackson–Vanik amendment to the Trade Reform Act of 1974 making expansion of trade and credits contingent on Moscow's permitting more Soviet Jews to emigrate. Protesting such interference in its internal affairs, Moscow rejected the conditional offer of economic aid.

That many Americans did not share the administration's enthusiasm for détente became increasingly evident. Hard-line anti-Communists opposed to any agreements with the Soviet Union along with critics of Soviet unwillingness to agree to end restrictions on emigration of Soviet Jews and dissidents, condemned détente as playing into the hands of the oppressive Moscow regime. In August 1975 maritime unions of the American Federation of Labor and Congress of Industrial Organizations (AFL-CIO) called a boycott against loading grain shipments bound for the Soviet Union. In Congress, Senator Henry Jackson (D., Wash.) led the attack on the Helsinki Declaration as "a sign of the West's retreat" from "a crucial point of principle," the right of the Baltic and Eastern European states to self-determination.

Carter's Efforts to Expand Détente

Although critical of the Ford administration's execution of foreign policy, in his victorious presidential campaign Jimmy Carter did not criticize détente as a means to peace. He believed that détente, made more comprehensive and reciprocal, would promote the national interest. Carter insisted that, as a first step in improving relations, Soviet leaders should live up to the 1975 Helsinki statement. Above all, Carter committed himself to the promotion of human rights. In the early weeks of his term he repeatedly expressed that commitment in such statements as: "I want our country to be the focal point for deep concern about human beings all over the world." Assuming that economic assistance could foster advances in basic human rights, the administration proposed a 20 percent increase in U.S. foreign aid for fiscal 1978 and an expansion of the program of the Agency for International Development (AID) for "new initiatives in human rights."

Cyrus Vance, the new secretary of state, saw the need after Vietnam to accept the limits of U.S. power and seek accommodation, while avoiding confrontation with the Soviets. Thus the Carter administration acted on several fronts to eliminate grievances and lessen tensions. The Panama Canal Treaties of 1978 (p. 67) and the Mideast Peace Agreement between Egypt and Israel in 1979 (p. 79) became major accomplishments in the face of great odds. Moreover, in the first two years of his administration, Carter attempted to negotiate multilateral curbs on international arms sales that he viewed as threatening "stability in every region of the world." The dramatic establishment of diplomatic relations with the People's Republic of China on January 1, 1979, foreshadowed by the 1972 Nixon opening of relations, followed by the abrogation of the 1954 Mutual Defense Treaty with the Republic of China (Taiwan), gave Washington a "China card" to play in negotiations with the Soviet Union. The success of the Carter–Vance approach was highlighted in an administration press release early in 1980 stating that no member of the U.S. armed service had been killed in combat in the Carter administration—the first such achievement since the Harding–Coolidge administration after World War I.

SALT II

Following the agreement in SALT I in 1972 the United States and the Soviet Union continued to negotiate during the next six years to achieve further limits on nuclear weapons. As a result, in June 1979 at a summit meeting in Vienna, Carter and Brezhnev signed SALT II. It called for each nation initially to limit itself to 2,400 strategic arms delivery vehicles, a number to be reduced to 2,250 by the end of 1981, and it established sublimits on launchers of land-based and submarine-based ICBMs equipped with multiple independently targetable warheads (MIRVs), and on aircraft equipped for long-range missiles.

Widespread criticism of the treaty as advantageous to the Soviets and a serious division within the administration played into the hands of the treaty's opponents. Carter's national security adviser, former Columbia University professor Zbigniew Brzezinski, denounced the Soviets for interference in the Ethiopia–Somali conflict involving control of the strategically important horn of Africa and for repeated behavior inconsistent with détente. Brzezinski wished to link U.S. support of strategic arms limitation with the withdrawal of Soviet and Cuban "military advisers" from the Ethiopian conflict and with restraint in the Soviet buildup of conventional forces in Europe. Vance, on the other hand, rejected linkage and favored negotiations on limitation of strategic arms independent of other issues. A chorus of hawkish voices, the extreme right-wing anti-Communists and those connected with the military and arms industry, charged that the Soviets could not be trusted. These critics pointed to the relative decline in military expenditures by the United States as evidence of a dangerous trend that Salt II would accelerate (see table).

Comparative Military Expenditures (current $ billions)

Year (Ending June 30)	NATO Countries	Warsaw Pact	United States Only	U.S.% World Total
1966	91	62	55.9	35
1968	110	73	79.4	37
1969	112	79	80.2	35
1970	111	85	79.3	32
1971	111	92	76.8	29
1972	117	98	77.4	29
1973	121	108	75.1	27
1974	135	122	78.6	26
1975	145	136	86.8	25

SOURCE: U.S. Arms Control and Disarmament Agency

COLLAPSE OF DÉTENTE

The sharp criticism of Salt II, growing suspicion of Soviet leaders' insincerity about improving human rights, and continuing East–West tension in the Third World demonstrated that serious differences over both goals and methods to achieve them threatened the future of détente. Soviet actions in 1979 and a U.S. presidential campaign in 1980 inflicted fatal blows.

Response to Soviet Invasion of Afghanistan

In late December 1979, Soviet combat troops invaded Afghanistan to prop up the communist government of that small, impoverished nation wedged between Iran and Pakistan on the southern Asian border of the Soviet Union. Shocked by Moscow's first armed invasion of a sovereign nation outside of Eastern Europe, President Carter warned that this act placed the United States "in a state of crisis" and it was "the most serious threat to world peace since the Second World War." He vowed to repel "an attempt by any outside force to gain control of the Persian Gulf region . . . by any means necessary, including military force." Named the Carter Doctrine, this tough stance won wide support from Americans worried about the dependence of the West on Persian Gulf oil and frustrated by the United States' seeming helplessness since the defeat in Vietnam and the recent seizure of American hostages in Iran (p. 79).

Salt II became a casualty of the Soviet invasion of Afghanistan. At the request of President Carter, the Senate shelved further consideration of the treaty. Moreover, the administration now decided to install medium-range cruise missiles in five NATO countries and Pershing 2 missiles in West Germany by 1983. A series of "get tough with the Soviets" measures replaced cooperative efforts. Carter now imposed an embargo on the shipment of 17 million tons of U.S. grain purchased by the Soviet Union, and Washington also banned the export of high technology exchanges instituted by the Nixon administration in 1972. Skeptics immediately pointed out that the Soviets would buy both grain and high technology in military weapons from allies of the United States, leaving the American farmer and manufacturer as the only losers. Yet Carter persisted; he organized a boycott of the 1980 Olympic Games in Moscow that kept U.S. athletes at home without interrupting the Olympics.

Renewed cold war rhetoric and the hard line against the Soviet Union sparked public enthusiasm for a buildup of U.S. military strength. The administration responded with a standby draft registration program, the organization of a Rapid Deployment Force (RDF), and a plan for mobile basing of the MX, the proposed new strategic ICBM. Carter also submitted to Congress a proposed 4 percent increase in his defense budget for fiscal 1981. To some Americans it appeared as though the administration had made a complete about-face from its conciliatory statements expressed only a few months earlier in support of détente.

RENEWAL OF COLD WAR

A Foreign Policy Based on Military Strength: The Concept of Deterrence

Reagan's election as president signaled a change in U.S. foreign policy with vast implications. In his campaign Reagan condemned détente as beneficial only to the Soviet Union, and he claimed that Carter had been "soft" toward the Communists. At his first news conference, on January 29, 1981, Reagan revealed his deep distrust of Soviet leaders. He charged that they "have openly and publicly declared that the only morality they recognize is what will further their cause, meaning they reserve unto themselves the right to commit any crime, to lie, to cheat, in order to attain that, and that is moral, not immoral." Administration leaders made clear that they intended to base policy on a massive rebuilding of the nation's military strength, especially its strategic deterrent. Secretary of State Alexander Haig, a career military officer, explained to the Senate Armed Services Committee that "there can be no easy distinction drawn between foreign and defense policy. They are inextricably linked."

The new administration, following the example of earlier post–World War II administrations, took its history lesson from the 1930s when the military weakness of Britain and France made it easy for Hitler and Mussolini to commit acts of aggression. Reagan and his advisers ignored another lesson from the pre–World War I era, in which the great powers engaged in an arms race with tragic consequences. Some critics of the proposed arms buildup questioned the validity of equating the Soviets of the 1980s with the Nazis of the 1930s. However, a majority of Americans, according to polls, acknowledged the need for increased defense expenditures.

The Reagan Arms Buildup

True to campaign promises, Reagan requested $1.3 trillion in defense spending over the next five years. This record peacetime military spending would consume about one-third of the annual expenditures of the United States and cause enormous budget deficits. To justify such expenditures the Defense Department

Changes in U.S./Soviet Strategic Levels, 1966–1980

SOURCE: Dept. of Defense Annual Report, FY 1982

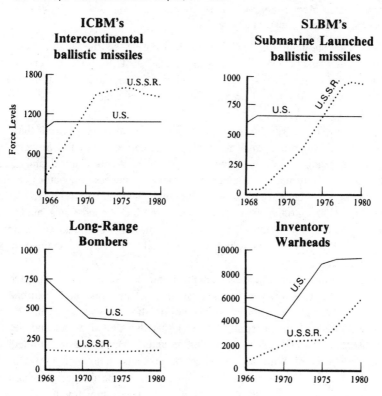

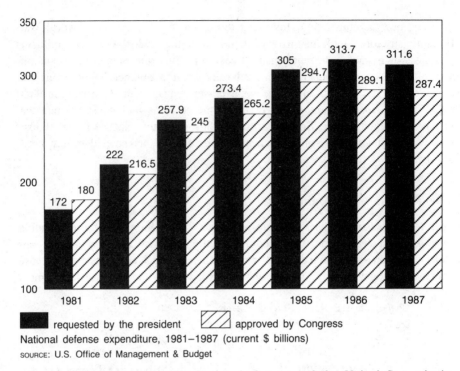

National defense expenditure, 1981–1987 (current $ billions)
SOURCE: U.S. Office of Management & Budget

released data showing that the Soviets had surpassed the United States in its strategic arms arsenal. Such claims of a loss of U.S. nuclear superiority, referred to by Reagan as opening a "window of vulnerability," strengthened his hand in pushing through Congress huge military budgets, as shown in the accompanying graph.

Assumptions about the Kremlin's intentions also influenced the Reagan administration's approach to arms control negotiations with the Soviets. In the words of Eugene V. Rostow, director of the U.S. Arms Control and Disarmament Agency, "intimidation and coercion and, if necessary, victory in nuclear war" lay behind the Russian's arms buildup. Such a worst possible scenario meant that Washington had to "maintain a credible second-strike nuclear capability so that the United States, its allies, and its other interests are protected at all times." Deterrence, according to this point of view, remained a viable strategic concept.

The administration's bellicose rhetoric and its use of unsubstantiated statistics comparing U.S.–Soviet stockpiles of nuclear weapons disturbed some Americans. George F. Kennan, advocate of the postwar containment policy (pp. 8–9), protested in the spring of 1981 that the United States and the Soviet Union were embarked on a "collision course." He urged an immediate 50 percent reduction of both nations' nuclear arsenals. The Union of Concerned Scientists attempted to alert the American people to the dangers in proliferation of nuclear weapons. In addition, the nuclear freeze movement, advocating a bilateral agreement with verifiable guarantees to stop further production and deployment of nuclear missiles, sprang up on college campuses and spread throughout much of the nation.

As support for arms reduction grew, Reagan announced in November 1981 a "zero-zero option" plan. The United States would cancel its proposed deployment of Pershing II ballistic missiles and ground-launched Cruise missiles in Western Europe if the Soviets would dismantle all their SS-4, SS-5, and SS-20 missiles. Moscow flatly rejected Reagan's proposal after pointing out that zero-zero did not include British and French nuclear weapons nor U.S. aircraft based in Europe.

Negotiations over reduction of intermediate-range nuclear forces (INF) in Europe resumed in Geneva in late November 1981. Instead of focusing on limiting future production of nuclear weapons the two sides now concentrated on reducing existing stockpiles—a significant change from SALT to START (Strategic Arms Reduction Talks).

Reagan also resorted to strong rhetoric to discredit the nuclear freeze movement and to win support for his position. In a March 1983 speech the president warned that "the freeze concept was dangerous for many reasons, notably because it would . . . leave the Soviets with nuclear superiority. So in your discussion of the nuclear freeze proposal, I urge you to beware the temptation . . . to ignore the facts of history and the aggressive impulses of an evil empire."

Strategic Defense Initiative

In the spring of 1983, Reagan presented a frightening picture of Soviet nuclear power and called on U.S. scientists to devise "the means of rendering these nuclear weapons impotent and obsolete . . . a vision of the future which offers hope." Influenced by a few scientists, notably Edward Teller, who had contributed to the development of the hydrogen bomb, the president asked Congress for $26 billion to support five years of research on an antisatellite (ASAT), that is a space-based ballistic missile. Identified by its supporters as the Strategic Defense Initiative (SDI), this new proposal quickly gained the label Star Wars from critics, who regarded the idea as pure fantasy. Robert McNamara, Defense Secretary in the Kennedy and Johnson administrations, ridiculed the proposal as "pie in the sky." Others charged that SDI would violate the 1972 ABM treaty (p. 120), although the Pentagon denied it. The new Soviet premier, Yuri Andropov, warned that Reagan was treading "an extremely dangerous path."

The warnings about the "evil empire" and the emotional appeals to build up U.S. military strength did not diminish the national propensity for practicality. In late August 1983 Washington signed a new grain deal with Moscow, whereby the United States agreed to sell 9–12 million tons of grain in each of the next five years—hardly an action one would take with a mortal enemy.

Moreover, the Reagan administration renewed the 1973 agreements on exchanges dealing with atomic energy and housing.

Collapse of START

With arms control negotiations stalled, in November 1983 the United States delivered the first Cruise and Pershing II ballistic missiles to Britain and West Germany, where organized protests failed to prevent deployment of these nuclear weapons. Soviet leaders responded by withdrawing from the two-year old INF talks in Geneva, and within three weeks forced the recess of START and the 10-year East–West talks in Vienna on reducing conventional armed forces. In reaction to the installation of Cruise and Pershing II missiles in Britain and West Germany the Soviets increased their deployment of SS-20s. Soviet leaders took the position that they would not negotiate an INF reduction until Washington reversed its deployments, whereas the Reagan administration supported resumption of negotiations until an agreement could be reached.

The prolonged haggling over numbers, the sharp rhetoric, the seemingly endless birth of new weapons with new acronyms, and the cessation of all negotiations disturbed many in both the United States and Europe. Some worried Americans agreed with the observation of Pulitzer-Prize-winning historian Barbara Tuchman that "the obstacle to progress is that the superpowers have got themselves into such a bind of mutual suspicion that they cannot divest themselves of a single missile. That will take a revolutionary change of attitude."

Continuing Arms Buildup, 1984–1986

Throughout the early months of the 1984 election year, the Reagan team campaigned for its special defense programs and an increase in the defense budget for fiscal 1985. A long relied upon approach involved alarming the public about Soviet power and intent and contrasting U.S. weakness. In mid-January, 1984 CIA Chief William J. Casey warned that "the growth in overall Soviet military power, unmatched by the West over the last 15 to 20 years, has encouraged them to try intimidation to split our allies away from us and undermine our credibility." Later in the spring, Defense Secretary Caspar Weinberger stated that the Soviet Union's "relentless arms buildup" is motivated by a quest for "world domination—it's just that simple."

Such arguments did not sway members of Congress skeptical about the wisdom of the administration's course and the validity of its data. Some critics believed that the Pentagon distorted reality and ignored widespread fraud and waste. Stories of corruption in the defense industry made headlines for several months. Public outrage grew with the revelation that defense contractors had charged $435 for an ordinary claw hammer and $600 for a toilet seat, and that the Air Force had paid $9,609 for a common wrench. Opponents of increased defense expenditures also pointed to huge amounts of unspent funds, $128 billion by mid-1984, appropriated in recent years for the Defense Department. As of May 1984, for example, the Pentagon had spent only $450 million of the $2.1 billion authorized in 1983 for 21 MX missiles. It required Vice-President Bush's vote to break a tie in the Senate to allow continued production of the MX.

Although the United States and the Soviet Union agreed, after Reagan's landslide reelection, to resume arms control talks early in 1985, the debate at home over SDI and MX continued. Defense Secretary Weinberger again revealed the administration's premises when he said, "The president's strategic defense initiative can contribute to curbing strategic arms competition by devaluing nuclear missiles and thus imposing prohibitively high costs on the Soviets if they continued in their quest for nuclear superiority."

Many Americans remained unconvinced of the need for either SDI or the MX. For example, some 700 members of the National Academy of Sciences, including 53 Nobel laureates, sent an appeal in May 1985 to Moscow and Washington to ban from space any weapon system, including the SDI. Mikhail Gorbachev, the new Soviet leader, sought to encourage such opposition by stating that U.S. development of SDI would not only end the Geneva Arms Talks, but would lead to "the scrapping of every prospect for an end to the arms race."

Rejecting such positions, administration officials returned to earlier warnings about the wicked nature of the Soviet system and the free world's need for effective defensive weapons. In July 1985, Weinberger asserted that "President Reagan was justified in calling the USSR an 'evil empire' because that spotlighted 'the coercive and tyrannical system of our Communist adversaries.' " The repeated themes—that the MX, or "peacekeeper," was an essential element of the nation's arms control strategy, and that SDI also served as a "bargaining chip" and would make nuclear weapons obsolete—eventually convinced Congress to approve funding of both programs.

Failures to Achieve Nuclear Arms Reductions

Meanwhile, the arms control talks in Geneva found the two sides still far apart on all key issues. A determined Gorbachev took the initiative in July 1985 by announcing a freeze on new Soviet nuclear arms testing beginning on August 6—the 40th anniversary of the dropping of the atom bomb on Hiroshima. Clearly he hoped to encourage the United States to do the same, but the Reagan administration did not follow Moscow's lead.

At the Geneva Summit in November 1985 President Reagan said that his main objective was "elimination of suspicion and distrust" between the two powers. The two leaders agreed to accelerate negotiations on 50 percent strategic arms reductions and on an interim INF pact. In addition, they endorsed increased cultural, scientific, and economic interchanges. As a result, shortly after the summit, four of the United States' biggest banks, as well as one British and one Canadian bank, agreed to lend the Soviet Union up to $400 million at unusually low interest rates to purchase U.S. and Canadian grain.

A fourth round of arms talks failed to produce any agreements on reducing the numbers of either medium-range missiles in Europe or ICBMs. Even though the United States continued to conduct testing of nuclear weapons, Gorbachev maintained his nation's freeze on such tests and offered to reduce Soviet strategic weapons if Washington agreed to adhere to the 1972 ABM treaty—clearly a move to stop SDI, Rejecting the Soviet proposals, in May 1986 Reagan announced the intention of the United States to abandon its technical observation of Salt II which it had never formally ratified (p. 124), because of continuing Soviet violations.

Nevertheless, Reagan accepted Gorbachev's invitation to meet in Reykjavik, Iceland in October 1986 to attempt to reach some agreement on nuclear arms reduction. After two days of proposals and counterproposals, Gorbachev rejected Reagan's offer to eliminate all ballistic missiles within 10 years because the United States refused to agree to limit SDI testing to the laboratory for the next 10 years. The president explained to the U.S. people that "the biggest disappointment in Iceland was that Mr. Gorbachev decided to make our progress hostage to his demands that we kill our strategic defense program."

Whereas the U.S. public at large also expressed disappointment at another failure to reduce nuclear weapons, hard-line hawks heaved sighs of relief as they denounced Reagan's proposed elimination of all ballistic missiles within 10 years as a major departure from the NATO strategy that had maintained peace. Senator Robert Dole (R., Kans.) expressed the viewpoint of those wary of making any concessions to the Soviets when he wrote in *Policy Review* in the fall of 1986:

> In fact, détente is a dangerous myth, based upon a phony premise: that there is more to our relations with the Soviets than a sum of parts; that if we cooperate with Moscow in enough ways and spheres we will create an atmosphere of good will that will be self-generating.

MILITARY–INDUSTRIAL COMPLEX

Some Americans wondered if the arms race could be halted. They recalled President Eisenhower's warning in his farewell speech in January 1961: "We must guard against the acquisition of unwarranted influence, whether sought or unsought by the military-industrial complex. The potential for the disastrous use of misplaced power exists and will persist." By the 1980s many citizens, deeply concerned by the failure to stop and reverse the arms buildup, suspected that the nation's political leaders had indeed allowed a military-industrial complex a dominant voice in making national policy. Several developments appeared to support this suspicion.

The Military Factor

By the end of 1983 the Defense Department had 359 overseas bases, manned by over 500,000 Americans, from Iceland in the North Atlantic to Diego Garcia in the Indian Ocean. In return for these bases Washington agreed to large grants of military aid, for instance to the autocratic and corrupt Marcos government of the Philippines for the use of Clark Field and Subic Bay naval base. At the same time the Defense Department maintained over 400 major military bases in the United States, wlth at least one base in each of the 50 states. Moreover, between 1976 and 1987 not a single major base was closed and 13 new ones were established. More than 800,000 service personnel, accompanied by their dependents, manned these bases. As a result, every state had military personnel stationed within its borders, ranging from about 100 in Vermont to over 200,000 in California.

The Industrial Factor

The Reagan administration encouraged the sale of arms to its allies and friendly governments worldwide. For example, it rescinded what Under Secretary of State James Buckley called "the Carter administration's so-called leprosy letter, which instructed U.S. officials not to assist businessmen seeking to meet the military needs of friendly states." Sales of arms overseas by U.S. firms surged—totalling over $23 billion in the 1982–1987 period. At the same time the Defense Department delivered over $50 billion in arms to foreign nations. Major purchasers included Saudi Arabia, Israel, Egypt, and Pakistan.

Millions of Americans relied on the defense industry for their livelihood. To equip the nation's military forces the Defense Department allocated contracts to firms in every congressional district in the nation. In 1987 companies in California had defense contracts totaling $24.5 billion, and even Wyoming firms received contracts worth $47 million. As a result, each state had a civilian work force—ranging from less than 1,000 in Vermont to over 130,000 in California—employed by defense industries. Moreover, in 1987 the Department of Defense itself employed 979,000 civilians nationwide.

Many U.S. corporations and small businesses depended on defense contracts to generate profits. A 1987 Navy Department study revealed that the nation's major defense contractors earned more than twice as much profit selling

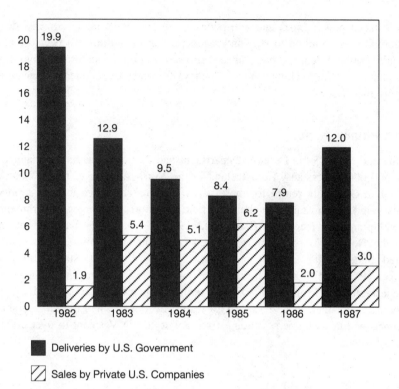

■ Deliveries by U.S. Government

▨ Sales by Private U.S. Companies

U.S. military exports to foreign nations (current $ billions)
SOURCE: U.S. Defense Security Assistance Agency

weapons to the Pentagon as they did selling products in the commercial market-place. Thirty-three large corporations, recipients of 52 percent of defense funds, had an average profit of 22.4 percent from filling military contracts, whereas they earned only 10.1 percent from the sale of nonmilitary products.

The great increase in defense spending by the Reagan administration made possible this bonanza for business and labor. According to the U.S. Arms Control and Disarmament Agency worldwide military expenditures reached $578.3 billion in 1980, with the United States accounting for 24.9 percent of the total. By 1984, when world military spending reached $880.2 billion, Washington spent 30.2 percent of the total.

The Political Factor

Given the prevailing international climate during the renewed cold war, a strong national defense against the "wicked, godless commies" served as the standard platform of many candidates for national public office in the 1980s. To be soft on defense invited defeat at the polls. Rare was the member of Congress who voted against a military appropriations bill or arms sale to another nation that would bring hundreds of million dollars to his or her district. The defense budget became a pork barrel to benefit constituents. With so much at stake, defense industry firms contributed heavily to the campaigns of friendly and influential members of Congress.

Few Americans expressed concern about or even awareness of these developments, but some did commit themselves to curb the military-industrial complex. Surprising events in the late 1980s would assist them.

WAGING THE COLD WAR IN DEVELOPING NATIONS OF ASIA AND AFRICA, 1981–1988

During the first phase of the cold war, 1946–1972, the United States fought two, long, costly, and frustrating wars—Korean and Vietnam—in East Asia against native communist forces. However, in the renewed cold war in the 1980s U.S. troops fought only limited engagements against local revolutionaries in Latin America and against terrorists in the Middle East. In addition, the United States furnished economic aid, as well as military equipment and training, to rebels in Nicaragua, Angola, and Afghanistan seeking to overthrow a communist regime, and to an anticommunist government in El Salvador resisting Marxist revolutionaries. Some saw great irony in the fact that whereas Washington condemned terrorism in the Middle East, it supported groups in Central America, whose adherents frequently resorted to terrorist acts against opponents, and refused to help groups in southern Africa resisting oppression and terrorism. Such policies generated sharp debate among Americans, and eventually led to the Iran–Contra Affair, which resurrected old questions about the right of the United States to interfere in the internal affairs of other nations and about the wisdom of congressional and public deference to the executive department's judgment in foreign affairs.

Support of the Afghanistan Resistance

When Moscow persisted in its relentless campaign against the Afghan guerrillas, Washington stepped up its economic aid and began to provide weapons covertly through the CIA, after a presidential finding, thereby avoiding the need for congressional approval. The Intelligence Oversight Act of 1980 allowed the CIA to bypass Congress in matters relating to covert activities. In fiscal 1985 the United States furnished over $250 million to the Afghan resistance forces. On the fifth anniversary of the Soviet invasion—December 27, 1984—Reagan stated that Moscow's action in Afghanistan "constitutes a serious impediment to the improvement of our bilateral relations." Public opinion polls indicated that most Americans approved support of the Afghan resistance. However, some Americans charged that the administration had not made an adequate effort to negotiate an end of the war because it viewed prolongation of the fighting as a costly embarrassment to the Soviet Union—a Russian Vietnam.

Support of Anti-Communists in Cambodia

Vietnam, with the backing of Moscow, invaded Cambodia in 1978 to oust the Khmer Rouge forces of Pol Pot supported by China. The United States faced difficult choices. Although the Khmer Rouge had killed over 1 million Cambodians during almost four years in power, the Carter administration imposed a trade embargo on Vietnam and withheld recognition from Vietnam's puppet government in Cambodia. Reagan continued these policies and furnished modest aid to a Thailand-based resistance coalition that included elements of the Khmer Rouge. Some Americans worried that the Reagan administration's policies might lead to the return of the hated Khmer Rouge to power, but the White House continued to give first priority to driving the Vietnamese out of Cambodia.

Constructive Engagement in Southern Africa

Reagan viewed the continued presence of Cuban troops in Angola as justifying the reluctance of the Republic of South Africa (RSA) to free Namibia, which served as a base for supplying the anticommunist, rebel Angolan forces of Unita under Jonas Savimbi. Employing a policy of "constructive engagement," Washington exerted quiet pressure on South Africa to end apartheid, and tried to set a timetable for the pullout of Cuban troops from Angola linked to South Africa's recognition of Namibian independence. In April 1981 the administration asked Congress to repeal the 1976 Clark amendment restriction against providing covert military assistance to internal factions in Angola.

After Congress, responding to administration pressure to support the Angolan "freedom fighters," repealed the Clark amendment in the summer of 1985 (p. 85), the Angolan government broke off talks with the United States. In November Reagan called for $15 million in covert aid to the Angolan rebels. Early in 1986, after Savimbi's visit to Washington, the administration privately decided to deliver Stinger anti-aircraft missiles to Savimbi's forces to pressure the MPLA to negotiate. During the rest of Reagan's presidency Washington continued to furnish covert aid while intensifying efforts to obtain an agreement on a date for the pullout of all Cuban troops without success.

The administration faced increasing pressure from Americans sympathetic to efforts by South African blacks to end apartheid and gain equal rights. Leaders of the African National Congress (ANC), which had campaigned since early in the twentieth century for a nonracial South Africa, argued that the East–

West conflict had no relevance to Africans segregated and oppressed by a white minority. That point of view disturbed leaders in the Reagan administration who tended to view all international issues in free world versus communist world scenarios. In 1986 Congress responded to public opinion polls showing overwhelming opposition of U.S. citizens to apartheid by voting to impose limited economic sanctions on the Republic of South Africa by a narrow margin over President Reagan's veto.

Support of Dictators in Zaire and Kenya

To assist the anti-Marxist rebels in Angola, Washington turned to President Mobutu Sese Seko of Zaire. Ignoring the fact that Mobutu's corrupt regime denied basic rights to the people, in four years (1983–1986) the United States furnished more than $400 million in military and economic aid to Zaire on the northern border of Angola.

Kenya also became important to U.S. policymakers because of its strategic location at the lower end of the Horn of Africa on the Indian Ocean (map, p. 83). Although Kenya fell under the domination of the undemocratic and corrupt government of Daniel arap Moi in 1978, it retained its capitalist economy and strong opposition to Marxism. Not only did the U.S. influence the World Bank to grant substantial loans to Kenya, but the Reagan administration also extended military and economic aid to the Moi regime totaling over $270 million between 1983 and 1986. Thus, as the cold war intensified, U.S. policymakers placed greater importance, even in the new nations of sub-Sahara Africa, on opposition to communism than on commitment to democracy and human rights.

NEW CRISES IN THE MIDDLE EAST, 1982–1986

War and Terrorism in Lebanon

Israel invaded Lebanon in June 1982, and the volatile Middle East erupted again (map, p. 77). The Israelis, apparently believing that Secretary of State Haig approved, sought to eliminate the capacity of the Palestine Liberation Organization (PLO) to carry out terrorist attacks on Israel from Lebanese bases. Israeli troops advanced rapidly to the outskirts of Beirut, a sanctuary for PLO forces and their Lebanese and Syrian allies. To save Lebanon from destruction, in August the United States arranged the evacuation of PLO and Syrian forces from Beirut under the supervision of an international force that included eight hundred U.S. Marines.

To frustrate any possible attempt by the Soviets to exploit the situation,

Reagan unveiled a Middle East peace plan in September 1982 calling for establishment of Palestinian self-government in the Israeli-occupied West Bank and Gaza in association with Jordan. Israel quickly rejected the U.S. initiative, which called for a freeze on Israeli settlement of the West Bank. King Hussein of Jordan and PLO leaders also rejected the U.S. proposal. Complicating the peace effort was the late September massacre of hundreds of Palestinian civilians in Beirut by Lebanese Christian militia permitted by Israeli military commanders to enter two Palestinian camps. At the request of the Lebanese government, Reagan, despite the unanimous opposition of the Joint Chiefs of Staff, sent 1,200 Marines to join French and Italian forces to "restore Lebanese sovereignty and authority over the Beirut area."

Efforts in ensuing months to negotiate both the Syrians and Israelis out of Lebanon failed as civil conflict broke out between Lebanese Moslem and Christian factions. Even though Reagan, in February 1983, pledged to take "all necessary measures to guarantee the security of Israel's northern borders in the aftermath of the complete withdrawal of the Israel army," the Begin government continued to reject Reagan's plan, as did the Palestinians and Jordan.

In April 1983 a truck laden with bombs crashed into the U.S. embassy in Beirut killing 63 persons, including 17 Americans. Outrage at this terrorist act strengthened Washington's determination to keep U.S. military forces in Lebanon until peace and stability prevailed. Sniper attacks and shellings against the Marines, hunkered down in barricaded positions at Beirut's airport, continued as efforts to end the fighting failed. In late August 1983 Washington authorized Marine commanders to shoot back. In mid-September Reagan ordered U.S. warships to shell the emplacement of the Druse militia that fired on the Marines.

In Washington a new controversy arose as many members of Congress, concerned about the safety of the Marines, fearful of the nation being dragged into another war through the action of the chief executive, and jealous of their constitutional powers, prepared to invoke the War Powers Act. Eager to avoid an official proclamation declaring that U.S. troops were in a combat or war situation, and unwilling to comply with the War Powers Act provision that he withdraw the Marines within 60 days unless Congress voted to extend the time period, Reagan acted to avoid a constitutional crisis. Finally, on September 20, 1983, negotiations produced a compromise that invoked the War Powers Act while authorizing the president to maintain the 1,200 Marines in Lebanon for up to 18 months.

Suddenly a dramatic act of terrorism challenged the case for the U.S. presence in Lebanon. On October 23, 1983, a terrorist crashed a truck laden with an estimated six tons of explosives into the Marine barracks at the Beirut airport, and killed 241 sleeping Marines. Americans denounced the unknown perpetrators of this tragedy, and President Reagan declared "these deeds make so evident the bestial nature of those who would assume power if they could have their way and drive us out of that area." He repeatedly expressed his determination to keep the Marines in Lebanon as "peacekeepers" until the establishment of a coalition government accepted by Lebanon's warring sects and tribes, and free of control by foreign troops. Many Americans, however, concluded that the Marines had become "sitting ducks" and should be immediately withdrawn. Journalists began finding parallels with Vietnam. A Harris public opinion survey early in December 1983 showed that 67 percent of the Americans queried thought that the loss of U.S. lives in Lebanon served no national purpose.

A Defense Department investigation of the terrorist bombing of the Marine barracks implied in a December report that the president should not have sent the Marines to Lebanon on an impossible mission. The statement also suggested that inadequate security measures had been taken at the Beirut barracks. Defusing any possible embarrassing response to this report, President Reagan declared: "I accept responsibility." But the continued presence of the Marines in Lebanon became an albatross for the president in an election year. By late July 1984 he had withdrawn all combat U.S. troops—implicit acknowledgment of the failure of U.S. policy in Lebanon.

Iran–Iraq War

Iraq's attack on Iran in September 1980 threatened to disrupt the flow of oil from the Persian Gulf states. Although the United States depended on the region for less than 10 percent of its oil, Washington worried about the consequences of any interruption in the oil supply of its European allies and Japan, and about the danger of the conflict spreading into a larger war. The United States did not have diplomatic relations with Iran or Iraq, and Congress banned arms sales to either side. Americans harbored ill-feelings toward Khomeini's Iran since its seizure of the hostages in 1979, and they also had little reason to support Iraq— long suspected of harboring terrorists and having strong Soviet ties. But, arms merchants in Europe and Asia, lured by the opportunity for huge profits, sold arms to both sides. Between 1983 and 1987 Iraq became the largest arms purchaser in the Third World. As indecisive fighting dragged on, the Reagan administration began to provide modest nonmilitary support to Iraq, and mounted a worldwide campaign to shut off the sale of arms to Khomeini's Iran.

In the spring of 1984, in response to Iran's threat to attack oil operations in Saudi Arabia and other Gulf States sympathetic to Iraq, Washington supplied the Saudis with Stinger anti-aircraft missiles and tanker planes. The president insisted there was "no way" the United States would permit Iran to carry out its threat to close the Strait of Hormuz. Before his second term ended, the president had to translate his words into action.

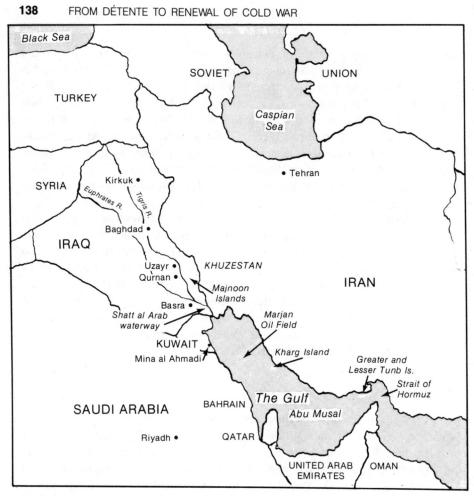

The Persian Gulf Region in 1984

Escalation of Mideast Terrorism

American actions in the Iraq–Iran conflict infuriated the fanatic supporters of Khomeini in the Mideast. Hezbollah, the pro-Iranian fundamentalist Shiite sect in Lebanon, resorted to new acts of terrorism against Americans. In March 1984 they kidnapped William Buckley, the CIA station chief in Beirut. Concerned that in a presidential election year terrorists might attempt to repeat the embarrassment inflicted on the Carter administration, Reagan signed a secret National Security Directive in April 1984 to expedite the launching of preventive strikes against international terrorist groups by infiltrating secret operatives into such organizations. Administration officials also continued to proclaim that the United States would not make concessions to terrorists. But U.S. words did not deter the fanatics in the Middle East. In September 1984 a Hezbollah terrorist drove a van loaded with explosives into the U.S. embassy annex in East Beirut, killing 24 persons, including two U.S. servicemen, and wounding 90, including the U.S. ambassador.

In the absence of a strong response from Washington, acts of violence against Americans multiplied. Mideast terrorists in 1985 seized and held as hostages two more U.S. citizens, hijacked two commercial airliners and an Italian cruise ship with U.S. passengers aboard, detonated a car bomb at a U.S. military shopping center in West Germany, and in December attacked travelers in airport terminals in Rome and Vienna. The year ended with 38 Americans killed, 139 wounded, and 2 taken hostage by terrorists.

Military Actions against Libya

The Reagan administration now concluded it must expand its covert efforts against Libya's leader Colonel Muammar al-Qaddafi, the prime suspect in the December attacks in Rome and Vienna. In order to condition the U.S. public to accept the use of military force to fight terrorism, Secretary of State Shultz contended in a news conference on January 16, 1986, that the United States should make it absolutely clear that it would "fight back" against terrorists.

But tensions did not subside. On April 2 a bomb exploded in a TWA plane over the Mediterranean and killed four Americans. Three days later an explosion in a West Berlin discotheque killed one U.S. soldier and wounded 204 persons, including 5 U.S. citizens. Washington believed that Libya was behind both acts of terrorism. After denouncing Qaddafi as "the mad dog of the Middle East," Reagan promised that the United States would respond if the evidence demonstrated Libya's responsibility.

On April 14, U.S. aircraft attacked three military targets near Tripoli, including the barracks where Qaddafi frequently stayed, and two military targets near Benghazi. Eleven and a half minutes later the U.S. bombers resumed the seven-hour return flight to their British base. The long 2,700 mile flight became necessary because France, Spain, and Italy had denied permission for flight through their air space. The attack damaged and destroyed civil as well as military installations, killed over 40 civilians, including Qaddafi's adopted infant daughter, and wounded hundreds. Reagan told the public that the bombing was in response to the attacks in West Berlin carried out on orders from Tripoli. The president claimed that "our evidence is direct, it is precise, it is irrefutable." U.S. officials explained that the attack did not intend to kill Qaddafi, and that they had honored the 1981 executive order prohibiting U.S. officials from engaging in assassination.

Public opinion polls indicated strong popular support throughout the nation for the government's action. Although Reagan's popularity at home soared, critics saw the president once again in a sure win situation against a very weak and much despised opponent. Four Democratic leaders in the Senate charged that the raid violated the War Powers Act of 1973. U.S. allies, except for Canada, Britain, and Israel, felt deceived, and expressed fears that terrorism would escalate as a result of the U.S. action. Demonstrations against the United States took place in major cities throughout Europe, and sharp protests came from several African countries and much of the Arab world. Three days after the attack, 12 foreign ministers of the European community met in Paris and called on the United States to avoid any further military action against Libya. Gorbachev called the air strike "militaristic and aggressive," and warned that such actions could damage relations between the Soviet Union and the United States. But, underlining the fact that the attack was a one time operation, 5 U.S. oil companies paid $2 billion a year in taxes and fees to the Libyan government and continued their operations in Libya through all the turmoil.

In the aftermath of the attack on Libya a rash of terrorist acts of vengeance occurred. By early 1987 terrorists had killed an American and two British hostages, and seized six more U.S. hostages.

THE COLD WAR IN CENTRAL AMERICA AND IN THE CARIBBEAN

Turmoil in the Middle East never distracted the Reagan administration from its belief that Marxists, particularly the Nicaraguan Sandinistas and the El Salvador rebels, and their supporters threatened to expand their influence and control in Central America and in the Caribbean. To convince a Congress—sensitive to widespread post-Vietnam public opposition to armed intervention in the Third World and divided in general along party lines as to the validity of the administration's analysis of the situation—the White House waved the flag, engaged in political arm twisting, and appealed directly to the voters. To defeat the enemy in Central America Washington exerted economic pressure, provided military and economic aid to local groups fighting the enemy, and periodically brandished the fist in military maneuvers and covert operations. Eventually, frustrations accumulating through more than four years of ineffective efforts to bring about the downfall of the Sandinista government in Nicaragua and to stop its alleged support of Marxist rebels in El Salvador pushed the Reagan administration into a secret operation that linked tactics in the Middle East and in Central America.

Responses to Civil Conflicts in El Salvador and Nicaragua

Two days after his election as president, Reagan told reporters:

> I don't think that our record of turning away from countries that were basically friendly to us, because of some disagreement on some facet of human

rights, and then finding that the result was that they have lost all human rights in that country—that isn't a practical way to go about that.

Reagan contended that such a sequence had occurred in Cuba before Castro's triumph and more recently in Nicaragua before the overthrow of the Somoza dictatorship in 1979 by the Sandinistas. Convinced that Sandinista leaders were exporting revolutionary ideas, suppressing basic freedoms, and funneling arms to leftist guerrillas in El Salvador to overthrow the coalition junta under President Duarte, Reagan cut off, in April 1981, $15 million remaining in economic aid promised by Carter to Nicaragua.

Administration officials also tried to convince the public of dangers in El Salvador so grave as to justify expanded U.S. support of the Duarte regime. Secretary of State Alexander Haig charged that "a well-orchestrated international communist campaign designed to transform the Salvadoran crisis from the internal conflict to an increasingly international confrontation is under way." Late in February 1981 the State Department claimed to have "definite evidence of the clandestine military support given by the Soviet Union, Cuba, and their communist allies to Marxist–Leninist guerrillas now fighting to overthrow the established government of El Salvador." The White House also argued that the Duarte government of El Salvador was committed to basic economic and political reforms, and merited increased military as well as economic aid from the United States. For the remainder of fiscal 1981 Reagan proposed doubling military aid to El Salvador in addition to a total of $126.5 million in economic aid. Thus the new administration set a pattern that it would pursue relentlessly for eight years.

Critics of Reagan's proposals suggested that historic political, economic, and social ills in the region caused the revolutionary uprisings and urged that discussions be held with rebel leaders and government officials of El Salvador to decide on measures to solve these problems. Some argued that no aid should be given to a government unable to control extreme right-wing death squads that had murdered hundreds of opponents and four U.S. churchwomen on errands of mercy.

Many Americans also worried lest the administration's actions lead to a repeat of the Vietnam experience, though Washington officials assured that "US personnel will not accompany Salvadoran units outside their garrison areas, nor will US personnel participate in any combat operations." Some members of Congress questioned the wisdom of sending any U.S. military forces, and in early March 1981 they advised the president that "any involvement of military personnel in hostilities in El Salvador requires compliance with the War Powers Act." Congress proceeded to pass legislation (Dodd amendment) making the provision of military aid to El Salvador contingent on the president's certification at 180-day intervals that the Salvadoran government was making progress in controlling the military and "in implementing essential economic and political reforms."

Early in 1982 President Reagan told the OAS that "very simply, guerrillas armed and supported by and through Cuba are attempting to impose a Marxist–Leninist dictatorship on the people of El Salvador as part of a larger imperialistic plan." Convinced that El Salvador was fighting the U.S. cause, Reagan certified that the Duarte government was "making progress in supporting human rights and political reforms," thereby clearing the way to send additional military aid in 1982.

Covert Action

To free its hands to undermine the Sandinistas in Nicaragua, the White House decided to avoid open requests for congressional approval of certain actions. In December 1981 Reagan signed a top secret finding authorizing political and paramilitary operations designed to curtail Sandinista support to various rebel movements in Central America. In Honduras, U.S. officials set up secret camps to provide military training for Nicaraguan rebels to interdict supplies sent by the Sandinistas to rebels of El Salvador. In accordance with existing law in regard to covert operations, the executive branch informed only the Senate and House Intelligence Committees, who were sworn to secrecy.

Boland Amendment

Disturbed by the executive branch's extension of control over foreign policy and apprehensive about possible U.S. military involvement in Central America, in December 1982 Congress adopted the Boland Amendment to the Intelligence Authorization Act. Sponsored by Congressman Edward Boland (D., Mass.), head of the House Select Committee on Intelligence, it forbade the CIA and Defense Department to use funds appropriated by Congress for the next year to furnish "military equipment, military training or advice, or support for military activities for the purpose of overthrowing the government of Nicaragua or provoking a military exchange between Nicaragua and Honduras." President Reagan signed the act with that clause into law.

In the spring of 1983 the president warned that "the national security of all the Americas is at stake in Central America. If we cannot defend ourselves there, we cannot expect to prevail elsewhere." To assure all of his acceptance of the Boland amendment, Reagan claimed at an April press conference that "we aren't doing anything to try and overthrow the Nicaraguan government. . . . anything we are doing in that area is simply trying to interdict the supply lines which are supplying the guerrillas in El Salvador."

Public opinion polls consistently indicated that a substantial majority of Americans (71 percent in a July 1983 Gallup poll) feared that the Reagan administration was leading the nation into a Vietnam-style involvement in Central America. The public agreed that humanitarian and economic aid might be justified, but not military aid, either to Nicaraguan rebels or to an El Salvadoran government unable or unwilling to control its death squads. Some opponents of the administration's policies found attractive the idea advanced by the Contadora group (Mexico, Venezuela, Colombia, and Panama) that neighboring Latin American nations take the lead in negotiating settlements of the issues—an approach for which Reagan officials had no enthusiasm.

Convinced of the validity of its assumptions about the situation in Central America and frustrated by congressional resistance to its requests for more military aid to the Nicaraguan opponents of the Sandinistas, the Reagan administration turned to other ways to help the rebels (contras). The president ordered naval units to the Caribbean for an extraordinary six months of maneuvers, and by September 1983 some three thousand U.S. combat troops had arrived in Honduras for military exercises. The White House also authorized secret diversion of military equipment from the Pentagon's inventory to the CIA to use in supporting the contras. To intensify the pressure on the Sandinistas, in September Washington sharply restricted imports from Nicaragua, stopped exports to Nicaragua, and blocked efforts by Nicaragua to obtain international loans.

Defending such actions, government spokespersons claimed that the executive branch obeyed the Boland amendment because the national purpose was not to overthrow the Sandinista government, but rather to persuade it to stop the flow of arms to the rebels in El Salvador. After intense lobbying the administration won congressional approval of $24 million to fund covert military operations of the Nicaraguan rebels for the period ending in June 1984. But, two days after Reagan signed the funding bill, speedboat teams of Central American mercenaries conducted a pre-dawn raid that blew up five Nicaraguan oil storage tanks in Corinto. When congressional intelligence committees learned that the CIA had secretly trained the raiders, Congress enacted a new Boland amendment in December, 1983. This amendment stipulated that neither the CIA nor any agency engaged in intelligence activities could spend any funds other than the appropriated $24 million to help any military operation in Nicaragua.

Providing Security for Caribbean Nations

The Reagan administration also viewed the protection of the small island nations of the Caribbean Sea as vital to the security of the United States. At a meeting of the Organization of American States (OAS) in February 1982 Reagan announced a Caribbean Basin Initiative to ensure the well-being and security of 27 Caribbean nations. In July 1983 Congress passed the key parts of Reagan's proposal in the Caribbean Basin Economic Recovery Act, offering a program of trade, economic, and tax measures to expand employment and raise living standards.

Invasion of Grenada

Before dawn on October 25, 1983, an assault force of 1,900 U.S. Marines and Rangers together with 400 soldiers from six small Caribbean island nations invaded Grenada, a small island about 100 miles northeast of Venezuela (map, p. 54). President Reagan said he acted in response to "an urgent, formal request from five member nations of Eastern Caribbean States to assist in a joint effort to restore order and democracy on the island of Grenada." He defended the action as necessary "to protect innocent lives, including up to 1,000 Americans, in Grenada." The president claimed that Cuban workers and soldiers in Grenada were building a 9,000-foot runway to help airlift arms to Nicaragua and that Cuba had just sent a high-level delegation to meet with leftist leaders of Grenada in possible preparation for a Cuban military buildup.

The surprise invasion of a 20-mile long island with a population of 110,000 came only two days after the American people had been shocked by the terrorist bombing of Marine headquarters in Lebanon (p. 77). The U.S. military, determined to avoid their Vietnam experience, barred the press from accompanying U.S. troops into Grenada, so the administration moved quickly to assure the public of the need for the military action. In a televised address to the nation, President Reagan said that U.S. forces had found that Grenada was "a Soviet–Cuban colony being readied as a major military bastion" and that "we got there just in time."

However, four days after the invasion began the Senate voted (64–20) to require the president to conform to the War Powers Act and withdraw U.S. military forces from Grenada within 60 days or ask Congress for a declaration of war. Critics claimed that the invasion violated the Rio Pact of 1947. Some skeptics wondered if the administration's need for an easy military win—after so much frustration in the Middle East and Central America—before the 1984 presidential election campaign accounted for the invasion of Grenada. They asked why Washington had rejected a political accommodation with Grenada and had opposed a $14.1 million loan to Grenada by the International Monetary Fund (IMF).

U.S. forces had won an easy victory with few casualties, and an ABC News poll on October 29 found that 90 percent of those queried supported their nation's action in Grenada. Even Democratic party leaders in Congress muffled their doubts, or spoke out in favor of the invasion. But worried European leaders and upset Latin Americans voiced disapproval of "gun-boat" diplomacy. The UN General Assembly voted 108 to 9 to condemn the action and the United States vetoed a similar resolution before the UN Security Council.

On December 15, 1983, the last U.S. combat troops left Grenada. In seven weeks 19 Americans had been killed and 115 wounded. At apparent small cost U.S. forces had achieved their objective, and President Reagan proclaimed that once again the nation "stands tall."

Congressional Resistance—More Administration Pressure, 1984–1986

In the four years, 1980 through 1983, the United States poured almost $800 million in aid to El Salvador. According to one estimate this aid amounted to $140,000 to be used against each of the estimated rebels. Speculation in the press that military intervention by the United States might be imminent prompted President Reagan in March 1984 to promise again not to "Americanize the war" by committing U.S. soldiers to combat.

Domestic debate over U.S. policy in Central America intensified after the revelation in April 1984 that the CIA had supervised covert mining of key Nicaraguan harbors. The fact that the mines had damaged a Soviet tanker, as well as merchant ships of U.S. allies, provoked critics to charge that the United States had violated international law. Congress passed a "non-binding sense of the Congress resolution" condemning the mining of the Nicaraguan ports. Senator Barry Goldwater (R., Ariz.), head of the Senate Intelligence Committee, in an angry letter to CIA director William Casey wrote that the mining was "an act of war. For the life of me I don't see how we are going to explain it." But the US Ambassador to the United Nations, Jeane Kirkpatrick, defended the mining as an act in "individual and collective self-defense against Nicaraguan aggression," and upheld the administration's refusal to accept the jurisdiction of the World Court in a case filed by Nicaragua against the United States. Many Americans disagreed and viewed the Reagan policy as based not on the needs and realities in Central America, but on domestic political considerations and an inflexible cold war mentality.

Dismissing the attacks on its policies, the administration sent $21 million to the contras, increased the number of U.S. military advisers in El Salvador and Honduras, and launched war games in the Caribbean involving over 30,000 U.S. service personnel. On May 9, 1984, Reagan took his case for emergency military aid to El Salvador directly to the U.S. people in a television address declaring that

> Central America is a region of great importance to the United States. And it is so close. San Salvador is closer to Houston than Houston is to Washington, D.C. Central America is America; it is at our doorstep. And it has become the stage for a bold attempt by the Soviet Union, Cuba, and Nicaragua to install Communism by force throughout the hemisphere.

In June a former CIA analyst stated that since 1981 the Salvadoran armed forces had "not intercepted a single clandestine weapons shipment from any foreign country on water or land." Congress responded at the end of the month by voting to delete $21 million included as part of the administration's urgent supplemental appropriation for the contras.

In his second term Reagan resorted to patriotic rhetoric to rouse popular support and thereby put on the defensive members of Congress who questioned his assumptions and opposed his policies in Central America. He extolled the Nicaraguan rebels as "freedom fighters," "our brothers," and "the moral equivalent of the Founding Fathers." Secretary of State Shultz warned that if Congress denied more aid to the rebels, then Nicaragua would fall into "the endless darkness of communist tyranny." Yet an April 1986 *New York Times*–CBS News poll revealed that only 38 percent of the people knew which side the United States supported in Nicaragua and that only 40 percent of those who knew favored military aid to the contras.

In June 1986 the World Court held (14–1) that U.S. aid to the contras violated international law and that Nicaragua was entitled to reparations for the mining of its harbor. A month later Washington vetoed a UN Security Council resolution calling for U.S. compliance with the World Court ruling. Sensational developments soon placed the administration's program in jeopardy.

IRAN–CONTRA AFFAIR

The Reagan administration had become deeply frustrated by its inability to free Americans held hostage by fanatic terrorists in Lebanon and by persistent congressional resistance to its Central American policies. Secret actions between May 1985 and November 1986 to resolve these problems produced an unexpected drama that thrilled some Americans, disturbed many, and embarrassed the White House. U.S. lives were lost, reputations damaged, folk-heroes created, illicit fortunes made, and fundamental questions raised about the constitutional limits that Congress might and should impose on the executive branch's conduct of foreign relations.

The Story Breaks

In July 1985 press accounts linked a staff member of the National Security Council (NSC), Marine Lt. Col. Oliver North, with a private network supplying military aid to the contras. But National Security Adviser Robert McFarlane denied that any NSC official had violated the law in dealing with U.S. assistance to the contras. Although rumors circulated about secret aid flowing to the Nicaraguan rebels, no clear evidence of such activities surfaced until July 1986 when Senator John Kerry (D., Mass.) presented to the Senate Foreign Relations Committee evidence of illegal actions in dealing with the contras. Soon thereafter North denied to the House Intelligence Committee that he had raised money for the contras or offered them military advice. Two months later—on October 5—Nicaraguan forces shot down a C-123 carrying arms and captured the surviving crew member, Eugene Hasenfus, a U.S. citizen. In custody, Hasenfus

told Nicaraguan officials that he worked with CIA employees and had participated in numerous flights to supply the contras.

As rumors about secret government actions in Central America swirled
throughout the nation, a startling new story came out of the Middle East. On
November 3, 1986—the day after the release of U.S. hostage David Jacobsen—
a Lebanese magazine reported that the United States had secretly supplied arms
to Iran. One day later the official Iran press agency asserted that Robert Mc-
Farlane, who had resigned in December 1985 as National Security Adviser, had
taken a U.S. delegation on a secret mission to Teheran in July. Although Reagan
said that the story in the Lebanese magazine had "no foundation," the White
House admitted working with other countries to obtain the release of hostages.
U.S. intelligence sources now revealed that 18 months earlier the president had
approved a broad plan for secret contacts with Iran to improve relations, end
Iran's support of terrorism, and help free the hostages.

In an effort to contain the uproar following these disclosures, Reagan told
the nation on November 13 that "we did not, repeat, did not trade weapons or
anything else for hostages—nor will we." However, he admitted to a "secret
diplomatic initiative" over an 18-month period involving the shipment of
"small amounts of defensive weapons and spare parts" to Iran. A suspicious
press and opposition leaders in Congress remained dissatisfied with the president's version of what happened. Senate and House Intelligence Committees
undertook to investigate alleged violations of laws and reports that Reagan had
ordered CIA director William Casey not to tell Congress about the secret sale of
arms. On November 20 the Majority Leader of the House, Jim Wright (D.,
Tex.), disclosed that he had learned from Admiral John Poindexter, the National
Security Adviser, that Israel with Washington's approval had shipped to Iran
anti-tank missiles and Hawk anti-aircraft missiles. For these weapons Iran had
paid $12 million, which was deposited in a Swiss bank account. The question of
what happened to that money was unanswered.

After a weekend of frantic behind-the-scenes activity, Attorney General
Edwin Meese announced the discovery of evidence in North's office revealing
the diversion of the Iran arms sale money to furnish arms to the contras without
the president's knowledge. Reagan dismissed North from his NSC post after
calling him "a national hero," and accepted the resignation of Poindexter as
National Security Adviser. A stunned nation demanded the complete story of the
Iran–Contra transactions.

Official Investigations and Revelations

In February 1987 a special commission appointed by Reagan to study the
operations of the NSC and headed by former Senator John Tower (R., Tex),
reported that "the Iran initiative ran directly counter to the administration's own
policies on terrorism, the Iran/Iraq war, and military support to Iran." Moreover,

"the price charged to Iran was far in excess of what was paid to the Department of Defense for the arms" and "most of these monies remain unaccounted for." The commission also revealed the involvement of the NSC in raising funds for contras from private U.S. citizens and foreigners. The Tower group concluded that "the President did not seem to be aware of the way in which the operation was implemented and the full consequences of U.S. participation. . . . At no time did he insist upon accountability and performance review."

President Reagan admitted to congressional committees that he was "very definitely involved in the decisions about support to the 'freedom fighters'—my idea to begin with." Although some saw this admission as a direct contradiction of previous statements, the president claimed that he did not break any law because in his view the congressional ban on contra aid in the Boland amendment did not apply to the NSC. The November 1987 report of the congressional committees concluded:

> The Iran–Contra affair was characterized by pervasive dishonesty and inordinate secrecy . . . officials viewed the law not as setting boundaries for their actions, but raising impediments to their goals. When goals and the law collided, the law gave way. The covert program of support for the contras evaded the Constitution's most significant check on executive power: The President can spend funds on a program only if he can convince Congress to appropriate the money. . . . If the President did not know what his national security advisers were doing, he should have. . . . It was the President's policy—not an isolated decision by North or Poindexter—to sell arms secretly to Iran and to maintain the contras "body and soul," the Boland amendment notwithstanding.

In order to avoid future misunderstandings and evasion of the law the report recommended that "the National Security Act be amended to require that Congress be notified prior to the commencement of a covert action except in certain rare instances and in no event later than 48 hours after a finding is approved."

After 14 months of investigation by the special prosecutor, Lawrence E. Walsh, a federal grand jury in March 1988 indicted North, Poindexter, and the two arms dealers. In May 1989 a jury found North guilty of three felonies—obstructing Congress, destroying documents, and accepting an illegal gratuity. In the trial of Poindexter early in 1990, ex-President Reagan testified on videotape that the transfer of arms to Iran "was a covert action that was taken at my behest" and that "I had no knowledge then or now that there had been a diversion, and I never used the term." In April a federal jury convicted Poindexter on five counts of destroying documents and lying to Congress. Judge Harold Greene sentenced Poindexter to prison for six months. Both men appealed their convictions, and in separate cases a federal district court judge dismissed all charges on the grounds that each case had been influenced by testimony given Congress under immunity.

The public record clearly documented that, although the Iran–Contra Affair violated laws and contradicted Reagan's proclaimed policies, the president endorsed the initiative. Reagan approved weapons sales to Iran in an effort to obtain the release of U.S. hostages. His subordinates circumvented Boland amendments by using third parties such as Israel to arm Iran and Saudi Arabia to fund the contras, and attempted to keep both operations secret. In effect a small group within the executive branch acted secretly in contempt of Congress and in violation of the constitution to carry out policies it believed to be in the national interest. Destruction of many important documents by North and others may mean that the full story will never be known. Fear of creating another Watergate and irreparably damaging the presidency weakened the determination of some to pursue the case wherever it led. Certainly the enduring popularity of Ronald Reagan discouraged elected politicians from attacking the chief executive. The media dubbed him the "Teflon" president, and even that unflattering label failed to stick.

Aftermath

The Iran–Contra Affair helped to convince a majority of Americans that further aid to the contras did not serve the public interest. Yet the administration continued to campaign for support for the "freedom fighters." In August 1987 Reagan dismissed the peace plan drafted by the presidents of five Central American nations because it failed to address U.S. security concerns in the region. In October he told the OAS that "as long as there is breath in this body, I will speak and work, strive and struggle for the cause of the Nicaraguan freedom fighters." When Premier Gorbachev, in private talks with Reagan in Washington in December 1987, offered to stop all military deliveries to the Sandinistas if the United States stopped financing the contras, the president failed to respond. In February 1988 Congress voted to end all military aid to the contras. Tensions relaxed when the contras and Sandinistas signed a 60-day truce effective April 1, 1988. Congress then approved $47.9 million in humanitarian aid to the contras.

Although the sale of arms to Iran did obtain the release of one U.S. hostage in 1985 and two in 1986, five Americans seized as hostages since 1984 remained captives. Moreover, as the Iran–Contra Affair unfolded in 1987, a new crisis in the Persian Gulf threatened U.S. interests in the region.

PERSIAN GULF CRISIS, 1987–1988

As the stalemated Iraq–Iran War entered its seventh year in 1987, a small, oil-rich neutral nation called Kuwait (600,000 population), located on the west side of the Persian Gulf, turned to Washington for help. Believing that the belligerents would respect the U.S. flag, the Kuwaitis asked the United States to fly its flag on Kuwaiti oil tankers. President Reagan had recently reiterated his commitment to maintain the flow of oil through the Strait of Hormuz (map, p. 138).

Late in February Washington learned of a threatening development—Iran's deployment of Chinese-made missiles near the Strait of Hormuz, an action placing all Gulf traffic in jeopardy. The White House responded by having the U.S. Navy escort Kuwaiti ships registered under the U.S. flag through the Gulf. To emphasize his commitment Reagan warned that "the use of the vital sea lanes will not be dictated by the Iranians." Still obsessed with fear of Soviet intentions in this critical area, the president added "these lands will not be permitted to come under control of the Soviet Union."

Debate over U.S. Policy

Opponents of the president's moves contended that the administration erred in responding to developments in the Middle East in "the bellicose idiom of the East–West struggle." They pointed out that the Soviet Union agreed to fly the Soviet flag on three oil tankers leased to Kuwait, thereby committing the Soviet Union to keep the Persian Gulf open to international commerce. Some observers concluded that U.S. policy aimed at regaining credibility with moderate Arab states shocked and angered by the Iran–Contra Affair. The debate over the wisdom of U.S. action became even more heated after two missiles fired by an Iraqi fighter plane on 17 May hit the U.S. frigate *Stark* killing 37 sailors and seriously damaging the ship. When Iraq apologized for "pilot error," some Americans wondered why the navy had failed to avert the disaster and why the administration continued to favor Iraq in the war.

In July, after a reregistered tanker flying the U.S. flag hit an Iranian mine in the Persian Gulf, some European nations, including the Soviet Union, announced plans to send minesweepers. In October an Iranian missile hit a Kuwaiti ship flying the U.S. flag and wounded 18 men, including the U.S. captain. A few days later U.S. Navy ships destroyed two Iranian oil platforms in the Persian Gulf. Supporters of Reagan's policies argued that Iran threatened the flow of vital oil to the United States and its allies, and that terrorists backed by Iranian fanatics had seized Americans and held them as hostages. They noted that ever since the seizure of 52 Americans in the U.S. embassy in Teheran in 1979 the regime of the Ayatollah Khomeini had flaunted its anti-Americanism. As a *Wall Street Journal* reporter pointed out, "Few US foreign policy actions win more domestic support than bashing Iran."

Many Americans, however, began to question the wisdom of their government's actions that placed the lives of U.S. service personnel at risk. Some called for a withdrawal of U.S. forces and an all-out effort for a negotiated settlement. Others pointed out that Iraq had started the war, used chemical weapons, initiated the attacks on commercial traffic in the Persian Gulf, and caused the deaths of 37 U.S. Navy personnel, yet Washington regarded Iran as the villain. The fact that the administration's actions had not denied the Soviets access to the area, but rather had enabled them to improve relations with Arab states on the Gulf convinced some critics that the old cold war premises did not apply in the Middle East.

End of the Crisis

Two disturbing incidents hastened the end of the Iraq–Iran War. In April 1988 an Iranian mine seriously damaged a U.S. Navy ship escorting tankers through the Strait of Hormuz and wounded 10 U.S. sailors. After consulting with congressional leaders about a proper response, the administration authorized the navy to strike a return blow. Four days later 6 U.S. warships crippled or sank 6 Iranian vessels and seriously damaged 2 Iranian oil rigs. In July another tragedy strengthened the case for peace. While on patrol duty in the Gulf a nervous crew of the U.S. cruiser *Vincennes* shot down an Iranian commercial airliner killing 290 civilian passengers. President Reagan called "it a terrible human tragedy," and stressed that the unfortunate incident proved the need to achieve the U.S. goal of peace as soon as possible. Before the month ended Iran announced acceptance of a UN Security Council 10-point peace plan and a cease-fire with Iraq on August 20. This promising development prompted the Defense Department in mid-September to urge the end of full-time U.S. escorts in the Persian Gulf.

Unresolved Problems

As the Reagan administration entered its final weeks the Middle East remained a trouble spot. Iraq had used chemical weapons against both the Iranians and its own people—the Kurds—in defiance of the 1925 Geneva protocol. Although members of Congress urged the White House to impose economic sanctions on Iraq until its government renounced the use of chemical weapons, the administration refused on the grounds that such actions would not be productive. High government officials still hesitated to pressure an Iraq whose friendship or neutrality they regarded as crucial in the Middle East.

Intensive efforts by Secretary of State Shultz to end the Arab-Israeli conflict by securing agreement to his proposal, whereby Israel would transfer to the Palestinians certain administrative powers in the West Bank and Gaza Strip, failed to win approval from either side. Acts of violence continued and terrorists in Beirut seized more hostages. The problems of the Middle East continued to thwart U.S. policymakers seeking to bring peace, economic stability, and a respect for basic human rights to that tumultuous region.

CHAPTER 6

Adjusting to a Changing
International Scene

"I find it difficult to believe that relations with the Soviet Union will ever be 'normal' in the sense that we have normal relations with most other countries."

George Shultz, February 1988

"I think there is quite a difference today in the leadership and in the relationship between our two countries, and I think we have held very productive meetings. . . . I think that enough progress has been made that we can look with optimism on future negotiations."

Ronald Reagan, June 1988

"The Cold War is over. In signing the Charter of Paris we have closed a chapter of history."

George Bush, November 1990

In the final two years of the Reagan administration dramatic developments in the Soviet Union and Eastern Europe sent encouraging signals to the United States and its NATO allies. Gorbachev's promotion of "glasnost" and "perestroika" heralded both a more open society and the restructuring of basic political and economic institutions. The Soviet leader's new internal policies suggested the need to reexamine long-held assumptions about Soviet intentions and the threat of international communism. Americans sensed that a glorious opportunity to relieve international tension beckoned the leaders of East and West.

ENDING THE COLD WAR

Bitterly disappointed by the failures at Reykjavik, representatives of the two powers reconvened strategic arms reduction talks in Geneva early in 1987. Although resumption of the testing of nuclear weapons by the United States in February caused the Soviets to end their moratorium on testing, Gorbachev instructed Moscow's negotiators to press on to eliminate all nuclear missiles. In addition to the goal of arms reductions, high-level Soviet and U.S. officials sought agreements on human rights, peaceful resolution of regional conflicts, settlement of the Afghanistan problem, student exchanges, and trade policies.

Progress in Reducing Nuclear Arms

At the Washington Summit in December 1987, Reagan and Gorbachev agreed to destroy medium-range nuclear missiles (300–3,400 miles) and to allow each side to station personnel outside the other's production plants to ensure that banned missiles and their components were no longer being manufactured. The two powers also agreed to limit the number of ICBMs deployed to 4,900 warheads. These unprecedented arms reduction agreements won the overwhelming support of the U.S. people. A delighted President Reagan proclaimed in an address to the nation: "We took a step—only a first step, but still a critical one—toward building a more durable peace. . . . Soviet-American relations are no longer focused only on arms control issues; they now cover a far broader agenda—one that has, at its root, realism and candor."

Nevertheless, some Americans did not applaud the president's actions. Howard Phillips, president of the Conservative Caucus, charged that Reagan had become "a useful idiot for Soviet propaganda." The normally pro-administration *Wall Street Journal* complained that "arms control . . . has become the heavy-metal music of Western foreign policy—a seemingly addictive pursuit of otherwise normal people." But the Senate responded to public opinion by voting 93–5 on May 27, 1988, to approve the arms reduction agreement.

Two days later Reagan and Gorbachev met in Moscow to sign the INF treaty and to seek agreements on the reduction of long-range strategic nuclear missiles. With less than seven months of his term remaining, Reagan hoped to crown his administration with a major achievement in arms reduction—a treaty restricting manufacture and deployment of ICBMs. Although four days of discussions failed to resolve significant disagreements, especially in regard to SDI, the two leaders "reaffirmed their solemn conviction that a nuclear war cannot be won and must never be fought . . . and their disavowal of any intention to achieve military superiority." Gorbachev's clear commitment to internal reforms coupled with the Soviet decision to pull troops out of Afghanistan persuaded Reagan to admit that he no longer believed that the Soviet Union was an evil empire. Additional reasons for optimism continued to appear.

Beyond Containment

Following the 1988 U.S. presidential election the new Bush administration found Moscow urging it to move quickly to make substantial reductions in nuclear arms. In a widely praised speech at the United Nations in New York in December 1988, Gorbachev announced the decision of the Soviet government to reduce its armed forces by 500,000 worldwide, to withdraw six tank divisions from Eastern Europe, and to make sharp reductions in military forces in the European republics of the Soviet Union. Gorbachev pointed out, "It is obvious

. . . that the use or threat of force no longer can or must be an instrument of national policy." To apply more pressure on Washington, Gorbachev announced in April 1989 that by the end of the year Moscow would close three reactors that produced plutonium and would also halt the production of enriched uranium. In May the Soviet president told Secretary of State James Baker that the Soviet Union would reduce its short-range nuclear missiles in Eastern Europe, and called on the United States to enter serious negotiations to reduce nuclear arms.

Many Western analysts interpreted Gorbachev's words as a sincere call for ending the cold war so that the Soviets could focus their resources on rebuilding their faltering economy. In general, Americans enthusiastically endorsed these moves by the Soviet leader and urged their government to respond positively. However, some hard-liners warned that Soviet arms reduction proposals would destroy NATO's capacity to defend Western Europe against Warsaw Pact conventional forces and would undermine recent security achievements.

Still harboring old suspicions of the Soviets and determined to avoid appearing indecisive in response to Moscow's initiatives, the Bush administration announced its intent to press on with SDI research and to proceed with plans to triple the range of its European-based Lance rockets equipped with nuclear warheads. The Kremlin responded that if Washington carried out that plan, then the Soviet Union would no longer feel bound by the recent INF treaty banning intermediate-range nuclear missiles. The maneuvering for advantage and the war of words continued as a Bush administration official accused the Soviets of tossing out arms control proposals in "a kind of drugstore cowboy fashion." Secretary of Defense Richard Cheney dismissed Gorbachev's offer to eliminate 500 short-range nuclear warheads in Eastern Europe as a "pittance."

At a meeting in Brussels in late May 1989 commemorating the 40th anniversary of NATO, Bush described it as "the best investment in peace that we have ever made," and called on the West to move "beyond containment" by ending the painful division of Europe and making it united and free. He expressed his belief that "we live in a time when we are witnessing the end of an idea—the final chapter of the communist experiment." Moving to control the agenda, Bush urged as a first step in arms reduction that the Soviets join the Americans in cutting conventional forces in Europe to a ceiling of 275,000 before proceeding to reduce short-range nuclear weapons. The strategic arms reduction talks (START), suspended late in 1988, reconvened in Geneva in June 1989.

By the end of 1989 popular uprisings had overthrown Communist party dictatorships in Poland, Hungary, Czechoslovakia, East Germany, Bulgaria, and Romania. In November Americans rejoiced as their TVs showed East Berliners tearing down the Berlin Wall erected in 1961 (p. 26). After Moscow took no action either to save the communist regime or to prevent free elections scheduled in the six Eastern European nations in the spring of 1990, many Americans concluded that the cold war had ended in victory for the West. Public opinion polls indicated a growing belief that the containment policy had become obsolete, and that Washington should reduce military spending and declare a "peace dividend" to meet a backlog of domestic needs.

The Bush administration continued to proceed cautiously in word and action. Although supportive of Gorbachev's efforts to reduce international tension and to make the Soviet Union a more open society, the president resisted pressure to extend direct economic aid to Moscow. However, at the Malta Summit Meeting in December 1989, Bush told Gorbachev that he wanted to help make perestroika work, and he promised to assist Soviet efforts to improve economic relations with the West. One year later, after Moscow eased its curbs on emigration, Bush lifted trade restrictions imposed by the Jackson–Vanik amendment (see p. 121).

Responding to a New Order in Europe

Some Americans criticized their government for its "spectator role" in the sweeping changes in Eastern Europe. Many began to question the necessity of maintaining nuclear deterrents and conventional forces in Europe to discourage aggression from a Communist bloc that no longer existed. A free Europe, no longer dependent on U.S. economic and military support, appeared imminent. Defending his course, President Bush said, "I would rather be called cautious than I would be called reckless."

In January 1990 he proposed a limit of 195,000 on U.S. and Soviet troops in Central Europe, but reserved the right to keep 30,000 U.S. forces elsewhere in Europe—a plan that Moscow soon accepted. In support of his national security policy the president, in February, claimed that U.S. allies "don't want to see the United States pull back into what would be perceived world-wide as some kind of neo-isolationist decoupling." As negotiations on the reduction of nuclear weapons in Europe continued, early in May Bush cancelled plans to base the new short-range Lance nuclear missiles in West Germany. Later that month, the Soviets joined the United States in agreeing to end the production of chemical weapons.

At the Washington Summit, May 30–June 3, 1990, Bush and Gorbachev narrowed differences on reducing strategic nuclear weapons while leaving the specifics to negotiation by experts from each nation. The Soviets agreed to purchase at least 10 million tons of grain per year in each of the next two years and also to encourage U.S. firms to invest in and open businesses in the Soviet Union. Before the summer ended, McDonald's, the fast-food chain, opened restaurants in Moscow. But Washington withheld most favored nation status in its trade relationship with the Soviet Union because of the Kremlin's crackdown on Lithuanians seeking independence from the Soviet Union and its continuing huge military expenditures. Although the two heads of state agreed as to the inevitability of the unification of Germany, Gorbachev refused to accept a united Germany as a member of NATO and insisted that the present East German–Polish boundary be accepted as permanent.

Dismissing such disappointments, Secretary of State Baker claimed that progress at this summit helped move the two nations from "a balance of terror" to "the steadier ground of balance of interests." In a press conference at the end of the summit, a delighted President Bush declared: "In my view, we've moved a long, long way from the depths of the Cold War." Four days later Washington and its NATO partners agreed to reduce controls on such high-tech exports as computers, fiber-optical communication equipment, and pharmaceuticals to Eastern European nations.

Administration leaders believed that they had avoided the pitfall of the "liberals," that is going too far too fast, especially in regard to arms reduction and NATO, some of whose members favored transforming the Western military alliance into more of an European political organization. Early in May Bush contended that "our enemy today is uncertainty and instability. So the alliance (NATO) will need to maintain a sound, collective military structure with forces in the field backed by larger forces that can be called upon in a crisis." Key administration officials also pushed hard for a $306.9 billion defense budget for fiscal 1991—only $2.7 billion less than it had requested for fiscal 1990, months before the upheaval in Eastern Europe. The budget request included huge sums for such favorites of the military-industrial complex as SDI, the Stealth bomber (B2), and the MX. Such gestures did not reassure the extreme conservative wing of the Republican party. Some charged "a sell-out" to the Soviets at the Washington Summit. Richard Perle, Assistant Secretary of Defense in the Reagan administration, suggested that "Mr. Gorbachev saw a President eager to keep him in power and willing to make concessions to do so." To blunt such arguments, late in June Defense Secretary Richard Cheney announced his opposition to economic assistance to the Soviet Union as long as it continued its heavy expenditures on arms.

After holding firm against Soviet efforts to delay for five years the recognition of one sovereign German nation and to make a united Germany a member of both NATO and the Warsaw Pact, Washington supported actions by the West German government that weakened the Soviet case. In July the two Germanys put into effect a common currency and established economic unity. Gorbachev now accepted the inevitable unity, and even dropped his opposition to NATO membership for the united Germany, which was officially proclaimed on October 3, 1990. The cold war map of Central Europe had become a relic.

These dramatic developments in Europe underscored a remarkable change in the United States' relationship with its closest postwar allies. As the cold war wound down, the nations of Western Europe became less dependent on U.S. economic and military aid and less willing to submit to domination by Washington. Thus, at the sixteenth annual economic summit of the six industrial powers (the United States, Britain, France, W. Germany, Italy, Japan) in Houston in July 1990, sharp differences surfaced in regard to trade policies, aid to the Soviet Union, and actions to protect the environment. President Bush acknowledged that in "a rapidly changing world," friendly nations no longer had to clear their policies with Washington. Evidence of this growing independence of the nations of Western Europe appeared in their efforts to create a single market based on a uniform currency and free trade, despite reservations by U.S. officials. Capitol Hill and Wall Street viewed such actions as a threat because the European community's refusal to reduce its subsidies on agricultural exports made it more difficult for the U.S. farmer to compete in the world markets and thereby worsened the United States' serious unfavorable balance of trade. Adding their voices to the opposition, hard-line hawks warned that moves toward European economic unity could undermine NATO and leave Western Europe vulnerable.

However, the movement to design a new order in Europe, initiated in Helsinki in 1975 at a Conference on Security and Cooperation in Europe (CSCE), gained momentum as cold war tensions subsided. In November 1990, CSCE met in Paris to endorse the results of 20 months of negotiations by representatives of 16 NATO nations and 6 Warsaw Pact nations. The United States and 33 nations (all of Europe except Albania, plus Canada and Turkey) signed a treaty that provided a charter for a new Europe and set up a secretariat to work for its goals. In addition, NATO and Warsaw Pact members signed a nonaggression pledge, and each side agreed to limit its conventional forces in Europe (CFE). President Bush joined Gorbachev and other leaders in declaring an end to "the era of confrontation and division in Europe" and in promising "a new era of democracy, peace and unity." The hoped-for millenium edged closer in July 1991 when the six Warsaw Pact members agreed to dissolve that 36-year-old political and military alliance.

PROGRESS TOWARD PEACE IN THE DEVELOPING COUNTRIES

The relaxation of East–West tensions in Europe assisted those seeking to end conflicts in the Third World between Marxist and anticommunist forces. Both Moscow and Washington began to encourage negotiations between warring factions in Latin America, Asia, and Africa to resolve long-standing conflicts exploited by the cold war rivals. Some notable successes resulted.

Peace in Nicaragua

The presidents of five Central American countries convinced the Sandinistas and contras to accept an accord in February 1989 providing for disbanding the rebel force and for open elections under supervision of international monitors within a year. President Bush, finding "troublesome elements" in the plan, continued the trade embargo on Nicaragua and convinced Congress to extend aid to the contras until elections took place. When the five Central American presidents insisted that the contra forces in Honduras be disbanded no later than December 8, Washington, after trying to stall the dissolution of the rebels until after the February 1990 elections, reluctantly accepted the timetable.

In their nation's first open and honest election, the Nicaraguan people in February 1990 chose as their president Violeta de Chamorro and handed Daniel Ortega, the Sandinista leader, an unexpected defeat. A delighted President Bush soon lifted the trade embargo on Nicaragua, urged Congress to grant $300 million in economic aid to the Chamorro government, and told the contras to disband and lay down their arms. In May the contras agreed to disarm—thereby ending a war that killed more than 20,000 Nicaraguans and ruined the nation's economy.

Peace in El Salvador

Despite aid totaling over $3.9 billion, or more than $1 million a day, during the Reagan years, the El Salvadoran government, backed by the military and upper class, still faced a determined rebellion. The conflict had resulted in the deaths of some 70,000 El Salvadorans and over 1 million exiles—many fled to the United States. The regime of President Duarte had failed to produce significant democratic reforms, and both sides routinely resorted to acts of terror. Elections in March 1989, boycotted by the Farabundo Marti National Liberation Front (FMLN), a group of rebel parties, resulted in the triumph of the conservative Arena party. The Bush administration, however, accepted the election as evidence of El Salvador's movement toward democracy and continued to support the government.

After the administration of new President Alfredo Cristiani rejected peace proposals by rebel leaders, the latter renewed their military offensive. On November 16, 1989, a group of armed persons wearing military uniforms killed six Jesuit priests and two servants—an act of terror widely attributed to the government's armed forces. Bush, nevertheless, labeled the Salvadoran government "a democracy" and urged it to track down and bring to justice "the terrorists." Following Cristiani's visit to the White House in February 1990 in quest of more support, Bush urged Congress to endorse the administration's request for a $50 million increase in aid in the 1991 budget. But revelations that the soldiers accused of slaying the Jesuit priests had received military training from the U.S. Armed Services strengthened the case of those favoring sharp cuts in aid to the Cristiani regime.

In April 1990 the Salvadoran government attempted to blunt criticism by taking into custody eight soldiers for killing the Jesuit priests and by agreeing to meet with FMLN under UN supervision. When several rounds of talks failed to produce peace, the Soviet Union joined the United States in October in urging the two sides to agree to a cease-fire and a political compromise. Congress applied pressure by voting to withhold 50 percent of the military aid allocated to El Salvador for fiscal 1991. But after the January 1991 killing of three U.S. military advisers by the rebels, who had launched a major offensive, and the continuing failure of the UN moderated peace talks, President Bush in June released half of the withheld aid as permitted by the congressional resolution of October 1990.

UN negotiations finally produced in September 1991 a plan for peace agreed to by President Cristiani and five guerrilla commanders and signed by them on January 16, 1992. El Salvador's 11-year ordeal, long regarded by some critics of U.S. policy as a proxy war between the United States and the Soviet Union, appeared over. In a remarkable appraisal of the terrible impact of the cold war on Third World people, Cristiani told the UN General Assembly that his compatriots had long been "easy victims of that abusive and irrational polarity that divided the world into inevitable bands on the basis of an artificial ideological fanaticism."

Progress toward Ending Cambodia's Civil War

The ending of the cold war in Europe also facilitated the gradual development of peace and freedom in Indochina. Although Vietnam ended its 11-year occupation of Cambodia in September 1989, opponents of the Vietnamese-created communist government in Phnom Penh continued to wage war against it after the failure of a 19 nation peace conference in Paris. To guard against the victory of a coalition that included the Khmer Rouge (p. 134), in November 1989 Congress imposed minor restrictions on President Bush's use of CIA contingency funds to arm Cambodians fighting to overthrow their government.

A sensational television documentary "From the Killing Fields," shown in April 1990, claimed that arms furnished by Washington to the opposition fighting the Cambodian government had been used by the Khmer Rouge to commit atrocities on the people. But a Bush administration spokesperson pointed out that the president remained "unalterably opposed to a return to power of the murderous Khmer Rouge" and that none of Washington's approximately $15 million a year of covert and overt aid went to them. Pressure from Congress and knowledgeable insiders convinced the White House to take steps to guarantee that the Khmer Rouge would not regain power. In July Secretary of State Baker announced that Washington was withdrawing its diplomatic recognition of the Cambodian coalition that included the Khmer Rouge, and was opening negotiations with Vietnam to settle the Cambodian conflict.

With the cold war ended, the Bush administration no longer found it desirable to base its policy in Cambodia on the standard premise that "an enemy's enemy is a friend," that is, that opponents of Moscow and Vietnam in Cambodia, whoever they might be, should be treated as allies. Thus in August 1990 the United States joined the other permanent members of the UN Security Council (Britain, France, the Soviet Union, China) in announcing agreement on a plan for a political settlement in Cambodia involving UN supervised elections that would take place following ratification of a peace treaty by the 19 nations involved in the war.

As this process advanced, the White House announced in December its intent to initiate formal talks with Vietnam on normalizing relations. In April 1991, the Bush administration said that it would furnish $1 million in humanitarian aid to Vietnam. Washington, however, would not lift its economic embargo until Hanoi agreed to the UN plan for free elections and an end to the civil war in Cambodia. Hopes for peace escalated after the Cambodian rebels and the government signed a cease-fire in June and began another round of peace talks hosted by China. In late September the UN Security Council approved a plan designed by all Cambodian factions for UN supervised elections in 1993. An end to more than a quarter century of conflict in Southeast Asia and Cambodia's 12-year civil war appeared imminent.

Peace in Angola

Late in the Reagan administration four months of negotiations by representatives of Angola, Cuba, South Africa, and the United States produced in October 1988 an agreement on the pullout of Cuban troops from Angola in the next 24–30 months. Before the year ended, Angola, Cuba, and South Africa signed a protocol providing for independence for Namibia pending the withdrawal of all 50,000 Cuban troops from Angola by July 1, 1991. But prospects for an early end to the conflict collapsed after the Reagan administration refused to suspend aid to the Unita rebels led by Jonas Savimbi, and Angola's Marxist government failed to make peace with the insurgents.

Accepting the premises of conservative advisers, who believed that only Unita could rescue Angola and Namibia from the Soviet-backed Angolan government, early in his term President Bush sought to increase covert military aid to the rebels. Although hopes for peace soared in June 1989 when the heads of 18 African nations persuaded the two sides in Angola to agree to a cease-fire,

Washington indicated its intention to continue to send arms to Unita "until there is a national reconciliation." By August the truce collapsed and heavy fighting resumed.

As the civil conflict persisted in 1990 hard-line U.S. conservatives, ignoring the end of the cold war, campaigned to convince the public that Angola's government survived only because of Soviet aid that greatly exceeded the paltry amount of aid furnished to the rebels by the United States. In September the House Intelligence Committee voted to continue covert aid to the rebels, and the Bush administration turned down Moscow's "triple zero option" calling for the Americans and Soviets to agree to stop all military aid to Angola and for the two Angolan sides to agree not to accept arms from anyone else. Although all but a small contingent of Cuban troops had withdrawn from Angola by late November 1990, the civil war continued. Before the year ended the United States and the Soviet Union coordinated efforts to persuade both sides to accept a cease-fire and end the 15-year conflict that had killed more than 300,000 people. In May 1991 the Angolan government and the rebels agreed to a cease-fire and to hold free elections in the second half of 1992. By the end of May the last Cuban soldiers had left, and the two sides had signed a peace treaty to be monitored by the United Nations. The *Wall Street Journal* called the agreement "another vindication of the Reagan doctrine."

Continuing Civil Conflict in Afghanistan

Neither Washington nor Moscow, acting alone or together, in the post-cold war era could produce peace in Afghanistan where deep local ethnic or religious divisions existed. Although the Soviets completed the withdrawal of their troops from Afghanistan in February 1989, the Mujahideen rebels refused to accept the offer of a coalition government and UN supervised elections, and continued their fight to overthrow the Soviet-installed government. Mindful of Washington's decade long support of the rebels, the Bush administration argued that the communist government should step down before the elections. When that did not occur, the United States continued to send annually about $300 million in economic and military aid to the Mujahideen, while the Soviets maintained their airlift of military supplies to the Kabul government. Deep disagreements over strategy and sectarian divisions among Islamic fundamentalists divided the rebels and frustrated the efforts of peace makers.

By mid-1991 developments in the Middle East, Eastern Europe, and in the Soviet Union caused Washington and Moscow to reconsider their support of favored Afghan groups. The Bush administration did not include in its proposed 1992 budget any funds for the Afghan rebels, and a Soviet Union beset by internal turmoil had few resources to send to the Afghan government. In September, a Soviet government, shaken by an attempted coup (p. 172) agreed with the United States to halt all arms sales to Afghanistan factions. The Afghan government then offered to negotiate an end to the civil war, but rebel leaders with a large stockpile of weapons, sensing a weakened enemy, rejected the proposal. But early in February 1992 three moderate Afghan rebel groups accepted a United Nations peace proposal. When Pakistan, the chief supplier of arms to the radical Islamic rebel groups, also backed the UN plan, Washington promised its support.

NEW DEVILS AND NEW CRUSADES

Many thoughtful observers of the human experience from the Crusades to the late twentieth century have noted the individual and group need for a devil. Perhaps no one expressed this more perceptively than the Renaissance political philosopher Niccolo Machiavelli, who in the sixteenth century wrote, "There are many who think that a wise prince ought, when he has the chance, to foment astutely some enmity, so that by suppressing it he will augment his greatness." In modern times one finds many examples of the masses coerced in a dictatorship that uses devils or scapegoats, but wooed in a democracy by appeals to their faith and patriotism to make sacrifices to fight a wicked enemy. Some have even suggested that leaders in democratic nations often decide that war against a foe, repeatedly portrayed as an evil threat, can distract the people from serious problems at home. Critics of U.S. foreign policy since World War II have pointed to U.S. invasions of the Dominican Republic in 1965 (p. 64) and Grenada in 1983 (p. 144), as well as to the armed attack against Libya in 1986 (p. 139), the Korean War (p. 37), and the Vietnam War (p. 86) as examples of the use of a devil by U.S. political leaders to gain popular support. Defenders of U.S. policy in each instance have denounced such an interpretation as cynical, prejudiced, even disloyal, and not based on fact. Two actions in the Bush administration reopened the debate.

Noriega and Operation Just Cause

Late Sunday evening December 17, 1989, President Bush issued a top secret order implementing a carefully designed plan to invade Panama to capture President Manuel Noriega. At 7:00 A.M. on December 20 the president appeared on national TV and radio to inform the American people that at 1:00 A.M. U.S. paratroopers, infantry, and marines had launched a coordinated assault across three fronts in Panama. The chief executive explained that he had taken such action "to protect the lives of American citizens in Panama, and to bring General Noriega to justice in the United States."

This sudden dramatic action, the biggest military operation by U.S. forces since Vietnam, had roots extending back many years. In August 1983, General Manuel Noriega became head of Panama's defense forces and thereby virtual dictator. Since his high school days in the 1950s, Noriega had worked secretly for the CIA providing information and logistic help. After gaining power he continued to cooperate with the CIA and with the U.S. Drug Enforcement Agency (DEA), even receiving a letter of commendation in 1987 from Jack Lawn, head of the DEA. The Panamanian leader also allowed the use of Panama as a base for the Reagan administration's campaigns against the Nicaraguan Sandinistas and El Salvador's rebels. As a reward for his years of assistance the United States, according to federal officials, secretly paid Noriega $322,000.

But there was another side to Noriega—a ruthless, corrupt man-on-the-make who cooperated with Colombian drug traffickers using Panama as a base for transshipments of cocaine to the United States and for laundering money gained from drug sales. In 1987 public protests in Panama accused Noriega of fraud and murder, and demanded that he step down. In February 1988 two federal grand juries in Florida indicted the Panamanian dictator on charges involving drug trafficking. A month later the Reagan administration froze $50 million in Panamanian funds in U.S. banks, and in April imposed economic sanctions on Panama.

Having inherited the Noriega problem, the Bush administration hoped that Panama's elections scheduled for May 7, 1989, would bring a new government to power. However, an electoral tribunal controlled by Noriega annulled the election of opposition leader Guillermo Endara as president. On September 1 the United States severed diplomatic relations with Panama. When Noriega continued to defy Washington and to strengthen his iron grip on the Panamanian people, a small group of Panama Defense Forces staged a revolt on October 9 and attempted to seize headquarters and take Noriega prisoner. But forces loyal to Noriega rescued him and executed the rebels. U.S. forces in Panama failed to help the rebels, and the unfriendly U.S. press once again caricatured Bush as a "wimp."

A determined president now proceeded secretly with a few top advisers and military officers to design specific invasion plans. In anticipation of an impending U.S. response the National Assembly of Panama on December 15 declared the existence of a state of war with the United States. Within 48 hours, Panamanian soldiers killed two U.S. soldiers in different incidents. Although Panama officials called the shootings accidents, President Bush condemned them as "an enormous outrage" and ordered 24,000 U.S. troops into combat to protect the lives of Americans.

U.S. forces in four days crushed Panama's troops that resisted. On January 3, 1990, General Noriega surrendered to U.S. officials, who took him to Miami. There he was arraigned on drug charges and brought to trial in September 1991 and convicted in April 1992. The vast majority of Americans (80 percent according to a Gallup poll) supported Bush's actions. A *New York Times* editorial deemed it "a personal triumph" for the president, and most congressional Democrats remained silent or praised the president. However, few of the nation's allies agreed. The OAS in a 20–1 vote "deeply regretted" the invasion, called by some another case of "gringo imperialism," as a violation of the Rio Treaty of 1947. The UN General Assembly, after the United States with the support of Britain and France vetoed a Security Council motion condemning U.S. action, passed a resolution (75–20 with 39 abstentions) denouncing the invasion as a violation of the UN Charter. On February 14 Washington announced that all of its invasion troops had been withdrawn.

What the U.S. government called Operation Just Cause had come at considerable cost and left serious problems. Twenty-three U.S. servicepeople lost their lives, over 300 were wounded; 50 Panamanian soldiers died, and an estimated 400 were wounded. The military action caused extensive property damage, and opened the way for over $1 billion in looting that followed the collapse of authority throughout Panama. Some confusion exists as to the number of Panamanian civilians killed, although official U.S. military reports estimated 300 to 400. The removal of Noriega failed to stem the drug trade in Panama. One year later, according to both U.S. and Panamanian officials, drug trafficking and money laundering continued unabated and may have increased after the seizure of Noriega. Yet most Americans continued to view favorably the action taken by their government in Panama.

Saddam Hussein and Operation Desert Storm

At 3:00 A.M. Baghdad time on January 17, 1991, squadrons of U.S. and allied planes took off from U.S. naval vessels in the Persian Gulf and bases in Saudi Arabia to attack Iraqi forces in Kuwait and military targets in Iraq. At 9:00 P.M. Washington time on January 16 President Bush on national TV informed the American people that "the world could wait no longer. . . . We will not fail." This resort to force climaxed a decisive change in U.S. policy toward a small Middle East nation.

The United States government had tilted toward Iraq in its 1980–1988 war against Iran because of deep hostility toward the regime of Ayatollah Khomeini and the regime's support of terrorism and anti-Americanism (p. 137). In November 1984, after Iraq expelled the Abu Nidal terrorist gang, the Reagan administration restored diplomatic relations with Iraq for the first time in 17 years. Although some Americans questioned the wisdom of abandoning strict neutrality in the Iraq-Iran conflict, many saw economic opportunity in selling the Iraqi government farm crops, industrial products, and surplus military goods, and in purchasing Iraqi oil.

Even after evidence surfaced following the end of the Iraq–Iran war that Saddam Hussein, president of Iraq, used poison gas against the separatist Kurds, the Bush administration rejected as "not in the national interest" Congressional requests for limited sanctions against Iraq. In 1989 Baghdad bought almost $1 billion of U.S. agricultural products, often at prices 10 to 15 percent above the market price. Furthermore, in the first six months of fiscal 1990 Iraq received $500 million in bank loans guaranteed by the U.S. government. Explaining Bush's position in testimony before a House subcommittee in April 1990, John H. Kelly, Assistant Secretary of State, said, "We are not prepared to see economic and trade sanctions legislatively imposed at this point. . . . A significant effect of suspending our export-promotion programs would be to deny U.S. exporters the ability to compete."

But criticism of Saddam Hussein escalated as stories of his brutal rule and threats against neighbors Israel and Kuwait appeared in the U.S. press. Newspaper accounts repeatedly referred to reports of Hussein's efforts to expand production of chemical weapons and to produce a nuclear weapon. Although the Bush administration condemned such actions by Iraq, it failed to call for any counter measures. The Iraqi leader's words and actions continued to give substance to the charge that he sought to be the dominant power in the Persian Gulf. In April 1990 he threatened to "burn up half of Israel." In July he accused Kuwait of costing Iraq billions in revenue by exceeding OPEC oil production quotas, and he demanded that Kuwait both cancel the $15 billion debt that Iraq owed and surrender specific oil fields to Iraq. Saddam Hussein repeatedly condemned the United States for its support of Israel and Kuwait. Responding to these developments, *U.S. News and World Report* in June featured a cover story characterizing Saddam Hussein as "The World's Most Dangerous Man."

Nevertheless, the Bush administration refused to take a stand against the Iraqi president and routinely approved sales of U.S. arms-related high technology to Iraq. On July 25, 1990, April Glaspie, U.S. Ambassador to Iraq, told Saddam Hussein that "we have no opinion on the Arab–Arab conflicts, like your border disagreement with Kuwait. . . . James Baker has directed our official spokesman to emphasize this instruction." In Washington Secretary of State Baker's chief assistant for the Middle East said that the United States had no obligation to come to Kuwait's aid if that nation were attacked. As Congress debated legislation to cut off $1.2 billion in loan guarantees to Iraq a State Department official said the administration believed "the kinds of legislative measures under consideration would not help us to achieve U.S. goals with Iraq."

At 9:00 P.M. August 1, 1990, President Bush received the startling news that Iraqi troops had swarmed across the Kuwaiti border (2:00 A.M. August 2 Kuwait time). A determined Saddam Hussein, apparently counting on only verbal reaction by Washington, had ordered Iraqi armed forces to seize control of Kuwait. At a news conference early the next day Bush called Iraq's action "naked aggression" and ordered tough economic sanctions. Although Congress voted to support sanctions, some members criticized the administration for failure to act earlier. Senator Alfonse D'Amato (R., N.Y.), normally a strong supporter of Bush, pointed out that the State Department had been "mollycoddling" and "appeasing" Saddam Hussein. On the same day in an emergency session the UN Security Council, whose support Washington now eagerly sought—in contrast to its opposition to any UN Council action in response to the invasion of Panama—voted 14–0 (Yemen abstained) condemning the invasion of Kuwait and demanding unconditional immediate withdrawal of all Iraqi forces from Kuwait.

As Saddam Hussein's troops quickly completed their conquest of Kuwait, U.S. intelligence officials on August 3 reported a buildup of Iraqi military forces on the Kuwait border with Saudi Arabia. A disturbed President Bush asserted: "This will not stand. This will not stand, this aggression against Kuwait." Washington proceeded to put together an unusual coalition of 27 nations that included long-time allies of the European Community, Cold War adversaries such as the Soviet Union, thirteen nations of the Arab League, and Israel. Administration officials, under the president's skillful direction, convinced the UN Security Council in late August to vote 13–0 to authorize enforcement of economic sanctions against Iraq until it withdrew its military forces from Kuwait.

The White House also ordered Operation Desert Shield—a major deployment of U.S. troops and jet fighters to Saudi Arabia to protect it from an "imminent threat" by Iraqi forces. Comparing Saddam Hussein to Adolf Hitler, Bush emphasized that American forces were sent for "defensive reasons" and that "a line has been drawn in the sand." To silence domestic critics, who claimed that Washington had not made clear why the defense of Saudi Arabia was of "vital interest" to the United States, the president explained:

> Our action in the Gulf is about fighting aggression and preserving the sovereignty of nations. . . . It is about our own national security interests and ensuring the peace and stability of the world.
> We are also talking about maintaining access to energy resources that are key—not just to the functioning of this country but to the entire world.

Public opinion polls indicated that most Americans supported their president's actions and strategy, but that a majority favored a diplomatic rather than a military solution to the crisis. Although Congress also backed the steps taken by Bush, members of both parties urged the administration to persuade allies to share the burden.

A war of words, maneuver, and counter-maneuver continuing throughout the autumn of 1990 raised the anxieties of the American people and their allies. The Iraqi leader gave no signs that he would withdraw. After Secretary of Defense Cheney stated that the United States had drawn up plans to strike targets inside Iraq if provoked, Iraqi leaders warned of possible terrorist attacks against U.S. troops. In appeals for Arab support Iraqi radio broadcasts portrayed the American soldier as a foreign invader breaking Arab laws and traditions by "drinking alcohol, eating pork, and practicing prostitution." President Bush responded by videotaping an address to the Iraqi people warning them that Iraq was "on the brink of war. . . . There is no way Iraq can win."

Meanwhile each side built up its military strength in the area. The U.S. Defense Department estimated in late September that Iraq had sent 360,000 soldiers to Kuwait. By mid-October the United States had 200,000 troops in the Gulf region. However, other nations in the alliance against Iraq failed to furnish many soldiers (Britain 6,000 and France 13,000 by mid-October), and contributed funds to defray costs of the operation far short of what many members of Congress thought appropriate.

The military buildup and bellicose statements by administration officials increased the fears of some Americans that their government might resort to the use of force to resolve the crisis. Such a possibility also disturbed many members of Congress who contended that Article I, Section 8 of the federal constitution specifically grants to Congress the power to declare war. Bush heated up the debate late in October when he stated: "History is replete with examples where the president has had to take action. I've done this in the past and certainly would have no hesitancy at all." Representatives of both political parties urged that he confer with Congress before sending troops into action and reminded the president that the American people opposed war. Whereas, according to polls, three out of four Americans supported the use of economic sanctions, less than a majority favored the use of military force against Iraq. The White House faced the problem of scaring Iraq into withdrawing from Kuwait without frightening the American people and Congress into demanding a peaceful compromise solution.

Concerned that sanctions and the defensive military forces already in place might not convince Saddam Hussein to withdraw from Kuwait, the Bush administration decided to increase the military pressure. Two days after the November elections the president announced a decision, made several days earlier, that U.S. troops would not be rotated until the crisis ended and that the size of the U.S. military force in the Gulf region would be increased "to ensure that the coalition has an adequate offensive military option." Thus the White House acknowledged for the first time that the U.S. military presence in the desert was not purely defensive.

Rejecting the testimony of respected former cabinet members, national security advisers, and two ex-chairmen of the Joint Chiefs of Staff, who argued that sanctions and diplomacy should be given a fair chance over a much longer period, Bush decided that the United States should obtain coalition agreement on a specific date for Iraq to withdraw or face expulsion by force. After vigorous lobbying by Washington the UN Security Council on November 29 voted 12–2 (China abstained, Yemen and Cuba opposed) to authorize the use of force to free Kuwait if Saddam Hussein did not withdraw his forces by January 15, 1991.

To appear willing to give diplomacy a chance, Bush offered 15 dates over the next three weeks for Secretary of State Baker to meet with Iraqi officials. When the Iraqis held out for January 12 as the only convenient date Washington rejected it as too close to the United Nations deadline. Meanwhile, three days of intensive lobbying by Bush and administration officials convinced Congress to authorize the president "to use United States armed forces pursuant to United Nations Security Council Resolution 678." Reflecting the widespread opposition throughout the nation to the use of force, the Senate approved the measure by a narrow 52–47 vote while the House voted in favor 250–183, with most of the dissenters being Democrats. Last-minute efforts by the UN Secretary-General and by the French government to achieve a peaceful settlement failed. On January 14 the Iraq parliament voted unanimously to fight rather than withdraw Iraqi forces from Kuwait.

In Operation Desert Storm allied planes and missiles pounded military targets in Iraq and Kuwait around the clock as ground forces assembled in Saudi Arabia. U.S. military spokespersons carefully managed all reporting of the war in order to guarantee that only positive accounts reached American eyes and ears. The public experienced no ambiguity, as during the Vietnam War, about the rightness of the nation's cause and the soundness of the tactics and strategy employed by its military leaders. The skill and bravery of U.S. fighting forces and the awesome, sophisticated military technology used by the allies appeared on TV each day in carefully censored vignettes. The fact that no draft existed and that for the first time in a war involving U.S. forces in the twentieth century only professional, all-volunteer personnel, both men and women, participated also reduced public opposition. A Gallup poll taken on the first day of the war indicated that 79 percent of the American people supported the decision for war. A rash of yellow ribbons prominently exhibited in every community, and patriotic stickers on motor vehicles, testified to the fact that most Americans backed the war effort.

After more than five weeks of air attacks failed to move Iraqi forces out of Kuwait, President Bush, having rejected Gorbachev's proposed mediation, secured allied approval to send Saddam Hussein an ultimatum. On February 22 Bush gave Iraq a deadline of noon the next day to begin a withdrawal to be completed within seven days or face an allied ground attack. When the Iraqi leader used delaying tactics as he tried to negotiate favorable peace terms with help of the Soviet Union, the allied ground assault began on February 24. One hundred hours later Bush halted the ground war and declared, "Kuwait is liberated" and "Iraq's army is defeated." An elated president also revealed a major reason for the war when he said: "It's a proud day for America and, by God, we've kicked the Vietnam syndrome once and for all." Incredibly low U.S. casualties—only 79 reported combat deaths—the humiliating withdrawal of Iraqi forces from Kuwait, the sharing of the war's cost (allies pledged $54 billion out of an estimated $61 billion total cost and furnished about 25 percent of the armed forces), pride in U.S. technology, and the demonstration that the United States was now the world's number one military power contributed to an immediate postwar euphoria.

Some Americans, however, began to worry about unforeseen consequences of the war. Burning oil fields in Kuwait, deliberately set afire by Iraqi forces, threatened severe ecological damage. Although a U.S. Air Force postwar survey of Iraq indicated that up to 70 percent of U.S. bombs had missed intended targets, a United Nations survey team concluded that in Iraq "most means of modern life support have been destroyed or rendered tenuous." Hundreds of Iraqi civilians had lost their lives in allied bombing attacks, and death by starvation or disease threatened thousands. In addition, the persecuted Kurds and Shiites of Iraq, encouraged by President Bush and allied leaders to revolt, faced ruthless suppression by Saddam Hussein's loyal military forces withheld from war combat. Fearing the breakup of Iraq and consequent instability in the region, U.S. policymakers ruled out military action to aid those rebelling against Saddam Hussein. Not only had the Iraqi leader survived the war and retained power, but evidence mounted that he had acquired most, if not all, the essentials for making nuclear weapons. A *Washington Post*-ABC News poll of April 3 indicated that 55 percent of those polled believed that the United States should have not have ended the war with Saddam Hussein still in power. Many wondered why their government left in control of Iraq a man portrayed as such a villain and the antithesis of all democratic institutions and values.

After the UN Security Council early in April passed a cease-fire resolution to stop Iraq's campaign against Kurdish and Shiite refugees, Bush agreed to airlift food and nonmilitary aid to them and ordered battalions of Marines to help them settle in northern Iraq. Saddam Hussein responded by accepting the terms of the United Nations cease-fire resolution. Within a month the U.S. military began to turn the supervision of the Kurdish refugee camps over to UN teams, and by mid-July all U.S. and allied troops had withdrawn. But President Bush and the United Nations would maintain sanctions against Iraq until the destruction of its ability to produce nuclear weapons and the replacement of Saddam Hussein.

DESIGNING A NEW WORLD ORDER

In his address informing the American people of the beginning of the air war against Iraq in January 1991 President Bush suggested, "We have before us the opportunity to forge for ourselves and for future generations a new world order, a world where the rule of law, not the law of the jungle, governs the conduct of nations." Support for the president's [goal] appeared in the unique composition of the alliance assembled under the UN to force Iraq to withdraw from Kuwait. That alliance, backed by the USSR, testified to the end of the East-West, Communist-anticommunist division of the Cold War era. The fact that Arab nations, notably Syria and Egypt, rejected Saddam Hussein's appeals and supported the UN alliance in an action that would benefit Israel also gave promise of a new era. Immediately after the war administration leaders moved to promote a new world order whereby any aggressor anywhere in the world faced overwhelming opposition.

In Quest of Peace in the Mideast

In March 1991 President Bush called for Israel to give up Arab lands occupied since 1967 in return for peace based on earlier UN Security Council resolutions. Secretary of State Baker made several trips to the Middle East to arrange a peace conference involving Syria, Lebanon, Jordan, and the Palestinians. Meanwhile the Israeli government persisted in constructing settlements in the occupied West Bank region to house Jewish immigrants from the Soviet Union. President Bush pressured Israel to stop such action and to participate in a peace conference by asking Congress to defer action on Israel's request for U.S. guarantees on $10 billion in loans. Baker eventually persuaded the five parties to convene in Madrid on October 30, 1991. Although the six-day Madrid Conference produced no agreement on divisive issues it set the stage for subsequent meetings by bringing the long-time enemies together in face-to-face for the first time since Israel's creation in 1948.

The Bush administration also acted to secure the Middle East against possible future aggression such as that launched by Saddam Hussein. The White House initiated negotiations with Saudi Arabia for developing a new security alliance patterned after NATO to protect the vital oil-producing regions of the Middle East. The Defense Department's proposal to place large stockpiles of weapons and station U.S. military personnel in Saudi Arabia led to the latter's demand that the United States provide training for Saudi military forces and arms to equip an offensive army. Although reluctant to build up a Saudi military force capable of offensive action, Washington in November 1991 waived its embargo on arms sales to the Middle East by agreeing to sell Saudi Arabia more than $3 billion of Patriot air defense missiles. But long standing ethnic and religious rivalries in the region imposed formidable obstacles to the establishment of a Mideast defense alliance.

Promoting Peace and Progress in Europe

The collapse of communism in Eastern Europe in 1989 stimulated sharp debates in Western Europe and the United States as to the validity of arguments justifying the continuation of NATO as a guarantee against aggression. Some leaders of the European Community (12 nations of western Europe) saw a political union combined with a single trading market and monetary union as the surest road to peace and prosperity for its 340 million citizens. To free Europe from its dependence on the United States for security, they advocated an independent defense and military policy based on a European "rapid reaction force." In order to prevent total disintegration of the Soviet Union and its retreat to authoritarian rule, some European leaders, notably Chancellor Helmut Kohl of Germany, also urged large amounts of economic aid to the Soviet Union and its eventual membership in the European Community. They envisioned a united, free Europe as the centerpiece of a new world order.

Sensitive to possible adverse consequences of European economic unity on the U.S. economy, and worried about security risks in an unstable Eastern Europe, the Bush administration defended continuation of NATO and suggested possible expansion of this successful collective security organization to include additional European nations. Washington also took the position that Soviet policies designed to achieve a free market must be in operation before the United States granted large amounts of economic aid. Proceeding cautiously, the administration in June 1991 approved both a temporary waiver of trade restrictions against the Soviet Union and $1.5 billion in loan guarantees to Soviet agriculture.

The cause of peace received a great boost when nine years of START negotiations finally produced the first agreement by the two rivals to make specific reductions in their nuclear arms arsenals. Gorbachev, under great pressure to improve domestic economic conditions by reducing military expenditures and gaining more U.S. aid, agreed to cut the Soviet nuclear stockpile from 10,846 warheads and bombs to 8,040 by destruction of 2,806 weapons. For its part the Bush administration agreed to destroy 1,686 weapons in reducing its nuclear arsenal from 12,081 to 10,395. At the Moscow Summit Meeting the two leaders signed the historic agreement on July 31, 1991. Bush then told Gorbachev that he would support most favored nation (MFN) trade status for the Soviet Union in U.S. markets. The president explained that "We want to ensure that our economic relationship expands as quickly as your reforms permit."

The Dissolution of the USSR and New Problems

Having based its Soviet policy on the assumption that Gorbachev would continue to lead a united Soviet Union, the Bush administration found itself caught with a potentially serious problem in mid-August 1991 when a small junta of high military, civilian, and KGB officials in the USSR staged a coup by placing Gorbachev under house arrest and moving to seize control of the Kremlin. Washington immediately suspended its economic aid programs and applauded Boris Yeltsin, president of the Russian Republic, who defied the junta and inspired hundreds of thousands in other Soviet republics to stand up against the coup.

The collapse of the coup after three days left the Soviet Union facing disintegration into separate republics, each independent and sovereign. The three Baltic republics declared their independence, and demands rose in many of the remaining 12 republics for far-reaching political and economic changes to replace the discredited communist system. President Bush responded to the triumph of the Soviet people over the hard-line communists who backed the coup by restoring agricultural loans and urging Congress not to overturn his grant of MFN status to Moscow. He also, after a delay of several days, gave full diplomatic recognition to the Baltic republics, as did the Soviets shortly thereafter. Secretary of State Baker on a trip to Moscow in September indicated that Washington intended to drop its insistence on clear evidence of a free-market economy in operation before extending economic aid.

Western leaders worried that the destruction of central authority in the Soviet Union meant that no one person or responsible group controlled all the nuclear weapons in place in several different republics. This concern over the security of Soviet nuclear weapons motivated President Bush to make a startling, unilateral move in late September 1991. On prime-time TV he announced that he would order "that the United States eliminate its entire worldwide inventory of ground-launched short range . . . nuclear weapons." In addition, the president promised to remove all tactical nuclear weapons on U.S. planes and ships, cancelled the mobile-based MX, and called all long-range U.S. bombers off 24-hour alerts. Soviet leaders had long pressed for the elimination of tactical nuclear weapons, and since they had withdrawn their military forces from east Europe, Bush saw no further need for the United States to maintain nuclear weapons in Europe.

Gorbachev called Bush's action "positive, very positive," and declared it a product of the "new thinking" he introduced into Soviet policy. A few days later he announced sweeping cuts in both tactical and strategic nuclear weapons and suggested that both sides remove nuclear missiles from all short- and medium-range military aircraft. The American people gave enthusiastic endorsement to these historic steps by the two leaders that promised peace and the diminution of the threat of nuclear holocaust.

Late in 1991 crucial decisions faced the United States as the central authority, notably the Communist party and KGB, that held together twelve diverse republics of the Soviet Union, collapsed. A worried Congress in November passed a Soviet aid package, that included the transfer of up to $500M from the Pentagon budget, to dismantle Soviet nuclear weapons based in the republics. To help forestall widespread famine in the coming winter, the Bush administration announced that it would send about $1.5 billion worth of food directly to Soviet republics. The White House also sent a strong message to the Kremlin and to leaders in the republics when on November 27, five days before a scheduled referendum on independence in Ukraine, administration officials revealed to the press that President Bush would recognize that republic's independence after it satisfied American concerns about human rights and arms control. This marked a dramatic reversal of Bush's statement during his August 1, 1991, visit to Kiev, the capital of Ukraine, warning against "suicidal nationalism."

In December, the presidents of the three republics—Russia, Ukraine, Belarus—that had established the Soviet Union in 1922 announced the end of the Soviet Union as "a subject of international law and a geopolitical reality." They proclaimed a new Commonwealth of Independent States and urged the remaining 9 republics to join. Washington responded by recognizing the Commonwealth and establishing diplomatic relations with Russia and 5 other republics as independent sovereign nations. President Bush said that the United States would establish diplomatic relations with the other 6 republics when they had made "commitments to responsible security policies and democratic principles." Although delighted with the demise of their long-time adversary, Americans remained anxious about the control of the former Soviet military forces and some 27,000 nuclear weapons in 4 republics. The Bush administration immediately sought guarantees that civil conflict within a republic or between republics would not result in the use of nuclear weapons.

Several dramatic developments in the next few weeks relieved U.S. anxieties. After Gorbachev resigned as president of the Soviet Union on December 25, he signed over the nuclear missile launching codes to Boris Yeltsin, president of Russia. The former Soviet republics then agreed that each could form a separate military force and keep nuclear weapons under a single command. Washington reacted by supporting Russia's takeover of the permanent UN Security Council seat of the Soviet Union and full membership of Russia and five other republics in the International Monetary Fund (IMF) and World Bank. In January 1992, President Bush urged Congress to approve $645 million in new aid for Russia and the other republics. The administration also proposed in its budget for the fiscal year 1993 a reduction of $10 billion in military spending, which included cancellation of production of long-range nuclear weapons originally designed to counter a Soviet threat. President Yeltsin reacted by outlining sharp arms cutbacks and plans to reduce strategic arsenals to levels well below those required by existing treaties. Then, in a speech to the UN Security Council on January 31, 1992, Yeltsin announced that he considered the United States and the West "not as mere partners but as allies." A new era beckoned.

PROBLEMS IN EAST ASIA

Washington's efforts to encourage development of a free and peaceful new order in Europe and in the Middle East did not lessen concerns about U.S. interests in other regions of the world. Trends in economic relations with Japan during the Reagan years and the growing challenge of China and Japan to U.S. influence in East Asia stirred some Americans to urge reexaminations of policies toward the nations of the Pacific Rim. Dramatic events in China early in the Bush administration led to vigorous debate over U.S. actions in East Asia.

Tensions in Relations with China

In early June 1989 the Chinese government's brutal suppression of mass protests by Chinese students and workers in Tiananmen Square in Beijing posed new problems for American policymakers. Eager to maintain strategic and economic relations carefully cultivated since Nixon's reestablishment of relations in 1972, and yet aware of the American people's dismay at the Chinese communist leaders' violation of basic human rights, the Bush administration proceeded cautiously. The president condemned the use of force against unarmed citizens, suspended all U.S. sales of weapons to the People's Republic of China, and persuaded the World Bank to postpone consideration of a new loan to China, but he did not stop Americans from trading with the Chinese. In July, Bush secretly sent two trusted advisers to Beijing to register the administration's opposition to the violent actions against peaceful demonstrations and to urge respect for human rights. No favorable response ensued.

Many Americans, distressed by scenes of horror in Beijing presented by U.S. television and by the refusal of Chinese officials to curtail their brutal policies, called on Washington to break all political and economic relations with China. Congress quickly passed legislation extending the visas of 40,000 Chinese students in U.S. colleges and universities afraid to return home. President Bush, however, vetoed the bill, and again sent his two advisers to Beijing to encourage Chinese leaders to modify their actions toward their own citizens. The White House also resisted pressure to suspend China's most favored nation (MFN) trade status, and congressional leaders failed to muster the votes necessary to overturn the president's action. In defense of his policies Bush pointed out that the Chinese "have a strategic position in the world that is important to us. . . . I do not want to isolate the Chinese people."

As a result of the continuation of trade on a most favored nation basis Chinese exports to the United States in 1989 rose 42 percent to a record $12 billion, and U.S. exports to China increased to $5.8 billion. That several American businesses profited from this trade influenced the president in May 1990 to renew China's MFN status despite strong opposition in Congress. The issue of renewal of MFN for China sparked sharp debate again in the spring of 1991. President Bush reminded the nation that many Americans benefited from trade with China and that Beijing had supported the allied cause in the Gulf War by abstaining from voting in the Security Council against the UN authorization for the use of force against Iraq. In neither year could congressional opponents of MFN agree on legislation making MFN contingent on China's guaranteeing basic rights to all its citizens.

The Bush administration applied pressure to encourage Chinese officials to abandon several objectionable practices. American spokespeople repeatedly denounced China's high tariff on imports competing with its domestically produced goods—an action contributing to an unfavorable balance of trade for the United States with China that reached $10.4 billion in 1990. Administration officials also condemned China's export of goods made by prison labor and Beijing's sale of missiles and nuclear technology to North Korea, Syria, Pakistan, Iran, and Algeria. In November 1991 Secretary of State Baker journeyed to China and informed its leaders that "the United States cannot turn a blind eye toward . . . human suffering or political repression." Baker's efforts failed to secure any promise to ease suppression of human rights, but Chinese officials indicated a willingness to allow some dissidents to leave the country and to cooperate in the international effort to control the proliferation of missile and nuclear technology. When the Chinese failed to modify their trade practices and piracy of U.S. patented inventions, U.S. trade representative Carla A. Hills recommended that Washington impose trade sanctions in 1992. Publication of a list of restricted imports that might be subjected to a 100 percent tariff aroused protests in both countries, and the effort failed. Forcing the communist leaders of China to conform to America's wishes proved to be a most difficult task.

Challenges from Japan

The amazing economic growth of Japan during the 1970s and 1980s threatened its harmonious relations with the United States. Many Americans believed that Japan progressed at America's expense. As evidence they pointed to their nation's unfavorable balance of trade with Japan. Totaling $43.5 billion in the five years 1975–1979, the unfavorable balance skyrocketed to $56.3 billion in 1987 alone, and totaled over $400 billion in the decade of the 1980s. U.S. critics of Japan also warned of the threat of large increases in Japanese investments in the United States (see p. 202). Some Americans also complained that although Japan paid a major part of the cost of maintaining a U.S. military force of 60,000 in Japan in 1988, Tokyo contributed little to mutual security interests worldwide. Bashing Japan became popular in America's business and political communities. As pressures mounted for the federal government to induce Japan to stop discriminatory import practices and the dumping of manufactured goods at discounted prices, Congress in 1988 passed the Omnibus Trade and Competitiveness Act. This law empowered the executive branch, after identifying unfair trade barriers, to negotiate their removal within 18 months. If negotiation failed the president could impose sanctions.

As domestic complaints about Japan's economic policies intensified the Bush administration turned to the Trade Act of 1988 to pressure Japan. U.S. trade representative Carla Hills on May 25, 1989, released a list of Japanese products that could face 100 percent duties. After President Bush cited Japan for placing unfair trade barriers on imports Tokyo agreed to participate in trade talks. When Prime Minister Toshiki Kaifu visited Washington late in August Bush warned him that negotiations must lead to significant changes by April 1990, or the U.S. government would be under pressure to retaliate. Four rounds of talks finally produced in April a modest package of concessions that enabled Bush to drop Japan from the list of unfair trading partners. A fifth and final round of negotiations ended in June 1990 with promises by each side to deal with their own economic shortcomings and to enable U.S. goods and services to compete fairly in the Japanese market.

Although the U.S. trade deficit with Japan in 1990 fell to $41.1 billion, the lowest in six years, the criticism of Japan did not subside. Some Americans believed that Japan, heavily dependent on mideast oil, should have contributed more than its pledge of $9 billion to defray the military costs of the Gulf War. When Tokyo forced the U.S. Rice Council to withdraw its exhibition from an international food fair in Japan in March 1991 a new round of "bashing" Japan followed. Frequent meetings of high officials of the two governments in subsequent months produced courteous exchanges but no substantive agreements to alleviate the anxiety of many Americans.

As the U.S. economic recession worsened and public opinion polls indicated that a majority of Americans believed President Bush was more concerned with foreign affairs than with the nation's economic problems, the administration acted before the presidential primary election campaign heated up. On December 30, 1991, Bush embarked on a 12-day visit to four Asian nations seeking to ease trade barriers and thereby increase U.S. exports and create "jobs, jobs, jobs."

After visits to Australia, Singapore, and South Vietnam, Bush—

accompanied by 21 executives of major U.S. corporations, including the presidents of General Motors, Ford, and Chrysler—spent three days attempting to convince Japanese officials to take concrete steps to reduce Japan's trade surplus with the United States. Although the heads of the three U.S. automakers and five representatives of the Japanese auto industry found few points of agreement, Bush and Prime Minister Kiichi Miyazawe pledged to "work together to maintain world peace and security, promote development of the world economy, support the world-wide trend toward democratization and market-oriented economies and meet new international challenges." The Japanese did agree to buy more U.S. cars and $10 billion more in auto parts in 1992—a pledge belittled by U.S. auto officials as "woefully inadequate and embarrassing."

A flood of sharp comments followed in each country. Each blamed the other country for the problems facing the U.S. economy. The speaker of Japan's lower house of parliament said that "the source of the problem is the inferior quality of U.S. labor." He called U.S. workers "lazy" and claimed that one-third of them "cannot even read." Some Americans responded with angry criticisms of the Japanese and demands that Washington restrict Japanese imports. Others acknowledged that the problem evolved largely because of the short-sightedness of U.S. corporate management and the failure to insist on producing quality products. Most Americans agreed that the federal government needed to act to strengthen the domestic economy. Being the top military power in the post-cold war world seemed less important than being number one at maintaining the economic and social well-being of U.S. citizens.

A NEW ERA

In the 1992 presidential primary, candidates of both major political parties emphasized the need for the federal government to shift from preoccupation with foreign policy to increased action on domestic problems. The American people faced a world without a powerful enemy possessing the military potential to threaten or to ignite a major conflict. Such previously identified devils as Castro, Qaddafi, and Saddam Hussein survived in a seriously weakened condition. The major international challenges in the final years of the twentieth century involved furnishing aid and hope "as an international angel of mercy" to Third World peoples deprived and oppressed by terroristic military regimes, encouraging the peaceful resolution of long-standing ethnic and religious conflicts, and assisting the peoples of the former Soviet Union to make the transition to democracy and a free economy.

In this changing world, many saw the original vision of the founders of the United Nations as realistic. The success of the UN coalition in the Gulf War of 1991 and the death of the Soviet Union encouraged the members of the Security

Council in January 1992 to agree to respond to possible "new risks for stability and security" by authorizing the secretary-general to make "recommendations on ways of strengthening and making more efficient . . . the capacity of the United Nations for preventive diplomacy, for peacemaking and for peacekeeping." No longer would a single nation or an alliance of a few nations have the awesome responsibilities they bore since the end of World War II.

CHAPTER 7

Prosperity and Its Limits

"Practical men, who believe themselves to be quite exempt from any intellectual influences, are usually the slaves of some defunct economist."
John Maynard Keynes,
The General Theory of
Employment, Interest
and Money

In the last months of 1945, troop ships docking in U.S. ports deposited thousands of soldiers at discharge centers. They filled out forms, and quickly changed back into civilians, headed home on the first train they could find. Within a year after Hiroshima, the size of the armed forces fell from 12 million to 3 million. These men and women returned to the richest and most powerful economic state in the history of civilization.

This U.S. horn of plenty contrasted dramatically with the rest of the world, including other advanced industrial countries whose economies had been crippled by wartime devastation. The war had cut the Soviet Union's productive capacity by 40 percent. Germany's and Japan's steel industries had been reduced to rubble. Many Europeans lived on fewer than 1,500 calories a day, and starvation was epidemic in Asia. Even in 1947, when European industrial reconstruction was well under way, the United States produced 57 percent of the world's steel, 43 percent of its electricity, and 62 percent of its oil.

Before the outbreak of war, the Roosevelt administration's New Deal policies—including social security payments, farm price supports, a minimum wage, and rural electrification had supported the concept that the federal government had some responsibility for the welfare of individual citizens. Federal attempts to stimulate investment, employment, and consumption, from the National Industrial Recovery Act to work-relief programs such as the Works Progress Administration (WPA), bolstered the morale of the unemployed and anticipated the active management of the economy after 1945. But the New Deal failed to bring general prosperity or get rid of high unemployment rates. In 1941, almost 10 percent of the labor force was still out of work.

Federal demand for military equipment and supplies and the contracts the government made with private corporations to obtain them, more than New Deal policies, ended the Great Depression. The steel industry, which produced an average of 22 million tons a year between 1931 and 1935, expanded its output to 90 million tons by 1944. Allied need for war matériel led to rapid advances in productive capabilities. At the height of the war, for example, the Kaiser shipyards in California could turn out a fully outfitted warship *every day*. The U.S. gross national product (GNP)—the total dollar value of goods and services produced in a given year—doubled from $100 billion in 1940 to over $210 billion in 1945.

The cost of fighting the war forced sharp upward revisions of the income tax. But in spite of higher taxes government expenditures far exceeded tax income. Between 1938 and 1944 federal tax revenues rose from $7 billion in 1938 to $40 billion in 1944—but during the same period federal expenses jumped from $8 to $100 billion. Consequently, the U.S. government turned toward vigorous deficit financing after 1941, a policy that Franklin Roosevelt and his advisers had used most reluctantly as a means of stimulating the economy during the 1930s. The United States issued short- and long-term bonds on its credit, in other words borrowed from individuals and businesses, to make up the difference between tax receipts and total expenses. Because of deficit financing, the country's national debt rose to about $280 billion by the end of the war, nearly six times what it had been at the time of Pearl Harbor.

As public and private demand for manufactured goods increased in the early 1940s, military service siphoned millions of workers out of the labor market. Suddenly, especially in occupations that required skill or technical knowledge, the labor surplus of the Great Depression turned into a severe labor shortage. In 1933, a quarter of the labor force was out of work. Ten years later, the unemployment rate had dropped to just over 1 percent, spawning a demand for labor strong enough to propel large numbers of women and black people into industrial jobs for the first time. Wages and salaries increased; most workers could count on overtime pay if they wanted to work more than 40 hours a week. Business enjoyed rising profits. Because of pressure to produce larger quantities of goods more quickly, factories tried to introduce more efficient managerial methods, assembly techniques, and machinery.

During peacetime prosperity, businesses ordinarily direct some of their high profits toward capital purchases—new and more equipment, offices, factories, and inventories. For their part, families take paychecks to buy consumer goods that they need or want and possibly could not earlier afford. During the 1930s businesses put off expansion or replacement of their plants and machinery because of declining sales and the uncertain future. In the same way, families with lower incomes "made do" with aging clothing, appliances, automobiles, and housing.

In the early 1940s, U.S. resources, as plentiful as they were, had limits; and until Allied victory, production of military necessities came first. Businesses channeled resources toward tanks and artillery instead of such goods as refrigerators and houses. Civilians with the disposable income to buy products they had foregone during the depression now ran up against shortages and rationing. In 1943 and 1944 fewer than a thousand passenger cars were manufactured for domestic use each year. Still, increasing jobs and profits during World War II meant that many Americans ate better, wore finer clothing, and had more money for recreation than they had during the 1929–1941 depression.

A large portion of the wartime income of businesses and families could not be spent on goods they needed, so both increased their savings—in the form of bank accounts, payroll savings bonds, and other government securities. These savings created a reservoir of purchasing power while helping to pay for war costs. At the end of the war, these savings together with pent-up capital and consumer demand heralded a 25-year period of vast prosperity.

THE POSTWAR ECONOMY

Prosperity and Pessimism

In 1945, the United States enjoyed an abundance of resources—food, energy, industrial plant, trained workers—unmatched in the world. In contrast to the economic wreckage abroad, the war had reactivated the U.S. economy. Seemingly unlimited reserves of oil and coal made fuel for industry, transportation, and heating extremely cheap. Industries such as aviation and electronics were still in their infancy.

Nonetheless, most business and labor union leaders, government officials, and economists had pessimistic views about the immediate economic future. The conventional wisdom held that depression would return as the federal government cancelled war contracts while millions of ex-soldiers looked for jobs and workers in defense industries were being laid off. In August 1945, the Office of War Mobilization and Reconversion forecast unemployment as high as 8 million, or 15 percent of the labor force, by the following spring. The fresh memory of the 1930s obscured the more serious problem of the postwar years: what to do about rising prices and demand for consumer goods in short supply.

The Employment Act

Laissez-faire, the concept that government should not regulate, subsidize, or interfere with private enterprise, had been on the wane in the United States since the time of the Civil War, even though "free enterprise" and "market economy" remained slogans for those who would minimize state regulation of the economy. In 1945, the expansion of federal power during the previous 12 years made many Republican leaders anxious to reduce the tendency toward centralized economic planning and "regimentation" that marked the New Deal and war years. To try to prevent a postwar downswing, President Truman and his advisers sought legislation to use the government's fiscal powers (its ability to raise funds through taxation or borrowing and its ability to reallocate and redistribute wealth as it buys goods or makes welfare payments) and monetary powers (its ability to regulate the amount of currency and credit).

Even free-enterprise Republicans in Congress, worried by the prospect of postwar depression, supported the Employment Act. Passed in February 1946, this act extended the government's economic responsibility *in behalf of* the private sector. According to the act,

> the Congress hereby declares that it is the continuing policy and responsibility of the federal government to use all practicable means consistent with its needs and obligations . . . in a manner calculated to foster and promote free competitive enterprise and the general welfare, conditions under which there will be afforded useful employment opportunities . . . and to promote maximum employment, production, and purchasing power.

The Employment Act stated goals rather than policy. But it made explicit the proposition that the federal government should ensure economic conditions to provide jobs and promote, if not guarantee, the social welfare of private citizens. The Employment Act made the president the chief economic manager of the nation, advised by a three-person Council of Economic advisers, obliged to submit an annual economic report to Congress to describe the current state of the economy and to make appropriate recommendations for the future. The act, in sentiment, confirmed the economic activity of the New Deal and implied that the Keynesian economics developed at Cambridge University in the 1920s and 1930s should be taken as a standard theory against which future public policy must be tested.

Keynesian Economics

John Maynard Keynes, a British economist, became a prominent economic voice in Great Britain after his brilliant and prophetic opposition to the vindictive, economically crippling Treaty of Versailles following World War I. Keynes argued for a government-dominated capitalism. Holding that the fiscal and monetary instruments of a government give it the power to counteract sharp downward cycles in the private sector of the economy, Keynes called for government intervention in the economic cycle. His viewpoint attacked the prevailing assumption of Keynes's generation—that capitalism, because of competition and self-interest, had a natural tendency to correct market imbalances.

According to Keynes, capitalism was not self-regulating. Supply and demand, prices and wages, savings and investment, he said, did not necessarily move toward an equilibrium that benefited the largest number of buyers and sellers, workers and consumers, families and businesses. Keynes maintained that during depressions, private capital investment might not take place even when funds could be borrowed at very low interest rates. Declining consumer demand could reduce profits or profit expectations to a point where investor ability and willingness to buy new or more equipment could dry up. Thus, said Keynes, both private investment and business activity could fall toward zero and not be able to revive themselves.

Keynes believed that the level of consumer spending determined the inclination of private investors to finance new capital projects. Likewise, consumer spending depended on the employment rate and security of workers who used their incomes to purchase what investors produced. When workers were laid off or frightened of the future, Keynes went on, corporate earnings would decline, resulting in more unemployment and possible investor panic.

The Keynesian solution was government expenditure to create jobs in bad times, to rekindle consumer demand and private production, and to stimulate greater private investment. However, because government tax revenues decrease in periods of rising unemployment and taxation tends to lower consumer purchasing power, Keynes advised tax cuts, borrowing, and deficit spending to counteract depressions. Government has the legal right to tax and collect revenue to pay off these obligations at a later time, so he felt this system of deficit spending did not necessarily endanger the fiscal security of the government.

President Roosevelt distrusted Keynesian economics; the first dramatic use of deficit spending came after Pearl Harbor. Although the Employment Act signaled a movement toward the Keynesian system, the "new economics" only entered the White House economic orthodoxy with the advent of the Kennedy administration in 1961. Previous presidents had used deficit financing skeptically and sparingly. By 1965, when Keynes appeared on the cover of *Time*, the nation's leading economists gave his ideas almost reverential treatment. Policy analysts in Washington, D.C. and elsewhere had come to regard Keynesian economics as a fully reliable instrument of economic stabilization, an engine of economic growth, and scaffolding for government management of the private sector. Keynes's theories seemed so reliable as to fall outside ideological argument or partisan politics.

The Problem of Inflation

In early 1946, the high unemployment rate that had worried President Harry Truman and Congress failed to materialize. Instead, prices began to rise suddenly when accumulated savings and a backlog of private demand for goods pushed spending far past national production capacity. Despite its effectiveness in stabilizing prices, the wartime Office of Price Administration (OPA), with its ration coupons, rent controls, profit restrictions, and wage and price ceilings, had become unpopular among buyers and sellers alike. Manufacturers and farmers, straitjacketed by price controls, wanted to exploit a seller's market. Consumers were ready to pay high prices for goods that had been restricted or unavailable during the war.

In June 1946, worried about the upcoming midterm elections, Congress dropped most OPA controls. Truman, trying to force Congress to pass a stronger anti-inflation law, responded by vetoing the bill. The immediate result was *no* price controls. Almost immediately, the relative price stability of the previous three years vanished. An annual inflation rate exceeding 18 percent on top of public impatience with wartime regulation helped to give the Republicans control of both houses of Congress in January 1947 after the November 1946 elections.

Labor Reacts

Postwar inflation, causing the rapid contraction of buying power, brought with it union discontent and spectacular strikes. In the last months of 1945, a wage dispute between Walter Reuther's United Auto Workers and General Motors led to a bitter 113-day strike. Then, about 700,000 steelworkers walked out. In April 1946, John L. Lewis took 400,000 coal miners on strike, demanding wage increases and pension protection. Coal was the country's main source of energy, so the strike had a catastrophic effect on the steel, transportation and electricity industries. In late May, a continental railroad strike loomed. The strike was the greatest threat to freight movements since the Pullman strike of 1894. With the rail system near paralysis and antiunion pressure rising in Congress, the president went on radio on May 24, 1946. "Pearl Harbor," he said, "was the result of action by a foreign enemy. The crisis tonight is caused by a group of men within our own country who place their private interests above the interests of their country."

The next day, Truman addressed a special session of Congress and asked for what amounted to a conscription of railroad workers and a federal takeover of the industry. Railroad leaders surrendered. The threat of federal action ended the strike just three minutes before the president delivered his speech. The Democratic House of Representatives, however, supported the president's proposal 306–13.

The Taft–Hartley Act

Senator Robert Taft blocked consideration of the railroad takeover and a draft of strikers in the Senate, saying that the proposal violated "every principle of American jurisprudence." Son of President William Howard Taft, and an articulate opponent of the New Deal, the Ohioan became majority leader of the Senate after the November elections. Joined by other Republicans when the new Congress met in January 1947, Taft set out to design a comprehensive labor bill that would modify the Wagner Act of 1935 and curb the power of organized labor, thus limiting the government's role in labor-management relations. The final Taft–Hartley Act, passed by Congress on June 23 over presidential veto, placed limitations on the rights and conduct of the trade unions, none of them as injurious to the future of organized labor as those who called it a "slave-labor bill" maintained.

The Taft–Hartley Act outlawed the *closed shop* (in which employers could hire only union workers) but permitted the *union shop* (in which nonunion employees had to join a union within 30 days if the majority of workers in a company voted for it). It forbade "unfair labor practices," including featherbedding (in which unions compelled employers to pay for jobs that had actually been eliminated by automation), jurisdictional strikes (arising from disputes between unions over which has the right to do a job), and union refusal to bargain with employers. The act allowed employers to sue unions for broken contracts, outlawed union contributions to political campaigns, and forbade strikes by federal employees.

Moreover, unions could not strike without giving 60-day notice of their desire to begin negotiations with employers. In 1932, the Norris–La Guardia Act had virtually outlawed the use of the labor injunction by federal courts to prevent strikes. Now, the Taft–Hartley Act gave the National Labor Relations Board (NLRB) and the president the power to ask for federal court injunctions, the NLRB to prevent violations of the law and the president to restrain a union from striking for 80 days when a strike jeopardized national health or safety. In addition, Section 14(b) permitted states to outlaw union shops, resulting in a rash of state "right to work" laws.

To unionists Section 14(b) and the rebirth of the labor injunction were the most fearsome aspects of the act. Labor leaders said that the 1947 act would cancel the gains of organized labor during the New Deal. Truman's veto and subsequent Democratic efforts to repeal the law reflected the increased power and political force of unions after the 1930s. Still, the enactment of the Taft–Hartley Act demonstrated declining enthusiasm for the labor movement and the rising prestige of business managers in the postwar United States.

THE ADVENT OF WELFARE CAPITALISM

The Employment Act of 1946 sanctioned vigorous economic management through the federal government's fiscal, monetary, and regulatory powers. This was a pivotal point in the evolution of welfare capitalism, an idea and specific policies set in motion during the 1930s to reach its apex in the 1960s and

1970s. Thus, government uses its power to control market imbalances and individual economic self-interest to insure minimal standards of living and services for all citizens. Government intervenes in private acquisition and production with the stated end of trying to create an equitable climate of private ownership.

In the postwar United States, public spending for domestic services rose sharply. Increasingly, the national government took the lead in social spending for health, education, and income maintenance. From the mid-1960s to 1980, such expenditures comprised the most expansive area of the national budget. When the Reagan administration came to power in 1981, the Republicans protected middle-class benefits such as social security payments and medical insurance. Democrats criticized the Republicans' callous indifference toward public assistance for the poor. But by the 1980s, the central issue was cost containment. Political leaders of all views were caught between the economic risks of federal deficits and the political risks of federal cutbacks. Ruthless competition for public funds at all levels of government raised the question of limits of public ability to sustain the customary expansion of services and subsidies. Still, President Reagan, who opposed the Tennessee Valley Authority and social security as late as 1964, extolled his predecessor, Franklin D. Roosevelt, in his first inaugural address. To the most conservative president elected in 50 years, welfare capitalism was a concept to be restricted, not abandoned.

The Fair Deal

The ongoing legacy of the New Deal began to take shape in the Truman era, three years after the end of global war. President Truman's unexpected reelection in 1948, coupled with Democratic majorities again controlling both houses of Congress, seemed to provide an opportunity to extend New Deal programs when Congress met in January 1949. In his State of the Union address that year, Truman declared that "every individual has a right to expect from our government a fair deal," a phrase that he used as a clarion call for advancements in the social security and farm programs, a higher minimum wage, repeal of the Taft–Hartley Act, the enactment of a national medical insurance plan, extension of public electrical power programs, federal aid to schools, and an increase in housing for low-income people.

In 1949 Congress enacted and enlarged more welfare programs than in any year since 1938. It raised the minimum wage from 40 to 75 cents, and the Housing Act of 1949 mandated the construction of 810,000 subsidized low-income housing units. In 1950, amendments to the Social Security Act extended coverage to more than 10 million new workers. On the other hand, President Truman failed to secure repeal of the Taft–Hartley law. His administration's proposal to substitute direct farm payments for crop restrictions to protect farm income and lower food prices never left Congress. The American Medical

Association mounted a successful campaign against national health insurance. The Roman Catholic church refused to support federal aid to education.

"Creeping Socialism"

Although President Eisenhower acquiesced in the idea that the federal government had some obligations to protect the economic well-being of citizens, he preferred that Washington advise and assist states, local communities, and individuals rather than expand the economic role of the federal government. Likewise, he deplored deficit financing and remained suspicious of Keynesian solutions throughout his years in the White House. Along with his key economic advisers, George Humphrey, secretary of the treasury, and Arthur Burns, head of the Council of Economic Advisers, he sought to curb the expansion of the national debt by balancing the budget. He also tried to reduce the scale of federal taxes and expenditures.

For the business leaders surrounding the president, achieving balanced budgets and reducing federal activity in the economy remained an elusive goal. From 1933 to 1953 most Republicans had shaken their heads over expanding federal government, as annual federal expenditures climbed in 20 years from about $5 to $74 billion, and as civilian employment in government grew from 600,000 to 2,400,000. But once in power, the Republicans found it difficult to make cutbacks. Pressure to increase military outlays and retain popular benefits such as farm subsidies and social security prevented them from making significant budget reductions. The Eisenhower administration achieved a balanced budget in only 3 of its 8 years.

The Eisenhower administration never really resolved its own confusion over the degree to which the federal government should support the welfare of its citizens. Although the executive branch remained philosophically at odds with the expanded role of the government in private lives, it established the Department of Health, Education, and Welfare (HEW) in 1953. Yet HEW's first secretary, Oveta Culp Hobby, opposed free federal distribution of polio vaccine in 1955, calling it "socialized medicine . . . through the back door."

The 1950s

The midcentury economy continued to benefit from the wealth, power, and productive capacity of the United States, leader in world industrial markets and provider of consumer goods unforeseen in history. The business cycle wavered, and there were brief recessions in 1954 and 1958. But in the 1950s 3 percent and 4 percent unemployment rates were typical, and they set the pace for the expansion of the U.S. economy through the the 1960s. For millions of Americans, the 20 years after World War II brought unexpected affluence and wealth.

The Keynesian Triumph

In January 1961, the Kennedy administration came to Washington, bringing with it an impressive roll call of college professors, social scientists, and Keynesian-oriented economists. The Keynesians, of considerable force in many university departments, had smarted in the 1950s at the Eisenhower administration's chilly reception to their ideas of economic management. They now enjoyed a committed friend in the White House. Under the leadership of Walter Heller, head of the Council of Economic Advisers, the "new economics" that had troubled and angered "small government" traditionalists for more than a generation became fashionable in the federal government. Although many southern Democrats and Republicans continued to voice strong opposition to growing levels of federal spending, congressional majorities supporting Keynesian economic management consistently outvoted them after 1963.

Anxious to "get the country moving again," in 1961, 10 days after his inauguration, President Kennedy proposed heavy federal spending to lower unemployment. Kennedy also led the way in trying to convince a skeptical Congress to lower taxes, allowing consumers and investors to keep more of their income. His administration wanted to keep federal expenditures steady through deficit financing, thus a tax reduction would stimulate private production and consumption. In 1962, Congress approved higher rates of depreciation for industry, resulting in lower corporate taxes. Congress also tried to give incentives to private investment by allowing a 7 percent tax credit on purchases of machinery. In 1964, under President Lyndon B. Johnson, Congress cut personal income taxes between 7 percent and 21 percent and corporate taxes by 4 percent, releasing during the next year more than $11 billion of private spending power. This helped to trigger rapid economic expansion in the middle 1960s. The greatest beneficiary of this new Keynesian policy was business. Said *Business Week*, "the lesson of 1964 is that fiscal policy needs to be used actively and steadily if balanced long-term growth is to be achieved."

The War on Poverty and the "Great Society"

Between 1950 and 1960 the nation's GNP rose from $286 to $506 billion. By 1965, it stood at $688 billion. Even after adjustments for increasing prices, annual national output almost doubled in these 15 years. But U.S. academics, political leaders, and voters became more conscious of millions not sharing in "the affluent society." Intellectuals and opinion makers "discovered" the conditions of life in the cellar of welfare capitalism—a world of malnutrition, illiteracy, and despair. According to Michael Harrington, whose *The Other America* (1962) had enormous infiuence on policy debate, "the fundamental paradox of the welfare state" was that "it is built not for the desperate, but for those who are already capable of helping themselves. . . . The poor get less out of the welfare state than any group in America."

In 1964, the Johnson administration, pursuing what it called the "Great Society," acted to reduce structural unemployment caused not by fluctuations in the business cycle but by the absence of marketable labor skills. The mainstay of this "War on Poverty" was the Economic Opportunity Act, passed in August 1964. When he signed the bill, President Johnson said, "For the first time in all the history of the human race, a great nation is able to make and is willing to make a commitment to eradicate poverty among its people." The Office of Economic Opportunity (OEO), under the direction of Sargent Shriver, former director of the Peace Corps during the Kennedy administration, oversaw a complex enterprise—including "community action" programs, training centers for unemployed youth, urban and rural poverty assistance teams, loans to acquire land for family farms, and loans to industries for hiring and training the perennially unemployed—with mixed results.

Despite annual appropriations of up to $1.5 billion in the mid-1960s, the OEO experienced declining popularity among Congress and the public. OEO agencies were attacked for spending funds sloppily. Many whites thought too much money was being spent on African Americans. Some believed that federal money was being used in black neighborhoods to organize antiwhite groups and fight "city hall." After 1967, as the Vietnam War absorbed a greater share of federal funds, OEO encountered considerable resistance in getting appropriations. By early 1973, the War on Poverty had faded into oblivion. Still, federal government expenditures for public aid—not including Social Security, pensions, housing, or education—doubled between 1968 and 1973.

Medicare

Johnson's health care legislation fared better. Back in 1945, Harry Truman had sought in vain a system of health insurance to pay for hospital and nursing costs. In 1960, Congress began making grants to states to help pay for the medical expenses of old people with low incomes. Then, in July 1965, Congress passed an act, popularly called Medicare, to provide compulsory health insurance under the Social Security program, allowing the elderly to pay only a small fee for each period of hospitalization. The new law also created a low-cost voluntary insurance program to help pay for doctors' fees. Medicare was to be paid for out of Social Security taxes. When President Johnson flew to Independence, Missouri to sign the bill with former President Truman, the two old New Dealers beamed as they posed for the news cameras. The American Medical Association, which had predicted medical anarchy if the act passed, did not support a threatened doctors' boycott. Eventually 95 percent of the medical profession joined the program. By the middle 1960s the position that the federal government had no responsibility for the economic and physical well-being of its citizens had been driven to the outer fringes of U.S. politics.

A GENERATION OF ECONOMIC GROWTH

Total household consumption rose every year in the 1950s, with purchases of houses, automobiles, and recreational goods—from television sets to sporting equipment—expanding at a rapid rate. The booming advertising industry reflected the growing need of businesses to manipulate and stimulate demand. In 1958, John Kenneth Galbraith, an eminent Harvard economist, dubbed the United States "the affluent society."

Corporate power and prestige grew in the 1950s. Manufacturing, retailing, and finance concentrated in larger companies. Small businesses, suffering from less efficient management and machinery, were burdened by higher per unit costs of production. Giant complexes—including older corporations like General Motors, newer corporations like IBM, financial networks like Bank of America and American Express, and retailing chains like Sears and Safeway—exerted awesome power in markets. A nostalgic sentiment for "free enterprise" remained, but the limited competition of corporations, so large that each seller had great influence in setting prices of goods and services, made the old notion of freewheeling competition obsolete. This market structure, called *oligopoly,* differed from the days of unregulated monopoly markets. In the postwar United States, General Motors competed with Ford, Chrysler, and American Motors through product differences and advertising as much as through pricing. In the 1890s a *monopoly,* Standard Oil, had enough market power to determine singly the price of oil products throughout the nation. Since World War II, the United States has become increasingly an economy of corporations large enough to have the power to administer prices. On the other hand, consumers have become more exacting in holding corporations responsible for the quality of life and the security of workers.

In 1954, Yale historian David Potter wrote *People of Plenty.* The influential book argued that the American character was shaped by the nation's abundance of natural resources. Because of plenty, Potter argued, class conflict over scarce resources—which had fueled social movements all over the world—had little meaning to the American mind. "The very meaning of the term 'equality' reflects this influence," Potter said. "A European, advocating equality, might very well mean that all men should occupy positions that are roughly on the same level in wealth, power, or enviability. But the American, with his emphasis on equality of opportunity, has never conceived of it in this sense." On the other hand, Potter believed that American expectations of abundance, expanding wealth, and upward mobility exacted a heavy psychological toll.

Four years later, in the widely read *The Affluent Society,* John Kenneth Galbraith added that the quest for private wealth resulted in the underallocation of resources for public goods and services, such as mass-transit systems and education. But in spite of such academic warnings, most Americans after World War II were enchanted by the panorama of products that stretched before them in department stores, showrooms, and supermarkets. Several forces—new construction, automobile production, technological advances, and public spending— contributed to a remarkable period of prosperity.

Construction

From the Crash of 1929 to the end of World War II, the building industry was flat. Then, pent-up demand for housing and commercial facilities was released, with tremendous expansionary impact on the economy. In densely settled areas, cities merged into "corridors" or "chains" of urban centers, industrial complexes, and suburban towns that stretched over whole regions, especially in the Northeast and California. New urban skylines appeared. Countryside and city blurred as developers and corporations bought open land for housing and commercial use; the center of gravity of cities and towns shifted away from downtowns and main streets to suburban satellites.

After 1945, the movement from cities turned into a mass migration. For millions of young families, owning a single-family home within commuting distance of work turned from a dream into a reality. Even blue-collar laborers began to enjoy wages high enough to allow them to leave dilapidated row houses and apartments in central cities and move toward urban peripheries. By 1960, about one-third of the nation lived in suburban areas. In the 30 years that followed, metropolitan and exurban areas grew even faster, as low-density, out-of-town housing, shopping malls, and commercial buildings dominated whole regions of the country.

The nation's population grew from 150 million in 1950 to 250 million in 1990. By the late 1980s, 37 metropolitan areas with at least 1 million people contained 49 percent of the nation's population. The New York City metropolitan area had about 18 million residents, followed by Los Angeles (14 million), and Chicago (8 million). Middle-class citizens were likely to live outside rather than in cities, but near cities nonetheless. Only 5 million Americans lived on farms.

While construction in suburban and metropolitan areas thrived, many central city neighborhoods declined, and aging housing stock fell into disrepair. Into these neighborhoods, abandoned by the middle class, had come millions of rural southern African Americans, Puerto Ricans, Mexicans, Asian immigrants, Jamaicans, Dominicans, Haitians, and others, seeking jobs and opportunities. But many of these new migrants were ill-trained for the demands of the commercial workplace. In many cities, industrial jobs were declining. In addition, the newcomers faced considerable prejudice and discrimination. Beset by shrinking tax bases, cities failed to invest in public infrastructure such as bridges, sewers, and waste disposal. From the 1960s, stark polarities of poverty and affluence widened in cities, and by the 1980s, miles of slums and housing projects often ringed gleaming office towers in downtown urban centers.

During the 1950s and 1960s, however, new roads and highways needed for housing developments, shopping centers, factories, and corporations located outside cities created a bonanza for construction companies. New expressways acted as links between commercial downtown buildings, suburban houses, and interurban areas. New roads proliferated throughout the expanding suburbs and metropolis.

Automobiles

By the late 1950s railroads, which 50 years earlier had been the most powerful industry in the nation, carried less than 50 percent of intercity freight traffic in the United States. Except for commuter lines, ever less able to support themselves without public assistance, railroads became insignificant in passenger travel. This victory of the automobile and highway began with Henry Ford's assembly line in 1909 and climaxed with the Federal Highway Act of 1956.

Congress financed federal highways as early as 1921. The WPA built over 650,000 miles of highways, roads, and streets. But in 1955, President Eisenhower, stressing defense needs, proposed a federally funded highway building program that heralded the full arrival of the automobile age. Myriad superhighways, connecting all major cities of the country, were financed by special taxes on gasoline and diesel fuel. The following year, in 1956, Congress approved the Federal Highway Act, the largest public works act ever passed, appropriating $32 billion for 41,000 miles of limited-access interstate highways to be built over the next 13 years.

In 1955, *Time* named H. H. Curtice, head of General Motors corporation, "man of the year." It had been a record year for the automobile industry—7.9 million new passenger cars sold and more than half of them made by General Motors. GM, with 514,000 employees and 119 plants, was the largest manufacturing corporation in the world. *Time* called the automobile the "quintessential" U.S. product. Between 1945 and 1955 national automobile registrations jumped from 26 million to 52 million. In 1989, the figure stood at 183 million, but by then a large number of U.S. drivers were driving foreign cars, a negligible part of the market before 1970.

From the 1950s to the 1970s, a quarter of all U.S. jobs had their sources in automobile-related manufacture. Automotive corporations were the base of the domestic steel, rubber, radio, and plastics industries. No industry was more affected by the automobile culture than oil. Expenditures for gasoline rose from $5 billion in 1950 to about $100 billion in 1990, and 63 percent of petroleum consumed the same year was used for transportation. From midcentury until the global oil shortages of 1973 and 1974, the price of gasoline remained remarkably low. In the 1980s, gasoline prices stabilized at much higher rates, but still remained far below market prices in the rest of the world. Although this cheap fuel promoted regional mobility and commerce, it also encouraged waste and increased U.S. dependence on imported oil.

New Technologies

Construction and transportation were older industries, that played an important role in postwar economic expansion. In the 1940s and 1950s new industries such as computers, aerospace, plastics, and electronics expanded, developing new products and productive techniques with amazing speed, in part through government expenditure for defense and space research.

After 1945, no manufactured product had more impact on economic organization than computers. Machines that stored, retrieved, and processed information had a profound impact on managing industry and systemizing record-keeping. Computers became standard in large corporations, government offices, and institutions. Inventors quickly realized the wide applicability of computers, especially when silicon-based microprocessing chips radically reduced the size of computer hardware and increased program and software capacities. From Route 128 in eastern Massachusetts to "Silicon Valley" near San Jose, California, many regional economies became tied to computer-related production and computer-based record-keeping.

Computerization was the enabling technology of the second half of the twentieth century, fundamental to economic growth and activity in other industries. During the 1980s, computers took over much of the nation's system of production and distribution. Led by the United States, the computer revolution altered global communications, finance, and enterprise. Personal computers became commonplace during the 1980s. In 1990, the United States still controlled more than two-thirds of the world market and had three times as much computer power per capita as Japan.

Great postwar advances also took place in aviation and aerospace. An infant industry in 1945, commercial aviation grew rapidly. In 1958, the Boeing Company introduced commercial jet aircraft, cutting interregional and international air travel time in half. Domestic airline revenues rose from $200 million in 1945 to more than $50 billion in 1990. In addition, Boeing, McDonnell Douglas, Lockheed, and other aerospace companies obtained lucrative government contracts for national defense and space exploration.

Chemical companies, including Du Pont, Monsanto, and Dow, developed and synthesized organic chemicals to produce a family of remarkably versatile and inexpensive materials. Oil-based plastics created a new family of human-made substances. The creation of these laboratory-developed "synthetics" introduced scores of light-weight, durable, resilient fibers and substances. Examples include nylon and fiberglass, which were introduced in 1938. In the 1940s and 1950s such materials replaced more expensive commodities in goods as different as clothing, containers, and furniture.

New electrical appliances, such as dishwashers, washing and drying machines, and air conditioners came into widespread use. They freed families from the drudgery of much household labor and made living conditions more comfortable. Factory prepared foods, juices, vegetables, meats, and cereals, elaborately packaged and often frozen, made household cooking faster and easier. But no single technology after 1945 had as much social and cultural impact as television. In 1946, 8,000 households owned television sets. In 1990, more than 98 percent of U.S. households owned a set. Television grew into the principal instrument of national communication, with transforming impact on U.S. politics, consumption, entertainment, and use of leisure time. From the Army–McCarthy hearings of 1954 to the coverage of the Persian Gulf War of 1991, the television camera repeatedly demonstrated its dominance as an instrument of opinion formation and arbiter of mass taste. Without television, Davy Crockett, Elvis Presley, the Superbowl, and MTV could not have become part of popular culture.

Public Spending

From the 1940s on, outlays by the federal, state, and local governments for public goods and services—not only new technologies—provided a motor of economic growth and private consumption. By 1990, government spending totaled about one-third of the GNP. Governments purchased privately produced goods, including school buildings and typewriters, missiles, and interstate highways. Governments also provided incomes. In 1990, federal, state, and local governments employed 17 million people, not including members of the armed forces. The salaries of diplomats, meat inspectors, police, and millions of others added up to a substantial share of consumer buying power. Government supplements to income, including Social Security, public assistance, unemployment insurance, and veterans' and farmers' benefits also boosted levels of private consumption.

AN ERA OF INSTABILITY

The birthrate in the United States, about 20 per thousand in 1945, rose sharply in the late 1940s and 1950s to about 25 per thousand before it returned to rates below 20 per thousand after 1965. During the 1970s, the birthrate dropped to about 15 per thousand. In other words, the number of young people in the United States between 1945 and 1970 was abnormally high as a segment of the general population. This "baby boom" helped to stimulate consumer demand for everything from diapers to schools.

These children, many of them born into an era of unprecedented economic growth, never seriously questioned the future of material expansion. As they grew older, some middle-class youth, unable to comprehend or sympathize with the economic uncertainty their parents had known in the Great Depression, often reacted with contempt to their parents' materialism, quest for security, and conformity.

The victory over McCarthyism after 1954 enhanced the prestige of liberal dissent in the late 1950s. In the early 1960s, when the "baby boom" began to reach college age, students at some of the nation's top colleges worked to register black voters in southern states. Some idealistic students, encountering racial discrimination and bigotry for the first time, discovered a United States that contradicted their comfortable childhoods. To them, this seemed to be another country, a land less just than the one they had read about in suburban schools. These young activists returned to campuses with grim tales of racism, political corruption, and economic inequity. By 1962, the year the radical Students for a Democratic Society (SDS) was founded, politicized students felt that abused minorities and the working class should have much more political and economic power, and a few urged violent revolution to achieve it.

Outright campus turmoil began at the University of California at Berkeley in the autumn of 1964. After the Oakland *Tribune* complained that student demonstrations against its alleged racial discrimination had been organized on university property, the Berkeley administration forbade student organizations to use campus property to distribute leaflets and solicit members. The ensuing Free Speech Movement (FSM) demonstrations electrified television audiences across the country, underscoring radical political activism that was growing in colleges from Berkeley to Ann Arbor to Cambridge.

The escalation of the Vietnam War in 1965 redoubled student dissent. At Vietnam Day demonstrations on campuses across the country that October, other students repelled by the war or opposed to military service joined the protests. Campus antiwar turmoil continued through the 1960s, reaching its most violent and convulsive point following the U.S. invasion of Cambodia in 1970 and the National Guard's shooting of students at Kent State University in Ohio. Political protest was but part of a broader cultural attack. An exotic radicalism spreading from the San Francisco Bay Area across the continent after 1966 challenged the community and habits of the middle class.

To describe this phenomenon, Theodore Roszak, a social historian, first coined the term *counterculture*. For Roszak, youth were revolting against their parents' "frozen posture of befuddled docility" and the social "ideal men usually have in mind when they speak of modernizing, up-dating, rationalizing, planning." Said Roszak, "Drunken and incensed, the centaurs burst in upon the civilized festivities that are in progress."

The counterculture was fascinated by the mystical and the occult. Its vision of a future free of rules and social obligations gave it an illusory sense of moral superiority. Wide use of marijuana and hallucinogenic drugs discredited firm reality. Youth glorified the irrational. Many sought new religious experiences. Logic and order seemed to be enemies rather than tools of understanding. "Reason, though dead," said the critic Leslie Fiedler, "holds us with an embrace that looks like a lover's embrace but turns out to be rigor mortis."

The counterculture's freedom in sex, dress, and behavior ultimately had as profound an impact on U.S. society as campus uprisings over race, constitutional rights, or war. The youth rebels of the 1960s initiated a revolution of manners. The consensus of the 1970s, that individuals generally have the right to do as they wish, was the counterculture's most potent legacy. Older social norms, such as what constituted pornography and obscenity, eroded, leaving the judiciary to decide the limits of personal freedom by court ruling.

Although many youth in the 1960s idealized a culture of poverty, they were the beneficiaries of middle-class prosperity. For them, affluence was a kind of birthright. Many rebels grew up so distant from the actualities of industrial production and the working class that providing for and distributing consumer goods seemed "irrelevant." The young, as much as their elders, valued their automobiles and stereo systems—and few bothered to ask where these came from. They were another generation of the "people of plenty," believing in an environment of limitless resources and automatic technological solutions to economic problems.

Many youth leaders attacked corporate America's faith in the efficacy of capitalism—and private enterprise's ability to produce the good life. The large industrial corporation, heralded during the postwar years as an engine of affluence, changed image. For anticapitalists young and old, the economic system seemed to endanger the well-being of workers and nature.

The counterculture left an indelible mark on social thought and policy. Its distrust of authority, indifference toward traditional forms of family, sexuality, education, and worship—coupled to popular quests for self-realization and social justice—affected U.S. attitudes and behavior in the 1970s and 1980s. In political form, student rebellion—itself derived from the civil rights movement—extended into new forms of protest and liberation. Moreover, the Dionysian impulse of the 1960s continued to assert itself in the popular arts, notably in television, film, and music, and more darkly in the vast and sinister underworld of drug abuse.

DECLINING ECONOMIC SECURITY IN THE 1970s

Uninterrupted prosperity in the 1960s made Keynesian economic management seem capable of sustaining indefinite growth. Economist Walter Heller wrote, "The cost of fulfilling a people's aspirations can be met out of a growing horn of plenty—without robbing Peter to pay Paul." Between 1960 and 1970 the GNP rose from $506 billion to $982 billion, an increase of almost $2,000 per capita in a period of relatively stable prices. This economic optimism faded in the first years of the 1970s. Inflation, rising sharply after 1968, averaged levels higher than 6 percent through the 1970s—coupled to high unemployment rates. A severe recession between 1974 and 1976 increased awareness of growing dependence on imports of foreign oil, the inability of economic policy to counter high rates of inflation and unemployment, and the declining power of the dollar in international money markets. By the late 1970s, a cautious, even ominous mood disturbed many Americans.

In stark contrast to the bouyant atmosphere of the postwar era, the 1970s gave way to worried, often alarmist, views of the capitalistic system's ability to sustain itself. Radicals—and many liberals—argued that the system was inequitable, exploitative, or simply doomed. In his analysis, *The Cultural Contradictions of Capitalism,* Harvard sociologist Daniel Bell argued that capitalism eroded its own most important values. In encouraging hedonistic behavior, said Bell, affluence undercut the restrained, ordered, prudent style of living that encouraged high productivity. At the same time the tempo of global production, competition, and distribution—dwarfing the scale of international trade before 1945—made the U.S. competitive edge abroad more crucial to its material welfare than at any time in memory.

Price-Wage Controls and Inflation

The prosperity of the middle 1960s was tied to government expenditure, both for increased social services and for the Vietnam War. Federal expenditure more than doubled between 1960 and 1970 from $97 billion to $208 billion, and national defense costs rose from $47 billion to $79 billion between 1965 and 1969. Because of domestic controversy over the war, presidents Johnson and Nixon were both unwilling to finance the Vietnam war through tax increases. They relied on government borrowing to pay for it. This deficit spending had strong expansionary impact on private spending. The military, relatively indifferent to costs, put vast sums of income into the hands of consumers, while directing production toward articles such as helicopters and artillery, which were neither capital investments nor goods that directly benefited consumers. This military spending contributed to an inflation rate rising to politically dangerous levels, from 1.7 percent in 1965 to 5.9 percent in 1970.

Consequently, in the Economic Stabilization Act of 1970, Congress empowered the president to fix prices and wages to counteract the declining value of the dollar. On August 15, 1971, President Nixon announced a general freeze in prices and wages—with important exceptions in the case of agricultural commodities, profits, dividends, and interest rates. The president wanted to curb increases of prices and incomes without antagonizing business leaders whose investments affected the rate of U.S. growth and whose support was the key to his continued political power. The announcement initiated the most direct federal management of wages and prices in two decades.

Price and wage controls remained in increasingly confusing and complicated "phases" until 1974. But at the urging of Secretary of Treasury George Schultz, the tendency by the end of 1972 was toward "decontrol." In January 1973, controls were virtually abandoned. A year later, the inflation rate had risen to an 11 percent annual rate. Economists debated the degree to which "decontrol" fueled inflation in 1973. But most agreed that the Nixon remedies for inflation were an unequivocal failure. Price increases did not abate during the Ford or Carter administrations. Inflation continued to sap public confidence and purchasing power, reaching an 11.3 percent annual rate in 1979 and 13.5 percent in 1980.

Troubled Agriculture

Aided by electrification, superhighways, and improved communications economic life in many rural areas improved. But like other small businesses, though it remained a mainstay of wishful Jeffersonian rhetoric, the family farm suffered. What became typical of agriculture in the 1970s and 1980s was the emergence of large, highly capitalized farm operations—"agribusiness"— prospering amid failing one-family farms.

For more than a century agricultural technology has threatened small producers by increasing productivity to a point where surpluses and resultant declining prices endangered small, indebted farmers with bankruptcy. After 1933, farmers became a specially protected minority with incomes supported by federal subsidies. The government calculated these subsidies from the average costs of farmers but allowed more efficient farms to receive government subsidies too. Highly mechanized farms on superior land had production costs far lower than the national average. Yet they enjoyed benefits equal to marginal farmers. Thus, income supplements to secure farmers indirectly encouraged larger scale farming.

Corporate farming—in which agricultural production was organized by syndicates of investors and managed by highly educated technicians—brought new economies of scale to big, automated farms. The average size of a farm rose from 151 acres in 1930 to 463 acres in 1987. At the same time, the farm population of the country declined from 25 percent to 2 percent. Farmers benefited from rising food prices during the 1970s. The devalued dollar encouraged exports. The Nixon administration's policy of "decontrol" contributed to increased food prices and farm income. Wheat prices rose threefold in 1972 and 1973 after the U.S. government agreed to sell large amounts of grain to the Soviet Union. Meat prices went up by 43 percent. Soaring farm earnings encouraged farmers to buy new machinery and farmland, thereby increasing their debt load and mortgage payments. By the late 1970s, renewed foreign competition and a higher priced dollar resulted in overproduction and falling prices. Large-scale, highly capitalized corporate farms with low production costs remained competitive and profitable. Many smaller, less efficient "family farms" became insolvent. The value of midwestern and southeastern farmland plunged. During the 1980s, agricultural earnings remained low, and a depressed economic state reigned in much of the rural United States.

The Energy Crisis

In 1973, the U.S. economy reeled from rising prices that followed "decontrol." From the end of the year to the spring of 1974, the country also faced a severe shortage of oil products, including gasoline, diesel fuel, and heating oil. This shortage had several causes. First, although demand for oil products increased in the early 1970s, the nation's refining capacity remained constant. In addition, after the United States supported Israel in the Yom Kippur War of 1973, Arab nations embargoed the export of crude oil to the United States for several months. The Organization of Petroleum Exporting Countries (OPEC), an international combine of oil-rich nations, quadrupled its price of crude oil.

The Recession of 1974

In 1974, the United States, with an annual inflation rate of over 11 percent and an unemployment rate of over 9 percent, entered a deep recession. In this downturn, both prices and unemployment rose, an especially unsettling economic condition because economists had once thought that this was impossible. Recent economic theory taught there was an inverse relationship between prices and unemployment. Many factors contributed to this inflation, including global demand for petroleum and grain, the power of corporations to set prices at a high level even when consumer demand dropped, and the buying power that unemployed workers received from unemployment benefits and easier consumer credit.

Despite inflation and credit, consumer demand dropped. The fear of unemployment increased household thriftiness and thus dampened production. Consumers cut back on "big purchases" such as houses, automobiles, and appliances. Housing starts, about 2 million in 1972, fell to 1.1 million in 1975. Automobile sales, 9.7 million in 1973, declined to 6.7 million in 1975. In the second quarter of 1976, two years after the beginning of the Energy Crisis, employment and consumer demand revived. Business, expecting further demand, increased its inventories for the first time in two years. The inflation rate, however, remained close to 6 percent.

A Second Recession

After the multiple setbacks of the early and mid-1970s, recovery of economic confidence proved elusive and patchy. Before large companies and household buyers regained their composure, another recession broke in 1979, intensifying during the early 1980s. After the Republicans captured the White House and control of the Senate in 1980, the federal government introduced fiscal and monetary policies designed to cut the interest rates and inflationary spiral that seemed to run out of control during the Carter administration.

Two basic industries suffered special blows. U.S. automobile and steel manufacturers lost their dominating power in domestic and international markets. After 1974, low-cost, well-designed, fuel-efficient Japanese cars captured a large share of trade. Between 1978 and 1980 U.S. automobile production plunged from 9.1 million to 6.4 million, with losses so catastrophic that the once mighty Chrysler Corporation remained solvent only through heavy federal subsidies and loan guarantees. Many steel mills closed permanently, unable to compete with foreign producers. The membership of the United Steelworkers union declined from 1.4 million to 700,000 workers between 1980 and 1983.

The future of petroleum supplies remained in doubt. The Energy Crisis of 1974 underscored U.S. dependence on imported oil. A second shortage and price hike in 1979 drove home the idea to many policymakers and industrial managers that the era of near-inexhaustible, low-cost energy had ended, though industrial and consumer appetites for oil products remained ravenous. Political instability in the Persian Gulf and OPEC's relentless price increases (until surpluses temporarily drove down global prices in the early 1980s) reminded some Americans of the nation's increasing dependence on foreign oil. Between 1960 and 1990 U.S. petroleum production declined from 33 percent to 15 percent of world output. During the same period, imports rose from about 10 percent to 45 percent of all crude oil consumed in the United States.

THE 1980s AND EARLY 1990s

In 1980, former California governor Ronald Reagan entered the White House, and Republicans set a new direction for the economy, full of hope that aggressive capitalism would reverse the nation's frightening economic decline of the 1970s. By 1980, runaway inflation endangered economic stability. The consumer price index soared to a 13.5 percent annual rate, eroding public confidence in the future and in government itself. The prime lending rate surged to an astonishing 18.9 percent. Washington seemed to be losing control of prices, and public faith in the Carter administration's regulative abilities lagged. The unemployment rate exceeded 7 percent, and during the late 1970s neither the Carter administration nor Congress offered any meaningful policies to counteract the new phenomenon of "stagflation"—the combination of rising prices, high unemployment, and anemic growth in the economy. Dominated by new Reagan policies, the economy in the 1980s became far more robust, in fact, introducing a period of great general prosperity. Yet the new decade saw no end to daunting social, cultural, and economic challenges, notably the global competition abroad and the underclass at home.

Economic Policy in the 1980s

President Jimmy Carter suffered from domestic economic problems and repeated disappointments in foreign policy. His 1979 declaration of a national "crisis of confidence" struck many voters as misguided and as evidence of ineffective leadership, not as a weakness in the American people.

An alternative course of macroeconomic policy popularly called "supply-side economics" gained converts among Republican politicians, policy analysts, and investors unhappy with the Carter administration's indirection. Supply-side economics hoped to stimulate production and growth by controlling inflation, lowering taxes for investors, deregulating industries, and shrinking federal domestic spending. In 1981, in the first year of the Reagan administration, Congress enacted a White House-sponsored tax law allowing faster depreciation for capital investment and offering other incentives to investors. Republican control of the Senate from 1981 to 1984, and conservative power in the House through 1983, helped to advance such initiatives. The Federal Reserve maintained high interest rates in order to restrain inflation. Deficit spending, designed to build up the nation's military arsenal, remained a far more significant force in expansion than most Republicans cared to admit, especially because this was a basic Keynesian and Democratic technique to stimulate the economy and because servicing the national debt was becoming an issue of deepening political concern.

A severe recession from the summer of 1981 through 1982 fell hard on indebted farmers in the Mississippi Valley and industrial workers in mature, automating, unionized industries in the Ohio Valley and Northeast. Battered by the collapse of oil prices and reckless real estate expansion, Texas, Oklahoma, and Louisiana entered a regional recession that persisted through the decade. The national unemployment rate rose rapidly in 1982, reaching nearly 10 percent. But the destabilizing inflation of the 1970s plunged, dropping below a 4 percent annual rate during 1983, the lowest rate since the 1960s.

In late 1982, economic expansion began again and lasted until 1990. Business activity bubbled as new tax policies and relaxed regulations gave a green light to investors. In turn, this spurred new projects and jobs; confidence returned. In 1984, the unemployment rate dropped to less than 8 percent, and by 1989 it was just 5 percent. During the early 1980s, high technology fields including computer electronics, telecommunications, pharmaceuticals, and health sciences expanded rapidly. Real estate ventures, including condominiums, shopping malls, and low-rise office buildings gave a new look to the metropolitan and exurban landscape. Still, the economic boom of the mid-1980s eluded many U.S. workers as the contraction of basic industries and expansion of global competition continued through the decade.

Globalism

Multinational production and distribution has been a motor for global trade and interdependence for almost half a century. Yet in the 1980s continued advances in communications and transportation accelerated the trend. Capital markets were reorganized, as computer- and satellite-driven communication made possible instantaneous global transfers of currency, capital, and ownership. Banking and securities markets became fully internationalized, as did some basic industries. For example, in Asia, production of textiles, automobiles, steel, electronics, computers, and other consumer goods expanded rapidly, competing with U.S. manufacturers, and creating new wealth from Singapore to Korea. Japanese capital moved with unparalleled force through world markets throughout the 1980s.

Japanese incursions into the U.S. economy provoked ill feelings, especially in California, where highly visible foreign investment in real estate alarmed state officials and business leaders. The Japanese purchase of New York City's Rockefeller Center and Los Angeles' Universal Studios in 1989 symbolized new Japanese power in the United States, as the building of a Disneyland near Tokyo signaled the force of U.S. culture there. The purchase of U.S. Treasury securities by Japan bothered some economists who felt that such foreign-held debt—coupled to the aggressive export policies of Japan—threatened U.S. sovereignty. The Federal Reserve lost some regulatory control over interest rates because of international money markets in Frankfurt and Tokyo, which determined the value of the dollar in relation to other trading currencies. The presence and power of U.S. capital throughout the world remained formidable, but transnational commerce ended that era of U.S. dominance of world industrial markets stretching from 1945 to the 1970s.

Indebtedness and Taxation

By the late 1980s, private and public indebtedness had reached alarming levels. In 1990, the Federal Reserve reported that consumer debt had reached $737 billion, a rise from about $300 billion 10 years earlier. Credit card debt had jumped to 29 percent of the total consumer debt, up from 18 percent in 1980. Public debt had grown at all levels. The national debt rose from about $900 billion in 1980 to $3.2 trillion in 1990. Federal expenditure to pay the interest on this debt grew from about 12 percent to 25 percent of the national budget between 1980 and 1990. State and local spending increased at even more rapid levels to pay for social services. The tax burden on the public included highly visible income and social security taxes, as well as ubiquitous sales, property, excise, gasoline, and use taxes.

The 1981 tax cuts were followed by the Tax Reform Act of 1986, which was the most thorough overhaul of federal tax law in over 50 years. The 1986 law attempted to erase special rules and exemptions ("shelters") that over the years had benefited industries, groups, and certain investors. But many middle-income taxpayers thought that income taxes nonetheless continued to shield the rich, and increasingly, they resented paying taxes when public services—as in the case of sanitation or schools—had evidently shrunk in quality, or when private alternatives had supplanted them—as in the case of security forces or transportation. Moreover, a growing number of taxpayers resented federal, state, and local expenditures that seemed to perpetuate a dependent welfare population in the cities.

The Money Society

In 1987, *Fortune* coined the term *the money society* to try to explain the new economic culture of the 1980s. The decade's gap between the very rich and the middle class seemed to widen. During the 1980s, financial engineering offered bankers and entrepreneurs vast opportunities to construct and "restructure" corporations. Exotic financial instruments, including leveraged buyouts and junk bonds, facilitated such complicated practices. In California and the Northeast in particular a new class of investment bankers, corporate officers, attorneys, and real estate developers made huge amounts of money very fast. Residential real estate in San Francisco, Los Angeles, New York, Washington, and Boston soared in value, as newly affluent young professionals (categorized as "yuppies") outbid one another for attractive houses and apartments.

Dealmakers like Donald Trump appeared on the scene during the marked economic recovery of 1982 and 1983. By the end of the decade, Trump had a real estate empire that included several Atlantic City gambling casinos, New York hotels and apartment buildings, and an airline company. His self-promotional 1987 best-selling book, *The Art of the Deal,* made him an icon of the money society. However, his grandiosity, greed, and gaudy private life left him few admirers by 1990, when his debt-based empire showed signs of collapse. A parade of speculators and investors like Trump working inside or with the nation's leading banks tested the edges of regulation, general accounting practices, and securities law. Sometimes in outright collusion, they were able to control markets and reap whirlwind profits, drain financial institutions of money, float risky bond issues, and reshuffle rather than create wealth.

The new breed of investors would buy a company with borrowed funds—bank loans—using the company itself as collateral. During the 1980s, the leveraged buyout became a preferred tool of grand corporate finance, whereby an investor syndicate might buy a company with funds borrowed through issuing high-yield ("junk") bonds. The dividends on the bonds issued were to be paid by the company's future revenues or asset sales. Junk bonds paid a high return because the revenue to pay for the bonds was not certain or secure since these companies were so indebted. The cost of obtaining this money was higher, as was the possibility of default on these bonds. Many of these bonds were issued and sold by Drexel Burnham Lambert, First Boston, and other financial institutions, often to insurance companies, pension funds, and savings and loan associations.

The legendary "junk bond" king Michael Milken reigned, seemingly invincible, in the Los Angeles offices of Drexel Burnham through the mid-1980s. Then, suddenly, disclosures by the Securities and Exchange Commission (SEC) of illegal financial activities by leading dealmakers—including Milken—rocked the world of investment banking. In 1986, high-flying investor Ivan Boesky agreed to pay a $100 million fine for trading stocks using illegal information from a Drexel Burnham banker. Two years later, Milken was charged with insider trading and fraud. In 1990, he was sentenced to 10 years in prison for illegal financial activities, and Drexel Burnham went out of business. The next year, yet another scandal erupted when it was revealed that Salomon Brothers, another leading investment banking house, had tried illegally to control U.S. Treasury bond sales and obtain favorable rates for itself. Thus, the credibility of U.S. financial markets was further undermined. On the other hand, the aggressive prosecutions by the SEC and the Federal Reserve between 1986 and 1991 showed that regulative agencies worked even during the Reagan and Bush administrations to protect the security of financial markets.

During the 1980s, alongside new money, came new attitudes that made comparisons to the Gilded Age of the 1880s appropriate. The glorification of power and conspicuous consumption among the newly rich social figures in financial capitals like New York and Los Angeles, and Tom Wolfe's *Bonfire of the Vanities*, the 1987 novel of an investment banker's fall from upper-class grace, savaged the excess and class pretension that marked the "money society." Even as incomes soared and paper-based fortunes accumulated among the leaders of the money society, most Americans felt pinched, even as they turned their televisions on to watch programs like "Dallas" and "Lifestyles of the Rich and Famous."

The Savings and Loan Disaster

The savings and loan debacle comprised one of the most massive transfers of wealth in U.S. history. The beneficiaries were homeowners, landowners, and real estate developers, all of whom profited from loose money and easy loans. Investment bankers and attorneys made huge fees on transactions. Billions of dollars poured into savings and loans banks that then pumped these assets into the hands of speculators, dealmakers, and other financial acrobats.

In the once-tame savings and loan industry, many local banks and financial institutions called "S&Ls" or "thrifts" traditionally took small deposits and made mortgage loans to individual home buyers. They were intended to provide a local system of real estate finance. During the early 1980s—influenced by prominent constituents, notably real estate developers—Congress relaxed the rules of savings and loan operations. Likewise, Congress increased the levels of deposit insurance, allowing higher interest rates and attracting new depositors. The White House and regulatory agencies acceded to the new rules, thus allowing savings and loan institutions to make big loans for apartment buildings, commercial real estate, and shopping malls. Savings and loans also bought large amounts of junk bonds. If these outstanding loans failed and junk bonds fell in value, S&L institutions would also fail. Still, savings and loans deposits were insured through Federal Savings and Loan Insurance Corporation (FSLIC). Thus, the federal government—and taxpayers—were obligated to pay.

Laxities of regulatory control became apparent by the mid-1980s. Reckless lending and inadequate insurance reserves were well known to investors, bankers, and regulators. Rash investments and overbuilding in real estate had become commonplace. But a huge amount of money was being made, and many influential citizens manipulated members of Congress through campaign contributions. The savings and loan industry epitomized a broad-based special interest pyramid with political muscle in the White House, on Capitol Hill, and in state capitals. Among investors, a cozy attitude existed in which money was to be made before a day of reckoning, a mood that permeated savings and loan finance, notably in the rapidly growing "sunbelt" states of Arizona, California, Florida, and Texas. The day of reckoning finally came when hundreds of savings and loan institutions became insolvent.

By the end of the 1980s, the nation needed an estimated $200 billion *before interest* to cover savings and loan losses. Estimates of total costs of the S&L debacle ran as high as $1.4 trillion because of long-term interest. In August 1989, Congress created the Resolution Trust Corporation to oversee the liquidation of failing thrifts and sell their remaining assets at a fraction of their market value of a few years before. Where the additional federal revenue was to come from, whether from U.S. Treasury bond sales or increased taxes, no one was quite certain. But the financial carnage the savings and loans failures had caused was sure to inflict long-term damage on middle-class taxpayers who had not benefited from the savings and loan spending spree of the 1980s.

The Crash of 1987 and Recession of 1990

In 1987, after five years of rapid growth, the stock market underwent a one-day collapse unseen since 1929. On October 14, 1987, the Dow Jones industrial index crashed 508 points, or more than 22 percent. The index, having risen during the 1980s economic expansion from about 800 to 2,700, lost almost a thousand points between August 1987 and the final October lows. Many economic analysts predicted a stiff economic downturn as a result. They were wrong. The pulse of credit and consumer spending maintained itself for three more years, but gradually weakened in 1990 as overextended credit, overbuilt commercial real estate, and surplus retail inventories became evident.

The sickening drama of the nation's savings and loans defaulting preceded major bank losses. By the late 1980s, banks were forced to raise their own capital reserves to make up for an increasing number of bad loans. The nation's largest banks had moved from straightforward practices into dealmaking in order to compete with investment banks and private investor syndicates. They also had made risky foreign loans, especially in Latin America. As commercial real estate and bond values declined in the late 1980s, large banks also became insecure. Suddenly, credit tightened. In 1990, the economic expansion of the previous eight years ended. The unemployment rate reached 7 percent the following year, and the Federal Reserve began to lower interest rates in an effort to stimulate consumer spending and private investment.

The recession of the early 1990s had greater impact on white-collar workers and managers than earlier economic downturns, especially in the Northeast and on the West Coast. Many financial institutions and corporations dramatically cut their professional work forces in their efforts to reduce costs. Lawyers, architects, accountants, and other beneficiaries of the 1980s found themselves suddenly unemployed. Real estate values declined, leaving homeowners feeling stretched and sometimes facing alarming equity losses. In addition, increasing concern about the environment, the underclass, and public safety eroded tax-payer confidence.

Environmentalism

The modern environmental movement originated in the 1950s. By midcentury, unpleasant side effects of economic growth and consumer appetites had become obvious in urban areas. Industrial and automobile exhaust fouled the air of cities from Pittsburgh to Los Angeles. In 1962, Rachel Carson's influential book, *Silent Spring*, documented potentially poisonous economic practices, especially the environmental damage inflicted by the use of the pesticide DDT. By 1970, environmentalism had become a major political force that continues to influence economic policy today. That year, Congress created the Environmental Protection Agency (EPA), which by 1990 had become the nation's largest regulatory agency. Attempts by the Reagan administration to roll back the EPA's regulatory power in the early 1980s were a political failure. By the 1990s, environmentalism reached beyond partisan politics.

Public worry over water pollution and shortages, nuclear and toxic waste, acid rain, global warming, ozone depletion, and asbestos poisoning mounted. Sometimes environmental advocates exaggerated the situation, relying on dubious statistics and media alarms to advance anticapitalistic views. But what to do with solid waste and garbage perplexed many communities, especially in densely populated areas of the country. The possibility of malfunctioning nuclear-fueled electrical power plants frightened even more Americans. These fears intensified in 1979 when equipment failure in a nuclear generator on Three Mile Island in Middletown, Pennsylvania led to a partial meltdown of its core. A more serious nuclear accident seven years later at the Chernobyl, Ukraine nuclear power plant in the Soviet Union spewed lethal radiation clouds and forced the evacuation of 40,000 people in the surrounding region. In March 1989, an oil tanker, the *Exxon Valdez*, struck a reef in Alaska's Prince William Sound. The oil spill that followed fouled thousands of miles of Alaskan coast-line. The state's fishing industry was temporarily wiped out, and pictures of dying birds and otters, soaked with oil, stunned the nation. The *Exxon Valdez* disaster again illustrated how human error could have catastrophic effects on a large geographic area.

In the early 1990s, environmental remediation, although evident in isolated areas, was by no means complete. The problem was inevitable trade-offs between ideals and economic interests, including corporate profits and consumer demand for cheap power, food, and products. The politics of water, for example, illustrated the difficulty of rational policy. Water pollution continued to escalate in localities around the country. The capacity of toxic wastes, pesticides, and organic salts to pollute water supplies was no longer disputed. In 1990, according to the EPA, 65 percent of river and stream pollution came from farms, in comparison to 7 percent from factories. Yet government policies have long protected agriculture. Powerful farm lobbies in Washington, D.C. and state capitals opposed increased water controls and regulations, as did the coal, chemical, and petroleum industries on account of increased production costs.

The Underclass

Some Americans were unaffected by the economic cycle, and many of them were virtually unemployable. The gap between coping middle-class workers and the urban lower class, disproportionately African American and Hispanic, continued to widen during the 1980s. This economic schism was aggravated by the breakdown of family structure, widespead illegitimacy and illiteracy, epidemic drug abuse, and despair. This urban underclass was unlike earlier generations of poor Americans because it lacked the education and work habits necessary for steady employment. Fewer unskilled jobs existed.

In the cities, poor people and vagrants spread into new territory, making streets and parks places of fear for the middle and working classes. High-rise public housing towers that had been the pride of urban renewal after the 1949 Housing Act had long lost their luster. Now, these projects seemed to breed economic insecurity, crime, and despair. Moreover, the mentally ill, drug addicts, alcoholics, and victims of rising housing costs in cities comprised a new urban element, called the "homeless." For the homeless, even unskilled jobs were out of the question. In urban slums, stable family life was vanishing. The underclass and the homeless raised profound and unanswered questions of civil rights, public safety, and government responsibility.

Older industrial cities suffered the most. Their tax bases were eroding and infrastructure run down, with fewer people to pay for its repair. For example, Detroit's dispersing population dropped from about 1.2 million in 1980 to 1 million in 1990, and whole residential neighborhoods were depopulated. What had been in the 1950s a vibrant city of almost 2 million people had become what *The New Republic* described as "a landscape of broken warehouses, factories, and rubble-strewn lots that seems to have no boundary." In the 1990s, New York City's welfare population exceeded 1 million, and in some cases represented a family's fourth generation on welfare. Not surprisingly, widespread disillusionment with the welfare policies of the New Deal and Great Society grew, because such programs seemed to breed rather than cure ill-being.

As early as 1983, *Fortune* reported that the middle class was "gradually being pulled apart," as economic forces propelled households toward the high or low end of the income spectrum, and as industrial jobs were eliminated through automation or foreign production. In the 1980s, some Democratic leaders called for trade restrictions to limit imported goods and exports of U.S. capital. Others called for an explicit "industrial policy" to give the federal government greater control over corporate planning and practices. A few economists, convinced of impending shortages of natural resources and environmental damage, endorsed aggressive state control of the economy.

Still, popular faith in private enterprise remained robust. Although even conservative Republicans believed in a "safety net," that is, public responsibility for social welfare, the degree and method remained open to question. Radical redistribution of wealth had little appeal outside a few research universities and think tanks. The lure of democratic capitalism was underscored by the revolutions in Eastern Europe and the Soviet Union after 1989. These revolutions rejected centralized economic authority and state planning in behalf of freer markets and individual autonomy. In the United States, in spite of daunting challenges in the 1990s, trust in private economic leadership was rooted deeply in the national folklore and in the nation's impressive long-term record of growth and prosperity.

CHAPTER 8

The Supreme Court, Individual Liberty, and Equality

"Ever since Hammurabi published his code to 'hold back the strong from oppressing the weak,' the success for any legal system is measured by its fidelity to the universal ideal of justice. Theorists beset us with other definitions of law: that it is a mask of privilege, or the judge's private prejudice, or the will of the stronger. But the ideal of justice survives all such myopic views, for as Cicero said, 'We are born to it.' "

Earl Warren, 1955

Although May 17, 1954, was a historic day for race relations and the Supreme Court, the decision the Court made then originated three years earlier. Linda Brown, a nine-year-old African American, was being bused past the front door of the white Summer Elementary School, seven blocks from her Topeka, Kansas home, to the all-black Monroe School, about a mile away. Her parents objected and decided to contest an 1867 Kansas law, which segregated Topeka elementary schools by race.

In 1954 the Supreme Court decided that the city of Topeka had denied Linda Brown her constitutional rights. The Court in *Brown v. Board of Education of Topeka, Kansas* ruled that "in the field of public education the doctrine of 'separate but equal' has no place. Separate educational facilities are inherently unequal. Therefore, we hold that the plaintiffs have been deprived of the equal protection of the laws guaranteed by the Fourteenth Amendment." The *Brown* decision held unconstitutional the school segregation laws of 17 states and the District of Columbia, which covered 40 percent of the nation's public school students. The Court's decision on public education climaxed more than 50 years of legal efforts to crack the walls of segregation and inaugurated the civil rights revolution of the 1950s and 1960s.

THE ROLE OF THE SUPREME COURT

Following the "court-packing" fight of 1937, the role of the Supreme Court in the U.S. constitutional process had by 1945 undergone great change. Basic policy decisions are usually made by the elected or "political" branches of government. Congress enacts laws and the president executes them. The Court's function is to interpret the law, but judges often disagreed as to the meaning of "interpret."

From the 1880s to the 1930s, the Supreme Court often protected corporate and other property interests by ruling that federal and state legislative efforts at economic and social regulation were unconstitutional. The Court, by exercising judicial review, acted as a restraint on the legislative and executive branches, but the only restraint of significance on the Court had to be self-imposed. As the Court overturned legislation, a potentially dangerous tension existed between popular rule by the people's elected representatives and rule by lifetime appointed, nonelected judges.

Many defenders of the New Deal's social and economic legislation believed the Court exceeded its proper function as the interpreter of the Constitution. They charged the Court was becoming a policy-making body and usurping the legislature's role. They held the Court was too "activist"; that it should exercise more "self-restraint." The Court seemed to stretch too far Chief Justice Charles Evans Hughes's maxim, "We are under a Constitution, but the Constitution is what the Supreme Court says it is."

After the court-packing fight, the justices exercised more "self-restraint" vis-à-vis the political branches of government and upheld New Deal social and economic legislation. As one observer put it, "The Court followed the election returns"; certainly the justices were influenced not only by Roosevelt's proposal, but also by the overwhelming popular majorities that the New Deal ran up at the polls.

By 1945, the Court modified its earlier role as a frequent defender of property adversely affected by government regulation. The judges limited their function and gave the political branches more freedom to regulate. The Court, however, indicated in 1938 that it would jealously guard, through its power of judicial review, certain "preferred freedoms." The Court would grant special protection to individual liberties singled out by the Bill of Rights and to "discrete and insular minorities." The Court held such liberties fundamental to the democratic process and the representation of minorities. Threats to such "preferred freedoms would necessitate "searching judicial inquiry." This view took on great significance in the Court's "judicial activism" of the 1950s and 1960s as the justices moved strongly to protect individual liberties and equal protection under law from government acts.

THE VINSON COURT

Under Chief Justice Frederick M. Vinson, from 1946 to 1953 the Court decided important cases involving such questions as free speech and the rights of the Communist party; church-state relations; and the civil rights of African Americans. But the Court rarely cast the issues in clear focus or ruled with unanimity or persuasiveness.

Free Speech

In 1940 Congress enacted the Smith Act, which made it unlawful to "advocate . . . overthrowing any government of the United States by force or violence," to publish printed matter or organize groups "advising or teaching" such overthrow, and to conspire to commit the foregoing acts. The so-called "membership clause" forbade "knowing" membership in any such group. Civil libertarians thought the law violated the First Amendment guarantees of freedom of speech, press, and assembly.

In 1949, as the cold war grew in intensity and a Gallup poll showed that 7 out of 10 Americans believed that membership in the Communist party should be forbidden by law, 11 leaders of the U.S. Communist party were convicted in a federal district court for violation of the Smith Act. The indictment did not charge an actual conspiracy to overthrow the government, but rather charged that the communist leaders had conspired to organize groups that advocated such violent overthrow. In 1919 a unanimous Court had ruled that only speech representing a "clear and present danger" could be suppressed by the government. Rigorous application of that precedent would have challenged the constitutionality of the convictions of the Communists. But the U.S. Supreme Court in *Dennis v. United States* (1951), in a 6–2 decision with 5 widely differing opinions, treated the indictments as charges of direct conspiracy—action, not simple association with speech—to overthrow the government.

The Supreme Court upheld the constitutionality of the "advocacy" section of the Smith Act, modifying the "clear and present danger" doctrine to read "clear and present or future danger." Chief Justice Vinson wrote for the majority, "Obviously, (the clear and present danger doctrine) cannot mean that before the government may act, it must wait until the rebellion is about to be executed." Vinson claimed the very existence of the communist conspiracy was the danger. Justices Douglas and Black dissented vigorously and called the Smith Act a "virulent form of prior censorship of speech and press." They did not see the U.S. Communist party of 55,000 members as an imminent threat to the U.S. government or as a criminal conspiracy beyond the protection of the Bill of Rights. More prosecutions and anticommunist legislation followed at federal and state levels, with convictions obtained in every federal prosecution brought on conspiracy or membership charges between 1951 and 1956.

Church and State

Between 1947 and 1952 the Supreme Court ruled in three cases on the First Amendment's words: "Congress shall make no law respecting an establishment of religion." The court viewed the main question as, what is an unconstitutional "establishment of religion?" Many Americans, often Roman Catholics or evangelical and fundamentalist Protestants, wanted public support for religious education. Others, Jews, mainstream American Protestants, and secularists, feared the entry of organized religions into public arenas and urged a strict separation of church and state. In 1947 the Court, in a 5–4 vote, upheld the use of New Jersey tax monies to bus children to parochial schools as a reasonable use of the state's power to support the general welfare of children. The next year the Court declared a religious education program, typical of programs in 40 states, privately run by religious groups, carried on in the public schools during the school day fell squarely under the ban of the First Amendment.

In 1949 a troubled and divided Court declared in a 6–3 ruling that "we are a religious people whose institutions presuppose a Supreme Being" and upheld a "released time" religious education program that allowed children with parental permission to leave schools, usually for one period per week, to attend churches for religious instruction. Ironically, in our secular age, issues of church and state have dogged the Court and divided Americans. The Jehovah's Witnesses flag salute cases in the early 1940s as well as school prayer, birth control, and abortion decisions in later decades sharply divided the U.S. public.

Civil Rights

For most of the twentieth century the Supreme Court and lower federal courts have been the major protectors of civil rights. The lawyers of the National Association for the Advancement of Colored People (NAACP) consistently attempted through the judicial process to guarantee African Americans the right of due process, equal protection of the laws, and the vote as set forth by the Fourteenth and Fifteenth Amendments.

The NAACP worked from its founding in 1910 to end grandfather clauses, poll taxes, literacy tests, all-white Democratic primaries, and other measures that kept African Americans from voting. In 1915 the NAACP won its first major legal victory when the Court ruled the grandfather clause, which denied the vote to individuals whose ancestors had not voted before the Civil War, unconstitutional as a blatant violation of the Fifteenth Amendment. The Court nullified the all-white primary in five decisions from 1927 to 1953, a noteworthy example of the gradualism of the judicial process.

In 1927 the Supreme Court ruled that restrictive housing covenants, those agreements by a buyer not to sell his home to an African American or a member of some other specified group, were private contracts and not forbidden by the Fourteenth Amendment's equal protection clause. But in 1948 the Court, though it continued to rule that restrictive covenants are private matters, ruled that such covenants could not be enforced by state courts, because such action would constitute a state denial of equal protection of the law. The restrictive covenant, the bulwark of housing segregation, was thus made unenforcible by legal means. After 1946 the Interstate Commerce Commission and the Supreme Court ruled against discrimination in interstate transportation.

In three cases between 1938 and 1950 involving graduate education, the Court chipped away at the South's segregated educational system. In 1938, the Court held that Missouri could not send a qualified black law school applicant to an out-of-state law school merely because Missouri had no public black law school. The Court held that the applicant had a right to go to a public law school in Missouri that was "substantially equal to those which the state afforded there for persons of the white race." In 1950 the Vinson Court decided that a hastily built black law school in Texas constructed to comply with the Missouri precedent was not the equivalent of the University of Texas Law School. The new law school was not equal in physical facilities or in the "intangibles" that make for greatness in a law school. Texas failed the "substantially equal" test. The Court decided, "We cannot find substantial equality in the education offered white and Negro students by the state."

In 1950, the Vinson Court also ruled against a series of state laws governing the University of Oklahoma, which required that African Americans sit in separate rooms adjoining the main classroom and at special desks in the library, and eat at a separate time in the cafeteria. The Court declared such restrictions impaired and inhibited the plaintiff's "ability to study, engage in discussions and exchange views with other students, and in general to learn his profession."

THE WARREN COURT

In September 1953, President Eisenhower appointed California's governor, Earl Warren, to replace Vinson—a heart attack victim—as Chief Justice. The president later called the appointment "the biggest damned-fool mistake I ever made." Nevertheless, the Warren Court from 1953 to 1969 left a mark on U.S. constitutional development and the daily lives of the U.S. people unequaled by any Court since the Marshall Court.

In 1953 Earl Warren, a popular 62-year-old California politician, had held public office since 1919 as a racket-busting district attorney, a tough attorney-general, and an unprecedented three-term governor. He won the Democratic, Republican, and Progressive party nominations for attorney-general in 1938 and governor in 1946. He supported progressive social and economic legislation. In light of his later rulings as Chief Justice in favor of racial equality, of due process for the criminally accused and of legislative reapportionment, there is irony in his early support for the evacuation and detention of 110,000 Japanese-Americans in World War II, his tough law enforcement record as a prosecutor, and his opposition to legislative reapportionment in California in 1948.

Chief Justice Earl Warren

Preferred Freedoms

In the Warren years the Court became noted as an activist Court, but not in the tradition of the pro-property activism of the Supreme Court from the 1880s to 1930s. The Warren Court exercised judicial review to protect "preferred freedoms" from federal and state legislative and executive abuses or from the repressive forces of private groups or organizations. Justice Hugo Black wrote in 1947 that the clause in the Fourteenth Amendment, "nor shall any state deprive any person of life, liberty, or property, without due process of law," "incorporated" the first eight amendments to the Constitution against actions by states as well as by the federal government. Traditionally, the Bill of Rights had limited only the federal government. But in 1925 the Court decided that the First Amendment provisions on freedom of speech and press also protect citizens from state actions that violate the due process clause of the Fourteenth Amendment. In the 1950s and 1960s the Court, by "selective incorporation," declared that most of the rights contained in the first eight amendments to the Constitution restrain actions by the states.

The Warren Court under the "due process" and "equal protection" clauses of the Fourteenth Amendment expanded individual rights under law and established new assurances of legal equality. These decisions nullified local, state, and federal government actions that violated citizens' constitutional rights, and, to right old wrongs, went on to order affirmative action—such as legislative reapportionment and school busing. Unpopular and often persecuted minorities with little chance to gain legal rights through election now believed they had solid constitutional arguments for their claims, so they turned to the Court for judicial remedies to their grievances.

The Court responded by a vigorous exercise of judicial review and orders of affirmative action, and in the process reversed between 1953 and 1960 an unprecedented 45 previous Supreme Court decisions. Supporters applauded this shaping of basic law through Court initiatives. They saw the Warren Court as the most important and innovative branch of the federal government in domestic affairs. But critics charged it with becoming a policy-making branch, usurping the functions of the people's elected representatives in the legislatures. Justice Harlan, in 1964, expressed reservations on the Court's initiatives when he wrote,

> These decisions give support to a current mistaken view of the Constitution and the constitutional function of this Court. This view, in a nutshell, is that every major social ill in this country can find its cure in some constitutional 'principle,' and that this Court should 'take the lead' in promoting reform when other branches of government fail to act. The Constitution is not a panacea for every blot upon the public welfare, nor should this Court, ordained as a judicial body, be thought of as a general haven for reform movements.

Some feared that the Court's rulings might cause a severe loss of popular support. Widespread acceptance of the Court's moral and intellectual reasoning for its rulings is vital. For unlike the Congress, which has the "power of the purse," or the president, who has the "power of the sword," the Court, unless strongly supported by the legislature and/or executive, has only the "power of its opinion."

The most significant decisions of the Warren Court centered on race relations, legislative reapportionment, and criminal due process. The Court also ruled on important cases with often controversial results in matters of church and state and freedom of speech, press, and assembly. And the Court set limits on the enforcement of the Smith Act and legislative investigations.

Church and State Relations

In 1962 the Court ruled by a vote of 8–1 that the New York Board of Regents prayer for public schools, "Almighty God, we acknowledge our dependence upon thee, and we beg Thy blessings upon us, our parents, our teachers and our Country," was "wholly inconsistent with the establishment clause." The Roman Catholic hierarchy and Protestant fundamentalists expressed shock and denounced the decision. Most Jews, many liberal Protestants, and secularists applauded the Court. The following year the Court on the same grounds ruled 8–1 against a Pennsylvania law requiring a daily reading in school of ten Bible verses and a Maryland law requiring a daily Bible reading and recitation of the Lord's Prayer. The 1963 decisions outlawed practices that existed in 37 states and the District of Columbia, and included 41 percent of the nation's school districts.

In 1965 in a 7–2 decision the Court in *Griswold v. Connecticut* held unconstitutional an 1879 Connecticut law that made it a crime for any person to use or advise the use of any birth control means. Justice Douglas asserted,

> We do not sit as a super-legislature to determine the wisdom, needs, and propriety of laws that touch economic problems, business affairs, or social conditions. . . . The present case . . . concerns a relationship lying within the zone of privacy created by several fundamental consitutional guarantees. . . .
> It concerns a law which, in forbidding the *use* of contraceptives rather than regulating their manufacture or sale, seeks to achieve its goals by means having a maximum destructive impact upon that [marriage] relationship. Such a law cannot stand. . . . Would we allow the police to search the sacred precincts of marital bedrooms for telltale signs of the use of contraceptives? The very idea is repulsive to the notions of privacy surrounding the marriage relationship. We deal with a right of privacy older than the Bill of Rights.

Thus the Court went beyond any specific guarantee or principle of constitutional law to develop a general "right of privacy."

Douglas argued that a "fundamental right of privacy" had roots in the "penumbras"—the shadows, the interstices—of the First, Fourth, Fifth, and Ninth Amendments of the Bill of Rights. Other justices found the right of privacy in the 9th Amendment or the "liberty" clause of the Fourteenth Amendment. But when Douglas wrote, "We deal with a right of privacy older than the Bill of Rights" he was referring to natural law and natural rights—universal rights that a rational person would find reasonable and just. Some would call such an argument for a constitutional right of privacy an example of the "new substantive due process," doing for privacy what the "old substantive due process" did for liberty of contract and laissez faire economics. Privacy became central to and a most controversial part of Court cases in the 1970s, 1980s, and 1990s involving abortion, homosexuality, and the "right to die."

Though some charged the Court had exceeded its proper role and was making, not interpreting, the law, the decision had strong public support. A Gallup poll in November 1964 revealed that 81 percent of the public believed birth control information should be available to anyone who wanted it.

Freedom of Speech and Press

In 1964 the Warren Court declared that "speech concerning public affairs is more than self-expression; it is the essence of self-government." The Court believed that by a forceful, uninhibited exchange of ideas, the truth could be uncovered and progress assured.

In 1964, in *New York Times v. Sullivan,* the Supreme Court overturned a conviction in an Alabama state court, which declared the *Times* guilty of libel. The paper ran an ad placed by some civil rights leaders, which the jury found to be false and defamatory to L. B. Sullivan, a city commissioner in charge of the Montgomery police. Sullivan was awarded $500,000 in damages. A unanimous Court held newspapers guilty of libel only if they publish material they know to be false or with reckless disregard of whether it is true or false. This principle was extended in 1966–1967 to include comment on most public figures as well as government officials. The ruling provided a strong preferred position to free expression in our system of self-government.

The Court did not strike down the Smith Act as contrary to the First Amendment, as dissenters Douglas and Black urged, but made successful prosecutions more difficult than under the earlier *Dennis* decision. In 1957 the Court held that the Justice Department must prove the defendants advocated actual violent overthrow of the U.S. government now or in the future, not merely that they held such a belief. In a 1961 decision, the Court ruled that to gain a conviction for "knowing membership" the prosecution must prove that the defendant understood the organization's revolutionary purpose and participated vigorously to that end. In *Brandenburg v. Ohio* in 1969, involving the prosecution of some Ku Klux Klan rabble rousers, the Court declared that for the speech to be illegal it must actually incite or produce "imminent lawless action," not merely advocate violence as an abstract doctrine. The Court had returned to the clear and present danger doctrine.

Curbing the Abuses of Legislative Committees

By 1957 the Supreme Court had moved to curb the abuses of congressional and state legislative investigations into "un-American" activities. Legislative committee investigations serve as a necessary part of the legislative process, to educate the legislators and the public about the problem, define the issues, get the facts, and aid the legislators in drafting corrective legislation. Committees are not criminal courts, however. The techniques and methods of Senator Joseph McCarthy in the early 1950s (see p. 293) led to charges that he damaged the reputations and violated the rights of many witnesses. The hearings directed by McCarthy often took the tone of a criminal prosecution, but the witnesses did not have the legal rights of due process. Sensational public hearings occurred in which witnesses suffered such penalties as loss of reputation, dismissal from their jobs, and loss of pension payments. Investigating committees made uncooperative witnesses liable to criminal contempt proceedings and possible jail sentences.

In June 1957, Earl Warren for the Supreme Court asserted, "The Bill of Rights is applicable to investigations as to all forms of governmental action." Warren asked, "Who can define the meaning of un-American?" The Court declared the investigative body must tell a witness the subject of the inquiry, and how the committee's questions relate to it. There should not be exposure simply for the sake of exposure.

SCHOOL DESEGREGATION

The May 17, 1954, *Brown v. Board of Education* decision broke new constitutional ground for the Supreme Court and ushered in the civil rights revolution of the next 15 years. In the arguments before the high Court, the states' lawyers had maintained that the Tenth Amendment—"the powers not delegated to the United States by the Constitution, nor prohibited by it to the states, are reserved to the states"—made education the exclusive concern of the states. The NAACP's lawyers supporting Linda Brown claimed the Fourteenth Amendment—"No state shall . . . deny to any person within its jurisdiction the equal protection of the laws"—forbade state segregation laws.

Debates in Congress and the ratifying state legislatures in 1866–1868 had not discussed in detail the Fourteenth Amendment and public education. In 1896, in *Plessy v. Ferguson,* the Supreme Court decided that an 1890 Louisiana intrastate train segregation law was not in conflict with the Fourteenth Amendment as long as the separate facilities were equal. That segregation precedent, the "separate but equal" doctrine, became the guiding rule for numerous state and federal court decisions from 1896 to 1954.

Chief Justice Warren now urged the Court to speak with one clear voice. He feared that concurring opinions and dissents would make public compliance difficult to obtain. Warren desired a brief decision in ordinary language, an opinion that every weekly newspaper could reprint in full and all citizens could read and understand. The new Chief Justice's position carried the day, and resulted in a unanimous decision, an achievement of judicial statesmanship. Warren phrased the Court's opinion in brief, clear, and unequivocal language.

> Today, . . . it is doubtful that any child may reasonably be expected to suc-
> ceed in life if he is denied the opportunity of an education. . . . It is a right
> which must be made available to all on equal terms.
>
> . . . Does segregation of children in public schools solely on the basis of
> race, . . . deprive the children of the minority group of equal educational
> opportunities? We believe that it does. . . .
>
> To separate [Negroes] . . . solely because of their race generates a feeling
> of inferiority . . . unlikely ever to be undone. . . .
>
> We conclude that in public education the doctrine of "separate but equal"
> has no place. Separate educational facilities are inherently unequal. . . . We
> hold that the plaintiffs . . . (are) deprived of equal protection of the laws
> guaranteed by the Fourteenth Amendment.

The Court also requested further argument to decide what method would be most effective to remedy the situation. On May 31, 1955, in the second *Brown* decision, *Brown II,* the Court ruled that primary responsibility for desegregation rested with local school authorities under the supervision of the local U.S. District Courts. The Court recognized that local conditions required different solutions. It called for "transition to a racially nondiscriminatory school system" and ordered that progress be made "with all deliberate speed."

Public Reaction

The immediate reaction to the Supreme Court's desegregation ruling was mixed. A Gallup poll in late May 1954, indicated that 54 percent of Americans ap-proved "that all children, no matter what their race, must be allowed to go to the same schools." In the South only 24 percent approved and 71 percent disapproved. Adamant opposition appeared only in the Deep South.

Political Reaction

President Eisenhower did not attempt to persuade the public to accept the *Brown* decisions. He refused even to say he agreed with the *Brown* decision. "I think it makes no difference whether I endorse it or not," he said in 1956. "The

Constitution is as the Supreme Court interprets it; and I must conform to that and do my very best to see that it is carried out in this country." In 1956 he privately told a speechwriter, "I am convinced that the Supreme Court decision *set back* progress in the South *at least fifteen years*. . . . It's all very well to talk about school integration—if you remember you may be also talking about social *dis*integration." During the presidential campaigns of 1956 and 1960, however, both major political parties gave support in their platforms to the desegregation decision.

Though many southerners grudgingly agreed that desegregation was inevitable, a lack of effective leadership at the national and local levels created a vacuum soon filled by opponents, such as James Byrnes, governor of South Carolina, and Senator James Eastland of Mississippi, head of the Senate Judiciary Committee. Byrnes raised the fear of racial intermarriage and miscegenation, and suggested that the states end public education in order to block integration.

White Citizens' Councils in the South organized popular opposition to the *Brown* decisions as early as 1956. Southern politicians dusted off old nullification doctrines, which called for states to interpose their power between the federal courts and local school boards in schemes of "massive resistance." These politicians promised to aid private schools with state subsidies and tuition grants. They also used pupil placement tests, local control laws, complicated legal steps for African American parents, multiple forms to fill out for transfer to all-white schools, and redistricting to thwart desegregation. By 1964 the southern states had passed 471 laws to evade or avoid compliance with desegregation. In 1954–1955 most moderate southerners became silent as an atmosphere of intimidation and fear led to the dismissal of some outspoken colleagues and neighbors from their pulpits, their classrooms, or their jobs.

By 1956 the spirit of resistance swept across the South, as 101 southern congressmen and senators signed a "Southern Manifesto." They denounced the Supreme Court and called for resistance to school desegregation by "any lawful means."

> We regard the decision of the Supreme Court in the school cases as a clear abuse of judicial power. It climaxes a trend in the federal judiciary undertaking to legislate, in derogation of the authority of Congress, and to encroach upon the reserved rights of the states and the people. . . .
> . . . The Supreme Court of the United States . . . undertook to exercise their naked judicial power and substituted their personal, political and social ideas for the established law of the land.

In the 1960s billboards appeared calling for the impeachment of Earl Warren as segregationists, militant anti-Communists, and "law and order" advocates condemned the Court.

Little Rock

In September 1957 national and world attention focused on Little Rock, Arkansas when the court-ordered desegregation of Little Rock's Central High School became the first great test of federal power versus state interposition, court-ordered desegregation versus white supremacy, and presidential authority versus a defiant southern governor.

On May 20, 1954, the school board of Little Rock had voted to desegregate its schools, starting with the high school, in 1957. But on the night of September 2, 1957, Governor Orval E. Faubus ordered the Arkansas National Guard to Central High School in Little Rock "to maintain order." In reality his goal was to block the entry of nine African American students to Central High School. On the next day President Eisenhower, in a press conference, said, "You cannot change people's hearts merely by laws." He added that there are people who "see a picture of mongrelization of the race." On the same day the federal district court ordered desegregation at Central High School to proceed "immediately." On September 21 the federal district judge ordered Governor Faubus and the Arkansas National Guard to stop blocking desegregation in Little Rock.

As desegregation began in Little Rock, an angry white mob rioted. The *New York Times* reported, "A mob of belligerent, shrieking, and hysterical demonstrators forced the withdrawal today of nine Negro students from Central High School." About 1,000 white supremacists—screaming "niggers," "nigger-lovers," and "lynch"—forced the Little Rock authorities to persuade the African American students to leave the building by noon. On September 24 President Eisenhower, carrying out his constitutional responsibility to "execute the law," ordered federal troops into Little Rock and called 10,000 Arkansas National Guardspersons into federal service to join with the U.S. Army to end mob chaos and to enforce the federal court's orders.

The troops stayed at Central High for the rest of the school year. Little Rock school authorities declared the situation at Central High School "intolerable"—one of "chaos, bedlam, and turmoil"—and asked the federal district court for a two-and-a-half year suspension of school desegregation. Chief Justice Warren ruled for a unanimous Supreme Court in September 1958, in *Cooper v. Aaron*, "Constitutional rights . . . are not to be sacrified or yielded to the violence and disorder which have followed upon the actions of the Governor and Legislature (in Little Rock). . . . Law and order are not here to be preserved by depriving the Negro children of their constitutional rights." There was to be no delay or retreat.

The President and Congress Act

The pace of school desegregation proceeded slowly in the 11 states of the Old Confederacy. In 1964, only 1.2 percent of African American children attended desegregated schools. A few courageous African American children and parents, civil rights organizations, and a few often isolated federal judges carried the burdens of school desegregation. They received no presidential or congressional aid.

In 1963 and 1964, presidents John F. Kennedy and Lyndon B. Johnson finally gave vigorous support to school desegregation and the civil rights movement. They pressured Congress to enact the 1964 Civil Rights Law, which allowed the U.S. attorney general to initiate school desegregation suits—a morale boost and a financial relief to hard-pressed African American parents and civil rights organizations. Title VI of the act required the U.S. government to end funding to all federally assisted programs where there was racial discrimination. This stipulation became a major tool for school desegregation for the rest of the decade, especially after Congress enacted a law in 1965 granting massive sums of federal money for elementary and secondary education. The cut off of federal funds under Title VI replaced the slower, case-by-case court litigation process of the previous decade. The legislative and executive branches finally joined the judiciary in the fight against racial segregation in the public schools.

School Desegregation in the 1960s

School desegregation struggles continued in the courts in the 1960s. In 1964, after a long series of court fights involving 56 Virginia laws to block school desegregation and the five-year closing of Prince Edward County's schools, the Court, in reference to *Brown II,* held "there has been entirely too much deliberation and not enough speed" in desegregation. The Court ordered the county's schools reopened and authorized the lower federal court to order county officials to levy taxes to run a desegregated school system. Defining what state and local governments could not do to segregate students, the Court told local governments to take affirmative action to right old wrongs, thereby raising judicial activism another degree. In 1968, a unanimous Court in *Green v. New Kent County* also struck down a rural Virginia county's racial freedom-of-choice plan as unconstitutional. The Court's rule striking down "freedom-of-choice" and its call for an "affirmative duty" by "whatever steps" to eliminate "racial discrimination . . . root and branch" granted federal judges sweeping power to issue desegregation orders, including busing.

LEGISLATIVE REAPPORTIONMENT

Chief Justice Earl Warren referred to the state legislative reapportionment decisions of the 1960s as the most important during his tenure on the Supreme Court. They dealt with the fundamental issue of who is represented and with what impact in the state legislature. Prior to 1962, the Supreme Court had avoided ruling on the apportionment of state legislatures. In 1946, Justice Felix Frankfurter, for the Court urged judicial restraint and warned that the judiciary "ought not to enter the political thicket" of Court-directed legislative reapportionment. He held the issue was a political one to be resolved by the political process. In the reapportionment decisions of 1962 and 1964, the Court rejected this approach.

For decades, and in some cases since the eighteenth century, many states had legislative representation plans that apportioned representatives on grounds other than equal population districts, at least in *one house* of the legislature. Proponents of judicial intervention argued that the federal courts had jurisdiction because citizens' "equal protection of the laws" was being denied by state action in violation of the Fourteenth Amendment. Should one man's vote be the equal of another's?

In the years since the drafting of state constitutions and the enactment of apportionment statutes, the nation's population had increased and moved from farms to cities and their surrounding suburbs. Most states did not reapportion their legislatures to keep up with these population changes. Rural voters held a stranglehold on most state legislatures. Rural legislators would not vote themselves out of office or their constituents out of favored positions. Reformers viewed the federal courts as the only hope to achieve proportional representation. By the mid twentieth century, public opinion strongly supported reapportionment as a reaffirmation of equality and majority rule. A study of the 1960 census disclosed that in 44 states, legislative apportionments permitted less than 40 percent of the population to elect majorities in the legislatures; in 13 states, one third or less could elect a majority of both houses in the legislature. Vermont's house of representatives had one representative from each town. Thus one town with a population of 38 cast the same vote in the state legislature as another with a population of 33,155. Vermont had not redistricted its house of representatives since 1793. People in metropolitan areas believed legislatures ignored urban needs—in favor of rural interests. They complained about "rotten boroughs" and "minority rule."

In 1962 in *Baker v. Carr,* the Supreme Court ignored Justice Frankfurter's warning and entered the "political thicket," holding in a 6–2 decision that it had jurisdiction in a Tennessee legislative reapportionment study.

The Alabama constitution of 1901 directed that both houses of the state legislature be apportioned according to population and be reapportioned after each census. But the legislature had not been reapportioned since 1900. On June 15, 1964, in *Reynolds v. Sims,* Chief Justice Warren spoke for a majority of eight to uphold a lower federal court order to the Alabama legislature to reapportion. Warren wrote,

> Legislators represent people, not trees or acres. Legislators are elected by voters, not farms or cities or economic interests. As long as ours is a representative form of government elected directly by and directly representative of the people . . . it would seem reasonable that a majority of the people of a

state could elect a majority of that State's legislators. . . . The Equal Protection Clause demands no less than substantially equal state legislative representation for citizens . . . an honest and good faith effort to construct districts, in both houses of its legislature, as nearly of equal population as is practicable.

Opponents' attempts to allow one house of a state legislature to be represented on a basis other than population by amending the federal Constitution, as well as the resolutions of 32 state legislatures to convene the first national constitutional convention since 1787, failed. By 1967, within three years of the *Reynolds* decision, all 50 state legislatures complied with the Court's reapportionment ruling—a victory for judicial activism and the popular "one person one vote" movement.

CRIMINAL DUE PROCESS

Due Process

Americans historically have prided themselves on their allegiance to "fair play" and the "rules of the game," concepts called "due process of law" in criminal law and justice. The Warren Court took major and controversial steps to assure due process to those accused of crimes.

The constitutional provisions of greatest importance in criminal cases are the Fourth, Fifth, and Sixth Amendments. The most relevant portions of the amendments follow (emphases added):

4th Amendment: The right of the people to be secure in their persons, houses, papers and effects against *unreasonable* searches and seizures, shall not be violated, no warrant shall issue, but upon *probable cause,* supported by oath or affirmation, and particularly describing the place to be searched, and the persons or things to be seized.

5th Amendment: No person . . . shall be *compelled* in any criminal case to be a *witness against himself.* . . .

6th Amendment: In all criminal prosecutions, the *accused* shall enjoy the *right* . . . to have *assistance of counsel* for his defense.

Such limitations on government police actions and safeguards for individuals had long been recognized in the federal courts. The Warren Court redefined these rights and extended their protection to individuals in state criminal proceedings under the Fourteenth Amendment—"nor shall any state deprive any person of life, liberty, or property, without *due process of law.*" But the unanimity of the Warren Court in the school desegregation cases and the strong majority in the legislative reapportionment decisions often gave way to deep and bitter division in the Court on these issues of due process.

Gideon v. Wainwright, 1963

On March 18, 1963, the Court in *Gideon v. Wainwright* held the Fourteenth Amendment's due process clause guaranteed all poor defendants free legal counsel in state felony prosecutions (crimes that are more serious and carry heavier punishments than those classified as misdemeanors). Florida had charged Clarence Earl Gideon, "a fifty-one-year-old white man who had been in and out of prisons much of his life," with robbing a pool room in Panama City, Florida in 1961. At his trial in the state court, his request for a court-appointed free lawyer was denied. Gideon defended himself, lost, and received a five-year jail sentence. He then sent a handwritten appeal to the Supreme Court. Although in 1942 in *Betts v. Brady,* the Supreme Court had denied free legal counsel to indigents in state courts, the Court took Gideon's case and appointed Abe Fortas, later a justice of the Supreme Court, to argue Gideon's claim. Fortas argued that counsel in a criminal trial is a fundamental right of due process enforced on the states by the Fourteenth Amendment. In the Court's unanimous 1963 decision overturning the *Betts* precedent, Justice Black wrote, "Any person hailed into court, who is too poor to hire a lawyer, cannot be assured a fair trial unless counsel is provided for him. This seems to us an obvious truth." Retried in 1963 with counsel in the same Florida courtroom and by the same judge as in the initial trial, Gideon was acquitted—after two years in jail.

The Miranda Decision

The historic *Miranda v. Arizona* case in 1966 raised two questions. First, did criminal suspects have the right to counsel before trial, such as during police interrogations? Second, if the right of counsel is denied, can the prosecution use "voluntary" confessions obtained in the absence of counsel at the trial or must the judge exclude such evidence on the grounds of the Fifth Amendment?

The Court delivered its answers in a controversial 5–4 decision on June 13, 1966, when it spelled out the "Miranda rule" for police to follow. On March 13, 1963, police arrested 23-year-old indigent Ernesto A. Miranda, a ninth-grade dropout and schizophrenic, for kidnapping and raping an 18-year-old girl in Phoenix, Arizona. The girl identified Miranda in a police lineup. Questioned by police, he did not request a lawyer, nor was he advised of his right to counsel. Two hours later he confessed and signed a written confession. At his trial Miranda's lawyer moved the confession be excluded as evidence. The lawyer argued that the use of Miranda's confession gained without his knowledge of his right to counsel violated his Sixth Amendment right. The judge allowed the confession to stand as evidence and Miranda lost. Miranda's lawyers appealed to the Supreme Court.

Earl Warren wrote the decision that stated:

> The prosecution may not use statements . . . stemming from custodial interrogation of the defendant unless it demonstrates the use of procedural safeguards effective to secure the privilege against self-incrimination. . . . As for the procedural safeguards . . . Prior to any questioning, the person must be warned that he has a right to remain silent, that any statement he does make may be used as evidence against him, and that he has a right to the presence of an attorney, either retained or appointed. The defendant may waive . . . these rights, provided the waiver is made voluntarily, knowingly, and intelligently.

Even if a defendant waived these rights, he could call for an attorney at any time during the interrogation. Warren held that "the constitutional foundation underlying the privilege is the respect a government—state or federal—must accord to the dignity and integrity of its citizens."

Four justices dissented with often bitter words. Police officials claimed "their hands were tied." Many charged the Warren Court with "coddling criminals," and moves to "Impeach Earl Warren" and "Curb the Court" spread.*

In 1967 in *In re Gault,* the Court extended the right of counsel to juveniles and held that in the pretrial interrogation juveniles must be told of their right of silence and that what they say can be used against them in juvenile court proceedings.

The Fourth Amendment—*Mapp v. Ohio,* 1961

In 1961 the Court in *Mapp v. Ohio* ruled to exclude all evidence from state criminal trials obtained by police in violation of the Fourth Amendment's restraints "against unreasonable searches and seizures."

At 1:30 P.M. on May 23, 1957, three Cleveland police officers rang the doorbell of Dollree Mapp. The police said they wanted to question her—they did not say on what subject. The police suspected "Dolly" Mapp was hiding a person wanted for questioning in a recent bombing and that she had illegal gambling materials. Miss Mapp called her lawyer, who advised her not to let the police in without a search warrant. She opened the second-floor window and asked if they had a warrant. They did not and she refused them admittance. They placed the Mapp house under surveillance.

---

* Miranda was retried, reconvicted, and resentenced to 20 to 30 years in prison. A good prison record, in which he completed two years of college by correspondence, earned Miranda a parole in 1972. He died of stab wounds in a barroom fight in 1976.

Three hours later seven police broke into Dolly Mapp's home. She demanded to see a warrant. A police officer held up a piece of paper, she grabbed it, and "placed it in her bosom." A struggle ensued. The officers recovered the piece of paper. The police did not find what they were looking for, but they did find "obscene materials," the possession of which violated Ohio law. Dolly Mapp was arrested, tried, and convicted for "knowingly having (possessed) . . . lewd and lascivious books, pictures, and photographs."

In the state trial no warrant was produced. The police entry, search and seizure were illegal. The Supreme Court faced the question, should it reinterpret the Fourteenth Amendment's provision that a state must not deny a person liberty without due process of law to exclude from state criminal trials evidence gained in violation of the Fourth Amendment?

Justice Tom C. Clark, attorney general under President Truman, wrote for a majority of five that material seized in violation of the Fourth Amendment is "inadmissable in a state court. . . . We can no longer permit (the Fourth Amendment) to remain an empty promise."

"Wiretaps" and "Bugs"—*Berger v. New York*, 1967

The Warren Court also took a strong stand against the abuses of the Fourth Amendment by the new electronic technology of "wiretapping" and "bugging." In *Berger v. New York* (1967), the Court declared unconstitutional a 1938 New York law that permitted police use of wiretapping and bugging. This decision overturned a Court ruling in 1928 that upheld wiretapping. Justice Oliver Wendell Holmes then called wiretapping a "dirty business." Many law enforcement officials, however, maintained that tapping and bugging served as essential police tools against organized and white-collar crime.

By 1967, the federal government and most states forbade indiscriminate wiretapping, although they did allow court-authorized wiretaps by police. Only seven states had any laws to forbid official or private bugging, and six of those allowed court-ordered bugs.

A 1938 New York law allowed electronic surveillance if the police could prove to a judge that "reasonable ground" existed that evidence of a crime might be obtained, and if the police named the particular person, conversations, and telephone to be tapped. The order would last for two months, but could be extended by the judge. In 1964, the New York police obtained information by a court-authorized "bug" and convicted Ralph Berger as a "go-between" in a bribe of the New York State Liquor Authority to get a license for a Playboy club.

The Supreme Court decided in a 5–4 vote that the New York law violated the Fourth Amendment as applied to the states by the Fourteenth. Justice Clark wrote, " 'The proceeding by search warrant is a drastic one' . . . and must be carefully circumscribed so as to prevent unauthorized invasions of 'the sanctity of a man's house and the privacies of life.' . . . New York's broadside authorization rather than being 'carefully circumscribed' . . . permits general searches by electronic devices." Four of the justices defended the New York law. Justice Black held that the Fourth Amendment forbids only "*unreasonable* searches and seizures," and does not erect walls of impenetrable "privacy," but his view did not prevail.

The Warren Court did allow police to "stop and frisk" a suspect on the street without a warrant. In *Terry v. Ohio* in 1968, Warren, speaking for the Court's majority said that police can stop "suspicious-looking persons" and "frisk them *for weapons*" when that is reasonably necessary for the safety of police and others. Any weapons or other evidence of crime produced in the frisk are admissable evidence in court.

Crime and the 1968 Presidential Campaign

From 1960 to 1967 the nation's crime rate rose 89 percent. Murders rose 40 percent; rape, 22 percent; assault, 55 percent; car theft, 52 percent, and robbery, 151 percent. A frightened public demanded safe streets and an end to the judiciary's "coddling of criminals."

In 1968, a presidential election year, the Vietnam War, race relations, and campus turmoil bitterly divided Americans. A Gallup poll showed that 63 percent of Americans believed the courts were too lenient on criminals. The Republican presidential nominee, Richard Nixon, called for a strengthening of the "peace forces over the criminal forces." In June 1968, Congress enacted a comprehensive "Safe Streets and Crime Control Act." It greatly increased federal aid to local police departments and authorized wiretaps and bugs by federal, state, and local law enforcement officers under court authorization and strict supervision. However, efforts in Congress to overturn *Miranda* and other Warren Court decisions on due process failed.

THE BURGER COURT

President Nixon appointed four justices to the Supreme Court in his first term in office. When Chief Justice Earl Warren retired in June 1969, Nixon named Circuit Court Judge Warren E. Burger to be chief justice. Burger was more conservative than Warren on the questions of "judicial activism" versus "judicial self-restraint" and on the rights of the criminally accused. The Democratic Senate rejected the nominations of two conservative southern federal judges, Clement F. Haynsworth in November 1969, by a vote of 55–45 and G. Harrold Carswell in April 1970, 51 to 45. Nixon finally succeeded in gaining the appointments of two federal judges, Harry A. Blackmun of Minnesota and Lewis F. Powell, Jr., of Virginia, and William H. Rehnquist, of Arizona, a former aide to Senator Barry Goldwater and Attorney General John Mitchell, to the Supreme Court. President Ford appointed an independent appellate judge, John Paul Stevens. In 1981, President Reagan named an Arizona state judge, Sandra Day O'Connor, as the first woman justice.

The first years of the Burger Court held some surprises for expectant conservatives. In 1971, Chief Justice Burger wrote two opinions for a unanimous Court. One upheld a lower federal judge's sweeping school desegregation order, including busing, in Charlotte-Mecklenburg, North Carolina, and the other, *Griggs v. Duke Power*, made a broad interpretation of the equal employment provision, Title VII, of the 1964 Civil Rights Act, resulting in affirmative action. In 1972 the Court unanimously rebuked the Nixon administration's claim of a right to wiretap Americans without a judicial warrant on assertion of national security needs. In 1973, the Court by a vote of 7–2 handed down the *Roe v. Wade* decision, arguably the most activist decision, as well as the most controversial since *Brown*, making abortion in the first six months of pregnancy a fundamental constitutional right based on a right of privacy and striking down all the state anti-abortion laws.

The four Nixon appointees did dissent in *Furman v. Georgia* in 1972, however, when the five Warren Court holdovers declared unconstitutional all the death penalty laws in the nation. Burger also dissented in the 1970 "Pentagon Papers Case" in which the Court, by a 6–3 vote, ruled that the Nixon administration's attempt at prior restraint to block publication of the classified government record of the Vietnam War violated the First Amendment's freedom of the press.

During his tenure as Chief Justice from 1960 to 1986, Burger grew more conservative, and the Court became more divided, with 6–3 and 5–4 decisions accounting for about 40 percent of all its rulings after 1972. In the post-Warren years, the Court demonstrated more deference to the executive and legislative branches, increased respect for state rights, and a preference that social issues be resolved in the political process, not by the judiciary. For example, the Burger Court modified its rulings on the death penalty. After breaking new ground in the 1972 *Furman* decision, the Court pulled back in 1976 and upheld new capital punishment laws in Georgia, Florida, and Texas.

The Abortion Issue

After *Roe v. Wade*, Congress passed a law in 1976 to stop all payments by Medicaid funds for abortions, except in cases of rape, incest, or when the birth of a child would place the mother's health in danger. In 1980, the Court in a 5–4 decison, *Harris v. McRae,* upheld the federal and several state laws that public funds need not be spent even for "medically necessary abortions." The Court ruled that though a woman had a constitutional right to have an abortion, the goverment is not compelled to finance the abortion. That ruling may have ended 250,000 to 300,000 abortions a year, as low-income women could not afford the financial costs. The decision aroused cries of discrimination against the poor. The Court left the issues of financing to the states, however, an example of judicial restraint.

In the 1980s and 1990s the abortion issue stirred continuous controversy in Congress, state legislatures, presidential elections, and court litigation. But in several cases, particularly in a 6–3 decision on an Akron, Ohio ordinance in 1983, and in a 5–4 vote on a Pennsylvania law in 1986, the Court strongly reaffirmed *Roe v. Wade* and struck down state restrictions.

School Desegregation

Much of the business of the Court, in the Burger years, as before 1969, revolved around issues of race. The Court, in *Alexander v. Holmes County Board of Education* in October 1969, unanimously rebuked the Nixon administration's attempts to delay school desegregation in Mississippi and ordered "every school district to terminate dual school systems at once and to operate . . . only unitary schools." In one year the percentage of African Americans attending formerly all-white schools in the South jumped from 18.4 percent to 38.1 percent. *Swann v. Charlotte-Mecklenburg Board of Education* in April 1971 upheld court-ordered busing to desegregate the Charlotte schools saying that busing was a legitimate tool to "dismantle the dual school systems." "Busing" and "neighborhood schools" remained issues throughout the 1970s as federal courts issued desegregation orders, including school busing in many large northern cities, notably Boston.

On July 25, 1974, in *Milliken v. Bradley,* the 20 years of unanimous, 9–0, Court decisions in school desegregation cases ended when the Supreme Court overruled a federal judge's order that Detroit and 53 surrounding suburbs must join in one metropolitan school district of almost 800,000 school children with massive busing to end school segregation. The Court split 5–4. The federal district trial judge had found that segregation existed by acts of city and state officials. The city's schools had become 67 percent African American; the suburban schools were 95 percent white. The trial judge ruled a metropolitan plan with large-scale busing the only way to end dual educational facilities and create a unitary system.

Chief Justice Burger, for the majority, including all four Nixon appointees, held that "disparate treatment of white and Negro students occurred within the Detroit school system and not elsewhere, and . . . the remedy must be limited to that system. . . . The constitutional right of the Negro . . . in Detroit is to attend a unitary school system in that district." He found no discriminatory action by the suburbs and thus ruled they could not be included in the desegregation order. The majority ruling barred any court-ordered busing across district lines for integration, except where both districts discriminated.

Justice Thurgood Marshall, the former chief counsel of the NAACP in the famous school desegregation cases of the 1950s and the first African American Supreme Court justice, wrote an impassioned opinion for the four dissenters. He charged the majority with "emasculation of our constitutional guarantee of equal protection." Marshall claimed the Court's order for Detroit to eliminate segregation in its schools and its ruling that the metropolitan plan was illegal resulted in a contradiction impossible to resolve—a system 67 percent African American could not be desegregated effectively.

In the 1970s and 1980s, private, whites-only educational institutions increased in the South. In 1970 the Internal Revenue Service had revoked these schools' tax-exempt status, but Bob Jones University in South Carolina refused to pay taxes. Burger, in forceful language, in *Bob Jones University v. U.S.* in 1983, ruled for a majority of eight that congressionally authorized tax exemptions applied to organizations that serve a "public purpose" and do not act "contrary to established public policy." He wrote that it was clearly the public policy of the United States since 1954 to end racial segregation. "There can no longer be any doubt that racial discrimination in education violates deeply and widely accepted views of elementary justice. . . . It would be wholly incompatible with the concepts underlying tax exemption to grant the benefit of tax exempt status to racially discriminatory educational entities."

In the first decade after *Brown*, the progress in racial-school desegregation was slow. Only 9.3 percent of the 3.4 million African American students living in the 17 states and the District of Columbia that had segregation laws in 1954, attended desegregated schools in 1964. With the strength of the civil rights movement and the vigorous support of the president and Congress from 1964 to 1968, especially Title VI of the Civil Rights Act of 1964, the pace quickened. By 1972, 46.3 percent of African American students in the Old Confederacy went to schools with a majority of whites. The South led the Border states and the North and West in school desegregation. In a major irony, the rural South, with its former rigid segregation and racial etiquette, slowly achieved the most desegregated schools. The 1968 *Green* decision outlawing "freedom-of-choice" combined with the administrative threat of Title VI to cut off federal funds to provide the impetus that led small southern towns with two schools and less housing segregation than the cities to move effectively to desegregate.

Northern cities now became the new centers of the school desegregation struggle, although evidence indicates that growing southern cities are "resegregating," with an increase in residential segregation and support for "neighborhood schools." After the 1970s every president, with the exception of Jimmy Carter, slowed the desegregation process. Title VI fell into disuse, and the Justice Department reduced its court suits. Congress became involved in passing various antibusing bills. More than 50 percent of U.S. school children rode buses to school in the 1980s and early 1990s but only 7 percent for purposes of desegregation. Total busing mileage in many southern states decreased after desegregation, because segregation required more busing. Students attending segregated private schools in the South required more busing in 1983 than those attending desegregated public schools. Yet the congressional rhetoric and antibusing bills continued.

The Reagan administration reached a new level of foot dragging on school desegregation. Reagan's support for Bob Jones University versus the Internal Revenue Service (IRS) and Reagan's opposition to affirmative action made his position clear, as did the budget cuts for enforcement of Title VI and the inaction and opposition to civil rights by the Department of Justice.

The Issues of Affirmative Action—Reverse Discrimination

In June 1978, in *Regents of the University of California v. Bakke,* a divided Court ruled on the question of affirmative action at the University of California Medical School at Davis. The medical school had set aside 16 of 100 admissions places exclusively for minority applicants, and some of those admitted had lower test scores than Allan P. Bakke, a 32-year-old white engineer. Bakke argued that the special quota reserved for African Americans, Asian Americans, and Hispanics denied him equal protection under the law in violation of the Fourteenth Amendment. Proponents of affirmative action called the quota not exclusionary, but a reasonable attempt to overcome the legacy of two centuries of slavery and years of segregation. The justices wrote six opinions and 153 pages of text—a far cry from the simple clarity of *Brown I.* Justice Powell ruled with four justices against the explicit reservation of 16 admissions places for minorities and ordered Bakke's admission; but Powell joined the four dissenters to form a majority that upheld affirmative action programs in which race may be a "plus," but not the sole factor in admission. The long-awaited decision was inconclusive, but the Court did uphold a "race-conscious" approach to admissions.

In related affirmative action employment cases, the Court in 1979, in a 5–2 decision, rejected a Louisiana white steelworker's claim of "reverse discrimination" and ruled "permissible" a voluntary affirmative action hiring program, including quotas, resulting from collective bargaining between private parties, a union and a company. But in July 1980, in *Fullilove v. Klutznick,* for the first time the Court upheld a congressional law requiring that 10 percent of a $4 billion public works apropriation go to "minority business enterprises." Chief

Justice Burger declared that Congress can recognize the legacy of job discrimination, need not be "color blind," and can legislate under the Fourteenth Amendment.

In 1984, the Court gave hope to the Reagan administration's anti-affirmative action efforts when it overruled a lower federal court that had declared Memphis could not lay off recently hired African American firefighters, but must obey affirmative action orders. The Supreme Court, in *Firefighters v. Stotts*, by a 6–3 vote, declared that "bona fide" seniority rules protect whites' jobs and do not violate Title VII of the 1964 Civil Rights Act. *Stotts* applied only to layoffs where there had been no proof of discrimination; but to advocates of affirmative action the decision brought fears of a basic shift in policy that would declare preferential treatment in hiring, promotions, and other employment practices "reverse discrimination" and a violation of the Fourteenth Amendment's Equal Protection Clause.

Two years later, in three decisions written by Justice Brennan, two 5–4 and one 6–3, the Court ruled for affirmative action in employment. The majority declared that a Michigan school board may give preference to African Americans in hirings and promotions and supported a judge's consent decree in Cleveland in which the city gave preferential treatment to hire and promote African American firefighters over whites with higher civil service scores and more seniority. The Court even upheld a U.S. district judge's order that Local 28 of the New York Sheet Metal Workers Union must hire a work force that was 29.23 percent African American and Hispanic by August 1, 1987. Brennan wrote that such a "race conscious goal" and order represented reasonable judicial remedies where there had been a history of "persistent and egregious discrimination."

Women's Rights

After a half century of efforts, Congress proposed the Equal Rights Amendment in 1972, but the ratification effort fell three states short of the constitutionally required three fourths in 1982. There was substantial progress, however, on the legal front on equality between the sexes. In 1963 Congress enacted the "Equal Pay Amendment" to the Fair Labor Standards Act of 1938; in 1964, Title VII of the Civil Rights Act outlawed sex discrimination in employment; and in 1972, Title IX of the Education Act banned sex discrimination in education.

A 1983 *New York Times* poll clearly showed a shift from 1970 in women's attitudes toward work outside the home as opposed to staying at home and raising a family. In 1970, 53% of women surveyed cited motherhood as one of the best parts of being a woman, but in 1983 only one quarter agreed. In 1970, less than 10 percent of women surveyed listed work outside the home as an enjoyable part of their lives; in 1983, 26 percent agreed. In 1983, 58 percent of

U.S. working women responded that they would rather work than stay at home even if they could afford to stay home, as did 31 percent of nonworking women. Forty-four percent of women in 1983 claimed there was discrimination in the workplace, where working women made only 62 cents to each dollar earned by men.

A follow-up 1989 *Times* poll revealed second thoughts by women on their expanding economic roles. Eighty-three percent of working mothers felt torn by conflicting claims from their jobs and families. In 1989, close to half of working women said they had to give too much to their jobs at the expense of their children and family life. But by then to attain or maintain a middle-class standard of living, the two-parent working family had become a necessity for most Americans. Between 1970 and 1989 the number of women doubled who said they worked primarily to support their families. In 1989, women made up 45 percent of the work force compared to 38 percent in 1970, and women's earnings had improved from 62 to 70 cents for each dollar earned by men. Economic opportunities also improved, and women entered once-closed professions such as lawyers, engineers, doctors, accountants, and business managers in large numbers. Women have significantly entered police work and the military, as seen in the 1991 Gulf War, and make up 50 percent of the nation's bus drivers. The same *Times* poll showed that working women fuel the women's movement, with special emphasis on public policies to aid the two working parent family, such as day care and parental leave. Equality in the workplace, however, remains working women's primary concern.

From 1971 to 1986, the Burger Court upheld Title VII of the 1964 Civil Rights law against sex discrimination. The Court ruled that employers cannot refuse to hire women solely because they have preschool children. Alabama could not refuse to hire women prison guards because they are not over 5'2" or weigh less than 120 pounds because size and strength requirements were not necessary to perform the job. The Court also held that employers cannot require working women to pay higher monthly pension contributions, nor pay retired women lower monthly annuity benefits than men based on women's longer life expectancy, because an employer cannot adopt a "fringe benefit scheme that discriminates on the basis of sex." In 1986 in *Meritor Savings Bank v. Vinson,* a unanimous Court decided that sexual harassment, defined as not only the loss of a job, but also as the creation of "hostile working environment," of a female employee in a District of Columbia bank by her supervisor constituted a violation of Title VII.

But in 1984, in *Grove City College v. Bell,* in a 6–3 decision, the Court narrowed the reach of Title IX banning sex discrimination in federally assisted colleges. The Court ruled, in support of the Reagan administration, that Title IX applied only to the specific department receiving the federal aid—in this case federal scholarship and loan funds; and not to the institution as a whole, as had been the practice since 1972. This ruling took the teeth out of Title IX on gender discrimination. The decision also boded ill for Title VI of the 1964 Civil Rights Act against race discrimination, Section 504 of the Rehabilitation Act of 1973, and the Age Discrimination Act of 1975, because all those civil rights laws had similar wording. These acts had given the U.S. government great power to end discrimination based on sex, race, disability, and age by the cutoff of federal funds. Congress, however, reversed the decision in 1988 when it passed the Civil Rights Restoration Act over President Reagan's veto and the opposition of the Republican nominee, George Bush. The new law makes clear that Congress instructs the executive to cut off all funds to an institution if there is any discrimination in these four areas in any single program at that institution.

In 1971 the Court for the first time applied the Fourteenth Amendment's equal protection clause to void a state law for sex discrimination. In *Reed v. Reed,* Chief Justice Burger wrote for a unanimous Court that Idaho's law granting men preference over women in administering deceased persons' estates violated the Fourteenth Amendment. Justice Brennan wanted to apply a tougher standard to all laws that classify people by gender. He wrote an opinion that all laws that treat women differently from men should be "inherently suspect"— that such gender classification should be treated as the Court treated racial classification. Brennan's view did not prevail, but the Court has frequently invoked the Equal Protection Clause to strike down state gender discrimination laws.

From 1974 to 1981 the Court also upheld certain laws that treated women differently—some would say protectively; others, unequally. The Court supported a Florida law that gave widows, but not widowers, a $500 property tax exemption, for there is "no dispute . . . financial difficulties of a lone woman . . . exceed those facing men." The Court upheld a California law that treated statutory rape as a crime when an older man has sexual intercourse with a girl, but not when an older women does so with a boy, for "only women may become pregnant" and "women suffer disproportionately . . . the consequences of sexual activity."

"Comparable worth" is a new concept advanced to establish equal pay among the sexes in comparable employment. Many jobs, traditionally held by women and thought of as "women's work," such as secretaries, nurses, and elementary school teachers, receive relatively low pay. Equal pay for equal work, though upheld by the Court, promised little improvement in women's income, because such occupations had few men. Advocates of comparable worth held the law still left a pool of low-paying "women's jobs." They based comparable worth on the equal employment opportunity provisions of the Civil Rights Act of 1964. Their proposal called for equal pay for different jobs of comparable value. The Supreme Court in a 5–4 decision in 1981 gave the comparable worth advocates hope. In that case, the Court overruled a trial court's rejection of a suit claiming discrimination brought by women matrons of an Oregon county jail for women who claimed that their salaries were $200 less a month than the salaries earned by the county's all-male deputy sheriffs.

In December 1983 the principle of comparable worth won a major victory when a federal trial judge in the state of Washington ordered the state government to pay its women workers $800 million to $1 billion in back pay and wage increases. In 1986, the state of Washington adopted the principle of comparable worth. Some women's incomes have doubled, and the gap between earnings by men and women dropped from 20 percent to 5 percent. There are still "women's jobs"—now better paid—and "men's jobs," and many workers in male-dominated jobs have left state employment for better paying jobs in private industry, leaving significant shortages in certain occupations. Reagan's Equal Economic Opportunity Commission unanimously ruled against comparable worth for federal employees in 1985, and Reagan's appointee as head of the Civil Rights Commission called it "the looniest idea since Looney Tunes came on the screen." Women's groups, unions, and many Democrats lined up on the other side. The Supreme Court has yet to rule on the constitutionality of several city and state comparable worth plans.

Criminal Due Process

The Burger Court both extended and curtailed the Warren Court's landmark decisions in criminal due process. In 1972, in a logical extension of *Gideon* the Court granted the right to counsel to indigents in all federal and state misdemeanor as well as felony cases if conviction could result in incarceration, but denied suspects the right to counsel in preindictment police lineups.

The basic *Miranda* rule stood unchanged until 1984, and in fact was extended to misdemeanor as well as felony cases. However, the Burger Court decisions from 1971 to 1980 whittled away at *Miranda*.

After 18 years, the Court in a 5–4 decision, *New York v. Quarles* in 1984, announced basic change in the *Miranda* rule. Justice Rehnquist, speaking for the majority, wrote that the police can ask questions first and give the warning later in a "situation where concern for public safety must be paramount." The police, after chasing a rape suspect, whom they had been told was armed, through an almost empty supermarket late at night, took him in custody and immediately asked him where the gun was. He answered, "The gun is over there." The lower courts excluded as evidence both the question and the gun at the trial as evidence obtained in violation of the *Miranda* rule. The Supreme Court's decision to overrule "blurs the edges of the clear line" of the *Miranda* rule and promised much litigation as to what constitutes a "public safety exception."

The Fourth Amendment's restraints on search and seizure and the 1914

Supreme Court "exclusion rule" extended to the states in the 1961 *Mapp* ruling—evidence illegally obtained must be excluded from a criminal trial— resulted in much litigation, split decisions, and legal confusion. Law enforcement officers, in attempts to stop the drug traffic and organized crime, found themselves in conflict with the Fourth Amendment and the exclusion rule. The Burger Court both supported and limited police.

In 1984, in a break with 70 years of precedents, the Court decided in *U.S. v. Leon,* a California drug dealing case, that some evidence obtained with defective search warrants can be used by prosecutors in criminal trials. The 6–3 decision declared that the exclusion rule should not apply when the police act in "objectively reasonable reliance" on a search warrant that at the time appeared to be valid, even though it later proved defective. Civil libertarians denounced the Court's ruling as a fundamental breach in the Bill of Right's protection of individual liberty and privacy.

First Amendment Decision

On First Amendment issues the Court rulings were also mixed, as illustrated by two early Burger Court decisions. In the 1971 "Pentagon Papers" case, *New York Times v. United States,* the high court decided 6–3 that the government could not exercise restraint prior to publication of information. The case involved the "leaking" of the Defense Department's "classified" history of the Vietnam War—the Pentagon Papers—to the *Times.* The Justice Department had obtained a lower federal court order to prevent the *Times'* publication of the material. Justice Brennan, for the majority, wrote "The First amendment tolerates absolutely no prior judicial restraints of the press predicated upon . . . conjecture that untoward consequences may result." The Court ruled in *Branzburg v. Hayes,* a 5–4 1972 decision, that the First Amendment does not grant reporters the privilege to refuse information subpoenaed by grand juries investigating criminal acts. The Court held that reporters who failed to comply could be jailed for contempt. The press claimed that if it could not keep its sources confidential, then sources would "dry up" and investigative reporting and an "informed citizenry" would be hurt.

Jefferson's "wall of separation between Church and State" received the Court's endorsement in decisions between 1973 and 1975. The justices disallowed state grants to nonpublic schools for building maintenance, state reimbursement of tuition or state tax credits for parents with children in nonpublic schools, and direct loans of instructional material, staff, and services to nonpublic schools. It held these practices violated the "establishment" clause.

In the 1980s, the Court zigged and zagged on church and state issues. In 1983, in *Mueller v. Allen,* a 5–4 decision upheld a Minnesota law that gave tax deductions for certain school expenses to both private and public school parents.

The lion's share went to parochial school parents who paid tuition. *Mueller* was the first time the Court endorsed any form of tuition aid to parochial schools. A year later, in 1984, the Court held, 5–4, that Pawtucket, Rhode Island could include the Christian Nativity scene as part of a tax-supported Christmas display. Chief Justice Burger wrote for the Court that the constitutional standard should be whether the challenged practice represents "a real danger of establishment of a state church." Burger referred to Thomas Jefferson's concept of a "wall of separation" as a "useful figure of speech," but not an accurate description or guide for "the relationship that in fact exists between church and state" in the 1980s. He concluded that "any notion that these symbols (the creche) pose a danger of establishment of a state church is farfetched."

In four decisions in 1985, however, contrary to the arguments of the Reagan Justice Department, the Court restored the "wall of separation." In one case the Court struck down Alabama's "moment of silence" at the start of the public school day because the legislative debate had made clear that the law represented an attempt to restore Christian prayer to the school. In another, the Court held that the 1965 Education Act that allowed public school teachers to teach remedial or enrichment courses in church schools violated the establishment clause.

THE REHNQUIST COURT

The Building of a Conservative Court

With the retirement of Chief Justice Burger in June 1986, President Reagan nominated the leader of the conservative wing of the Court, Justice Rehnquist, to be the new Chief Justice. A stormy confirmation hearing in the Senate Judiciary Committee followed. Several senators raised tough questions about Rehnquist's opinions on abortion, affirmative action, equality for women, free speech, church-state relations, and due process for those accused of crime. They claimed his "extreme" philosophy on the role of the Court in matters of individual liberty and equal protection under the law threatened fundamental U.S. rights and values. The Senate finally confirmed Rehnquist, 65–33, the 33 "no" votes being the largest number ever cast against a confirmed justice. Reagan then nominated, and a weary Senate unanimously approved, an arch-conservative federal circuit court judge, Antonin Scalia, to fill Rehnquist's former seat.

President Reagan's "social agenda," his pledges to end abortion, restore prayer in the schools, block the Equal Rights Admendment (ERA), check affirmative action, and get tough on criminals and pornography, had failed to gain congressional support. The Justice Department, especially under Attorney General Edwin Meese, turned to the Court and argued vigorously for Reagan's agenda. In a speech in 1985, Meese charged that the Court had become the maker, not the interpreter of the laws. The Court, he claimed, should exercise restraint and be faithful to the Founding Fathers' words and their "original intent," and should not create constitutional law where, he said, it does not exist, such as a right to privacy. Opponents retorted that Meese, frustrated by the inaction of Congress on the Reagan agenda, wanted to politicize the Court and make it the forum to promote a right-wing ideology. Meese's critics further argued that original intent is impossible to discover. Many held, with Justice Brennan, that the simple injunction to determine and apply original intent was "arrogance masked in humility." Also, they joined with Jefferson to rebuke the call that the present generation be ruled by the "dead hand" of the past. For example, should the Fourth Amendment's restraints on "unreasonable search and seizures" not apply to wiretapping because the authors of that amendment could not have foreseen changes in technology, such as modern telecommunications? Meese went on to say that Congress in 1789 did not intend that the Bill of Rights should limit the states. His critics responded that Meese was ignoring the Civil War and Reconstruction era, especially the Fourteenth Amendment and its due process clause, which the Court in the twentieth century has held to incorporate the Bill of Rights as restraints on state action. Should the Court view the provisions of the Constitution literally, as fixed provisions of a finished document, or as a set of general principles to be interpreted by the Court relative to changing times and circumstances? Justice Brennan made a public speech, unusual for a sitting justice, to rebut Meese.

When the moderate "swing" justice, Lewis Powell, retired in 1987, President Reagan nominated Robert H. Bork, a former Yale law professor, U.S. Solicitor General, and U.S. Circuit Court Judge in the District of Columbia. An outspoken and controversial conservative and an advocate of original intent, his nomination caused a storm of protest from a variety of civil rights, civil liberties, and women's groups as well as liberal senators. They feared that his confirmation would tip the bench 5–4 against the Warren Court's major precedents. After acrimonious televised hearings, with heated charges about the politicalization of the Court and a battle over judicial philosophies, the Senate rejected Bork by a vote of 58–42, the largest margin of defeat for a U.S. Supreme Court nominee in history. Next, Reagan nominated Douglas H. Ginsberg, a little known federal judge, but withdrew his nomination when it became known that he had smoked marijuana with students while teaching at Harvard Law School. Reagan finally succeeded in gaining confirmation of federal circuit court judge Anthony M. Kennedy, less controversial but a reliable conservative.

In July 1990 Justice William J. Brennan, Jr. retired after 34 years on the bench at the age of 84. If Earl Warren had been the moral conscience of the Warren Court, William Brennan had been its intellectual architect. Brennan had continued to gain majorities for his views for 21 years after Warren's retirement. In 1990, President Bush nominated a former New Hampshire state judge, 50-year-old David H. Souter, to succeed Justice Brennan. Souter, a reserved, little known, conservative New Englander, was presented by President Bush as a judge "who will interpret the Constitution, not legislate from the bench." In the 1990–1991 session, Souter joined the Court's majority in a tough law and order stance to overturn five precedents in the area of criminal due process. With the Warren Court justices gone, the question now concerned the Court's position on its major decisions and its general philosophy of jurisprudence in U.S. life.

Race Relations

Affirmative action became a central, and emotional, focus for the Court in race, and, increasingly, gender relations. In 1987 and 1990, Justice Brennan led slim majorities furthering unprecedented affirmative action policies. In 1987, the Court affirmed an Alabama federal judge's order to promote African Americans in the Alabama state police force; upheld an unprecedented municipal California transportation agency's voluntary action to promote a white woman over a man with test scores two points higher than the woman's; affirmed the power of Congress to favor African Americans and other minorities to acquire ownership of radio and television licenses; and upheld a federal judge's order to the Kansas City school board to raise the local property tax to pay the costs of a school desegregation plan, thereby intruding on the traditional legislative power of the purse.

For a decade, however, opponents of affirmative action argued that the equal protection clause protects individuals, not groups. They also held that affirmative action should be limited to cases in which the record proved specific instances of past discrimination and where the remedy was "narrowly tailored" to right the wrongs for the specific victims of discrimination. The advocates of affirmative action pointed to a pervasive history of societal discrimination and urged judges to exercise broad powers in fashioning remedies. The debate became inceasingly heated. One side charged "reverse discrimination" and "quotas." The other argued for special policies to overcome the heritage of slavery and racial discrimination and called for transitional numerical "goals."

Defeats for Affirmative Action

From January to June 1989, however, the Rehnquist Court took a strong anti-affirmative action position in five cases, four by 5–4 rulings. The majority included Chief Justice Rehnquist, and justices O'Connor, White, Scalia, and Kennedy.

In the first three of these decisions, Justice O'Connor wrote for a 6–3 majority that a Richmond, Virginia, City Council ordinance setting aside 30 percent of public works contracts for minority businesses violated the Fourteenth Amendment. Such a racial classification violated the equal rights of nonminority businesses. The Court held that to deny the constitutional rights of white contractors, there must be a "compelling state interest." O'Connor held that there must be (1) evidence to prove an actual pattern of "prior racial discrimination" and (2) that any remedy must be "narrowly tailored" to "fit the compelling goal." O'Connor found no specific discriminatory evidence in the record. There was obvious irony in the Supreme Court striking down an affirmative action plan voted by the elected city council of the former capital of the Old Confederacy.

In 1989 the Court, in a 5–4 decision, overruled the unanimous 1971 decision in *Griggs v. Duke Power* on "disparate impact" in employment. Chief Justice Burger had written in 1971 that the North Carolina utility's diploma and test requirements, though neutral on their face, had little relation to actual job performance, acted as "built in head winds" for African Americans, and had a racially discriminatory impact. The key for the Burger Court under Title VII of the 1964 Civil Rights law was not *intent*, but *impact*. If the African American plaintiffs could prove statistically that the employment practices had a racially disparate impact, then the burden of proof shifted to the employers to prove that the employment practices served a "business necessity." Such proof is usually difficult to establish and often leads to costly court fights. Many employers chose to take voluntary steps to redress striking racial and gender imbalances in their work forces. In the 1989 case, *Wards Cove v. Atonio*, arising from the complaints of Native Americans and Asian Americans in Alaskan salmon canneries who were relegated to nonskilled, low-paying jobs and to segregated housing and dining halls, Justice White, for the majority of five, wrote that despite the statistical evidence of a racially disparate impact, the burden of proof continues to rest with the plaintiffs.

In the third 1989 decision, an Alabama case, *Martin v. Wilks*, the Rehnquist Court undermined the binding force of consent decrees ordering affirmative action in hiring and promotion. Federal judges had issued consent decrees that had the force of law after minorities sued city governments on the grounds that African Americans had been discriminated against in public employment, most often by municipal police and fire departments, and after affirmative action programs had been adopted. Over 200 local governments settled such disputes by court consent decrees, and the decrees in these civil rights cases were long regarded as immune from later legal attacks by third parties. But in a Birmingham case, Chief Justice Rehnquist ruled for the Court that an eight-year-old consent decree mandating the hiring and promotions of African Americans and whites in equal numbers in the city's fire department until the firefighters approximated the racial composition of the local work force was not binding on employees hired after the decree. Rehnquist held that consent decrees binding on future third parties represented reverse discrimination and could be challenged by individuals, in this case whites, who were not parties to the original dispute and settlement. The ruling overturned consent decrees around the nation, invited renewed litigation, and the revival of old disputes.

Congress, urged by civil rights and women's groups and led by Senator Edward Kennedy (D., Mass.), drafted legislation to rewrite the laws and overturn the Court decisions (all except the Richmond case, which would take a constitutional amendment or a different Supreme Court interpretation of the Fourteenth Amendment). Again there was irony, for in the first half of the twentieth century civil rights leaders had placed little hope in the Congress, and, instead, had looked to the Court's reinterpretation of the Reconstruction amendments for assistance. Congress responded and passed the Civil Rights Bill of 1990. But in 1990, George Bush became the first president in history to veto successfully a civil rights bill, because the Senate failed by one vote to gain the two-thirds majority to override. Bush charged that the bill would force employers to adopt quotas. The bill's supporters denied the charge and pointed out that the bill ruled out quotas as a remedy for discrimination. In 1991, Bush backed down from his quota charges and signed the Civil Rights Act of 1991 that overturned 8 Rehnquist Court decisions, including *Wards Cove v. Atonio* and *Martin v. Wilks* and extended to women the right to sue for damages in cases of sex discimination or sexual harrassment in employment, a right long held by racial minorities.

Women's Rights

In 1988 the Court upheld a 1984 New York City law requiring the admission of women to private clubs that play an important part in business and professional life. Earlier, the Court had unanimously approved a Minnesota law ending sex discrimination in the Jaycees, and a California law that opened Rotary Clubs to women. In 1989, in *Price Waterhouse v. Hopkins*, Ann Hopkins won a discrimination suit on job promotion using Title VII. She charged that the intent of her employer was to discriminate, and the Court declared the burden of proof that her claim was false lay with Price Waterhouse, and the company could not sustain that proof.

Criminal Due Process

The Court continued to expand the exceptions to the *Miranda* and exclusionary rules. In decisions from 1981 to 1990, the Court held that the police must follow the basic procedural safeguards of *Miranda*, but the courts accepted confessions gained by deceptive means, such as a police officer posing as a prison inmate and getting another inmate to talk about crimes he or she committed. Moreover, Court decisions allowed law enforcement officials to present evidence in prosecutions gained in warrantless searches of people's trash and by surveillance from airplanes.

It was the death sentence, however, that drew the most attention. Most Americans in the 1980s and 1990s supported the death penalty. An Associated Press poll in January 1988 revealed that 86 percent of Americans supported capital punishment; in 1967 only 47% supported it. Thirty-six states enacted capital punishment laws after the 1976 Supreme Court decision approved newly drafted laws in Florida, Georgia, and Texas, but 22 had not yet held an execution by 1990. As of 1988, 75 percent of all executions had been carried out in six states—Florida, Georgia, Louisiana, Texas, Alabama, and Virginia. By mid-1991, more than 2,500 inmates sat on death row in 36 states, whereas only 167 had been executed since 1976.

Capital punishment proponents in 1988 cited the stark statistics of more than 20,000 murders a year in the 1980s in contrast with 8,464 in 1960, the popular desire for a strong deterrent, and society's right to self-protection. Yet states with the death penalty have higher murder rates than states without it. Opponents, having given up on the "cruel and unusual punishment" argument, claimed that the death penalty was meted out in an unfair and discriminatory manner and thus violated due process of law. Between 1977 and 1987, half of all U.S. homicide victims were African Americans, but of the 68 people executed in those 10 years, 92 percent had killed whites. Researchers in Georgia revealed that killers of whites were 11 times more likely to be sentenced to death in Georgia than killers of African Americans. Twenty-two percent of African Americans in Georgia who murdered whites were sentenced to death; 3 percent of whites who killed African Americans received the death sentence. But in 1987 in a 5–4 Georgia case, *McClesky v. Kemp*, the Court declared that statistics showing race-related disparities in the imposition of the death penalty were not significant enough to sustain due process challenges to state death penalty laws. In 1989 the Court, again split 5–4, held the Constitution permits states to execute murderers who are mentally retarded or who were 16-year-old juveniles when they committed murder.

The Retreat from the Right of Privacy

In the 1986 *Bowers v. Hardwick* case, the Court upheld Georgia's antisodomy law as applied to homosexuals to convict two consenting male adults for having sexual relations in the privacy of the defendant's house. In 1990, in *Cruzan v. Missouri*, the Court recognized a patient's right to refuse life-sustaining treatment, but also upheld the Missouri Supreme Court's denial of the Cruzan family's request to remove the nutrition and hydration tubes that had kept their

32 year-old daughter Nancy alive for seven years in a "persistent vegetative state." The Cruzans's arguments that they be allowed to remove the tubes rested on their claim to constitutional rights of family privacy. The Court, however, respected Missouri's most demanding "clear and convincing evidence" standard, an example of judicial deference to the states. Missouri's standard requires a written statement of intent before patients become incompetent to express themselves. Nancy's statements to her sister and her roommate that she would never want to live as a "vegetable" were ruled insufficient.*

In 1989, in the months after Ronald Reagan left office, much of his agenda was on the way to judicial implementation. In those months the Court handed down its anti-affirmative action rulings, upheld the death sentences of a juvenile and a mentally retarded person, and in *Webster v. Human Reproductive Services*, finally broke with its line of decisions that had strongly reaffirmed *Roe v. Wade*. In the 16 years since 1973, the abortion issue had become increasingly divisive, at times leading to acts of violence. Probably no decision except *Dred Scott v. Sanford* and *Brown v. Board of Education, Topeka* aroused such deep public emotion as *Roe v. Wade*. In *Webster* the Court upheld a Missouri law restricting abortions. The Court approved Missouri's law (1) to ban the use of public hospitals or other tax supported facilities to perform abortions not necessary to save the mother's life, even if the woman were willing to pay the full cost; (2) to ban all public employees—such as doctors, nurses, and other health care providers—from performing or assisting in any abortion not necessary to save the mother's life; and (3) to require that a doctor must perform tests on any fetus he or she suspects may be 20 weeks old to measure fetal age, weight, and lung development to determine if the fetus is "viable." The *Roe* precedent had held that viability only began in the third trimester. Medical experts had testified that 20-week-old fetuses could not be viable. The tests could also work an unequal hardship on the poor. Though the decision did not overturn *Roe*, it made clear that a majority of the justices no longer held that an abortion is a woman's fundamental constitutional right. Justice Blackmun, the author of *Roe*, read his dissent from the bench in a somber voice, "For today, at least, the law of abortion stands undisturbed. . . . But the signs are evident and very ominous, and a chill wind blows."

The *Webster* decision placed the issue of abortion back in the political arena of state governments. To the surprise of many, the pro-abortionists, using the cry of "pro-choice," defeated the anti-abortion "right to life" forces in several major political confrontations in 1989. Pro-choice advocates helped elect

---

* In December 1990, Missouri Probate Court Judge Charles E. Teel, who had first ruled in 1988 that the Cruzans had the right to remove the feeding tubes, ruled again that the Cruzans could remove the tubes and allow Nancy to die. Missouri did not challenge the Cruzans's request or Judge Teel's ruling.

pro-choice candidates, including the first African American governor of Virginia, L. Douglas Wilder; a Catholic governor of New Jersey, James J. Florio; and the first African American mayor of New York City, David N. Dinkins. In 1990, Connecticut's legislature enacted *Roe v. Wade* into state law under the Connecticut state constitution to assure women the right to an abortion in Connecticut, even if the Supreme Court overruled *Roe*. Pennsylvania, Utah, Guam, and Louisiana, however, enacted tough anti-abortion laws that will give the Court another clear opportunity to address the constitutionality of *Roe*. In 1991 the Court upheld the Reagan administration's 1988 ruling that medical personnel in federally funded family planning clinics cannot discuss abortion with pregnant women. Critics claimed the ruling violated the free speech of medical practitioners and the doctor-patient relationship, but the Court held the government need not finance abortion. Congress enacted a bill in 1991 to end the "gag rule," but the House fell 12 votes short in an attempt to override President Bush's veto.

The First Amendment and Religion

Cases involving religion and the schools continue to occupy the Court. It ruled for and against religious fundamentalists' goals in public education. In 1987, the Court declared unconstitutional a 1981 Louisiana law that required the teaching of the "creationist" theory of humanity's origin alongside the theory of evolution. The law's "pre-eminent purpose," wrote Justice Brennan, "was clearly to advance the religious viewpoint that a supernatural being created humankind." The federal courts also overruled an Alabama federal judge who, responding to fundamentalist pressures, ordered 40 history and social studies textbooks removed from the state's public schools on the novel ground that those books established the religion of "secular humanism." In a 1990 Iowa case, the Court declared that the federal Equal Access Law of 1984 was constitutional and not a violation of the establishment clause and that students under that law have the right to organize Bible study and political discussion clubs on school premises on the same basis as other extracurricular activities. In a 1989 Pittsburgh case, the Court claimed to "clarify" the 1984 Pawtucket Creche ruling. The Court held that a nativity scene standing alone in a courthouse violated the establishment clause, but that a display of an 18-foot-tall Hanukkah menorah alongside a 45-foot-tall Christmas tree a block away on the steps of the Pittsburgh city hall did not. The difference was the context, wrote Justice Blackmun, because the first appeared to give state endorsement to a religion, whereas the second was part of a festive celebration of the winter holiday season that has attained a secular status in U.S. society!

The First Amendment and Flag Burning

In 1989 the Court ruled that a Texas law (and similar laws in 47 other states) outlawing the desecration of the U.S. flag violated the First Amendment's protection of "symbolic" free speech and expression. Justice Brennan wrote, "We do not consecrate the flag by punishing its desecration, for in doing so we dilute the freedom that this cherished emblem represents." In an unusual move, two of the Court's most conservative members, Scalia and Kennedy, joined the liberal core of Brennan, Marshall, and Blackmun to form a 5–4 majority. A public uproar was led by President Bush who called for a constitutional amendment to protect the flag because it is the symbol of our national unity. But Congress, hesitant to change the 200-year-old Bill of Rights, enacted a law making it a crime to burn or deface the flag. In 1990, the same coalition of justices, speaking again through Brennan, found the new law "suffers from the same fundamental flaw" as the Texas law.

The End of a Supreme Court Era?

On June 27, 1991, Justice Thurgood Marshall, 82 and in failing health, retired after 24 years on the Court. Over six decades Thurgood Marshall had crafted much of the twentieth century's civil rights law. For 23 years he was the chief counsel of the NAACP Legal Defense and Educational Fund, winning 29 of 32 cases before the Supreme Court involving racial discrimination, notably in housing, voting, and education. Marshall greatly expanded the meaning of the equal protection clause and furthered the rights of minorities, women, and the poor. When Marshall joined his close friend and colleague William Brennan in retirement, the Court lost its last real tie to the Warren Court. Often in dissent since 1975, Marshall, in his last opinion in 1991, thundered against the new majority's overruling of established precedents, "Power, not reason, is the new currency of this Court's decision-making. . . . Neither the law nor the facts [have changed] . . . only the personnel of this Court did."

President Bush responded by nominating Clarence Thomas, a 43-year-old conservative African American Circuit Court judge and a beneficiary of Marshall's life work in civil rights. Thomas represented a striking change from Marshall. A child of poverty from rural Georgia who was raised by his sharecropper grandparents and Catholic nuns, and a graduate of Holy Cross College and Yale Law school, Thomas achieved his conservative credentials as head of Reagan's Equal Economic Opportunity Commission (EEOC) from 1982 to 1989 where he opposed affirmative action, dragged his feet on age discrimination cases, and spoke out against abortion. The NAACP, the AFL-CIO, women's groups, the elderly—a coalition similar to the anti-Bork movement of 1987—formed to block the Thomas appointment, while the White House, Senate Republicans, and conservatives rallied to Bush's nominee. After the Judiciary Committee concluded its hearings and divided 7–7 on Thomas, and two days before the scheduled full Senate vote on Thomas, a news report appeared that stunned the Senate and the nation. An African American University of Oklahoma Law School professor, Anita F. Hill, also a Yale Law School graduate and a former aide to Thomas at EEOC, responded to a routine FBI investigation of the nominee ordered by the Judiciary Committee. She alleged that Thomas had verbally sexually harrassed her at work at the EEOC. For three days the U.S. public watched and heard Hill's testimony and Thomas's denials on TV before the all-male Judiciary Committee in a volatile combination of race, sex, and bitter political infighting. The Senate, whose procedures appeared to have run aground, confirmed Thomas by the closest vote in the history of the Court, 52–48, in effect rejecting the word of the African American woman and asserting its marginal confidence in Clarence Thomas to succeed Thurgood Marshall.

The question became how far the Court of the 1990s might go to reverse precedents of the Warren and Burger Courts in areas of abortion, affirmative action, privacy, criminal due process, and First Amendment areas of speech, press, and religion. One might expect a conservative judge to respect precedent, but the conservatives of the Rehnquist Court, critical of the earlier Court's "policy-making," seemed willing to reverse precedents in order to return policy-making to the elected branches of government. Like Franklin D. Roosevelt in the late 1930s, Ronald Reagan and George Bush fundamentally changed the composition and the role of the Supreme Court for years to come. Proponents of civil liberties and equal protection of the law now looked increasingly to elected legislatures, and particularly to state lawmakers and state supreme court judges. For example, by 1991, courts in eight states had found a right to privacy, including reproductive choice, within their state constitutions. If *Roe* were reversed, the legal right to an abortion would stand in those states as a state constitutional right. Whatever the outcome, during the years from 1950 to 1990, the U.S. Supreme Court had played the central role in making individual liberties and equal protection of the law growing realities in U.S. life.

CHAPTER 9

The Struggle for Racial Justice

"We'll walk hand in hand, we'll walk hand in hand, we'll walk hand in hand someday
Oh, Deep in my heart, I do believe, We Shall Overcome Someday"

Civil Rights Song

The place—Montgomery, Alabama, the capital of the Confederacy, a black belt antebellum city. The date—December 1, 1955. Mrs. Rosa Parks, a seamstress in a downtown department store, refused a bus driver's order to give her seat to a white man. The police arrested Mrs. Parks for breaking the city segregation ordinance. The court found her guilty, and fined her $14. In response, the angry black community conducted a one-day boycott of buses with almost 100 percent success. A group of black ministers organized the Montgomery Improvement Association (MIA) and led a subsequent 382-day boycott struggle to desegregate the buses.

The black people of Montgomery pushed their leaders into a test of strength with the white segregationists who ran the city. A 27-year-old Baptist minister, Martin Luther King, Jr., was chosen to lead the MIA. A newcomer to Montgomery, he united the factions that divided the black community, brought the once apathetic black middle-class minority into the movement, persuaded the black churches to become socially active, and sustained the black citizens in their vigorous and courageous boycott. His leadership and oratory, as well, inspired the black community.

The next month, unknown terrorists bombed King's home. The bomb shattered the front porch and damaged the living room, and his wife and child narrowly escaped injury. A crowd of African Americans quickly gathered in front of the bombed house, and nervous city officials and police watched. King quieted the angry crowd and rallied their spirits. The young minister shaped a powerful social movement with such words as: "We must meet violence with nonviolence. . . . We must love our white brothers no matter what they do to us. . . . Remember . . . God is with the movement."

Through the Montgomery boycott, courageous African Americans found a new way to take direct action against racial injustice. They need not wait on others—lawyers, politicians, or judges—for their deliverance. Many African Americans hoped massive, nonviolent direct action would lead them beyond tokenism to real integration.

RACE RELATIONS IN THE 1940s

The Balance Sheet, 1940

Some events of the 1930s gave hope to black America, but the old problems of legal segregation, disenfranchisement, and systematic discrimination remained. The New Deal liberals could not even muster enough votes to enact a federal anti-lynching law. The balance sheet of black progress in 1940 might have listed on the negative side: in the South, disenfranchisement, de jure segregation, racism, economic subordination, and discrimination; and in the North, the growth of ghettos and their many problems. On the positive side: the consolidation in the 1930s of the tradition of racial solidarity, self-help, and economic development bequeathed by Booker T. Washington; the existence of civil rights organizations such as the National Association for the Advancement of Colored People (NAACP); the growth of black institutions such as presses, churches, fraternal organizations, and businesses; the impact since 1914 of the migration of African Americans from southern farms to northern cities and urban-industrial developments that broke down the traditional social relationships of rural life; the growth of a vigorous black culture led by the Harlem Renaissance; the newly won political leverage of African Americans in key northern electoral states and in the Democratic party; and the interracial unionism of the CIO.

The Legacy of World War II

As World War II ended in 1945, African Americans returned to the battle of fighting racism on one front—at home. The opening of the Nazi torture chambers of Buchenwald, Dachau, and Auschwitz, and the numbing revelations at the Nuremburg trials educated the world to the horrors of "racism." The U.S. government had made ringing declarations for human rights in the Atlantic Charter of 1941 and in Roosevelt's Four Freedoms speech. Hopeful, but still skeptical, African Americans demanded deeds as well as words.

Life, or at least the vision of what life might be, changed for some African

Americans dramatically during World War II. Many young black men committed to that vision went to war and saw the world, but they chafed at the humiliations of a completely segregated life in the U.S. military. On the home front, A. Philip Randolph, president of the Brotherhood of Sleeping Car Porters and Maids, threatened an all-black march on Washington to gain jobs for African Americans. He gained a presidential order in 1941 from Franklin D. Roosevelt to forbid discrimination in defense industries and to establish a Committee of Fair Employment Practices (FEPC) to oversee the order. The black press became more militant. The NAACP increased its membership from 50,556 to 450,000 during the war years. In 1944 the Supreme Court ruled against discrimination in Pullman cars and the denial of black voting in southern primaries.

Postwar Developments

International events of the late 1940s stirred the U.S. civil rights movement. Afro-Asian peoples broke the hold of Western imperialism and moved to national independence. The new status of black African nations increasingly inspired African Americans in the 1950s and 1960s. In 1948 the UN Commission on Human Rights, headed by Eleanor Roosevelt, drafted a charter, the Universal Declaration of Human Rights, which encouraged the disinherited everywhere. The ideological cold war between the West and the Communist bloc was fought in terms of "freedom" versus "totalitarianism." The gap between U.S. racial practices and rhetoric became a significant issue in the international propaganda contest. At home the migration of African Americans to the cities continued; industrialism relentlessly eroded the old social order with its fixed racial relationships; and urban African Americans exercised increased political power. Such international and domestic pressures worked to change U.S. racial patterns.

PRESIDENT TRUMAN, THE NAACP, AND THE COURT

Truman and Civil Rights

Harry S. Truman was the first president sympathetic to the broad expansion of civil rights for African Americans. In 1946 in response to racial violence, Truman created by executive order the President's Committee on Civil Rights. In 1947 the committee issued a report, *To Secure These Rights,* recommending "the elimination of segregation . . . from American life." The report became a blueprint for civil rights reformers for the next two decades. Truman asserted, "We must make the Federal government a friendly, vigilant defender of the rights and equalities of all Americans." The president sent a package bill to Congress in February 1948, urging the creation of a permanent civil rights commission, a joint congressional committee on civil rights, and a civil rights division in the Justice Department; a strengthening of existing civil rights laws and passage of a federal anti-lynching law; guarantees of voting rights, and specifically, the abolition of the poll tax; a fair employment practices commission; an end to discrimination in all interstate transportation facilities; and home rule plus voting rights in presidential elections for citizens of the District of Columbia.

Congress, however, controlled by a coalition of Republicans and conservative southern Democrats, did nothing. In June 1948, the president issued another executive order to force an end to segregation in the armed forces. Ironically the military, a basically authoritarian organization built on a chain of command, now took the lead in equal employment and promotion practices. Truman also issued an order for fair employment in the federal government.

In the election of 1948, Truman pushed civil rights to the point where many southerners walked out of the Democratic party convention and formed the Dixiecrat party, which carried four southern states for its presidential candidate, J. Strom Thurmond, governor of South Carolina. But Truman's actions earned him the support of African American votes in the big electoral states of the North—votes that proved decisive in his upset victory over the Republican candidate, Thomas E. Dewey.

Truman's successes in civil rights came through executive actions. Congress, with its seniority system that favored the entrenched southern Democrats, its rural bias, its cumbersome rules of procedure, and its Senate filibusters, passed no civil rights legislation from 1875 to 1957.

The NAACP and the Supreme Court

The NAACP Legal and Educational Defense Fund lawyers, headed by Thurgood Marshall initiated major new steps in U.S. race relations. The Supreme Court was the branch of government that took the lead. Lawyers and judges used Reconstruction amendments, the Fourteenth and the Fifteenth, as the primary instruments of change.

Since its founding in 1910 by W.E.B. DuBois, the NAACP emphasized political lobbying, public information, and court litigation to advance the rights of African Americans. The NAACP realized that a despised minority had less chance of progress through the political process under majority rule than through court litigation under the constitutional guarantees that no state may deny "due process," or "equal protection of the law," or the right to vote "on account of race." The climactic moment for the NAACP lawyers, led by Thurgood Marshall, came on May 17, 1954. In *Brown v. Board of Education of Topeka,*

Kansas, a unanimous Court speaking through Chief Justice Earl Warren, ruled that legal segregation in public education was unconstitutional.

For the next 10 years, in the face of growing white southern resistance, and in the absence of effective presidential leadership or congressional support, African American children and parents, civil rights lawyers, and the federal courts led the fight to end racial segregation. Change came slowly. There was token compliance in part of the Upper South and a defiant "never" in the Deep South and Virginia.

THE MONTGOMERY BUS BOYCOTT AND MARTIN LUTHER KING

The Montgomery bus boycott of 1955–1956 began a new era in U.S. race relations. Massive, nonviolent, direct action campaigns presented a new strategy and tactics. Martin Luther King, Jr., and other civil rights leaders inspired not only African Americans, but also other groups who had been discriminated against or excluded from the mainstream of U.S. society, including Hispanics, Native Americans, the poor, and women.

Martin Luther King, Jr.

Martin Luther King, Jr. was born in Atlanta, Georgia, on January 15, 1929, the son of a successful minister and the grandson of a sharecropper. Though a member of Atlanta's comfortable African American middle class and from a closely knit religious family, young King learned of discrimination and racial injustice early; in the 1930s Atlanta was a "Jim Crow" city. He had the advantage of an excellent education, first at Morehouse College, then at Crozer Theological Seminary and Boston University, where he earned a doctorate in 1954. Shortly thereafter he and his wife of one year, Alabama-born Coretta Scott, decided to "go South," and he accepted a pastorate in Montgomery, Alabama.

King's Movement toward Nonviolence

King's personal philosophy and strategy for social change had many roots. He made the words and deeds of Jesus Christ his lifelong guide. As a student at Morehouse, he read Thoreau's *Essay on Civil Disobedience.* He agreed that an individual should remain true to his conscience, even to the point of breaking unjust laws, and yet he should show his respect for law by accepting the penalty of imprisonment. In seminary King made a personal commitment to make the church as concerned with the improvement of conditions in this world as with the salvation of souls. While at Crozer, King was moved by a lecture on Mohandas Gandhi. The leader of India's massive nonviolent civil disobedience campaigns against British imperialism, Gandhi met hate, violence, and force with love and suffering. King came to see the redemptive power of love and unearned suffering as powerful forces for social change. He also accepted the view of Hegel, a nineteenth-century German philosopher, that history is a process in which all progress comes through struggle and that "historical figures" move history in accord with the world spirit.

To King the Christian community of love was to be achieved by Gandhian means of nonviolent resistance against evil. One should actively and directly protest against the evil actions of people, not against the people themselves. One should neither hate nor seek to humiliate an oppressor, for King's method of nonviolent resistance sought to awaken the moral conscience of the oppressor and to promote reconciliation. In his eyes, the suffering inflicted on innocent people by oppressors could be redemptive both for the sufferer and the oppressor, who could be converted by the victim's courage and righteous cause. Thus, one should abstain from all violence, both physical and spiritual. Love is central to nonviolence. To King love meant understanding, acceptance, and a recognition of the fundamental humanity of all persons. To do violence to one's brother was to do violence to oneself. Love, nonviolent direct action, and redemptive suffering would heal the divisions and bring peaceful reconciliation and the triumph of justice in the human community. King believed that there existed a "creative force in this universe that works to bring the disconnected aspects of this reality into a harmonious whole." Such was King's intellectual "pilgrimage to nonviolence." He noted that the experience in the Montgomery bus boycott of 1955–1956 "did more to clarify my thinking on the question of nonviolence than all the books that I have read."

The Montgomery Bus Boycott

In the Montgomery bus boycott African Americans refrained from using the buses for over a year. African American citizens urged on their leaders, and their leaders sustained the people. Initial negotiations with the bus company, private citizens, and the city council proved fruitless. The police arrested and jailed King for "speeding." Terrorists bombed his home. Police harrassed, arrested, and jailed African Americans on all sorts of minor charges. A grand jury indicted 115 African Americans for breaking a 1921 Alabama antilabor law against boycotts. When African Americans organized a car pool to get to work, the city government requested a local court injunction against the car pool as a "public nuisance" and an illegal "private enterprise." Each repressive step solidified the African American cause. The NAACP, claiming the Montgomery segregation ordinance violated the Fourteenth Amendment's "equal protection" clause, brought a legal suit to support the boycotters' direct action campaign. On November 15, 1956, the Supreme Court provided a major victory for African Americans and King's nonviolent approaches by striking down the Montgomery bus segregation ordinance as a violation of the Fourteenth Amendment. In 1957, King and his associates in the black ministry organized the Southern Christian Leadership Conference (SCLC) to coordinate and spread the new tactics throughout the South.

The Student Nonviolent Coordinating Committee (SNCC)

On February 1, 1960, black students staged a sit-in at a "whites only" lunch counter in Greensboro, North Carolina. By the end of March, student sit-ins, stand-ins, kneel-ins, wade-ins, and lie-ins had spread throughout the South. So began the civil rights revolution. Young black students now went beyond gradualism and the tactics of the older leaders. Inspired by King and the success of the Montgomery bus boycott, they adopted direct nonviolent confrontation to oppose southern segregation. In April 1960, at Shaw University in Raleigh, North Carolina, they organized the Student Nonviolent Coordinating Committee (SNCC).

SNCC workers, living among African Americans in the South, became the shock troops of the civil rights revolution. Most accepted nonviolence only as a tactic of social change rather than as a philosophy of life. They thought more in terms of political conflict, and they talked of "power structures." SNCC hoped to build a black–white "populist" coalition to alter radically U.S. society and values in order to bring not only increased equality of opportunity but also more equality of results. They hoped to empower the powerless, to redistribute wealth more equitably, to make all people political participants, and to make those on the "outside" into "insiders" in a new society. Students worked in racist black belt counties in voter registration, freedom schools, organization of sharecroppers, and the building of economic cooperatives and political action groups. SNCC led the effort to crack the bastion of segregation, Mississippi. The task culminated in the voter registration and community action projects of the Mississippi Summer Project of 1964.

In 1961 African American and white northern and southern "freedom riders" rode buses through the South to force compliance in Alabama and Mississippi with earlier federal rulings nullifying segregation in interstate travel. Violent mobs met the buses in Alabama, burned a bus, and beat riders. The police provided little or no protection. The Kennedy administration sent in hundreds of federal marshalls to protect the riders and their rights. Attorney General Robert Kennedy persuaded the Interstate Commerce Commission to implement the Supreme Court's ruling banning segregation in interstate carriers and terminals.

THE BIRMINGHAM DEMONSTRATION

The big 1963 civil rights story centered in Birmingham, Alabama, the South's leading industrial city and a center of racial oppression. City commissioner and police chief, Eugene "Bull" Connor, symbolized police brutality toward African Americans. In the state capital in Montgomery, sat defiant segregationist governor, George C. Wallace, who in his inaugural address early in 1963 declared, "I draw the line in the dust . . . segregation now . . . segregation tomorrow . . . segregation forever."

King concluded that if "Birmingham could be cracked, the direction of the entire nonviolent movement in the South could take a significant turn. It was our faith that as 'Birmingham goes, so goes the South.' " His SCLC planned its attack on Birmingham for months. These plans became so detailed they even counted the number of lunchcounter stools in each city diner. Bypassing the politicians, in the spring of 1963 King made three specific demands of Birmingham's business leaders. The demands called for: (1) desegregation of lunch counters, restrooms, fitting rooms, and drinking fountains in variety and department stores; (2) the upgrading and hiring of African Americans on a nondiscriminatory basis throughout the business and industrial community of Birmingham; and (3) the creation of a biracial committee to work out a timetable for desegregation in other areas in Birmingham. These negotiations with white business leaders failed. On April 3 the demonstrators made a few probing sit-ins, and arrests for marching without a permit began.

On April 10 Connor acquired a local court order enjoining all demonstrations until the right to demonstrate had been established in court. On Good Friday, April 12, King and others defied the court order and marched on City Hall. Police arrested King, and for two days he had no communication with the movement, his lawyers, or his family. In response to a public statement by eight white clergy in Birmingham that King was an outside agitator and a dangerous extremist, King wrote *A Letter from a Birmingham Jail,* a powerful reaffirmation of his nonviolent direct action philosophy. To the request that he wait for a more appropriate time, King replied, "justice too long delayed is justice denied." He added,

> I submit that an individual who breaks a law that conscience tells him is unjust, and who willingly accepts the penalty of imprisonment in order to arouse the conscience of the community over its injustice, is in reality expressing the highest respect for law.

He denounced "the silence of the good people."

King was released after eight days in jail, but the demonstrations continued. On May 2, a new tactic broke the stalemate. King sent 1,000 black

The Birmingham Demonstration, 1963
SOURCE: AP/Wide World Photos

children into the demonstration. Bull Connor met them at the barricades with firehoses, electric cattle prods, police dogs, and clubs. King sent students in wave after wave; soon more than 2,500 filled the jails. Black Birmingham stood united and defiant. Daily scenes of police brutality on the front pages of newspapers and on television newscasts shocked the nation and the world. In the

1960s, television made these racial confrontations, as well as expóses of poverty, social activism, and acts of violence part of the nightly television fare of most Americans. Birmingham could not be ignored. Gallup polls in May and June 1963 showed strong support outside the South for school and housing desegregation, and for an end to discrimination in public accommodations and employment; but those polls also showed strong opposition in the South to all such proposals. A June poll, however, showed 83 percent of southern whites believed desegregation of public accommodations and schools was inevitable, and 49 percent believed such desegregation would come within five years.

On May 10, King and the city's business leaders signed an agreement that accepted African Americans' limited demands on lunch counters, jobs, and formation of a biracial committee. And the Birmingham story included more than this limited agreement. King became the leading spokesperson for African Americans. His tactics worked. The civil rights movement became a militant mass protest under black leadership. In 1963, 930 protest demonstrations took place in 115 cities in 11 southern states. There occurred more than 20,000 arrests, 10 deaths, and 35 known bombings.

Eventually on June 11, 1963, President John F. Kennedy on national television threw the full moral force of his office behind civil rights. Kennedy responded to a growing tide of public opinion that clearly urged forceful federal action, saying

> We face . . . a moral crisis. . . . It cannot be met by repressive police action. . . . It is time to act in the Congress, in your state and local legislative body, and above all, in all of our daily lives. . . . This nation will not be fully free until all its citizens are free.

Kennedy asked Congress for the most far-reaching civil rights legislation since Reconstruction.

March on Washington

On August 28, 1963, 250,000 African Americans and whites marched on Washington to urge Congress to enact the civil rights bill. Major civil rights organizations, churches, students, some trade unions, and various liberal groups formed a civil rights coalition. African Americans called for "freedom now." They demanded the vote and equal access to public accommodations, jobs, education, and housing. Martin Luther King, Jr., captured the mood of the day with a moving statement of African American aspirations in his "I Have a Dream" speech: "I have a dream that one day this nation will rise up and live out the true meaning of its creed: 'We hold these truths to be self-evident, that all men are created equal.' "

But violence and tragedy marked the fall of 1963. On a September Sunday morning, a bomb exploded at the Sixteenth Street Baptist Church in Birmingham, killing 4 black girls and injuring 21. In November, a sniper shot down President Kennedy in Dallas, Texas. The new president, Lyndon B. Johnson, called for quick passage of the civil rights bill as a memorial to the slain president. An aroused public opinion, the legislative skills of President Johnson, the memory of the martyred Kennedy, the lobbying of churches, labor unions, and civil rights groups all worked to break a southern filibuster in the Senate and to pass the omnibus Civil Rights Act in July 1964. Finally Congress had joined the Supreme Court and the presidency to assert federal guarantees of civil rights.

The Civil Rights Act of 1964

Congress went beyond the Kennedy–Johnson recommendations. The act outlawed discrimination in most public accommodations and in all government facilities. It established a federal Equal Employment Opportunities Commission, a fulfillment of the FEPC movement of the 1940s. The act provided federal assistance for communities trying to desegregate schools. Title VI gave the federal government the power to end all financial assistance to state and local programs that did not meet federal desegregation guidelines. This provision made it possible to desegregate by administrative orders and to avoid much of the court litigation that had previously slowed desegregation to a snail's pace. The law empowered the attorney general to initiate federal court suits against discrimination in public accommodations, public facilities, education and employment. This grant of authority to the attorney general aimed at releasing poor African Americans and the civil rights organizations from the financial and legal burdens of continual litigation. The 1964 Civil Rights Act placed the federal government clearly on the side of the civil rights activists. Although the law strengthened the voting rights acts of 1957 and 1960, additional legislation was still needed to secure the right to vote for all African Americans.

THE NEW EQUALITY

The summer of 1964 saw increased civil rights agitation in the North against job and housing discrimination and de facto school segregation; riots against ghetto conditions in New York, Rochester, and Philadelphia; and passage of the Economic Opportunity Act—the beginning of the War on Poverty. Civil rights issues presented more than a question of due process and equality before the law. Many Americans began to view the race problem in national terms, involving great social and economic needs. African Americans called for an end to segregated housing, inferior inner city schools, high unemployment, poor police–community relations, and inadequate health care. Actions to end the powerlessness and despair of African Americans seemed imperative for real black advancement and social stability. Some Americans saw not only poverty, but also a culture of poverty that imprisons the poor from generation to generation. The black revolt pushed these issues onto the national agenda and created a new black consciousness that challenged traditional U.S. social, political, and economic systems.

The War on Poverty and the Great Society

On January 8, 1964, President Lyndon B. Johnson told the nation and Congress, "This administration, today . . . declares unconditional war on poverty in America." In August, Congress established the Office of Economic Opportunity (OEO). The U.S. economy and technology seemed to make possible the production of enough goods and services for all. Books such as John Kenneth Galbraith's *The Affluent Society* and Michael Harrington's *The Other America* had made many Americans conscious of an impoverished minority in the midst of plenty. In 1959, over 39 million Americans, or 22.4 percent of the population, lived in poverty (defined by the government in 1959 as an annual income for an urban family of four of less than $3,022). And more than 11 million of the poor were members of minority groups. That meant 56.2 percent of all minority persons lived in poverty.

The War on Poverty combined good politics and good morality. Even conservatives backed Johnson's proposals, which hopefully would get people "off welfare rolls and on the tax rolls." Some conservatives even supported Head Start, the Job Corps, the Neighborhood Youth Corps and other OEO programs, because they feared aggrieved minorities were "social dynamite." The black revolution forced the federal government to face up to questions of economic want as well as civil rights, because Lyndon Johnson understood that if his administration pushed civil rights, then it should also combat poverty. He believed poor and lower middle-class African Americans and whites must move forward together or fight each other for limited jobs, housing, medical care, education, and other social services. This old New Dealer hoped the War on Poverty would be the major mark of his presidency. Poverty must be fought, he said, "because it is right that we should." On May 22, 1964, President Johnson told a University of Michigan audience, "We have the opportunity to move not only toward the rich society and the powerful society, but upward to the Great Society. The Great Society rests on abundance and liberty for all. It demands an end to poverty and injustice." Tax reform and the Civil Rights and the Economic Opportunity Acts of 1964 would soon be followed in the Eighty-ninth Congress by a flood of social legislation, unequalled since 1935.

LBJ's Howard University Speech and the "New Equality"

In President Johnson's most impassioned, and possibly most perceptive, statement on race relations in the United States, he told a Howard University audience on June 4, 1965,

> It is not enough just to open the gates of opportunity. All of our citizens must have the ability to walk through those gates. This is the next and more profound stage in the battle for civil rights. We seek not just freedom but opportunity—not just legal equity but human ability—not just equality as a right and a theory, but equality as a fact and as a result. . . . Equal opportunity is . . . not enough.

Once legal segregation ended, many Americans believed that African Americans could and should make it on their own. Although most whites thought that African Americans would follow the pattern of earlier white immigrant groups, the situation of African Americans was different. White migrants came to the United States willingly and full of hope; African Americans came in chains and despair. White immigrants brought cultures and family ties that sustained them as strangers in a new land. By contrast, slave owners systematically destroyed the slaves' cultures—languages, religions, and folk ways. The slave family had no legal standing, and the auction block was a constant threat to family life. White owners denied black men the father's role as provider and authority. Two and a half centuries of slavery and a hundred years of segregation, disfranchisement, economic discrimination, and subordination and "judge lynch" represented unparalleled disadvantages.

European immigrants flooded into the United States, and especially the cities, from the 1840s to World War I when unskilled labor was in great demand, and a strong back and firm will made economic progress likely. But southern rural African Americans moved to the cities after World War I to find few unskilled jobs available in an age of industrial technology. Black sharecroppers shifted from the harsh life of the plantations and tenant farms after emancipation to the despairing life of the city ghettos.

Johnson's Howard University speech called for a "new equality." In the period of transition from racial oppression to racial justice, it appeared that "special treatment," "affirmative action," what some termed "reverse discrimination," would be necessary to provide African Americans an equal chance. To achieve real equality required special job training, intensive recruitment efforts by employers and educators, and a variety of such affirmative action programs, enforced by governments. The black revolution provided the primary initiative for change, but there was need for special efforts by the whole society. Lyndon Johnson's call for bold action in 1965 found only a small minority of white supporters.

SELMA AND THE VOTING RIGHTS ACT OF 1965

Martin Luther King, Jr. took his crusade to Selma, Alabama, in January 1965 to expand African American voter registration. Many held that African Americans' right to vote, especially for local officials who directly and immediately affect every person's life—such as sheriffs, school board members, and tax assessors—was essential to progress. Others believed that equal opportunity represented the key to progress. Those who worked for the advancement of African Americans long argued over the relative importance of the vote and equality of economic opportunity. Local civil rights organizations had tried to register African Americans using the cumbersome voting rights provisions of the 1957, 1960, and 1964 civil rights acts. In Alabama in 1947 only 6,000 African Americans had registered to vote and, in 1964, 110,000 had done so; but African Americans of voting age numbered 370,000, which meant that 70 percent were not registered. Voter registration efforts made almost no progress in the black belt. In Dallas County, Selma being its county seat, African Americans made up 57 percent of the population, and yet only 335 African Americans were among the 9,878 registered voters. In neighboring Lowndes and Wilcox Counties, where African Americans outnumbered whites four to one, not a single black citizen was registered. Intimidation, economic coercion, unfair administration of literacy tests, fears and apathy, and uncooperative local registrars (the Selma registrar opened his office two days a month) all accounted for low black registration.

The Selma Demonstrations

Local activists and SNCC began work on voter registration in Selma in 1962. In the winter of 1965 3,300 demonstrators were jailed in Selma. Sheriff James G. Clark arrested demonstrators daily as they marched to the courthouse to register. The demonstrators responded with prayers and songs. King called for a march to Montgomery to present demands to the state government. Governor Wallace refused permission for such a march, but, in keeping with the nonviolent defiance so characteristic of the movement, the march began. On 7 March under Wallace's orders to stop the march, 100 sheriff's deputies and 50 state troopers met the marchers at the bridge on Route 80 in Selma. An observer, Benjamin Muse, wrote, "The police moved in with tear-gas bombs and night sticks—the horsemen mounting what resembled a cossack charge—and drove them back to Selma." "Bloody Sunday" outraged much of the nation. Clergy, labor leaders, students, and many political leaders, from all over the nation, rallied to the cause of Selma African Americans. According to a Gallup poll taken at the height of the Selma demonstration, 76 percent of Americans favored strong federal legislation to guarantee the right to vote for all Americans.

On March 15, 1965, President Johnson addressed a special session of Congress and called for new voting rights legislation to guarantee "every American citizen . . . the right to vote . . . (we) must overcome the crippling legacy of bigotry and injustice." As he concluded, the president raised his head, paused for emphasis, and spoke the words of the anthem of the African American revolution, "And we *shall* overcome."

But white violence and police brutality continued in Selma. On March 17 a federal court approved King's Selma-to-Montgomery march and ordered the state to provide police protection. President Johnson nationalized the Alabama National Guard and the federal government provided security for the five-day march. On March 25 Martin Luther King, Jr. spoke from the Capitol steps where Jefferson Davis took the oath of office as president of the Confederate States of America in 1861. King spoke in triumph and called for more marches—on segregated schools, on poverty, and on "ballot boxes until race baiters disappear from the political arena."

The Voting Rights Act of 1965

The civil rights movement reached a peak of moral influence and political power when Congress passed the Voting Rights Act on August 4, 1965. This act substituted faster administrative procedures for lengthy court litigation to secure the vote for all. It ended all literacy tests and other voter qualifying tests used to disfranchise African Americans in all states and counties where they existed on November 1, 1964, and where fewer than 50 percent of the people of voting age voted or were registered to vote in the presidential election of 1964. This provision banned such tests in Louisiana, Mississippi, Alabama, Georgia, South Carolina, Virginia, Alaska, 26 counties in North Carolina, and one county in Arizona. The law empowered the attorney general to send federal registrars to replace local officials and to register voters. The law also authorized him to send poll watchers to observe the fairness of elections. The Twenty-fourth Amendment ratified in February 1964 abolished poll taxes as a qualification for voting in federal elections. But the poll tax remained as a restriction for voting in state and local elections in Virginia, Alabama, Mississippi, and Texas. The 1965 Civil Rights Act expressed Congress' opinion that such taxes were unconstitutional and requested that the attorney general test them in the courts. In 1966 the Supreme Court ruled that such use of the poll tax in these four states did violate the Fifteenth Amendment.

The Broad Consequences of the Civil Rights Movement

The philosophy and strategy of massive, nonviolent resistance and civil disobedience as practiced by the civil rights workers of the South had an effect that went far beyond race relations and the South. The 1950s had been an era of apparent social stability; years of economic growth—the "affluent society"; and years in which material acquisitions, the "move to suburbia," and conformity to middle-class values seemed the norm in white America. The 1950s also began with the Red Scare of McCarthyism, which labeled many dissenters and reformers as un-American or subversive. In that atmosphere, the Montgomery Bus Boycott, SCLC, and SNCC defied the status quo.

White students returning from the southern civil rights protests began the Free Speech Movement at the University of California at Berkeley in 1964, and the student movement influenced higher education for almost a decade. The anti-Vietnam War movement later adopted many of the civil rights movement's tactics. Welfare recipients, Native Americans, Hispanics, feminists, the disabled, homosexuals—those who felt oppressed or excluded adopted the spirit and many of the tactics of the civil rights movement. For example, the 43 million disabled, the nation's largest such group, shifted from being passive recipients of institutional largess and paternalism to demand a full role in society. In 1973, after two Nixon vetoes, Congress passed Section 504 of the Rehabilitation Act, which barred discrimination against the disabled by any entity receiving federal funds. In the 1980s, the disabled, increasingly organized as a political lobby and as activists in the streets, allied with traditional civil rights and feminist groups. After extending the antidiscrimination provisions of the housing laws in 1988 to include the disabled, Congress enacted the landmark Americans With Disabilities Act in 1990, the most sweeping civil rights law since 1964. Its provisions required that new trains, buses, and subway cars and new or renovated hotels, retail stores, and restaurants must be accessible to people in wheel chairs. All existing "public accomodations," from amusement parks and zoos to dry cleaners and doctors' offices, must serve the disabled and be made accessible unless the business can prove that would create an "undue burden." Telephone companies now had to provide relay services allowing hearing- and voice-impaired people with special telephones to place and receive calls from ordinary phones. And by 1992, businesses with more than 25 employees could no longer discriminate against the disabled in hiring and promotions.

But some in the 1960s, disillusioned with the pace of social change, gave up on social activism and dropped out of society to experiment with a variety of individual and communal life-styles. In many ways then, the southern civil rights movement helped create a different society, an open, freer, more tolerant, and, according to some, more permissive society.

THE GHETTO AND RACIAL VIOLENCE IN THE NORTH

From August 11 to 17, 1965, a week after the passage of the Voting Rights Act, the Watts ghetto of Los Angeles exploded in rioting. The riot signaled the end of one phase of the civil rights movement; at least it challenged the nonviolent direction King had given the movement from the Montgomery bus boycott of 1955 to the Selma-to-Montgomery march of 1965. Watts in 1965, Newark and Detroit in 1967, Washington, D.C., in the hours after King's assassination in 1968, and scores of other U.S. cities were torn by violence. In spontaneous upheavals, the rioters attacked primarily white businesses and the police. Time, exhaustion, and overwhelming police and military forces finally ended each riot. The riots expressed the hostility of many African Americans against the existing order. The rioters forced the nation to take notice, but they brought few benefits or substantive changes to the inner city.

The Inner City

During the 1950s and early 1960s many African Americans in northern cities gave money and support to the southern civil rights activists. They rejoiced and suffered with the victories and defeats of the southern African Americans. They welcomed the court decisions, the civil rights acts, the presidential orders and speeches, and the War on Poverty. Northern African Americans, however, came to realize that the civil rights victories, mainly southern, had changed little in the lives of inner city black families.

More northern African Americans attended segregated schools in 1965 than in 1954. In 1965 relative unemployment, African Americans to whites, was higher than in 1950. The gap between the wages of African American and white workers had widened. More African Americans lived in all-black neighborhoods in 1967 than at the time of the school desegregation decision of 1954, and almost 30 percent of all African Americans in 1967 lived in slum housing. The average African American received about half the income of the average white. African Americans suffered an infant mortality rate twice as high as whites (see pp. 278–280).

The Black Muslims

In the early 1960s a variety of African American nationalist groups, particularly the Black Muslims under Elijah Muhammad, offered a black separatist alternative to the biracial, integrationist civil rights movement. Muhammad preached that the white man's rule was ending and that African Americans would soon rule. The Black Muslims glorified blackness, using the slogan "black is beautiful." They pointed to black Americans' African heritage with pride. The Muslims preached a rigid moral code. They denounced liquor and drugs, and stressed good work habits and the patriarchal family. They also preached hate for whites and Christianity. They advocated obedience to the law. They did not advocate violence, nor did they carry weapons. But they supported all action necessary for self-defense.

Elijah Muhammad held out a vague promise of a future separate black territory in the United States. Although the Muslims avoided all political activity, they supported a separate black economy and denounced all black-white relations. "Why integrate with a dying world?"

The Muslims, their ministers, and their temples located in inner city neighborhoods, appealed to the young, to males, to the lower class—to those most alienated in black America. Muhammad's religion offered a rebirth. The Muslims offered a new name in place of the slave name—an X; a new religion—Islam; a new language—Arabic; a new homeland; and new black cultural and moral values. The movement grew from a few hundred in World War II to between 100,000 and 250,000 in the early 1960s.

Malcolm Little, a former thief, drug dealer and addict, pimp, and convict, known as Big Red, converted to the Nation of Islam while in prison. As Malcolm X he became the minister of Temple 7 in New York. A great organizer and powerful street-corner speaker, this product of northern ghetto life became the leading and most powerful voice of black urban America.

In 1964 Malcolm X broke with Muhammad and founded the Organization of Afro-American Unity. Unlike Muhammad, however, Malcolm X came to emphasize political action and social revolution, and he held out the possibility of coalition with radicals of all colors. He was developing his new position when unknown African Americans assassinated him on February 25, 1965. Both the Muslims and the appeal of Malcolm X reflected the frustration and "black rage" in the inner city.

After 1965 African Americans watched the Vietnam War escalate and the War on Poverty de-escalate. Funds, manpower, and the attention of government leaders were now focused on Southeast Asia. African Americans also deplored the lack of vigorous enforcement of civil rights laws at home. The defiance of southern politicians, the violence of segregationists against nonviolent demonstrators, and the mockery of justice in certain southern courts led many ghetto blacks to a cynical view of the law, democratic procedures, and due process. Some African Americans saw no effective alternative to violence as a way to redress grievances or "move the system."

The Kerner Commission

After the 1967 riots, President Johnson appointed the "Kerner Commission," headed by Illinois Governor Otto Kerner. The president charged the commission with the study of three vital questions in the civil disorders. What happened? Why did it happen? What could be done to prevent it from happening again? The commission's report stated:

> Race prejudice has shaped our history decisively; it now threatens to affect
> our future. White racism is essentially responsible for the explosive nature

(of) . . . our cities. . . . What white Americans have never fully understood—but what Negroes can never forget—is that white society is deeply implicated in the ghetto. White institutions created it, white institutions maintain it, and white society condones it. . . . This is our basic conclusion: our nation is moving toward two societies, one black, one white—separate and unequal.

King in Chicago in 1966 and "White Blacklash"

Martin Luther King, Jr. wrote in the spring of 1968:

The decade of 1955 to 1965—with its constructive elements—misled us. Everyone underestimated the amount of violence and rage Negroes were suppressing and the amount of bigotry the white majority was disguising.

King moved into Chicago in January 1966, to begin a nonviolent, direct-action campaign against segregated slum housing, job discrimination and unemployment, and de facto segregated schools. Chicago represented the first test for his nonviolent techniques in a big northern ghetto. In the South, King had clear and well-defined targets—legalized segregation, disfranchisement, and brutality. The movement had the air of a morality play with good guys and bad guys. King could arouse the nation's conscience. But northern de facto segregation, economic and political exploitation, subtle discrimination, and institutional racism presented more difficult targets to dramatize. Many African American youths in the northern ghettos were alienated and angry at society. King wrote, "Black nationalism is more fitted to their angry mood. . . . The critical task will be to convince Negroes driven to cynicism that nonviolence can win."

On July 10, 1966, at a mass rally King announced his demands on education, housing, jobs, transportation, public services, health care, and a guaranteed annual income. Chicago's ghetto erupted in riots on July 13. King's marches into white Chicago neighborhoods brought angry, often violent responses from lower middle-class and working-class whites of recent immigrant backgrounds. They saw King's demands as a threat to their jobs, neighborhood schools, and property values. Many whites, who had recently climbed out of urban poverty, bitterly resented a coalition of poor African Americans and upper-class whites that appeared to threaten their new, and still marginal, status as homeowners and secure jobholders.

Chicago's mayor Richard J. Daley did not make the clumsy mistakes of the Bull Connors and Jim Clarks of Alabama. Daley ordered the Chicago police to protect King and his demonstrators. On August 5 a mob of 4,000 whites in Chicago attacked King and 600 demonstrators, despite the protection of 960 police. King, hit in the head by a stone and knocked down, had met the northern white blacklash.

Three weeks later, King, Daley, and the religious, real estate, and banking interests of Chicago reached a 10-point agreement to open housing opportunities for African Americans. But the agreements turned out to be paper promises that Chicago's leadership did not fulfill. King and his nonviolent tactics failed in Chicago.

The Vietnam War and Civil Rights

Shifting his attention to the war in Vietnam, King called the U.S. government "the greatest purveyor of violence in the world today." In his opinion the continuation of the war diverted the money, energy, and national leadership needed to resolve the twin problems of race and poverty. The war, he claimed, siphoned off resources and attention from the War on Poverty and the struggle for civil rights at home. Not only did the ghettos suffer from a lack of attention at home, but African Americans fought and died on the front lines of Vietnam in disproportionate numbers. Some civil rights leaders criticized King for joining the peace movement and claimed his activities would dilute the civil rights movement's energies, alienate the Johnson administration, and arouse public hostility. King replied that as a Christian apostle of nonviolence he could not condone violence at home or abroad.

"Black Power"

King's leadership was challenged in the South at Greenwood, Mississippi, on June 16, 1966. Stokely Carmichael, a leader of SNCC, yelled to a crowd of African Americans, "We want black power!" The response came in a chant, "Black power! Black power!" Some disillusioned civil rights veterans questioned nonviolence and biracialism in the movement. King responded that he opposed violence in principle, and added that in a violent encounter African Americans would be slaughtered. He reaffirmed the biracial nature of the movement on moral grounds, noting that whites had suffered alongside African Americans. He also pointed out that African Americans made up only 10 percent of the total population and that white allies were necessary to form a coalition to alter the character of U.S. society, the society African Americans had to live in.

What did Black Power mean? Black separatism? Riots and rebellions? Guerrilla warfare? To most whites, Black Power represented an antiwhite cry. Disillusioned with the failure to fulfill the dream in their lives, many African Americans called for racial solidarity and pride, organization of African American cooperatives and credit unions, and creation of African American political action groups.

Black Power advocates called on African Americans to define themselves, design their futures, and gain control over their communities. Hopefully, African Americans acting as a group would have the power to bargain on a more equal basis with white America. Deploring the dependency and powerlessness of most African Americans, they called for a restructuring of U.S. values and institutions. Black Power leaders, who still supported integration as a final goal, insisted that it be the integration of proud new African Americans into a radically different U.S. society. Although most did not support violence, they justified its use in self-defense. African Americans told whites who wanted to work in the civil rights movement to go into the white communities and combat racism there. The Black Power leaders argued that integration as practiced simply took token individuals away from the black community, did nothing for African Americans as a group, and soothed the consciences of upper-class whites.

Black Power shifted from rhetoric to programs after 1967. The movement helped bring about the election of black mayors and city councilors, the creation of private all-black experimental schools; the winning of black community control, or at least influence, over public schools; the growth of black cooperatives and businesses; and the articulation of a black community voice in urban renewal and the decentralization of city governments.

The Assassination of Martin Luther King, Jr.

In the last year of his life, King continued to strive to resolve the problems of race and poverty. Working to rebuild the civil rights coalition, he attempted to unite the poor of both races. With far-reaching proposals on education, jobs, housing, welfare, social services, and community participation, in the spring of 1968 King planned a Poor People's March on Washington. African Americans, Hispanics, Appalachian whites, Native Americans—the disinherited of all groups prepared to march. In early April he went to Memphis, Tennessee, to help win union recognition and a living wage for striking municipal garbage workers. On April 4, 1968, as King stood on the balcony of his motel, he was shot and killed by a white man. His remarkable career ended as it had begun—in 1955 he stood up for a department store seamstress and her right to remain seated on a bus, and in 1968 he died in a struggle to assure garbage workers a decent life. Many African Americans and whites mourned and wondered if his violent death meant that nonviolent approaches to racial change were impossible in U.S. society.

Moments after the assassination the black communities in 125 cities erupted in violence. These outbreaks contradicted all King had preached. But African Americans felt angry, hurt, and bitter. Stokely Carmichael told African Americans to "get your guns." Police, 21,000 specially trained federal troops and 34,000 members of the National Guard—a record number for any domestic civil disturbance—eventually ended the riots. The president sent federal troops into Washington, Baltimore, and Chicago. Over 15,000 troops sealed off the District of Columbia. Riots between 1965 and 1967 took the lives of 225 people, wounded 4,000, and cost $122 billion in property damage. As the inner cities burned, the gulf between black and white seemed wider than ever. And King was dead.

The riots of April 1968 concluded the widespread racial violence of the 1960s. A realization that mainly African Americans were killed, wounded, or arrested, and black neighborhoods burned, as well as the overwhelming force of the white-controlled government may have ended the cycle of violence. The road of violence seemed to end in black futility. Energies in the black community now turned inward to build local institutions, to work for economic development, and to construct political organizations.

The Civil Rights Act of 1968

On April 11, 1968, Congress, partly in tribute to King, passed another major civil rights act. The law outlawed discrimination in the sale or rental of 80 percent of all housing by January 1, 1970. To gain congressional passage of the law, two exceptions were made. Owner-occupied apartment buildings of four or fewer apartments, and the private sale of a single-family home without a broker were not included in the antidiscrimination rule. The law empowered the attorney general to initiate suits if there existed a "pattern" of housing discrimination. The law also made it a federal crime to intimidate, injure, or kill a civil rights worker—a goal of southern civil rights activists for years. The Senate tacked on the so-called "Rap" Brown Amendment that made crossing a state line with intent to incite to riot a federal crime. This reflected the fear of "outside agitators" and "incendiaries." Rap Brown, a SNCC leader, had said, "Violence is as American as cherry pie" and had allegedly incited riot and arson in 1968 in Cambridge, Maryland. Ironically the Rap Brown Amendment would first be applied in the prosecution of the "Chicago Seven"—all white—for inciting a riot at the Democratic National Convention of 1968.

To further the irony, the Supreme Court, two months later, ruled all discrimination in the sale or rental of housing unconstitutional on the basis of the 1866 Civil Rights Act. The Court declared the Reconstruction law had been constitutionally enacted to enforce the Thirteenth Amendment and abolish "all badges and incidents of slavery." The law said all citizens have the right "to inherit, purchase, lease, sell, hold and convey real and personal property."

The "Poor People's March"

King's successor at SCLC, the Reverend Ralph D. Abernathy, led a "Poor People's March." Thousands arrived in Washington in April 1968, not to demonstrate and leave, but to camp on the mall near the Lincoln Memorial. They built Resurrection City out of tents and plywood, but the spring rain soon turned "Tent City" into a sea of mud. King's dream of massive demonstrations and civil disobedience to make the War on Poverty more than a slogan soon fizzled. The "dream" seemed dead, the leader gone, and the SCLC soon became more of a memory than a reality.

THE "BACKLASH"

The Election of 1968

In November 1968, Richard Nixon won the presidency and called for retreat, which one of his aides called "benign neglect," in the struggle for civil rights. In the campaign, Nixon sensed the popular demand of most whites for social order—the fears of racial riots, antiwar demonstrations, campus turmoil, street crime, and the uneasiness with the life-styles of the counterculture and the young. The great majority of voters were "unyoung, unpoor, and unblack; they were middle-aged, middle-class, and middle-minded." Nixon ran against Johnson's vice-president, Hubert H. Humphrey, a long-time civil rights advocate. Nixon played on the fears of the white backlash and spoke against "forced busing." He competed with George C. Wallace, running on a third-party ticket, for "blue-collar, working-class, ethnic" voters. They both believed the "ethnics" had become openly racist as the civil rights movement moved into northern cities. The Republican candidate supported "law and order" and "neighborhood schools," code words with clear racial appeals. Adopting a "Southern Strategy," Nixon named Spiro Agnew, governor of Maryland and an outspoken opponent of black militants, as his running mate; pledged to appoint a "law and order" attorney general; promised to name "strict constructionist, states' rights conservatives" to the Supreme Court; and campaigned successfully in the South. Nixon won 43.4 percent of the popular vote to Humphrey's 42.7 percent. But Wallace's 14 percent added to Nixon's signaled a clear majority in favor of a slowdown in civil rights. Humphrey lost all the southern states except LBJ's Texas—but won 85 percent of the black vote.

Nixon and the Retreat on Civil Rights

To implement the promised retreat, President Nixon named John Mitchell to be attorney general and appointed "strict constructionists" to the Supreme Court. On July 3, 1969, the Nixon administration announced that it would minimize the use of Title VI of the 1964 Civil Rights Act to cut off federal funds to compel school desegregation and would rely on the slower method of case-by-case court suits. In August 1969, the Nixon administration asked a federal court to delay desegregation in 31 Mississippi school districts. For the first time since

Brown I, the Justice Department sided with a southern state to thwart desegregation. The Supreme Court quickly rebuked this action and ordered desegregation "at once."

In 1970–1971 Nixon continued to speak for "neighborhood schools" and against "busing." His position seemed good "backlash" politics because a Gallup poll in August 1971 showed that 82 percent of Americans opposed the busing of African American and white school children from one school district to another. The Justice Department also prosecuted and effectively ended the radical Black Panther party in a series of shootouts and criminal conspiracy prosecutions. The party, a small group mixing Marxism and radical black nationalism, first appeared in Alabama after Bloody Sunday at Selma in 1965, then later moved to Oakland. The angry cries of young urban African Americans, photographs of armed African Americans and fearful whites, and the Panthers' breakfast programs for school children and violent encounters with local police marked the party's history.

Repression of African American militants developed at the state and local level too. In September 1971, at Attica state prison in upstate New York newly politicized inmates, 54 percent African American and deeply influenced by Malcolm X and the Black Panthers, rioted and took 39 hostages to protest overcrowding, deplorable living and working conditions, and the institutional racism of the prison system. The prisoners requested that Governor Nelson A. Rockefeller meet with them and discuss 30 "demands." He refused, and ordered an assault by state police and prison guards using helicopters, gas, and automatic weapons, which killed 10 hostages and 29 inmates, and left 4 hostages and 85 prisoners wounded. A state investigation called Attica "with the exception of Indian massacres of the late nineteenth century . . . the bloodiest one-day encounter between Americans since the Civil War."

The Nixon administration awarded many contracts to southern businesses and increased federal spending in the South. But benign neglect served as the policy for African Americans. The Office of Economic Opportunity was dismantled in 1973, and the War on Poverty ended. The Supreme Court upheld the precedent of *Brown* but as the Detroit (see p. 231) and *Bakke* decisions (see p. 233) demonstrated, it broke no new ground. Many of the Great Society programs of the 1960s, such as federal aid to education, Medicare-Medicaid, and job training continued on a reduced scale, but the experimentation, the commitment, and the cutting edge of federal reform disappeared.

A Southern President

In 1976 Jimmy Carter, a Georgian white "peanut farmer" from the black belt won the election. With a 94 percent vote from the black community, Carter represented a "New South." No race-baiter, he supported civil rights, and as Georgia's governor and as a candidate for president pledged racial justice. African American voter registration had grown dramatically since 1960, especially in the 11 states of the Old Confederacy, where there were 1,463,000 registered African American voters—or 29.1 percent—of the eligible black voting population in 1960, and 4,149,999—or 63.1 percent—in 1976. Jimmy Carter won back the "Solid South," with the crucial aid of black votes.

President Carter nominated more black judges and recruited more African Americans for important federal jobs than did his predecessors. Yet many African Americans believed Carter was moving too slowly on civil rights, urban issues, and social legislation. In their eyes, the Carter administration did not move vigorously on school or residential desegregation. The economic plight of African Americans grew worse as the president struggled with budget deficits and inflation rates of 7.6 percent in 1978 and 11.3 percent in 1979. The administration made lower prices its top priority, and restrictive fiscal and monetary policies led to worsening double-digit unemployment for African Americans. However, in 1980, given the alternative of Ronald Reagan, African Americans, more than any other group in U.S. society, voted for Carter, but in lesser numbers than in 1976.

African Americans as Office Holders

Many African Americans saw "Politics as our first hurrah." Indeed the right to vote and hold office had become one of the most visible changes in African American life after *Brown*. Race-baiters, such as Senator Strom Thurmond of South Carolina and Governor George Wallace of Alabama, now changed their rhetoric and courted the vote of African Americans. Their vote made an impact—Mississippi and Alabama led the nation in the 1980s in the number of black office holders. African Americans held 17 congressional seats in 1980 and 25 by 1991, compared to none between 1901 and 1928. In 1980 there were almost 5,000 elected African American local, state, and national officials; in 1990, there were 7,370. In 1965 African American officials numbered only 300. African Americans won the mayors' chairs in Newark, Detroit, Atlanta, New Orleans, Los Angeles, and Washington, D.C., and added such major cities as Chicago and Philadelphia in 1983 and New York in 1989. African American mayors supported affirmative action and advocated more equitable law enforcement in cities that found themselves with fewer financial resources, growing problems of poverty, and reduced federal aid. In 1989, L. Douglas Wilder became the nation's first elected African American governor, winning in the Old Dominion, Virginia. The strong candidacy of Jesse Jackson in the 1984 and 1988 campaigns for the Democratic presidential nomination increased African

American voter registration and activism. Jackson even won primaries in South Carolina, Alabama, and Mississippi, the core of the Confederacy.

But politics was not a panacea. In 1983, African Americans still held less than 1 percent of the nation's political offices, and 3 percent in the South, despite making up 20 percent of that region's population. In presidential election years between 1972 and 1988, African Americans registered and voted at a rate about 10 percent less than whites. The reasons behind these statistics were not always easy to understand. Some theorized that people in poverty often have low voting records, that African Americans are alienated from politics and still suffer the legacy of past exclusion. Whatever the reasons, though the political impact of African Americans is significant and increasing, African Americans are not yet as politically active as whites.

Ronald Reagan: "The Bottom"

The election of Ronald Reagan represented a disaster for African Americans. Reagan went beyond familiar backlash rhetoric to action. His major budget cuts in publicly subsidized housing, education, medicaid, food stamps, and other social services hit all the poor, especially African Americans.

Under Reaganomics, Americans in 1982 slid into the worst economic depression since the 1930s. The black community, as usual the hardest hit by economic hard times, responded with a resigned fatalism, if not cynicism. Nor did many African Americans share in the economic recovery of the mid-1980s as tax, spending and credit policies favored the rich and worked against the poor.

The Justice Department, long the champion of civil rights, became the center of the Reagan backlash, and, for example, argued for tax exemption for segregated Bob Jones University. But the Court rebuked the administration. In 1984, the Justice Department successfully argued before the Supreme Court against affirmative action layoff policies adopted by Memphis for firefighters. After some Court "setbacks," the Reagan administration's arguments carried the day in the Rehnquist Court's five major decisions against affirmative action in 1989. The administration cut civil rights enforcement activity by budget and staff cuts in the Department of Justice and Labor and the Equal Employment Opportunity Commission.

The Reagan administration did little to enforce school desegregation under Title VI. In unprecedented action, Reagan removed and replaced the chairperson of the U.S. Civil Rights Commission, fired three of its six members, and, after a wrangle with Congress, gained a Reagan majority on the commission. Congress, fighting rear guard actions, expanded the Voting Rights Act in 1982, and, in 1988 overturned the *Grove City College* decision and a Reagan veto to enact the Civil Rights Restoration Act. The 1988 law made clear that there would be a cutoff of all federal funds to an institution if there is discrimination in any part of the institution.

THE STRUGGLE FOR RACIAL JUSTICE: IN RETROSPECT

The civil rights movement had obvious achievements. Court decisions and legislative actions swept away legal segregation, voter disfranchisement and blatant denials of due process. Americans went far to ensure African Americans legal equality of opportunity. African Americans took control of the civil rights movement in the 1960s. African Americans developed new pride and hope. The movement seemed to change U.S. racial relations and attitudes, and a greater tolerance developed. The latter half of the 1980s, and early 1990s, however, saw an increase in racial tension, from the campuses of the nation's most prestigious universities to street murders in Howard Beach and Bensonhurst in New York City.

But people disagree as to whether the civil rights struggle and the War on Poverty brought substantial economic and social progress for African Americans. A good reporter could give a commonsense judgment by walking the streets, talking to people, and looking around. A more scientific judgment might be reached by analyzing numbers from sources such as the Bureaus of the Census and Labor Statistics. Such an analytical effort, despite its traps and its impersonality, provides a factual basis in judging whether African Americans made progress, held their own, or fell back. (See the tables on pp. 278–282.)

A Positive View

Two statisticians and social commentators, Ben J. Wattenberg and Richard M. Scammon writing in *Commentary* magazine in April 1973, wrote, "Large and growing numbers of American blacks have been moving into the middle class, so that by now these numbers can reasonably be said to add up to a *majority* of black Americans." They claimed that 52 percent of African Americans had "safely put poverty behind them." Wattenberg and Scammon documented that African Americans had made substantial progress in income, employment, types of jobs, and education.

Scammon and Wattenberg credited African American progress to the War on Poverty, a full employment economy, the Great Society programs, and particularly the black-led civil rights movement—especially in the years 1963 to 1967. They admitted, however, serious setbacks in African American family breakdown and a frightening picture of the ravages of crime. They held the narrowing of the economic class gaps was the fundamental step needed to bring the "only realistic solution to the race problem, integration."

"A Dream Deferred"

In 1983, the Center for the Study of Social Policy published a study, *A Dream Deferred: The Economic Status of Black Americans*. The study showed little economic progress by African Americans *relative* to white Americans in the years from 1960 to 1980. Despite progress in legal equality, voting, and education, "the economic gap between blacks and whites remains wide and is not diminishing. On measures of income, poverty, and unemployment, wide economic disparities between African Americans and whites have not lessened or have even worsened since 1960."

In 1960 the median family income of African Americans was 55.4 percent that of whites, in 1975, 61.5 percent, and in 1981, 56.4 percent. The unemployment rate for African Americans since 1960 was consistently twice that of whites. Black adult male employment dropped significantly between 1960 and 1982 from 74.1 percent of black males 16 or older to 55.3 percent. The figures for whites were 75.7 and 69.1 percent. Households headed by single women made up 47.1 percent of all African American households in 1982 compared with 21 percent in 1960. The white figures were 13.9 percent and 6.0 percent. In 1980, 23.7 percent of black householders with four years of *college* earned less than $15,000 a year—about the same proportion as white householders with four years of *high school,* 26.1 percent.

These economic conditions produced predictable social consequences. In 1979, the infant mortality rate for African Americans was double that of whites, and in childbirth black women died at four times the rate of white women. In 1981, 45 percent of all black children under age 18 lived in poverty, whereas 14.7 percent of all white children were below the poverty line. Though African Americans made up 11.9 percent of the population, African Americans represented over two-fifths of the prison population, more than half of the victims in crimes against persons, and were more than six times as likely as white men to be murder victims. The study's authors concluded, "There is a chronic and structural flaw in the American social order."

Class and Family in Black America

Census data in 1986 revealed that the top 20 percent of the population received over 50 percent of the household income, and the bottom fifth received 4.9 percent. There were a few big winners in the 1980s and some major losers; after five decades of shrinkage, the gap between rich and poor widened. The major losers were children under 18, teenage mothers, high school dropouts, female-headed households, the homeless of all ages and races, and unemployable young African American males. African Americans represented a disproportionate share of these losers, a group the media called the "black underclass."

In an essay published by the National Urban League, "The State of Black America 1990," sociologist Andrew Billingsley described the changes in class structure and family life in black America since the 1960s. Billingsley identified an upper class, almost a tenth of African American families, which had substantial wealth and high incomes. A middle class of well-educated men and women in professional, technical, and managerial occupations with family incomes above the national median represented a second group, which has doubled in the last two decades to include about a quarter of all African American families. Often the first members of their families to "make it," their economic status is tenuous, as they often climb the economic ladder with one hand while aiding needy relatives with the other. The most recently analyzed census material from 1988 household wealth illustrated the narrow margin on which most African American families live and the chasm between African American and white median family net worth—$4,169 for African Americans as to $43,279 for whites. A recession or an illness pushes African American families out of the middle class at a faster rate than whites. The traditional backbone of the African American community, the blue-collar working-class families with incomes above the poverty line, dropped from 44 percent of African American families in 1969 to 34 percent in 1986. The fourth group included workers with marginal jobs that left them in poverty, even in two-parent families where both spouses worked. This group comprised a steady 14 percent of African American families from 1969 to 1983. Billingsley's fifth group was the underclass, "where no family member has a secure or productive niche in the workforce." (The underclass and the working class poor comprised 30 percent of African American families in 1986. There were 2.1 million poor African American families in 1986 compared to 1.9 million in 1959.) These members of the so-called underclass were often the hard-core unemployed, unemployable young African American males, teen-age mothers, and female-headed families living without a future. Ravaged by drugs, particularly "crack" cocaine, with its devastating effects on family life, child abuse, and infant mortality, they also suffered 27 percent of the nation's AIDS cases and bore a disproportionate share of the nation's violence. More African Americans died in homicides in the city of Detroit than were killed in the same four days during the ground conflict in the Gulf War of 1991. The significant decline in the African American community of the once broad-based blue-collar working class and the rapid rise of the underclass attests to the despair and anger in Black America.

The 1968 Kerner Report described two societies—black and white—moving in opposite directions. The United States has always had class distinctions, but in the 1980s the distances between the classes widened. In Black

America a similar, but more exaggerated process took place. A 1988 study from the Center on the Budget and Policy Priorities reported, "The income gap between lower- and upper-income black families is now wider than at any point on record. Income inequality is now significantly greater among African American families than among whites."

The following "cold statistics" tell part of the story of black and white America.

STATISTICS ON AFRICAN AMERICANS AND WHITE AMERICANS

Population

	1950	1960	1970	1980	1990
Total	152,271,000	180,671,000	205,052,000	227,757,000	250,122,000
White	135,150,000	160,023,000	179,644,000	195,571,000	210,221,000
African American	15,045,000	19,006,000	22,801,000	26,903,000	31,047,000
African American as % of total	9.9	10.5	11.1	11.8	12.4

Median Family Income in 1989 Dollars

Year	All Races	White	African American	Hispanic*	African American Family Income as a % of White Family Income
1960	23,543	24,444	13,531	NA	55.4
1965	27,386	28,544	15,718	NA	55.1
1970	31,534	32,713	20,067	NA	61.3
1975	31,620	32,885	20,234	22,013	61.5
1980	31,637	32,926	19,073	22,145	57.9
1985	31,962	33,595	19,344	21,927	57.6
1989	34,213	35,975	20,209	23,446	56.2

*Hispanic persons are not identified by race in census.

Persons below the Poverty Level

Poverty (Nonfarm Family of Four in 1989—Poverty Level Was $12,675)

	% of All Persons	% of All Whites	% of All African Americans
1959	22.4	18.1	55.1
1966	14.7	11.3	41.8
1970	12.6	9.9	33.5
1975	12.3	9.7	31.3
1980	13.0	10.2	32.5
1982	15.0	12.0	35.6
1985	14.0	11.4	31.3
1989	12.8	10.0	30.7

Female-headed Households

	1950	1960	1970	1980	1989
As a % of all white families	2.8	6.0	7.8	11.6	13.0
As a % of all African American families	8.3	20.7	30.6	40.3	43.5

Persons in Female-headed Families Living in Poverty

	All Families	Whites	African Americans	Hispanics
1959	49.4 percent 7,014,000	40.2 percent 4,232,000	70.6 percent 2,416,000	*
1966	39.8 percent 6,861,000	29.7 percent 3,646,000	65.3 percent 3,160,000	*
1971	38.7 percent 7,979,000	30.4 percent 4,099,000	56.1 percent 3,587,000	53.5 percent 773,000
1976	37.3 percent 9,029,000	28.0 percent 4,463,000	55.7 percent 4,415,000	56.6 percent 1,000,000
1981	38.3 percent 11,051,000	29.8 percent 5,600,000	56.7 percent 5,222,000	55.9 percent 1,465,000
1989	35.9 percent 11,668,000	28.1 percent 5,723,000	49.4 percent 5,530,000	50.5 percent 1,902,000

* Bureau of the Census began keeping separate statistics on persons of Hispanic origin in 1972. Hispanics are not identified by race.

Aid to Families with Dependent Children (AFDC)—1969–1989

Number of AFDC Recipients and Percentage of Various Population Groups*

	1971	1975	1983	1989
Total recipients	10,043,000	11,131,000	10,569,000	10,799,000
AFDC child recipients	7,303,000	7,952,000	6,967,000	7,287,000
AFDC recipients as percentage of total population	4.86	5.17	4.51	4.35
AFDC recipients as percentage of total child population	10.46	11.84	11.10	11.37
AFDC recipients as percentage of children in poverty	69.2	71.6	50.1	57.9

* Data from U.S. House Ways and Means Committee—1991 *Green Book*

AFDC Characterictics—Recipients by Ethnic Group

	1971	1975	1983	1989
% of families with dependent children				
Whites	1969—NA*	39.9	41.8	38.4
African Americans	45.2	44.3	43.8	40.1
Hispanics	NA*	12.2	12.0	15.9

	1971	1975	1983	1988
Race as % of total population†				
Whites	1970—87.6	86.9	85.2	84.3
African Americans	11.1	11.5	12.0	12.3
Other races	1.3	1.7	2.8	3.4

* Not available
† Hispanics are not identified by race in census.

Education (Median Number of Years of Schooling Completed)

	1960	1970	1980	1989
African American men	7.7	9.4	12.0	12.4
White men	10.7	12.1	12.5	12.8
Hispanic men	NA	9.3	11.1	12.0
African American women	8.6	10.0	12.0	12.4
White women	11.2	12.1	12.6	12.7
Hispanic women	NA	10.6	10.6	12.0
Total African Americans	8.0	9.8	12.0	12.4
Total Whites	10.9	12.1	12.5	12.7
Total Hispanics	NA	9.1	10.8	12.0

Unemployment (percentage)

	1960	1965	1970	1975	1980	1982*	1989
Total in U.S.	5.5	4.5	4.9	8.5	7.1	9.7	5.3
African American & other races—male	10.7	7.4	7.3	13.6	13.2	18.2	11.5 †
White male	4.8	3.6	4.0	7.2	6.1	8.8	4.5
African American & other races—female	9.4	9.2	9.3	13.9	13.1	16.4	11.4 †
White female	5.3	5.0	5.4	8.6	6.5	8.3	4.5
Total African American & other races	10.2	8.1	8.2	13.8	13.1	17.3	11.4 †
Total white	4.9	4.1	4.5	7.8	6.3	8.6	4.5
Ratio African American & other races to white	2.1	2.0	1.8	1.8	2.2	2.0	2.5 †

* Unemployment in 1982 reached highest levels since the Great Depression of the 1930s
† Figures just for African Americans, not African Americans and other races

Life Expectancy at Birth in Years

	1960	1970	1980	1989
White male	67.4	68.0	70.7	72.6
White female	74.1	75.6	78.1	79.1
African American and other races—male	61.1	61.3	65.3	67.5
African American and other races—female	66.3	69.4	73.6	75.7

Infant Mortality Rate Per 1,000 Births

	1960	1970	1980	1988
Total	26.0	20.0	12.6	10.0
Whites	22.9	17.8	11.0	8.5
African Americans and other races	43.2	30.9	19.1	15.0
African Americans	44.3	32.6	21.4	17.6

Elected African American Officials

	Total	U.S. and State Legislators	County and State Officials	Law Enforcement	Education
1964		115			
1970	1,479	179	719	213	368
1974	3,007	256	1,607	340	804
1980	4,963	326	2,871	534	1,232
1984	5,700	396	3,367	657	1,445
1990 (Jan.)	7,375	440	4,481	769	1,602

SOURCE: Data in the preceeding tables from *Historical Statistics of the United States*, Vols. I and II; *Statistical Abstract of the United States, 1976, 1977, 1981–1991; Money Income and Poverty Status of Families and Persons in the United States: 1977, 1981; Money, Income of Households, Families and Persons in United States: 1977–1979, 1982; Money Income and Poverty Status in the United States: 1988–1989;* Department of Commerce, Bureau of the Census; *Economic Indicators*, 1981–1991, Council of Economic Advisors; *The State of Black America 1990*, National Urban League; *Overview of Entitlement Programs—1990 and 1991 Green Books*, Committee on Ways and Means, U.S. House of Representatives.

CHAPTER 10

The Presidency: Politics and Power

"The Buck Stops Here"
> *a paperweight on President Truman's desk*

"We have a cancer, close to the Presidency, that's growing" —
> *John Dean to President Nixon, March 21, 1973*

Shortly after 2:00 A.M. on June 17, 1972, a former CIA agent, James W. McCord, and four Cuban Bay of Pigs veterans were arrested for breaking into and bugging the Democratic National Committee (DNC) offices at the Watergate, an apartment-office complex in Washington, D.C. The two leaders of the burglary, G. Gordon Liddy, a former FBI agent and then-legal counsel of the Committee to Re-elect the President (CREEP), and E. Howard Hunt, a former CIA agent involved in the Bay of Pigs invasion and responsible for security at CREEP, watched from a motel room across the street as police arrested the burglars. President Nixon's press secretary quickly dismissed the break-in as a "third-rate" burglary, and most Americans during the 1972 campaign saw the burglary, as "just politics." But "Watergate" soon became the word used to describe the most ugly political crimes in U.S. history.

THE U.S. ELECTORATE

U.S. Voting

In a discussion of the U.S. presidency, one begins with an examination of the source of sovereign political power in the United States—the voters. In 1937, during the Great Depression, 50 percent of the voters identified themselves as Democrats, only 34 percent as Republicans, and 16 percent as Independents. The Democrats held their command in party allegiance, except for 1946, even

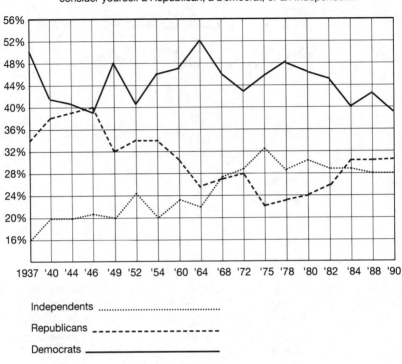

In response to the question, "In politics, as of today, do you consider yourself a Republican, a Democrat, or an Independent?"

Independents ....

Republicans _ _ _ _ _ _ _ _ _ _ _ _ _ _ _ _ _

Democrats _____

Party identification

SOURCE: Gallup Poll (released August 8, 1991)

during the Eisenhower years of the 1950s. The Democratic margins remained large during the Johnson–Goldwater campaign of 1964 and in the post-Watergate years, until the 1980s.

The number of Independent voters increased from 16 percent in 1937 to 28 percent in 1990. The Republicans' talk about political realignment and the emergence of a majority Republican party in the 1980s did not become a reality. However, in the 1980s, the number of Democratic voters declined, and there was a marked increase in converts to the Republicans, especially among voters under age 40, and Republicans have won the presidency in five of the last six elections.

Failure to Vote

In presidential elections in the post-World War II era the vote increased each year, from 48,794,000 in 1948 to 92,653,000 in 1984, but dropped in 1988 to 91,595,000. The percent of eligible voters actually voting ranged from lows of

51.1 in 1948 and 50.2 in 1988 to a high of 62.8 in 1960. It is popular opinion that Americans take their politics seriously, but the figures show a decline in participation in recent decades.

A Democratic Majority in Congress

The Democrats held a majority of seats in the House of Representatives in 40 of the 44 years from 1946 through 1990, with the exception being 1946–1948 and 1952–1954. Since 1964, the Democrats have held wide margins in the House, often majorities of more than two to one. The Democrats held similar leads in the Senate from 1958 to 1980, but with the election of Ronald Reagan in 1980, the Republicans gained a majority in the Senate, which they kept until the election of 1986.

An Elite Electorate

Elections demonstrated clearly that whites are more likely to vote than African Americans; fifty-year-olds vote at twice the rate of 18-year-olds; city people vote slightly more than country people, northerners and westerners more than southerners; and college graduates and the employed vote in substantially higher percentages than high school dropouts and the unemployed.

The Black Voter

A major change in the electorate between 1960 and 1988 was the increase in African American voters in the South. According to the Voter Education Project (VEP) in Atlanta, in 1960 in the eleven states of the Old Confederacy, 61.1 percent, or 12,276,000, of the voting age whites were registered to vote compared with 29.1 percent, or 1,463,000, of the voting age African Americans. In 1988 67.9 percent of whites reported they were registered to vote compared with 64.5 percent of African Americans, and 59.1 percent of whites reported they voted compared with 51.5 percent of African Americans. Though VEP's figures are incomplete for 1988, they reported that in 1984 5,596,000 African Americans registered, and 63 percent of those registered voted. In every one of these southern states between 92 percent and 97 percent of black voters favored Democrats. In 1988, excluding Texas, where 870,000 African Americans registered in 1984, there were 4,623,032 registered black voters. There was a total of about 5,500,000 registered black voters in 1988 in these eleven states. Jesse Jackson's candidacy in 1984 and 1988 and the Reagan administration's anti-civil rights policies provoked African Americans to use the 1965 Civil Rights Act to register and vote. Black voters, concentrated in northern cities in big industrial states and newly enfranchised in the South, became a force to be reckoned with.

Women's Political Activism

Women made a strong appearance at the Miami Democratic Convention in 1972, and the "new women's movement" grew politically in ensuing years. The Center for the American Woman and Politics at the Eagleton Institute at Rutgers University reports that in 1980, 1984, and 1988, for the first time, a larger number of women and a higher percentage of women of voting age voted than did men. Since the keeping of figures began in 1964, there have been more women than men of voting age and more women registered to vote, except in 1976. Women have made continuous grassroots gains in office holding. The number of women holding state and local office jumped from 7,089 in 1975 to 17,784 in 1990. Women members of Congress increased from 10 in 1970 to 28 in 1991. But in 1991 women held only three governorships and two Senate seats. Walter Mondale broke a precedent in 1984 when he chose Representative Geraldine A. Ferraro as his vice-presidential running mate.

The Decline of Party Loyalty and the Rise of Independent Voting

Despite Democratic dominance in voter preference in the post–World War II years until the GOP's resurgence in the 1980s, the Democrats have won only one overwhelming presidential election victory since Roosevelt in 1936—Lyndon B. Johnson's record 61.1 percent of the vote over Barry Goldwater in 1964. In the postwar years, the Republicans won five of six presidential victories by large majorities: Eisenhower in 1952 and 1956, Nixon's landslide over McGovern, 60.7 percent to 37.5 percent in 1972, Reagan's victory over Carter in 1980, and Reagan's record electoral triumph, 525 to 13, in 1984.

Voters have become increasingly independent when they vote for president. U.S. political parties are not disciplined national organizations committed to certain principles. They are loose coalitions of local and state organizations and personal followings held together by quadrennial presidential elections with their months of primaries, conventions, and hoopla of campaigning.

With the changes in U.S. society in the post–World War II years Americans became increasingly independent voters. First, Americans changed their voting habits as they moved—and move they did. For example, in 1975 48.5 percent of Americans lived in a house different from the one they lived in in 1970. Throughout the years since World War II many Americans moved from the North and East to the South and West—to the Sunbelt—and from the country and the city to the suburbs. Second, Americans acquired more education—in 1940 the average American over 25 had finished 8.6 years of school; in 1988, 12.7 years—and became more independent of party leaders. Third, the old city ethnic party bosses who traded favors and jobs to unskilled immigrants for votes lost influence as their old immigrant base changed and some of their traditional roles disappeared. The 1,218,500 immigrants of 1914 dropped to annual averages in the 200,000 range in the 1950s, but then rose steadily to 643,000 in 1988. There has also been a major change in the origin of recent immigrants, with only 10 percent coming from European nations and 85 percent almost equally divided, now coming from Latin America and Asia. Politicians have had to adjust to and attract these new immigrants and meet their expectations. Most government jobs have long required civil service examinations and thus reduced political parties' patronage. Moreover, the federal government's social welfare programs increasingly replaced the ward boss's handouts of coal, Christmas bundles, and emergency aid. In 1930 the federal government spent $817 million on social welfare (social insurance, health, housing, education) or 0.9 percent of the gross national product; and despite the "Reagan cuts" the figure in 1987 was $500 billion or 11.0 percent of the GNP. Fourth, union halls in the 1940s–1960s replaced political clubs as places to gather and gain help, and union membership increased from 3.7 million in 1934 to 22.8 million in 1980. The strongly Democratic labor union movement, however, has recently lost strength as union membership in the nonagricultural work force declined from 34.7 percent in 1954 to 14.2 percent in 1988, and the percentage employed for wages and salaries who belong to unions dropped from 23.2 percent in 1977 to 16.8 percent in 1988. The increase in independent voting will, no doubt, be further affected by such continued changes in immigration and union membership.

TV, Polls, Money, and the New Politics

In presidential campaigns candidates use techniques that reduce the role of party organizations. Television has been the primary cause of this change. TV, which first covered national conventions in 1948, allows candidates to speak directly to the voters. TV can be a major vehicle for serious public discussion on policy issues, as Adlai Stevenson demonstrated in 1956 with thoughtful policy statements on nuclear testing and public education, or, as in 1988, it can be the vehicle for "negative" or trivial "30 second sound bites." Sophisticated polling techniques provide candidates ready access to voter attitudes and wants. Direct and continuous communication flows both ways—from the voters to the candidates via polls and from the candidates to the voters via TV. No longer must a candidate work primarily through a chain of command of state committees, district leaders, ward bosses, and precinct captains. Increasingly, candidates have built personal organizations to do these jobs. Such organizations as "Citizens for Eisenhower," the extraordinary Kennedy "machine," and Nixon's Committee to Re-elect the President (CREEP), have become the norm.

The new battleground for votes in recent decades has been the rapidly growing suburbs. Candidates fly in by helicopter, "press the flesh" at shopping malls, and get on the local evening television news. Such techniques have replaced the railroad "whistle stop speech" and partisan exhortation to the regulars in the political clubhouse.

The "New Politics" still demands solid organization, hard work, voter registration, and doorbell ringing to "get out 'our' vote." But the old party politicians have been replaced by a new breed of "professionals for hire"— campaign managers, TV image-makers, sophisticated pollsters, computer experts, and, possibly most important, fund raisers to garner the vast sums of monies required for the new campaigning, especially for costly ads on TV. By the 1982 off-year election, a record $300 million poured into congressional campaigns from individuals and interest groups. By the 1980s a new sophisticated politics, conducted by professional "hired guns," and bankrolled by special interests, used the new technologies of TV, polling, and computers to create images and manipulate public opinion for candidates. Politicians have always practiced these arts, but the new techniques have made them more of a science. The political process as well as the electorate has thus changed markedly.

The "Vital Center"

Until the victory of Ronald Reagan in 1980, the U.S. electorate had been in the "middle of the road since World War II," rejecting the politics of the Left and Right. One historian described these moderate voters as the "vital center," representing the majority of U.S. voters. In foreign affairs, that majority favored a "responsible" internationalism and containment of Soviet expansion. At home, this majority of Americans supported the consolidation, but not the radical expansion of, the New Deal's role of the federal government as the protector of social security and regulator of the economy. Most Americans also supported a gradual expansion of civil rights guarantees, and, usually, protection of the civil liberties of the Bill of Rights. The minority on the extreme Left downplayed the cold war, favored an accommodation with the Soviets and supported a greatly expanded welfare state and vigorous defense of civil rights at home. The Right shifted from an isolationist, fortress U.S. policy to a militant anticommunism. It opposed the growth of the federal government's power in the social and economic lives of Americans. The Right favored free enterprise and states' rights, and gave little support to or opposed federal guarantees of civil rights or constitutional rights invoked by dissenters. Reagan adopted the rhetoric of the Right, and won major tax and nonmilitary spending cuts that reversed the expansion of the social service state and favored free enterprise. He denounced the Soviet Union as an "evil empire" and forged the biggest military buildup in the post–World War II years. Even Reagan and Bush, however, sounded moderate on some issues when appealing for votes, and downplayed the Right's more extreme proposals to cut Social Security or sell the Tennessee Valley Authority (TVA).

Harry S. Truman won his upset victory of 1948 while renouncing splinter groups on each flank of the Democratic party, the Henry Wallace Progressives on the Left and the Strom Thurmond Dixiecrats on the Right. In 1952 Eisenhower won a victory for "moderate Republicans" in the GOP convention over the conservative favorite, Robert A. Taft. In 1960 both John F. Kennedy and Richard M. Nixon appealed to the middle. In 1964 LBJ seized the center and won a smashing victory over a candidate regarded by many as a right-wing ideologue, Barry Goldwater.

By 1968 U.S. society was torn by the Vietnam War, urban riots, campus turmoil, the counterculture, and racial conflict. The center seemed to collapse. But two old political warhorses, Hubert Humphrey and Richard Nixon, played the game as usual and attempted to win the moderate majority. In 1972 Nixon carried 49 states and won the second highest percentage of the popular vote in the twentieth century by portraying Democratic candidate George McGovern as an irresponsible radical. In 1976 Jimmy Carter and Gerald Ford attempted to restore legitimacy to a government subverted by Vietnam and Watergate. They both stood for honesty, efficient government, and traditional values. In the 1980 campaign, Ronald Reagan successfully courted the Right, the center, and disaffected Democrats by presenting a conservative program in a manner and style, learned in long hours before the camera, which the voters found appealing. He downplayed his right-wing image, and came across to the voters as a "reasonable, responsible leader." Only 1 in 10 Reagan voters said they voted for him because he was conservative. In 1984, Reagan stood as a popular, charismatic, and decisive president who represented an optimistic patriotism and faith in traditional U.S. values. George Bush's victory in 1988 over Michael Dukakis was a triumph of peace, prosperity, Reaganism, and the expert use of the tools of the manipulative new politics. A centrist approach to presidential politics made sense in these years when most voters appeared to dislike the extremes of the Right or Left.

PRESIDENTIAL POLITICS AND THE USES AND ABUSES OF POWER, 1945–1991

Presidential Powers

In Franklin D. Roosevelt's administration (1933–1945), the powers of the presidency expanded greatly. Congress delegated, and the Court upheld, extraordinary powers to the president to combat the depression and to lead the nation in World War II. Some powers, such as those of commander-in-chief, are defined by the Constitution; others by act of Congress; and some by history, such as the role of political party leader. The presidency is the focal point of the U.S. political process. During the cold war, Congress and the U.S. people looked to the president to protect national security in a nuclear age. As a result, executive powers grew, some critics charged, to the point of creating an "imperial presidency" by the 1960s.

Some observers have argued that the essence of presidential power, however, is the *power to persuade*, not the legal right to command. To succeed, the president must sense the moods of the public and understand the powers of the presidency and its limits. The president needs to persuade the American people, members of the administration, the bureaucracy, the party, a majority in Congress, Washington insiders, the media, leaders of corporations, unions, universities, special interest groups, foreign heads of state, and people in other lands that the proposals of the President of the United States are right, possible, and reasonable.

THE TRUMAN ADMINISTRATION, 1945–1953

President Truman

On April 12, 1945, Vice-President Harry S Truman was called to the White House where Eleanor Roosevelt informed him of President Roosevelt's death: "Harry, the President is dead." The stunned Truman answered, "Is there anything I can do for you?" Mrs. Roosevelt replied, "Is there anything we can do for you? For you are the one in trouble now." Truman confronted many critical decisions in foreign affairs (see Chapters 1 and 2). At home, the new president faced the pressing problems of demobilizing the nation's armed forces and converting the economy to peacetime production. The list of problems seemed endless, including a rash of strikes, shortages of many raw materials and consumer goods, and inflation (see Chapter 7). In November 1946, the Republicans took political advantage of popular discontent and won the congressional elections for the first time since 1928. In foreign affairs, the Republican Congress led by Senator Arthur H. Vandenberg continued the bipartisanship begun in 1940 and supported bold administration initiatives such as the Truman Doctrine, the Marshall Plan, and NATO; but at home the 80th Congress was conservative and even saw socialist dangers in federal aid to school lunch programs. Truman's vigorous support of civil rights and his attempts to expand the Roosevelt New Deal failed.

The Election of 1948

In 1948 the Democrats faced a strong Republican challenger, Thomas E. Dewey, former governor of New York and the GOP presidential nominee in 1944. The Democratic party appeared to be badly split. Some, who believed Truman's policy toward the Soviets was too antagonistic and had caused the cold war, rallied to the banner of the Progressive party led by former Vice-President Henry A. Wallace, who pledged better relations with Stalin's Soviet Union and radical extensions of the New Deal at home. Truman's bold support of civil rights antagonized many southerners and led to the formation of the Dixiecrat party under Governor Strom Thurmond of South Carolina (see Chapter 9). Fearing defeat, some Democrats wanted to draft General Eisenhower.

But Truman won the nomination and went on to blast the "Do-Nothing 80th Congress" and the Wall Street "gluttons of privilege," as he crisscrossed the country on the presidential train in an old-fashioned "whistle stop" campaign. The Democrats lacked money, and all the polls indicated a certain Dewey victory, but the Missourian did not quit. He gave "sharp speeches fairly criticizing Republican policy and defending New Deal liberalism, [he] mixed [the criticism] with sophistries, bunkum piled higher than haystacks, and demagoguery."

Truman had advantages that are more obvious in hindsight. He was the incumbent; the Communists' brutal coup in Czechoslovakia and the Soviet

A Jubilant Harry Truman, a Decided Underdog in the Presidential Election of 1948, Enjoys the Last Laugh the Day After the Election

SOURCE: AP/Wide World Photos

Berlin blockade hurt Wallace; only four of the Deep South states followed Thurmond "into exile"; and the New Dealers finally rallied to Truman. The powerful legions of the AFL and the CIO worked tirelessly for Truman, the vetoer of Taft–Hartley. Farmers voted for Truman and his farm subsidies. African Americans, crucial in closely contested big electoral states, supported Truman in response to his strong civil rights position. Jewish voters backed Truman's recognition of Israel. In the previous decade the New Deal programs seemed dangerously radical to many, but now these same programs had many supporters who benefited from them and feared victorious Republicans would repeal their hard won gains. Last, and possibly most important, the candidates presented markedly different personalities. Truman campaigned as the underdog that Americans love. A former farmer, a World War I artillery officer, a haberdasher, a Kansas City machine politician, Truman was a plain-speaking, straight-

The Election of 1948

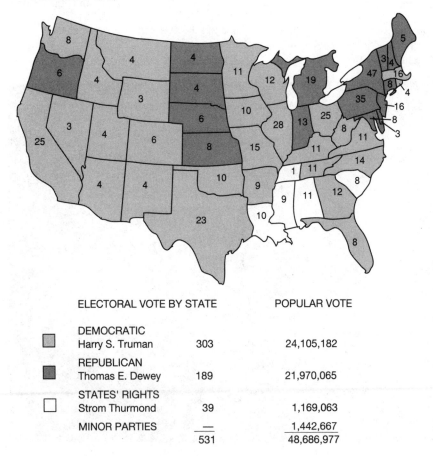

	ELECTORAL VOTE BY STATE	POPULAR VOTE
DEMOCRATIC Harry S. Truman	303	24,105,182
REPUBLICAN Thomas E. Dewey	189	21,970,065
STATES' RIGHTS Strom Thurmond	39	1,169,063
MINOR PARTIES	—	1,442,667
	531	48,686,977

forward, next-door-neighbor sort of man. To many voters, Dewey appeared cold, egotistical, and overconfident. For example, he announced his Cabinet before the election. Truman won with 49.6 percent of the popular vote and 303 electoral votes to Dewey's 45.1 percent of the popular vote and 189 electors. Thurmond captured only South Carolina, Alabama, Mississippi, and Louisiana, whereas Wallace won less than 2 percent of the vote. The voters gave the courageous underdog from Independence one of the greatest upset victories in U.S. history.

The Fair Deal

Truman pledged to the Americans a "Fair Deal," an expanded New Deal with the addition of federal aid to education, national health insurance, sweeping civil rights proposals, a bold new farm plan, and a greatly expanded federal housing program. But Truman won passage of only the last proposal and the extension of some New Deal measures, as congressional Republicans joined conservative southern Democrats to block him.

Corruption, Communism, and Korea

The Truman era ended on sour notes. Republicans charged the administration with petty corruption, with using bribes of mink coats and deep freezers, and creating a "mess in Washington." The worst scandal involved the Internal Revenue Service—nine persons eventually went to jail and most of them were Truman's cronies to whom he remained loyal too long. In February 1950, the junior Republican senator from Wisconsin, Joseph McCarthy, delivered a speech in Wheeling, West Virginia in which he made sensational and unsubstantiated charges of communist infiltration into the State Department. The American language added a new word: "McCarthyism." A Red Scare, overshadowing that of 1919–1920, absorbed the attention of the U.S. people and government for the next four years. Opponents now accused the Truman administration of being "soft on communism" and guilty of "losing China" in 1949. The Korean War settled into a deadly stalemate in 1951 and became "Truman's War" (see pp. 37–46), a seemingly endless and futile bloodletting. The Republicans raised cries of "Corruption, Communism, and Korea."

Executive Orders—Civil Rights

Though often frustrated in his efforts to persuade Congress to enact his domestic proposals, President Truman found a major source of power in the constitutional authority to issue executive orders. For example, he took the initiative in civil rights by executive orders. In 1946 he created the President's Committee on Civil Rights, which produced *To Secure These Rights* in 1947 (see pp. 251–252), a blueprint for civil rights action for the next two decades. In 1948, as commander-in-chief he ordered the desegregation of the armed forces, and as chief executive he ordered fair employment practices in the federal government.

Loyalty Programs

The House Un-American Activities Committee (HUAC) held sensational hearings in 1946. The Committee was established by congressional conservatives in 1938 to investigate "un-American" activities on the eve of World War II, and, many liberals feared, to harass New Dealers. To head off congressional witch hunts, to protect himself from charges of "being soft on communism," and to prevent communist infiltration of the federal service, Truman, by executive order in 1947, established a loyalty review program in federal employment. The order permitted dismissal if "reasonable grounds exist for belief that the person involved is disloyal to the Government of the United States." The attorney general also compiled a list of 82 subversive organizations; past or present membership in any of these organizations could be grounds for dismissal. The nuclear doomsday weapons and fears of the Soviets led to extraordinary executive secrecy measures and loyalty procedures to protect national security and prevent the employment of "security risks." But what was the meaning of "un-American," "subversive," or "disloyal"? Did they involve only actions, or also associations and beliefs? The national obsession reached new depths in 1953 when the Atomic Energy Commission denied security clearance to physicist J. Robert Oppenheimer, the "father of the atom bomb."

Though Truman's loyalty program allowed appeals, it violated traditional U.S. rules of fair play. The program failed to define disloyalty clearly. Those accused had no right to confront their accusers and cross-examine them or to examine the FBI's incriminating files. A person could lose his or her job and reputation by an administrative procedure without a day in court. The attorney general's list seemed to some an "executive bill of attainder" that by 1953 secretly branded over 200 organizations. Individuals were judged untrustworthy because of their political ideas and associations, motives attributed to them, or suspicions about their future conduct. During the Korean War, Truman expanded the executive loyalty program. Although the Truman administration checked on 4,750,000 employees, only 26,000 cases went to loyalty board hearings, and 7,000 quit the service or withdrew job applications while under investigation. Most received loyalty clearance, and only 560 persons were removed or denied employment on loyalty charges. Truman may have tried to blunt the public and congressional red hysteria, but the loyalty programs demoralized the federal service and encouraged a bland conformity to safe ideas in the bureaucracy.

Powers as Commander-in-Chief

In foreign affairs the president's constitutional authority as commander-in-chief and "chief diplomat" provided the greatest opportunity to exercise power. On June 25, 1950, the cold war turned hot in Korea. President Truman, acting as commander-in-chief and in response to UN Security Council resolutions, sent troops into combat in Korea. Truman acted without asking for congressional authorization, and thereby set a precedent for later "presidential wars." In 1951 Truman also sent four divisions of U.S. troops to Europe to fulfill a U.S. commitment to NATO (see p. 13), claiming the power to deploy such troops as commander-in-chief.

The Steel Seizure Case

In 1952 the Supreme Court, in *Youngstown Sheet and Tube Co. v. Sawyer*, ruled unconstitutional President Truman's unprecedented takeover of the strike-threatened U.S. steel industry during the Korean War. Truman cited the need for steel production for the war effort and claimed power to act "under the Constitution and laws of the United States and as Commander-in-Chief." Truman also argued that the use of such power was inherent in his constitutional office of chief executive. But in an unprecedented judicial–executive clash, the Supreme Court held that Truman's seizure was an unconstitutional usurpation of legislative power in violation of the separation of powers between the legislature and the executive. The Court rejected Truman's claim to inherent unenumerated executive powers and also held that a president could not seize a private industry under the commander-in-chief clause without congressional authorization. The president complied with the Court's decision and restored the steel industry to its corporate owners.

THE EISENHOWER ADMINISTRATION, 1953–1961

The Eisenhower Triumphs of 1952 and 1956

In 1952 Republican regulars favored the isolationist Ohio senator Robert A. Taft; but the managers of a "citizens' movement" for Dwight D. Eisenhower won the "battle of the delegates" at the Republican convention and nominated the military hero of World War II. A committed internationalist and a moderate on domestic issues, the 61-year-old Eisenhower—above politics, well-connected to the eastern establishment, and little known to the party professionals—balanced the ticket with thirty-nine-year-old California senator, Richard M. Nixon, who reassured the party conservatives by his hardnosed partisanship and his anticommunist record. The Democratic convention drafted Adlai E. Stevenson, governor of Illinois. Though detractors called him indecisive, to his admirers Stevenson combined rare qualities of brilliance, elegance, and wit. He pledged to "talk sense to the American people." His finely honed rhetoric, however, did not win the people. Eisenhower, popularly known as Ike, pledged "to go to Korea" and to clean up the "mess in Washington." Other Republicans lashed at "Communists in government." Crowds yelled "We like Ike," and on election day he won handily. Almost 13,000,000 more people voted in 1952 than in 1948, a 27 percent increase. "Corruption, Communism and Korea," and especially the magic of the Eisenhower personality brought out the big vote. Ike received 33,936,234 popular votes or 55.1 percent and 442 electors; Stevenson trailed with 27,314,992 votes and carried only nine southern states.

Although the Democrats lost control of Congress by the narrow margin of 1 seat in the Senate and 10 seats in the House, the Republican victory represented a tribute to the personal popularity of Eisenhower, not a resurgence of the Republican party. From 1955 to 1981, the Democrats controlled both Houses of Congress, and in Eisenhower's last 2 years from 1959 to 1961 their margin stood at 283 to 153 in the House and 64 to 34 in the Senate. Yet in a rematch with Stevenson in 1956, Eisenhower rolled up an even greater victory than in 1952: 35,590,471 to 26,022,752. Eisenhower negotiated an end to the Korean War, kept the nation out of any new wars, enjoyed a general prosperity (interrupted by recessions in 1953–1954 and 1958) and ran a pro-business administration. In the 1950s, Eisenhower presided over a period of governmental consolidation, without bold new starts nor repeal of the New-Fair Deal legislation.

Executive Privilege and Secrecy

Eisenhower, as a response to the cold war and to thwart McCarthyism, increased his powers by claims of executive privilege and secrecy to withhold classified information from Congress and the public. In the Truman administration in 1949 a Department of Justice attorney claimed that the president and cabinet heads had the right to withhold secret confidential papers and information from a congressional investigation. He claimed that the president's "uncontrolled discretion" had long been upheld by the Court. Court precedents did not support his claim, however.

Such executive action could be used not only to block irresponsible congressional investigators, but also to stop Congress from fulfilling its constitutional role to inform itself and the public of presidential folly or wrongdoing—a two-edged sword. Eisenhower ruled privileged all material generated by the internal deliberative processes in the executive branch of government, not just presidential conversations with aides. In 1958, Attorney General William P.

Rogers made the Justice Department attorney's memo of nine years earlier a constitutional doctrine—*executive privilege*. Later presidents Johnson and Nixon invoked it increasingly in the late 1960s and early 1970s.

While presidents exercised executive privilege to thwart Congress, the post–World War II presidency also invoked a rule of secrecy relative to the press and public on matters of "national security." Again, presidents, beginning with Truman, cited cold war dangers to establish this policy by executive orders, not laws passed by Congress. Most Americans believe that the government requires secrecy in certain ongoing diplomatic negotiations, active military preparations, and intelligence activities, but they also hold that the people have a right—in fact a need—to know in other areas if self-government is to work. Executive officials could also invoke secrecy to bury errors, cover up crimes, manipulate public opinion, and abuse presidential powers. But secret operations by later presidents, such as Johnson's escalation of the Vietnam war in the mid-1960s, and Nixon's bombing of Cambodia in 1969–1970, created a "credibility gap"; such secrecy seemed intolerable. By the late 1960s and early 1970s many Americans believed that presidents were improperly withholding information and misleading the public.

The Freedom of Information Act

Congress reacted to presidential claims of the need for secrecy by enacting the Freedom of Information Act of 1966. The law declared free disclosure to be the rule and that the burden of proof for withholding a document rested on the government, not on the person who requested it. The act, however, did allow for secrecy in matters deemed necessary by the chief executive concerning national defense or foreign policy. However, the law opened a flow of information to the public and investigative reporters.

Eisenhower's Global Anticommunism

President Eisenhower, though he practiced executive restraint at home, significantly increased presidential power abroad. Under Truman, the establishment of NATO and dispatch of military forces to fight in Korea changed the cold war from one of finely tuned economic and political containment of Soviet expansion to an increasingly military policy. The Eisenhower administration saw a responsibility to resist communism around the globe, maintained enormous military forces abroad, and made commitments, military pacts, and agreements with almost 50 nations (pp. 49, 70). In the Formosa Strait in 1955 and in the Middle East in 1957 Eisenhower obtained from Congress authority to use military force if certain "contingencies" arose. The cold war fears of the nuclear age led public opinion and Congress to support such contingency authorizations.

The Election of 1960

The Republicans in 1960 nominated Richard M. Nixon. A child of poverty, raised in rootless southern California, he saw his life as a series of lonely struggles and crises. Unlike Eisenhower, Nixon was a partisan campaigner and often charged his opponents with being "soft on communism." He used this technique to win election to the House in 1946 and the Senate in 1950. He gained a national reputation as a member of the House Un-American Activities Committee (HUAC) in its investigation of Alger Hiss in 1948. In the presidential campaign of 1952 he called Stevenson, "Adlai the appeaser . . . who got a Ph.D. from Dean Acheson's College of Cowardly Communist Containment." Many Democrats never forgot nor forgave such charges. Nixon campaigned for Republican candidates year-in and year-out, and he earned the support of delegates at the Republican National Convention in 1960.

Nixon, however, knew he had to gain Democratic and Independent votes to win the White House. In the 1960 campaign, he tried to put the "red-baiting, hatchet-man" image to rest and posed as a "New Nixon." Eisenhower gave Nixon a more prominent role than previous vice-presidents by sending him on numerous diplomatic trips abroad, thus Nixon presented himself as an experienced leader, knowledgeable in foreign affairs, who would continue the peace and prosperity of the Eisenhower years.

The Democrats nominated a young Massachusetts senator, 43-year-old John F. Kennedy. Kennedy, the grandson of an immigrant Irish Catholic Boston politician, son of a wealthy financier, schooled at Choate and Harvard, and World War II hero of P.T. Boat 109 symbolized the arrival of a new generation and style in U.S. politics. He won in primary battles against a trio of senators, Lyndon B. Johnson of Texas, Stuart Symington of Missouri, and Hubert H. Humphrey of Minnesota, and the still-willing Adlai Stevenson. Kennedy assembled a superbly organized and well-financed presidential campaign. Kennedy put to rest the Catholic issue by publicly pledging to support separation of church and state. This issue haunted many old-line Democratic leaders wishing to avoid a repeat of the 1928 race in which Republican Herbert Hoover easily defeated Democrat Al Smith, a Catholic from New York. Kennedy called on Americans to face the challenges of a "New Frontier." He brought a new generation that came to maturity in the depression, World War II, and the cold war into politics. His youth and his call for sacrifice contrasted strikingly with the Eisenhower presidency. Kennedy, also a practical politician, chose Texas Senator Lyndon Johnson as his vice-presidential running mate. The Catholic Kennedy from the urban Northeast needed Johnson to hold the South in the Democratic column.

In the campaign both Kennedy and Nixon proclaimed support of the cold war abroad and civil rights at home. They pledged vigorous exercise of presidential power. Kennedy, however, attacked the Eisenhower administration for not

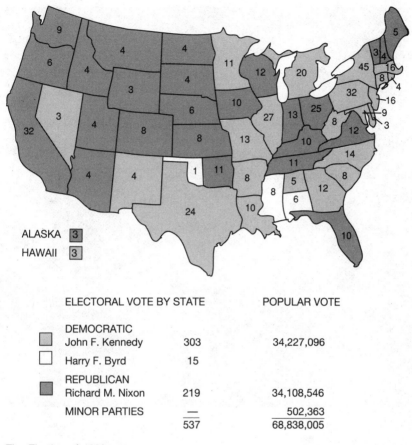

The Election of 1960

ELECTORAL VOTE BY STATE		POPULAR VOTE
DEMOCRATIC		
John F. Kennedy	303	34,227,096
Harry F. Byrd	15	
REPUBLICAN		
Richard M. Nixon	219	34,108,546
MINOR PARTIES	—	502,363
	537	68,838,005

being tough enough against Castro's Cuba. Kennedy inaccurately charged that the Eisenhower administration had allowed a "missile gap" to grow between the United States and the Soviet Union and claimed that the United States was losing the cold war. The Democratic candidate pledged to increase the U.S. rate of economic growth, to expand space efforts, and to support civil rights, medicare, and federal aid to education. Kennedy saw the federal government as the vehicle to achieve these goals and the presidency as the initiator of action.

Four televised debates, viewed by about 70 million Americans, became the high point of the campaign. In the first debate, Kennedy spoke with confidence to television viewers; Nixon—thin from a recent illness, his TV makeup running under the hot lights, his five o'clock shadow showing—busied himself debating Kennedy, not talking to the viewers. Many radio listeners thought Nixon won, but the vast television audience named Kennedy as the winner. Kennedy's show-

Kennedy-Nixon TV Debate, 1960
SOURCE: AP/Wide World Photos

ing neutralized Nixon's primary strength, that of more diplomatic experience and mature leadership. The campaign was fiercely contested and extremely close. Of the almost 69 million votes cast, Kennedy won by only 118,574 votes—no mandate. Kennedy, like all Democratic presidents since 1938, faced a conservative Republican–southern Democratic congressional opposition.

THE KENNEDY ADMINISTRATION, 1961–1963

The "New Frontier"

The "Thousand Days" of President Kennedy were marked more by promise than achievement. Though the Kennedy style captivated many Americans, the president faced a stalemate with Congress. In foreign affairs, he stumbled badly in the Bay of Pigs fiasco, was thwarted by the Berlin wall, and slid into increased involvement in Vietnam (pp. 98–100). But as 1963 dawned, JFK displayed a new confidence after his victory in the Cuban Missile Crisis and the Democratic support he gained in the 1962 congressional elections. On June 10, 1963, in a speech at American University, in response to popular concern over radioactive fallout from nuclear testing, pressure from much of the international scientific community, and his own sense of responsibility as the leader of a nuclear power, President Kennedy pledged that the United States would conduct no further atmospheric nuclear testing unless other nations did so first. He went further and called on Americans to "reexamine our attitude toward peace . . . reexamine our attitude towards the Soviet Union . . . reexamine our attitude towards the Cold War." His initiative resulted in the Test Ban Treaty signed in Moscow on July 25, 1963, and approved by the Senate that fall (p. 64). He attempted to lead Congress to enact major bills to guarantee civil rights and to adopt Keynesian economic policy (see pp. 182–183) with tax cuts to stimulate economic growth. The president had his economic advisers draft a major program to combat poverty. Then on November 22, 1963, Kennedy was assassinated in Dallas, a symbol of the irrational violence of the 1960s.

THE JOHNSON ADMINISTRATION, 1963–1969

LBJ

Lyndon B. Johnson took the oath of office beside blood-spattered Jacqueline Kennedy on Air Force One as it flew back to Washington from Dallas. This big, energetic, earthy man seemed born to lead. From the hill country of Texas, Johnson graduated from Southwest Texas State Teachers College. A master politician in Congress from 1937 to 1960, the vice-presidency frustrated him. His old Texas friend and former Vice-President John Nance Garner once described the vice-presidency as "not worth a pitcher of warm spit." In 1963 many regarded Johnson as one of the best prepared politicians, at least in domestic affairs, to assume the presidency since Teddy Roosevelt. At home Johnson planned to follow the humanitarian policies of the New Deal. Abroad he set himself against appeasement and the "communist menace."

The "War on Poverty" and the "Great Society"

Johnson acted decisively to pull the nation together. Backed by a strong majority of congressional and popular support, in 1964 the new president invoked the memory of his martyred predecessor and used all his legislative skills to push Kennedy's tax cut and civil rights bills through Congress, the first pieces of domestic legislation to break new ground since 1938. In his first State of the Union Address, Johnson called for an "unconditional war on poverty." He soon named his program the "Great Society," and convinced Congress to establish the Office of Economic Opportunity to wage the "war" in August 1964.

The Election of 1964

In the 1964 election committed right-wing ideologues took over the Republican party and nominated their favorite, Senator Barry Goldwater of Arizona. Goldwater, an amiable man, had written a book, *The Conscience of a Conservative*, which denounced the welfare state at home and called for victory over communism abroad. For the first time since 1932, the Republicans dropped their centrist position and "me too" stance and gave the voters a "choice not an echo." Goldwater captured the spirit of his supporters in his acceptance speech with the words, "Extremism in the defense of liberty is no vice! . . . Moderation in the pursuit of justice is no virtue!" The Goldwater nomination represented the triumph of the new wealth of the Sunbelt over the older Republican establishment of the Northeast. Goldwater fundraisers raised and spent over $16 million, 60 percent more than any previous presidential candidate. Some moderate Republicans, such as Governor Nelson A. Rockefeller of New York, "sat on their hands" in November or voted Democratic.

President Johnson, relishing the Goldwater challenge, pictured himself as the successor of the martyred Kennedy and the mastermind behind the legislative majority that enacted major tax, civil rights, and antipoverty laws. Goldwater, who had voted against civil rights and the War on Poverty, gave Johnson a chance to do battle with a self-styled conservative who talked of selling TVA, ending Social Security, and defoliating trees in Vietnam with "tactical atomic weapons." The Goldwaterites' slogan, "In your heart you know he's right" was twisted by some Democrats to "In your guts you know he's nuts." Johnson campaigned in favor of social reform at home and against war abroad, especially in Vietnam!

Johnson won the highest percentage of popular votes of any presidential candidate in U.S. history, 61.1 percent. Goldwater won his home state of Arizona and five states of the Deep South. The Johnson landslide carried in an 89th Congress with overwhelming Democratic majorities, 295 to 140 in the House and 68 to 32 in the Senate. LBJ nurtured a broad public consensus to support legislation to implement New Deal-Fair Deal-New Frontier economic, social, and civil rights programs. Congress, eager to enact LBJ's Great Society proposals, passed bills such as medicare, federal aid to education, voting rights, air and water pollution controls, model cities, rent supplements, and War on Poverty measures—legislative action without parallel since 1935.

LBJ and the Dominican Republic

In foreign affairs, however, Johnson demonstrated less knowledge and control, and his use and abuse of presidential powers eventually had disastrous consequences. In 1965 President Johnson sent 22,000 troops into the Dominican Republic (see p. 64). The administration claimed it sent the troops to rescue U.S. citizens from revolutionary violence, but in reality the troops' job was to prevent another Castro revolution in the Caribbean. Unfortunately, Johnson's "successful" use of military force in the Dominican Republic gave his administration the false belief that using sufficient military force could achieve its political goals in the Third World. This belief was to be painfully disproved in Vietnam.

LBJ and Vietnam

Presidents since Truman had sent economic and military aid and advisers to Vietnam and used the CIA and, under Kennedy and Johnson, the "Green Berets," to contain or defeat the communist Vietminh of Ho Chi Minh and the Vietcong rebels (see pp. 98–100). After Johnson assumed the presidency, he said, "I am not going to lose Vietnam." During the presidential election of 1964, the "peace candidate," Johnson, manipulated the Tonkin Gulf incident (pp. 86–87) to gain congressional passage of the Tonkin Gulf Resolution. He regarded Truman's failure to gain such congressional authorization in the Korean War as a political blunder. Johnson viewed the congressional resolution as good politics and as constitutional authorization to send troops into combat in Vietnam (525,000 by 1968). In LBJ's second administration, the war escalated into a seemingly endless and—to many, unwinnable—senseless nightmare of death and destruction. Johnson's conduct of the war and his uses and abuses of presidential power destroyed his broad base of popular support and created bitter divisions in the nation.

Power as Commander-in-Chief

Johnson argued that with or without the Tonkin Resolution he had the constitutional authority as commander-in-chief to commit troops to battle in Vietnam as part of his power to wage war in defense of the United States. The administration asserted "an attack on a country far from our shores can impinge directly on the nation's security," and the president alone has the power to determine if the situation is so threatening to the United States "that he should act without formally consulting with Congress." This expansive view of presidential power gave the chief executive very broadly defined war-making authority.

Confrontation Replaces Consensus

The euphoria of the Great Society of 1964–1965 was soon replaced by disillusion in northern inner cities with the failure of the War on Poverty and the civil rights movement to fulfill rising expectations. Racial riots tore at the fabric of urban life from 1964 to 1968. This endless violence and the misery of Vietnam, viewed nightly on the television news, crushed the hopes of many Americans. Confrontational politics in the streets replaced Johnson's efforts to build broad-based popular and legislative majorities.

The Election of 1968

As 1968 began, the country appeared as divided as at any time since the Civil War. In the Republican party a "New, New Nixon" made an extraordinary comeback from his defeats in the presidential race of 1960 and the California gubernatorial election of 1962 to gain the nomination. Nixon appealed to Republican Party regulars and played on public fears. He campaigned for "law and order" and appealed to what he called the "silent majority," Americans who feared racial violence, antiwar protesters, campus turmoil, and the life-styles of the counterculture. He actively sought southern votes by a "Southern Strategy," and he courted the northern "white backlash" vote (see pp. 271–272). Nixon raised over $25.4 million in campaign funds, a 64 percent increase over Goldwater's record fund in 1964, and more than twice the amount raised by the Democrats.

The third-party candidacy of Alabama segregationist Governor George C. Wallace appealed to racists North and South, lower middle-class ethnic groups who felt ignored, those who demanded victory in Vietnam, and those who blamed the government for their problems. He blasted the "pointy-headed intellectuals," "the briefcase totin' bureaucrats," and yelled, "Ah hadn' meant to say this tonight but yew know, if one of those hippies lays down in front of mah car when Ah becomes President." The end was usually drowned out by his audiences' roaring response. He told them to "send Washington a message"—one of rage, bitterness, resentment. Civility had disappeared from U.S. politics.

The ferocity of the "Tet offensive" launched by the Vietcong and North Vietnamese on January 29, 1968, shocked Americans (see pp. 107–108). Senator Eugene McCarthy of Minnesota seriously challenged President Johnson on the war issue in the New Hampshire primary on March 13. Robert F. Kennedy, President Kennedy's younger brother, joined the race three days later. Johnson announced on March 31 that he would not run for reelection. An assassin killed Robert Kennedy in Los Angeles in June after an apparently decisive Kennedy victory in the California primary. The Johnson administration candidate at the Democratic party convention in Chicago was Vice-President Hubert H. Humphrey, who had been one of the nation's leading supporters of working people and the underprivileged. In foreign policy, Humphrey stood firm as a cold warrior, and a "hawk" in Vietnam. Despite antiwar demonstrations in the streets and the impassioned "peace forces" in the convention hall, the administration rammed through a pro-war plank, and the delegates nominated Humphrey. In the streets, police brutally attacked youthful protesters as the nation watched on TV. The events of Chicago tore the Democratic party apart.

Wallace's candidacy threatened to deny any candidate an electoral majority and to throw the election into the House of Representatives where Wallace could bargain for his constituency and himself. Nixon took the high road and called for "law and order," whereas the Republican vice-presidential candidate Spiro T. Agnew's slashing rhetoric led some critics to call him "Nixon's Nixon." With only 43.4 percent of the popular vote, a mere 0.7 percent more than Humphrey,

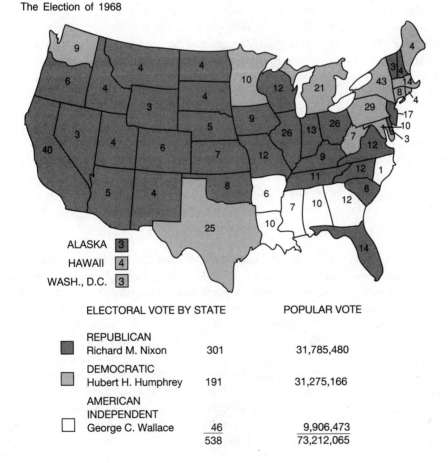

The Election of 1968

ALASKA 3
HAWAII 4
WASH., D.C. 3

ELECTORAL VOTE BY STATE		POPULAR VOTE
REPUBLICAN Richard M. Nixon	301	31,785,480
DEMOCRATIC Hubert H. Humphrey	191	31,275,166
AMERICAN INDEPENDENT George C. Wallace	46	9,906,473
	538	73,212,065

Nixon won the presidency by a majority of 110 in the electoral college. Republicans, revived from the Goldwater debacle of 1964, also made gains in the South. Humphrey held the old New Deal coalition in the North, but he carried only Texas in the once Solid Democratic South.

THE NIXON ADMINISTRATION, 1969–1974

Richard Nixon and Vietnam

President Nixon gradually deescalated the Vietnam War, but he did not withdraw all U.S. troops until March 28, 1973. In fact, the Nixon administration expanded the war by secret bombing raids in Cambodia in 1969–1970, and a covert war by the CIA against communist forces in Laos.

Accepting Congress' repeal of the Tonkin Gulf Resolution in 1971, Nixon justified his military actions in Southeast Asia under his constitutional authority as commander-in-chief. He argued that when he assumed the presidency, there were over 500,000 U.S. troops in Vietnam and he had the constitutional power and moral duty to do everything necessary to protect those troops until the last soldier was withdrawn. President Nixon, going beyond Johnson, argued that a *potential* attack on U.S. troops anywhere in the world justified a president to wage war. He used this reasoning to justify the massive invasion of neutral Cambodia in 1970 (see p. 112) to protect U.S. troops in Vietnam. Nixon acted and simply told Congress and the nation of his actions. Johnson and Nixon expanded the presidential power to make war to a degree that led critics to talk of an "imperial presidency." All efforts in Congress to end the war in Southeast Asia by cutting appropriations failed.

Richard Nixon at Home

Nixon said he would bring Americans together, but antiwar protests exploded with Nixon's invasion of Cambodia in 1970. Public anger increased with the 1970 shootings of protesting students at Kent State University and Jackson State College. Nixon had called youthful protesters "bums," offered African Americans "benign neglect," lashed his Democratic critics as "radicals," and put together an "enemies" list. Ironically, though Nixon opposed busing, the War on Poverty, and much of the civil rights agenda, he and Congress expanded spending on food stamps, welfare, Social Security and disability pensions, and accelerated the environmental movement. These actions and his foreign policy achievements such as the "opening to China" and "detente" with the Soviets (see pp. 118–120) became overshadowed by his self-imposed political isolation and criminal actions to protect his power.

The Election of 1972

President Nixon, however, won a smashing victory over the Democratic candidate, Senator George S. McGovern of South Dakota in 1972. The Republicans renominated Nixon and Agnew in a carefully staged performance in Miami. The Democrats presented a very different story. In May the political violence of the 1960s spilled over into the 1972 campaign. At the Maryland Democratic primary, a lone stalker shot and permanently crippled Governor George Wallace, removing him from the Democratic race. The little known McGovern won a first-ballot nomination. A January 1972 Gallup poll showed McGovern had only 3 percent of the Democratic support, but 23 primaries later, McGovern held a majority of the delegates. In the process, strange things happened. Letters appeared. One letter to a New Hampshire newspaper, appearing just before that state's first-in-the-nation primary, accused the front-runner, Senator Edmund S. Muskie, of bigotry toward French-Canadians, a big bloc of voters in the New Hampshire Democratic party. The same letter suggested Mrs. Muskie drank heavily. Next, prior to the Florida primary, letters on "Citizens for Muskie" stationery to supporters of Senator Henry M. Jackson, a leading candidate, accused him of fathering an illegitimate child in 1929 and of arrests for homosexuality in 1955 and 1957. Former Vice-President Humphrey's backers received letters on the same stationery that accused him of drunken driving in the company of a prostitute in 1967. The letters were phonies—part of the "dirty tricks" campaign orchestrated from the White House, paid for by a secret fund, and carried out by Donald Segretti. The use of sabotage, spies, wiretaps, and bugs culminated in the break-in and bugging of Democratic National Committee headquarters at the Watergate in Washington by employees of CREEP, former CIA and FBI agents and Cuban refugees, on the night of June 17, 1972.

McGovern, long an opponent of the Vietnam War, attracted many from the groups who had entered politics in large numbers in the previous decade— African Americans in 1964, young people in 1968, and women in 1972. The Democratic party rewrote its party and convention rules to welcome the newcomers. "McGovern's army" won within the party, but the demands of African Americans, Hispanics, feminists, and the counterculture, the liberation rhetoric, the militant antiwar activists' stance and the newcomers' appearance at the Miami Convention alienated much of the middle class. In the older cities many of the ethnic groups and trade unionists, the backbone of the Democratic party for decades in the big industrial states, felt forgotten, if not discriminated against, by the McGovern forces. Many of these traditional Democrats "sat out" the 1972 campaign; many others voted Republican.

McGovern made campaign mistakes. He pledged welfare reform with a federal payment of $1,000 per American, but he could not say how he would finance it. He chose Missouri Senator Thomas F. Eagleton to be his vicepresidential running mate. When he learned that Eagleton had been hospitalized for mental illness, McGovern said he backed him "1000 percent," and then he dropped him and selected Sargent Shriver, President Kennedy's brother-in-law. The Democratic organization became demoralized and desperate for money. Republicans pictured McGovern as a dangerous extremist. The Democrats brought a suit against CREEP for $1 million for the Watergate burglary, and McGovern denounced the Nixon administration as "the most corrupt in history." Few listened. A Harris poll in October revealed that 62 percent of the voters dismissed Watergate as "just politics."

Nixon, the picture of a head of state after his trips to China and Russia early in 1972, took the high road as Agnew and the agents of CREEP slugged it out. The CREEP organization raised $60.2 million, the previous record being $25.4 million. Nixon won 49 states, losing only Massachusetts and the District of Columbia, while piling up a record 47,167,319 votes to McGovern's 29,168,509. Yet the Democrats continued to control Congress, 239 to 192 in the House and 56 to 42 in the Senate.

"WATERGATE"

As 1973 and 1974 wore on, seemingly endless Watergate revelations shocked Americans and paralyzed government. Most political corruption in the past had involved more ordinary crimes, bribe-taking and kickbacks, but in their grasp for power the "President's Men" attempted to subvert U.S. constitutional procedures and end the rule of law.

The June 17, 1972, Watergate burglary was simply the tip of the iceberg of corruption of the Nixon presidency. Eventually, because of two young *Washington Post* investigative reporters, Robert Woodward and Carl Bernstein; a tough federal judge, John J. Sirica; a tenacious guardian of the Constitution, Senator Sam J. Ervin (D., N.C.); two relentless special prosecutors, Harvard Law professor Archibald Cox and Houston lawyer Leon Jaworski; a little-known Newark member of Congress, Peter W. Rodino (D., N.J.); the presidential "tapes"; the U.S. Supreme Court—and some good luck—the White House "horrors" came to light, President Nixon resigned, and his principal aides went to jail.

Wiretaps and "Enemies"

The Nixon administration used wiretaps and bugs widely to find out who was leaking information to the press and to gain advantages in the political infighting in the White House. The administration, between May 10, 1969, and February 10, 1971, without court authorization, wiretapped and bugged 13 government officials—10 on the White House staff, 5 reporters, and even the president's brother, Donald Nixon. The Supreme Court in 1972 ruled such unauthorized electronic surveillance an unconstitutional "search" in violation of the Fourth Amendment. In the years 1969–1971 the White House staff mirrored President Nixon's view that the government was under a "state of seige" from waves of antiwar protesters, campus radicals, and African American militants. They believed it necessary to take drastic steps to stop their "enemies" before a mob forced the president from office—just as they believed a mob forced out Lyndon Johnson in 1968. John Mitchell's Justice Department prosecuted a number of "conspiracy cases" against African American militants, radicals, and antiwar activists but without success. The White House compiled an "enemies list" of some 200 people and 18 organizations—mostly liberals, such as Senator Edward Kennedy, but also professional football player Joe Namath and the Harvard Law School. Nixon planned, after the 1972 election, to use the CIA, the FBI, and IRS to "screw our enemies."

Nixon and the Court, Congress, the Bureaucracy, and the Press

Though all presidents have tried, to a degree, to control or manipulate the courts, Congress, the bureaucracy, and the press, Nixon acted with unprecedented vigor and hostility. He demonstrated his contempt for the Supreme Court by his nominations of Haynsworth and particularly Carswell (see p. 229). The president impounded $15 billion that Congress appropriated for 100 federal programs, creating an absolute veto over legislation. He refused to cut off federal funds to desegregate schools as directed by the 1964 Civil Rights Act, and directed an aide to dismantle the Office of Economic Opportunity before its legal life expired in 1973.

Nixon, long at odds with the "liberal" press, had Vice-President Agnew blast the networks and the "eastern establishment press." In 1971 he requested a court injunction to prevent publication of the Pentagon Papers, a Defense Department history of the Vietnam War, which had been leaked to the *New York Times*. The Supreme Court ruled unconstitutional this attempt at "prior restraint." The administration tapped reporters' phones, pressured editors to fire reporters, and won a Supreme Court decision forcing the press to reveal confidential sources in grand jury investigations. The war against the press was systematic and thorough.

The Huston Plan and the Plumbers

In 1970 Nixon, upset that the FBI was not "doing the job" of exposing press leaks, approved a young White House aide's plan to use wiretaps, bugs, illegal mail openings, campus informants, and "surreptitous" entries—breaking and entering—to stop them. The so-called Huston Plan involved clearly illegal and unethical activities and FBI chief J. Edgar Hoover balked, fearing bad public relations and the "jackals of the press." The CIA, the FBI, and the Secret Service, however, had long carried on such covert illegal activities in the United States in the name of national security.

After Daniel Ellsberg leaked the Pentagon Papers to the *New York Times* in June 1971, the White House quickly set up a secret Special Investigations Unit nicknamed the "plumbers" after their job of "fixing leaks." The plumbers hired G. Gordon Liddy and E. Howard Hunt, and they went far beyond leaks. They tried to get "dirt" on the leading Democratic challenger, Senator Edward Kennedy; they forged and leaked a cablegram to "prove" President Kennedy ordered the assassination of President Diem of South Vietnam; they broke into the office of Ellsberg's California psychiatrist to get damaging information to "destroy" Ellsberg; and, finally, they broke into the Watergate Democratic National Committee headquarters. That break-in had the approval of the head of CREEP, former Attorney General John Mitchell. The "dirty tricks" of the CIA and the cold war had come home to U.S. politics.

Containing Watergate—or Obstructing Justice

The administration denied any involvement in the burglary, and put John Dean, the legal counsel to the president, in charge of efforts to "contain" Watergate during the 1972 campaign. The administration launched a public relations campaign to down-grade the break-in as a "third-rate burglary" and claimed to push the "most strenuous criminal investigation in history." In fact, on June 23, 1972, the president ordered the CIA to head off the FBI investigation into monies found on the burglars, which could be traced through a Mexican "laundering" operation back to CREEP. Nixon found willing political appointees in the CIA and the FBI who carried out these orders from June 23 to July 5, 1972. John Dean sat in on FBI interrogations, counseled CREEP officials on perjury before the grand jury, received all FBI field reports, and obtained daily reports from the assistant attorney general on the progress of the investigation. Nixon's private lawyer arranged to pay the seven burglars "hush money." After a sloppy job of investigation, the federal prosecutors on September 15, 1972, gained a grand jury indictment of only the seven burglars. CREEP, the White House, and Nixon seemed safe and that afternoon Nixon congratulated John Dean for "containing" Watergate. On November 7, 1972, Nixon won his landslide presidential election victory.

Judge Sirica and Woodward and Bernstein

Five Watergate burglars pleaded guilty, and the other two were tried and convicted in January 1973. But Judge Sirica announced that he was "not satisfied that all the pertinent facts that might be available . . . have been produced before an American jury." The Republicans raised $60.2 million for the 1972 campaign, and almost $2 million of this was in untraceable cash. *Washington Post* reporters Woodward and Bernstein, at the suggestion of a mysterious informant, "Deep Throat," traced brand new $100 bills found on the burglars through a Miami bank to Mexico to CREEP. The Nixon campaign was awash in money. Prosecutors later convicted 17 corporations of illegal contributions. Numerous corporate individuals gave a total of $1,433,830 to the Nixon campaign, some illegally. From August to November 1972, Woodward and Bernstein wrote articles about the CREEP–Watergate money connections, the secret funds of Haldeman and CREEP officials, and the White House ties to Donald Segretti and "dirty tricks" in the campaign. Few took heed.

McCord Cracks, Dean Talks, Ervin Investigates

On February 7, 1973, the Senate unanimously established the Select Committee on Presidential Campaign Activities under Senator Sam Ervin. In March, as sentencing day for the Watergate burglars approached, one of the burglars, James W. McCord, cracked and told Judge Sirica that there had been political pressure, perjury in the trial, and undisclosed criminal involvement by higher-ups. On the same day, March 21, 1973, John Dean told President Nixon that "we have a cancer—within—close to the Presidency, that's growing." He told Nixon of Hunt's demands for executive clemency and more money, that the blackmail might last two years and cost $1 million, and that many high officials were guilty of obstruction of justice. Nixon's response was "you better damn well get that [payment to Hunt] done, but fast. . . . Well, for Christ's sake get it." Nixon told John Mitchell the next day, "I want you all to stonewall it, let them plead the Fifth Amendment, cover up or anything else, if it'll save it— save the [cover up] plan."

The administration put out public relations stories and erected constitutional defenses. Citing the confidentiality of presidential deliberations and the separation of powers, the attorney general announced that the president could invoke executive privilege for all 2.5 million employees of the executive branch, past and present. But with the cover-up crumbling, Dean talked to the prosecutors on April 8 and entered into plea bargaining in return for his complete testimony. Others soon followed his example.

New Developments

On April 17 Nixon announced new Watergate "developments" and presented himself as a vigorous investigator. Throughout Watergate, Nixon "the criminal" posed as Nixon "the investigator," two irreconcilable roles. The public relations scenarios that the president's aides hoped would "play in Peoria" changed so often that Nixon, as the tapes would later reveal, confused the truth with the numerous cover stories. On April 30, 1973, in a dramatic TV speech, Nixon accepted the resignation of John Dean, regretted the resignation of "two of the finest public servants it has ever been my privilege to know," Haldeman and Ehrlichman, and announced the appointment of a new attorney general, Elliot L. Richardson, with the right to name a "special supervising prosecutor" to get to "the bottom of Watergate." He waived executive privilege for White House aides before the Ervin committee.

Dean Versus Nixon—the Tapes

In five dramatic days in June, John Dean told a detailed story of the cover-up, including the role of President Nixon, to the Ervin committee and a spellbound national TV audience. It became a test of Dean's word against Nixon's. Then, on July 13, 1973, a presidential aide stunned the TV hearings by revealing that President Nixon had installed automatic taping equipment in the White House, the Executive Office Building, and at Camp David. He had bugged himself. On July 23 Senator Ervin and the special prosecutor, Archibald Cox, obtained subpoenas for nine key tapes. The president refused to surrender the tapes and invoked executive privilege based on presidential confidentiality, the constitutional separation of powers, and a plea to protect national security. Cox requested a court order, claiming that the president was not above the law and could not withhold evidence in a criminal proceeding. Judge Sirica and the Circuit Court of Appeals ordered Nixon to give over the tapes.

On October 20, 1973, Nixon fired Cox and abolished the special prosecutor's office in what became known as the "Saturday Night Massacre." A "firestorm" of public protest compelled Nixon to name a new special prosecutor, Leon Jaworski, with added assurances of independence. Nixon delivered the tapes, but two could not be found and a third, a conversation between Nixon and Haldeman on June 20, 1972, three days after the burglary, had a mysterious erasure, an "eighteen-and-one-half-minute gap." General Alexander M. Haig, Jr., Nixon's new chief of staff, attributed the erasures to "some sinister force," but experts later testified that the erasures had been done by hand.

In November Nixon told newspaper editors in Disney World, "I am not a crook." Spiro Agnew, clearly a crook who had taken bribes while mayor of Baltimore and even as vice-president of the United States, resigned in October. Congress quickly confirmed the nomination of Representative Gerald R. Ford to be vice-president in December. As the year 1973 ended, the Nixon administration launched a new public relations campaign, "Operation Candor," to "get out in front" on Watergate, while the House Judiciary Committee under Peter W. Rodino began an impeachment inquiry.

The Special Prosecutor and House Impeachment

The special prosecutor and the House Judiciary Committee moved ahead relentlessly. It came down to Dean versus Nixon, and the tapes were the "best evidence." On February 29, 1974, a grand jury indicted Mitchell, Ehrlichman, Haldeman, and four others for conspiracy and obstruction of justice, and named Richard M. Nixon an "unindicted co-conspirator," though the latter did not become public knowledge until June. The special prosecutor believed a grand jury, under the constitutional separation of powers, could not indict a sitting president.

On April 29, 1974, Nixon went on TV to "tell all." He presented 1,254 pages of transcripts of the tapes. When the public learned that these tapes were edited to make the president look innocent, many expressed outrage. The House Judiciary Committee rejected the edited tapes and voted that Nixon's refusal to deliver the original tapes as subpoenaed blocked the House from carrying out its constitutional duty.

U.S. v. Nixon

Nixon tried to quash Jaworski's subpoenas, but on May 20, 1974, Judge Sirica again ordered the president to hand over the tapes. Nixon refused. The Supreme Court accepted Jaworski's request that the Court hear the case on immediate appeal to resolve the nation's constitutional and political crisis. The special prosecutor again argued that the tapes represented the "best possible evidence" and that no one is above the law. Nixon's lawyers reiterated previous arguments that the president had immunity from judicial orders. The president, they held, was responsible only to the contitutional impeachment proceedings in the House of Representatives. (Nixon had already refused to comply with the House's subpoenas.)

On July 24, in *U.S. v. Nixon*, a unanimous Supreme Court brushed aside Nixon's legal defenses and in effect declared that no one is above the law. Chief Justice Burger wrote,

> It is imperative to the function of courts that compulsory process be available
> for the production of evidence needed either by the prosecution or by the
> defense. . . . The generalized assertion of privilege must yield to the demonstrated, specific need for evidence in a pending criminal trial.

The Court ordered the president to deliver the subpoenaed tapes to Judge Sirica. Nixon complied.

In the closing days of July 1974, the House Judiciary Committee voted three articles of impeachment for obstruction of justice, abuse of presidential powers, and refusal to obey a House subpoena. The committee votes were bipartisan, 27–11, 28–10, and 21–17. On Monday, August 5, 1974, the tapes became public, and the revelation of Nixon's June 23, 1972 order to the CIA to block the FBI Watergate investigation destroyed the White House cover-up. Facing certain impeachment, the president resigned on August 9, 1974. The jail doors soon closed behind 29 of his colleagues.

Post-Watergate Politics

Watergate, following on Vietnam, further undermined Americans' confidence in the political process. The percentage of eligible voters voting in the congressional election of 1974 reached the lowest level, 35.9, since the war year of 1942. In 1978 fewer than 35 percent voted and the numbers fell to a post–World War II low of 33.4 percent in 1986. Even in the so-called apathetic 1950s, 41.7 percent and 43 percent voted in the off-year elections of 1954 and 1958. The percentage of eligible voters voting in the presidential elections of 1976 dropped to 53.5 and reached 50.2 in 1988, the lowest turnout since 1924. In the 1960s presidential elections always drew at least 60.9 percent of the eligible voters. Cynicism about politicians and apathy about politics became the norm. Congress did write new codes of ethics, conflict of interest and financial disclosure laws. Congress's major post-Watergate reform came in 1974 in a law to limit individual campaign contributions, tighten reporting and disclosure rules, and establish public financing of presidential campaigns. But the 1974 law also allowed private organizations to form Political Action Committees (PACs). PACs grew to 4,286 in 1988 with "collections" of $369.5 million in 1987–1988. As both incumbents and challengers spent increased time raising funds to run expensive computerized, professionally managed, TV campaigns, citizens became more cynical of "government by special interests." Also, incumbents became almost unbeatable as they gained the lion's share of PAC funds. The reform of campaign financing, though much talked about, made no headway. How could reformers pressure incumbents to vote for reforms contrary to the incumbents' interest? This question continued into the 1990s. Americans wondered if this pattern of cynicism, decline in voter participation, increased special interest money, and manipulated elections would continue, or if Americans would take a renewed interest in public life and reclaim the political process.

A RESURGENT CONGRESS

As Congress moved to check the abuses of Watergate, it also made efforts to end the war in Southeast Asia. After many fruitless attempts, Congress finally used its power of the purse to stop all bombing in Cambodia in August 1973, months after the United States had pulled out of Vietnam. After the war, in the mid-1970s, Congress took steps to limit presidents' ability to make war, and to rein in the CIA's "dirty tricks." At home, Congress acted to reclaim its authority in the budget process.

The War Powers Act

In November 1973, Congress took a major step to curb abuses of power by the president when it passed the War Powers Act. The act declared the president may send U.S. military forces into combat, but the president must immediately inform Congress of this action, and Congress must pass a resolution to support the war within 60 days or the president must end U.S. fighting. The president can continue the fighting another 30 days, if need be, to ensure a safe withdrawal of U.S. forces. Congress can stop U.S. military involvement before the 60 days are up by a simple majority vote, which the president cannot veto.

Reining in the CIA

Congressional investigations in 1975 and 1976 revealed CIA actions to assassinate heads of state and elaborate schemes to overthrow foreign governments or manipulate other countries' elections (see pp. 65–66). Congress established special congressional oversight committees to monitor the activities of the CIA and the intelligence community. The CIA's budget, personnel, and activities still remained secret, so it was impossible for the public to know what the agency might be doing. The public still had to trust in the president and congressional oversight. This trust seemed misplaced when an illegal effort masterminded by CIA director William J. Casey and directed by National Security Council members like Oliver L. North led to the Iran–Contra Affair in the 1980s. (See pp. 146–149.) Even at the time, some critics declared that congressional efforts were insufficient and made legal such abuses as presidential wars and the CIA's covert operations, the so-called "dirty tricks." Yet presidents Ford, Carter, and Reagan complained that the new laws made effective presidential leadership in foreign affairs difficult.

The Budget and Impoundment Control Act of 1974

In 1974, Congress enacted the Budget and Impoundment Control Act to restore Congress to some sort of parity with the president in its traditional sphere of legislative authority over "the power of the purse." In 1921, Congress, believing that it could no longer levy taxes and appropriate funds without presidential leadership, had mandated that the president present Congress with a budget. As a result, the White House, through the budget prepared by the Office of Management and Budget (OMB), came to control the budgetary process. The process reduced Congress' role to that of trimming or expanding the budget the president presented to them. The 1974 law restored power to Congress by creating a congressional budget office with staff and resources comparable to the OMB. This office was to provide information to the new budget committees in each House as they hold hearings and make recommendations on the president's budget. The law also directed the Congress to adopt a resolution on revenue and spending targets for each year by May 15, instructed the various congressional appropriations committees to set spending within those budget targets, and required Congress to pass a final budget resolution—"reconciliation"—by September 15 for the fiscal year beginning October 1. If the president impounds (refuses to spend) a congressional appropriation, both houses must approve this action by majority vote in 45 days or the impoundment will be cancelled and the money spent. Although the new law worked to provide more discipline and coherence in the congressional budgetary process and to stop President Nixon's impoundment practices of the 1970s, it failed to achieve fiscal order in the 1980s.

THE FORD ADMINISTRATION, 1974–1977

Gerald Ford

Ford, a one-time football star at the University of Michigan, had been a Republican regular during his years in the House from 1949 to 1973. Though partisan, most saw him as a friendly and decent man, who, from 1974 through 1976, did much to restore Americans' trust in their government. In September, 1974, however, in an act of compassion for a man he believed extremely ill and thoroughly discredited, Ford granted a presidential pardon for any illegal acts Nixon may have committed while president. Many cried "deal" and now feared the complete story of Watergate would never come out. The act of clemency undermined Ford's primary asset, his personal credibility and moral authority. Moreover, Ford made no progress with the backlog of unsolved problems he inherited, particularly the twin economic crises of the worst inflation since 1946 and the highest unemployment since the 1930s.

The Election of 1976

In 1976 President Ford used the powers of incumbency to beat back a right-wing challenge from Ronald Reagan. The Democrats, eager to contest the wounded "party of Watergate," chose a dark horse, Jimmy Carter. A former Georgia governor, an Annapolis graduate and peanut farmer, Carter first showed his strength in the Iowa caucuses and then fought through the primaries to a first-ballot victory at the national convention.

Carter was the first Southerner to be nominated by either major party since 1848. (LBJ was a Westerner from the hill country of west Texas.) An "outsider," untainted by the corruption of Washington, Carter promised never to lie to the American people. He pledged to reorganize the mammoth federal bureaucracy, cut the budget, and make the government more efficient and responsive. Carter assured Americans he would reduce the pretentions of the "imperial presidency."

Both candidates stressed honesty, trust, and character and set themselves apart from the taint of Watergate. That proved difficult for the long-time Washingtonian and Nixon's hand-picked successor and pardoner, President Ford. Even a series of TV debates could not enliven the dull campaign that Jimmy Carter won with 50.1 percent of the vote to Ford's 48 percent. The Democrats maintained control of Congress, 292 to 143 and 61 to 38.

The Election of 1976

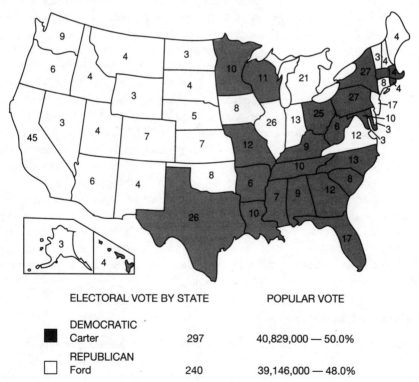

ELECTORAL VOTE BY STATE		POPULAR VOTE
DEMOCRATIC Carter	297	40,829,000 — 50.0%
REPUBLICAN Ford	240	39,146,000 — 48.0%

THE CARTER ADMINISTRATION, 1977–1981

Carter spoke boldly for human rights and by midterm he had several successes in foreign affairs (see pp. 121–122). He succeeded in getting ratification of the Panama Canal Treaties in 1978. In September of that year President Carter achieved a major breakthrough on the Middle East. He hosted a 13-day conference at Camp David, attended by Egypt's president Anwar Sadat and Israel's prime minister Menachem Begin, which produced unprecedented "accords" between the old enemies and culminated in a formal peace treaty in 1979. In late 1978, President Carter, building on earlier Nixon–Kissinger initiatives, announced the establishment of full diplomatic relations with Communist China. The administration also signed a treaty with the Soviet Union to limit offensive nuclear weapons (SALT II); although the Senate failed to approve the treaty, the two sides agreed to abide by its provisions.

On the domestic side, the unemployment rate from 1977 to 1980 fluctuated between 5.8 percent and 7.1 percent. For those four years the consumer price index rose by annual percentage increases of 6.5, 7.7, 11.3, and 13.5, largely because of OPEC agreements and turmoil in the Middle East that raised the price of oil. Carter had no success in reforming the "welfare mess" or in implementing his campaign pledge on national health insurance. He continued his posture as the Washington "outsider," thus alienating the Democratic leaders of Congress. By mid-1979, Carter's standing in the polls reached a low comparable to Truman's in the worst days of the Korean War and Nixon's at the bottom of Watergate. A CBS–*New York Times* poll of June 1979, showed fewer than 30 percent of Americans thought Carter was doing a good job. Carter's pollster found 50 percent of Americans pessimistic about the future. Public frustration mounted as the energy crisis worsened and gas station lines lengthened. In July, President Carter summoned leaders from all walks of life to 10 days of "summit talks" at Camp David to discuss the economy, energy, and his presidency. His subsequent July 15 TV speech had a program, of sorts, on energy, but Carter's key message was his claim that the nation's real problems were a "crisis of confidence by the American people" and the greed of "special interests." He appeared to shift the responsibility for the nation's woes from himself to the U.S. public. The press quickly dubbed the TV address the "malaise speech." The administration hoped the U.S. people would see new vigor and leadership in the speech and a cabinet shake-up he carried out. Instead many saw political confusion, ineptitude, and a "contrived crisis."

Iran and Afghanistan

By November 1979, the inflation rate reached levels unknown since 1946, and Senator Edward M. Kennedy announced he would challenge Carter for the 1980 Democratic nomination. In Iran the followers of Ayatollah Khomeini stormed the U.S. embassy and held 52 American hostages from November 4, 1979, to January 20, 1981—444 days (see pp. 79–80). In December, the Soviets invaded Afghanistan (see pp. 123–124). In the eyes of some Americans, President Carter and the "American giant" appeared helpless. Carter's diplomatic and military moves proved to be ineffective in checking Khomeini and the Soviets.

A Divided Democratic Party

The public, however, rallied to the commander-in-chief in a surge of patriotism, and in a couple of weeks Carter moved ahead of Kennedy in an ABC–Harris poll among Democrats and Independents, 48 percent to 46 percent. Kennedy's marital problems, the public memories of "Chappaquiddick," and Carter's successful use of his incumbency led to Kennedy's failure in the early primaries. By the time Kennedy focused his campaign and won primary victories in New York, Michigan, and California, Carter had enough delegates to gain a first-ballot nomination.

But the economy worsened. Interest rates rose to levels not seen in over a century, and literally choked off new construction and auto sales. Another year of double digit (13.5 percent) inflation and worsening unemployment painted a grim picture. Then, in April 1980, a secret military effort to rescue the U.S. hostages ended in a tragic fiasco in the desert of Iran when a helicopter and transport plane crashed killing eight soldiers. To many Americans in mid-1980, the events demonstrated the ineptitude of the Carter administration. Carter plummeted again in the polls.

Ronald Reagan

The Republicans quickly narrowed their field of seven to former California governor Ronald Reagan. Born in Tampico, Illinois in 1911, at 69 Reagan would be the oldest president ever elected, and he projected the traditions and values of his origins. In 1933, despite the depression, he was a $100-a-week sports broadcaster; in 1946, he worked as a $3,500-a-week Hollywood actor; and in the 1950s, he had become a $150,000-a-year TV spokesperson for General Electric by delivering a free enterprise, anti-welfare state message. In 1964, Reagan made a national television speech for Barry Goldwater, and denounced Social Security, Medicare, the 1964 Civil Rights Act, and TVA. To some voters Reagan's positions seemed more extreme than Goldwater's, but Reagan's masterful television presentation and his looks, voice, and down-home manner made the program and the speaker appear more responsible and acceptable than Goldwater. The speech delighted the political Right. Some conservative wealthy southern Californians, in the aftermath of the 1965 Watts riots, backed him to two terms as governor.

Reagan's Platform

Reagan called for a stronger military to stand up to the Soviets. At home, he wanted to "get the government off the backs of the American people," and unleash the free enterprise system to solve the economic problems in which Americans seemed trapped. He called for a 30 percent cut in the income tax, spread over three years, and tax credits for business to stimulate investment, production, and jobs, and to reinvigorate the U.S. competitive position in the world economy. People soon called these policy goals "Supply Side Economics" or "Reaganomics." Reagan urged deep cuts in federal spending on social programs and a massive increase in spending on defense. He claimed that economic growth would increase government revenues even with lower tax rates and thus balance the budget by 1983. A Republican primary opponent called Reagan's tax cuts, increased spending, and balanced budget promises "voodoo economics." Reagan forgave his critic, George Bush, and selected him as his vice-presidential running mate.

The 1980 Campaign

President Carter tried to divert the public's attention from his own record by hammering at Reagan as a "mad bomber" in foreign affairs and an "Ebenezer Scrooge," who would repeal 50 years of social progress. Carter also accused Reagan of racism. He slashed at Reagan's alleged incompetence and intellectual sloth and attempted to paint Reagan into a corner as a right-winger surrounded by Jerry Falwell's "Moral Majority," oil barons, and the National Conservative Political Action Committee. But Carter, whose main political assets were his supposed integrity, character, and decency came across to many as a mean, shrill campaigner. Reagan, after some initial gaffes, impressed many voters as "presidential," a leader with a positive economic program and a tough anticommunist. In the campaign's lone debate, Reagan's concluding comment was telling:

> Are you better off than you were four years ago? Is it easier for you to go and buy things in the stores than it was four years ago? Is there more or less unemployment in the country than there was four years ago? Is America respected throughout the world as it was? Do you feel that our country is as safe, that we're as strong as we were four years ago?

The issue at campaign's end was Carter and the Carter record. Pundits joked about the "evil of two lessers," and polls showed only a bare majority "highly favorable" toward either candidate. Only 52.6 percent of the eligible voters turned out.

The Results

Reagan won a substantial victory with 51.6 percent of the popular votes and 489 electoral votes to Carter's 41.7 percent and 49 electors. Reagan ran well throughout the country, winning 44 states. The only part of the Democratic coalition that held for Carter was the African American vote but even there the numbers fell. The Republicans won the Senate, 54–46, for the first time since 1952. In the House, the Republicans picked up 33 seats, still trailing by 243 to 192, but a coalition of Republicans and conservative southern Democrats promised Reagan a working majority. Most postelection analyses indicated the vote was anti-Carter and a call for a new economic policy. If Reagan had a mandate, it was to be "different from Jimmy Carter."

THE REAGAN ADMINISTRATION, 1981–1989

Reaganomics

During his first year in office, Reagan dominated Congress and pushed through his supply side economics programs. He gained a 25 percent income tax cut: 5 percent in 1981; 10 percent in 1982; and 10 percent in 1983. In March 1981, he presented a budget calling for major cuts of over $40 billion in more than 300 domestic programs. The proposed cuts hit social programs such as Medicaid, food stamps, student loans, public housing, job training, federal aid to education, and free school lunches. He proposed major increases in military spending (pp. 125–126, 333).

As early as February 17, 1981, Reagan issued Executive Order 12291 to deregulate U.S. business and encourage the productive forces of free enterprise. The order gave the Office of Management and Budget oversight of executive branch agencies to discourage "excessive regulation," to create a "true free market economy." The administration took steps to stop "unnecessary harassment" of U.S. business by the Environmental Protection Agency (EPA), the Occupational Safety and Health Administration (OSHA), and the Consumer Product Safety Commission. These agencies were established in the previous 15 years to promote safe work places, safe products, and a healthy environment. By the end of 1981, Reaganomics was in place.

The economy, however, collapsed in 1982. For the first time since the Great Depression, unemployment remained above 10 percent from September 1982 to June 1983. Tax cuts and increased military spending caused federal budget deficits to soar from $127.9 billion in fiscal 1982 to $207.8 billion in fiscal 1983. Congress and the 1974 Budget Act failed to stop the flow of red ink. The federal government's need to borrow to finance the deficit competed with private borrowers, and the combined demand for credit helped drive interest rates to levels not seen since the Van Buren administration (1837–1841). The Federal Reserve raised interest rates to curb inflation and the government's need to borrow. The prime interest rate (the rate the big banks charge their best customers), which had reached 21.5 percent in December 1980, stayed above 20 percent—except in the spring of 1981—until late September 1981. Such high rates for borrowing cut off capital investment and put the automobile, construction, and durable goods industries in the doldrums.

Unemployment and reduced demand cut inflation from its 13.5 percent rate of 1980 to 6.2 percent in 1982, and the stock market rallied in August 1982. The Dow Jones passed 1,000 for the first time in 1982, the beginning of the Bull Market of the 1980s. Reagan's deficit budgets eventually stimulated the economy, and recovery in production and employment resumed early in December 1982. Unemployment fell from a recession high of 10.6 percent in December 1982 to 8.1 percent in December 1983, the largest decline in unemployment in any single year since 1950. Unemployment continued to fall to a low of 7.0 percent in June 1984. The inflation rate for 1983 dropped to 3.2 percent, and reached a low of 1.1 percent in 1986.

Percentage Change, Annual Rate of Inflation: Consumer Price Index (CPI)

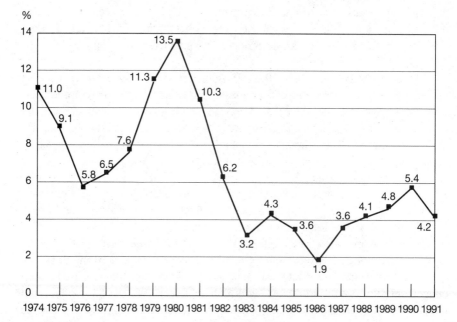

Year

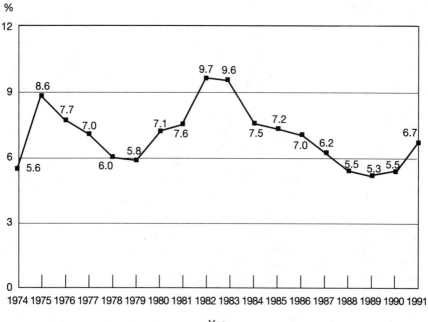

Annual Unemployment Rate: Civilian Workers

U.S. Budget Deficits

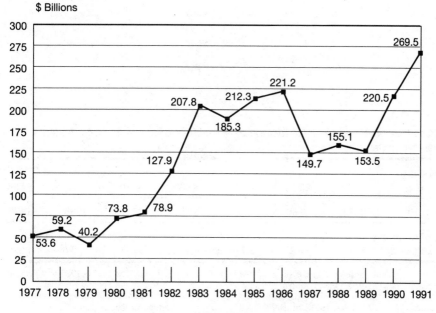

Fiscal Year

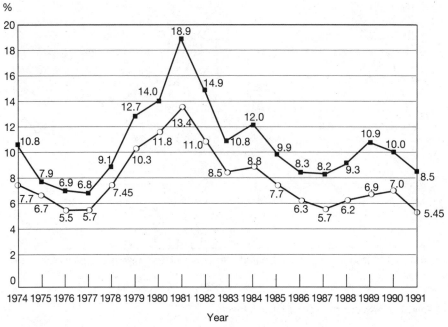

%

1974 1975 1976 1977 1978 1979 1980 1981 1982 1983 1984 1985 1986 1987 1988 1989 1990 1991

Year

■ Prime Rate   ○ Discount Rate

Interest Rates—Annual Averages: Prime Rate and Discount Rate

Gross National Product (GNP): Total Dollar Volume of Goods and Services Produced in the United States per Year

$ billions							
1,016	1,598	2,742	3,180	3,802	4,545	4,908	5,525
1970	**1975**	**1980**	**1982**	**1984**	**1987**	**1988**	**1990**
1987 $ billions							
2,863	3,193	3,823	3,796	4,175	4,545	4,726	4,895

SOURCE: Data in the preceding graphs and table from *Annual Statistical Digest*, 1974–1986 and *Federal Reserve Bulletin*, 1983–1990, both published by the Board of Governors of the Federal Reserve System; *Economic Indicators*, 1981–1991, Council of Economic Advisors; and *Statistical Abstract of the United States*, 1976, 1977, 1981–1991, the Department of Commerce, Bureau of the Census.

The Congressional Election of 1982

But the good economic news of the mid-1980s came too late for Republican candidates in 1982. The voters responded to a 10.1 percent unemployment rate on election day 1982 by giving the Democrats a 26-seat gain in the House, a standoff in the Senate, a pickup of 7 governorships (for a 35–15 state-house-margin), and control of 34 state legislatures. The Republican defeat in the House was the worst for a first-term incumbent president since 1930. But 48 percent of voters in exit polls blamed bad economic conditions on actions by past Democrats. Only 38 percent blamed Reagan.

The Court's Rebuffs

The Supreme Court rebuffed President Reagan on deregulation. For example, in 1983 the Court ruled 9–0 that the Reagan administration in 1981 illegally revoked a federal regulation that new cars be equipped by 1983 with air bags or automatic seat belts. Earlier in 1981, the Court overruled the administration and upheld an OSHA ruling to limit cotton dust, a cause of brown lung disease, in textile manufacturing. The Court upheld OSHA's standards as in accord with congressional law.

The Reagan Administration and the Environment

The Reagan administration followed a deregulation, pro-business, pro-developer policy and subverted the nation's largest regulatory agency, the EPA. Scandals in the EPA came to light in 1983 and forced 20 top officials, including EPA director Anne Burford, to resign. Secretary of the Interior James Watt, the cabinet officer most responsible for the nation's resources, but in fact the chief architect of the deregulation, pro-developer policy, resigned in 1983.

Lebanon, Grenada, and the War Powers Act

In 1983, President Reagan sent 1,200 Marines to Beirut, Lebanon to support the Christian government of President Amin Gemayel against various Lebanese Moslem factions supported by Syria (pp. 135–136). Congress passed a resolution invoking the War Powers Act for the first time and Reagan signed the resolution, but Congress authorized the marine presence for an extended 18 months, or until after the 1984 election. Later in 1983, Reagan ordered 7,000 troops to the Caribbean island of Grenada (p. 144), and Congress again invoked the War Powers Act. Reagan complied, but not before the military evacuated the U.S. medical students in Grenada and removed the Cuban presence.

The Evil Empire

In March 1983, speaking to the National Association of Evangelicals in Orlando, Florida, Reagan skillfully combined statements of religious beliefs, support for school prayer, and denunciation of "abortion on demand" with a warning about the Soviet threat. He cast the cold war in terms of right and wrong—"sin and evil"—and urged his audience not "to ignore the facts of history and the aggressive impulses of an evil empire." With the U.S. introduction of Pershing II and Cruise missiles to Europe in December 1983, the Soviets broke off all discussions of arms control, conventional and nuclear, and the cold war rhetoric reached a level of acrimony and hostility not seen since the late 1940s (pp. 124–128).

The 1984 Election

By July 1984, former Vice-President Walter F. Mondale emerged as the Democratic choice from a field of eight candidates. He held a large early lead in the polls, with fund-raising and endorsements from traditional Democrats, especially the AFL-CIO, in the industrial states. Mondale overcame a surprising series of early primary victories by Senator Gary Hart of Colorado. Hart, with a strong appeal to young, educated, urban professionals, the so-called "Yuppies," claimed to represent a new generation and new ideas. Jesse Jackson, a product of the civil rights movement, emerged as the first strong African American presidential candidate. Jackson greatly increased African American voter registration and presented a new voice to U.S. politics. In comparison, Mondale, a veteran liberal Democrat from Minnesota appeared cautious and bland. He excited many Americans, however, by choosing a three-term member of congress, Geraldine Ferraro, as his vice-presidential running mate. Ferraro's nomination signaled the "doors are now open" for women to be president. But Mondale probably lost more votes when he said in his acceptance speech that increased taxes would be necessary to get the budget under control.

Republicans rallied behind Reagan. His personality, mastery of television campaigning, and an improving economy made him a clear favorite. The 18-month economic recovery that began in December 1982 broke as many records on the plus side as the economic plunge of 1981–1982 had set on the negative. The 13.5 percent inflation rate of 1980 dropped to 4.3 percent in 1984. In November 1984, unemployment fell to 7.2 percent, below the 7.5 percent of election day 1980. The record federal budget deficit, unprecedented foreign balance of payments deficits, and increases in interest rates made economists and administration officials nervous. But most U.S. voters enjoyed the inflation-free boom, refused to worry about deficits at home or abroad, and applauded Reagan's repeated pledges not to raise taxes.

When Mondale tried to "talk issues"—arms control, problems in the Middle East and Central America, his proposal to raise taxes and reduce deficits, the environment, future appointments to the U.S. Supreme Court, "fairness" in the distribution of income, enforcement of civil rights, the gender gap—he had few listeners.

Reagan read correctly the upbeat mood of most Americans, talked about values, not specific issues, spoke in sweeping optimistic terms of the U.S. future, and appealed to patriotism. Reagan achieved a level of popularity with voters that had not been seen since Ike. After the traumas of Vietnam and Watergate, the social turmoil of the 1960s, the continuous economic troubles of the 1970s, and a string of "failed" presidents, a majority of Americans welcomed Reagan's announcement that they could "stand tall" again. With a landslide of 59 percent to 41 percent of the vote, Reagan won 49 states and the most electoral votes in history. He even won a majority among traditional Democratic Catholics and blue-collar workers. He repudiated the claims of a "gender gap" and won the women's vote, 57 percent to 43 percent. The Mondale–Ferraro ticket carried only African Americans (90 percent), Jews (66 percent), Hispanics (65 percent), and the unemployed (68 percent).

A "Resurgent" Presidency

Reagan had the confidence of the U.S. people and had restored luster to the presidency. A *New York Times* poll in November 1983, revealed that the majority of Americans saw the present as better than the past and the outlook for the future as significantly better than the present. Men and women, African Americans and whites, families with incomes over $20,000 and those under $20,000, Republicans and Democrats all expected the future to be better than the present.

A Supreme Court decision also reasserted the president's power. In June 1983, in a 7–2 decision, the Court reversed the post-Vietnam and Watergate flow of power from the White House to Congress, holding the 50-year-old "legislative veto" unconstitutional as a violation of the separation of powers. Congress often delegated authority to the president, but maintained the power to check the president and retake that power by a simple majority vote. Congress had passed 196 laws with 295 legislative veto provisions between 1932 and 1983, more than half of them since 1973. Many saw the use of legislative vetoes as a way for presidents and Congress to work out compromises on politically controversial issues. Others saw such vetoes as a healthy check on the growth of the national regulatory state in which the legislature in the past half century delegated great powers to the executive branch. After Vietnam, the veto was written into the 1973 War Powers Act to check presidential "international adventurism," and although the Court did not rule on the 1973 law, its 1983 decision raised serious questions as to the law's constitutionality.

Reagan worked hard to make the Republicans a national conservative majority party, but the Democrats, though in confused disarray as to how to capture the White House, continued to hold a strong majority political position. In 1985 the Democrats controlled 66 of 98 state legislative houses, 34 of 50 governorships, held a 253 to 182 edge in the House of Representatives, and had narrowed the GOP majority in the Senate to 53–47. Some political realignment trends, however, occurred in 1984. A majority of young, first time voters went for Reagan, and they also preferred Republican House candidates. Only one-third of white Americans voted for Mondale. Republicans continued to make gains in the South at the state and congressional levels. One commentator warned the Democrats that to regain the presidency they "must find a way to recapture the vast middle constituency that was set on the road to prosperity by the New Deal and then used that road to march in Mr. Reagan's parade."

Reagan's Second Term

Second-term policy mistakes and political troubles, in the pattern of FDR, Johnson, and Nixon, followed Reagan's smashing victory in the 1984 election. President Reagan, though a decisive leader in the 1981 tax fight and the Strategic Defense Initiative (SDI), lacked interest in details and often delegated great powers to subordinates. The president's second-term problems peaked in the Iran–Contra Affair of 1986–1987 (pp. 146–149), but three foreign policy actions in 1985–1986 foreshadowed trouble.

When Reagan visited Germany in May 1985 to memorialize the 40th anniversary of VE Day, he chose to go to a German cemetery to commemorate the dead soldiers of all nations. When news stories revealed that some of Hitler's murderous SS troopers were buried there, a public outcry arose. In April 1986 came the abortive attempt to kill Colonel Muammar al-Qaddafi of Libya (pp. 139–140), and the muddled summit on nuclear disarmament with Soviet leader Mikhail Gorbachev at Reykjavik, Iceland (p. 152) followed in October 1986. In November the revelation of the Iran–Contra Affair stunned the nation. To add to Reagan's woes in 1986, despite his vigorous campaigning, the Democrats widened their margin in the House by 6 seats to 258–177 and captured the Senate 55–45 for the first time in Reagan's presidency.

Further Setbacks for Reagan

In July 1987 the FBI and a U.S. attorney revealed multibillion dollar scandals in the Defense Department's procurement of materials and letting of defense contracts (p. 128). From 1983 to 1990, 25 of the 100 largest defense contractors were found guilty of fraud, with 16 guilty pleas or convictions involving 14 of the nation's largest weapons manufacturers in 1988–1990. In November 1987 the Senate resoundingly rejected Reagan's conservative Supreme Court nominee, Judge Robert H. Bork and, at least temporarily, frustrated the president's attempt to reshape the Court. In December 1987 Michael K. Deaver and in February 1988 Lyn Nofziger, Reagan's close friends and political advisers from California days to the White House, were convicted of illegal lobbying and perjury under the 1978 Ethics in Government Act. Attorney General Edwin Meese III narrowly escaped independent counsel and grand jury investigations, and a lengthy series of congressional queries. The press now referred to the "sleaze factor" in the Reagan administration.

An uninhibited pursuit of money seemed to pervade U.S. society in the 1980s with well-publicized villains like Ivan F. Boesky, the Wall Street "insider," Michael R. Milken, the "junk bond king," Jim and Tammy Faye Bakker, the money-making TV evangelists, and even the national baseball hero, Pete Rose. The Pentagon and savings and loan scandals of the second administration dwarfed the EPA scandals of the first four years.

To add to the president's and the nation's troubles, on October 19, 1987, the New York Stock Exchange crashed 508 points on the Dow-Jones, from 2,247 to 1,738, or 22.6 percent, for the worst one-day fall in the history of the exchange. The nation's longest and most vigorous bull market on record that began on August 12, 1982, at 788 on the Dow had peaked at 2,722 on August 25, 1987. During those years, however, the national debt and foreign trade deficit continued to climb to record highs, and in 1985 the United States became a debtor nation for the first time since World War I. The nation's financial house had fallen into disorder. The president blamed Congress for failure to cut spending for domestic social programs, whereas Congress blamed the president for failure to propose tax increases or defense cuts. The government appeared to be stuck in some kind of gridlock, and no elected official seemed to know the way out.

The Iran–Contra Affair

The Iran–Contra Affair of 1986–1987 (pp. 146–149) caused the president the greatest embarrassment and seemed to show him to be inept, out of touch, or deceiving the U.S. people. On November 25, 1986, Attorney General Meese, with President Reagan beside him, announced that U.S. arms had been sold to Iran with the profits placed in secret Swiss bank accounts and then "diverted" to the contras, the rebels fighting the Sandinista Nicaraguan government. These acts violated U.S. law and official policy.

In January 1987 Reagan told investigators he did approve the sale; in February he said he did not approve it; and then on February 20 he wrote, "I don't remember, period." The story remains confused. We do know that CIA director Casey, two national security advisers, Robert C. McFarlane and John

M. Poindexter, and an NSC staffer, Marine Lieutenant Colonel Oliver L. North, were the prime movers in the affair. It is also clear that Congress in 1984–1986, with broad public support, enacted several versions of the Boland amendment to stop military funding of the contras.

Reagan fired Poindexter, transferred North back to active duty with the marines, and appointed a bipartisan group, the Tower Commission, to investigate. The Tower Commission reported in February 1987 that "the ultimate responsibility for the events of the Iran–Contra Affair must rest with the president. If the president did not know what his national advisors were doing, he should have."

In the summer of 1987, Congress held televised hearings to learn what had happened. The ensuing report criticized the secretive, illegal, and poorly thought out executive conduct of foreign policy. Congress ended all military aid, covert or overt, to the contras in February 1988. Former federal judge Lawrence E. Walsh, a Republican, was named independent counsel to investigate and prosecute criminal actions. And by 1990, seven, including McFarlane, Poindexter and North, had been found quilty of criminal acts. However, on appeal, the federal appellate court raised the question of "tainted" evidence given by witnesses influenced by testimony given under congressional grants of immunity in the 1987 TV hearings. Unable to use MacFarlane's testimony against North, Walsh dropped the North prosecution in September 1991, and in November the federal appellate court threw out the conviction of Poindexter.

The White House continued to block access to key documents, including 200 pages of North's journal, by classifying them as "top secret." Nagging questions remained in 1991, however, as to what the president and vice-president knew and when they knew it. Who, indeed, was conducting U.S. foreign policy? Who was in charge in the White House?

Some saw the Iran–Contra Affair as a more serious scandal than Watergate because it involved the secret subversion, by a "rogue force in the White House," of announced U.S. foreign policy in two crisis areas of the world, and the executive's defiant violation of recently enacted congressional laws. But the popular president escaped any real threat of impeachment, or the permanent ignominy of Nixon after Watergate.

SDI and the INF Treaty

Though Ronald Reagan delegated much of the conduct of foreign policy to his subordinates, he did adopt one basic policy as an almost personal project, the Strategic Defense Initiative (SDI). (See pp. 127–128.) Reagan believed it a perfect weapon—a technological defensive shield to protect U.S. democracy against missiles from an evil empire by harmlessly destroying attacking nuclear weapons in outerspace. Critics questioned whether SDI would work or could even be tested; others charged that SDI threatened the strategic nuclear equilibrium with the Soviet Union.

But powerful historical forces were ending the totalitarian character of the Soviet Union. In 1985, reformist Mikhail Gorbachev rose to power, and in December 1987 Gorbachev and Reagan signed a historic treaty to destroy all Intermediate Range Missiles in Europe and to allow on-site inspection to implement the agreement (p. 153). This treaty foreshadowed the end of the cold war and restored some of Reagan's popularity. Was it Reagan's famous luck? Did Reagan's military buildup economically break the Soviet economy? Or were the main causes the predictable historical developments within the Soviet Union forecast by George Kennan in 1947 at the onset of the cold war? (See pp. 8–9.) Whatever the causes, in June 1988 the world watched the previously unthinkable unfold on TV as Reagan and Gorbachev strolled through Red Square engaged in jovial conversation. People everywhere felt relief with the lifting of the threat of nuclear annihilation.

THE REAGAN LEGACY

Admirers believed the Reagan legacy made a new conservatism acceptable and respectable. But Reaganism seemed to critics a "capitalist heyday," in which technocrats, entrepreneurs, developers, and "get rich quick" financial schemes took precedence over long-term global environmental warning signs; ignored or worsened racial, ethnic, religious, gender, and generational tensions; and neglected or violated international law and morality. Still other critics pointed to his nominees to the federal judiciary, especially the Supreme Court, and the major impact those judges will have on U.S. law and policy well into the twenty-first century. But Kevin Phillips, a leading Republican conservative ideologist and strategist, in his 1990 study, *The Politics of Rich and Poor: Wealth and the American Electorate in the Reagan Aftermath*, declared Reagan's legacy to be the public policies that redistributed income and made the rich richer and the poor poorer for the first time since the 1920s.

Phillips analyzed public policies on federal taxing and spending, interest rates, national debt and international trade, and described the shifts from a production to a service economy, the rise of the global economy, and the resulting winners and losers. Phillips argued that the history of U.S. politics and policy is the story of the struggle over the division of wealth—"the politics of money"—a conflict, he contended, more basic than those over region, religion, race, or gender. He concluded that "since the American Revolution the distribution of American wealth has depended to a large degree on *who controlled the federal government, for what policies, and in behalf of which constituencies*" (italics added).

Tax Policies

The Reagan administration's tax policies clearly benefitted the top 20 percent of Americans on the income scale at the expense of the rest of the population. The White House supported major reductions in the federal graduated income tax brackets. In 1946 the tax code had 14 tax brackets graduated according to income; after 1987, there were two brackets. The 1946 top bracket rate, 91 percent, on incomes over $100,000, despite many loopholes, remained in place until 1964. In 1972 the top bracket rate on earned income dropped from 70 percent to 50 percent; in 1981 that same reduction was extended to unearned income, a great boon to the small number of Americans who derived most of their incomes from interest, dividends, and rents. In 1986 the top rates on earned, unearned, and capital gains were set at 28 percent, the lowest since Calvin Coolidge.* Also in 1983 the percentage of tax receipts going to the U.S. Treasury from corporate income taxes fell to 6.2 percent, an all-time low. That figure was 32.1 percent in 1952 and 12.5 percent in 1980.

Social Security tax policy became a second major factor created a growing gap between the rich and the poor. In 1970 individuals paid into Old Age and Survivors' Insurance and Medicare a tax of 4.8 percent on their first $7,800 in income, for a maximum of $374 a year; in 1989 the tax rate had been raised to 7.51 percent on the first $48,000, for a maximum of $3,650—an increase of 976 percent. A person, such as Michael R. Milken, with a U.S. record salary and bonuses of $550 million in 1987 paid the same $3,650 as the plumber who earned $48,000. The Social Security income tax always has been a regressive tax, unrelated to ability to pay. The higher the income, after the base maximum ($53,400 in 1991), the lower the proportion paid in taxes. In 1991 the tax was 7.65 percent on the first $53,400 whether you were a Milken or a plumber.† Of the total federal receipts as a percentage of gross national product, social security taxes in 1945 amounted to 1.6%; in 1988, 7.0%. The comparable figures for non-social security tax receipts were 19.7% in 1945 and 12.0 percent in 1988—a major shift in the tax structure and burden. (By 1991, two out of three families paid more in Social Security taxes than in federal income taxes.)

The Congressional Budget Office reported a major shift of income in the years 1980 to 1988 from the lower 80 percent of the population to the top 20 percent. From 1977 to 1988 the bottom 10 percent lost 14.8 percent in average family income in 1987 dollars. Though the bottom 80 percent of families lost in

---

* The budget act of 1990 raised the top income tax rate to 31 percent, but left the capital gains (profit earned from the sale of real estate, stocks, and bonds) rate at 28 percent.

† The budget act of 1990, however, did raise the taxable portion of income for the Medicare part of Social Security—1.45 percent—to the first $125,000.

family income, the top 10 percent gained 16.5 percent; the top 5 percent, 23.4 percent; and the top 1 percent, 49.8 percent. In those years the top 1 percent increased its share of the national income from 7 percent to 11 percent. The most rational argument for such a tax policy held that it would stimulate new investment, economic growth, world trade, research and development, jobs, even more tax dollars to balance the budget. However, budget and trade deficits expanded, productivity slumped, and consumption, not investment, made the more significant growth.

Government Spending, Deficits, and Interest Rates

Federal fiscal policy on cuts in domestic spending* and increases in defense spending also influenced the redistribution of income. From 1980 to 1987 national government spending on defense increased from 23 percent to 28 percent of the national budget, whereas spending on human resources (excluding Social Security and Medicare) declined from 28 percent to 22 percent. Defense spending jumped 50 percent after inflation between 1980 and 1986, from $140.7 billion to $281.4 billion, the largest increase in peacetime history. Such policy choices redistributed income with obvious major gainers and losers.

On the other hand, the federal government chose to forego increased taxes to balance the budget in the 1980s, and in fact cut income taxes 25 percent from 1981 to 1983. Washington chose to borrow money to pay the annual deficits. That public policy resulted in an enormous growth in the amount of money paid annually in interest to foreign and U.S. bondholders—the wealthiest 20 percent of Americans, those who had also received the major tax cuts. As in the days of Alexander Hamilton, annual interest payments, which grew from $96 billion in 1980 to $216 billion in 1988, were paid by middle-income tax payers to well-to-do bondholders.

The U.S. government's voracious appetite for spending without comparable taxing has forced the U.S. Treasury to borrow trillions of dollars. To attract foreign and domestic bond buyers, the treasury has had to pay very high interest rates, about 14 percent in 1981 while Germany and Japan paid between 5 and 6

---

* The federal cuts and shifts of programs to the states led to increased state taxes, usually property taxes and regressive taxes such as sales taxes, not income taxes, to pay the spiralling costs of health care, education, prisons, and other social services. In the recession of 1991, costly in terms of lower revenues and increased spending to the unemployed, a decade after Reagan's Tax Act of 1981, states raised their taxes over $20 billion. In 1990 state and local taxes rose to an estimated 40 percent of all taxes, excluding Social Security taxes, as compared to 32 percent in 1960. In 1990 Americans paid 32.6 percent of GNP to the government compared to 31.3 percent in 1980, and 30 percent in 1975. And the greatest burden was borne by middle-income families—those earning $20,000 to $60,000—whose payroll tax deductions rose by roughly one-third since the mid-1970s.

percent. U.S. Treasury interest rates were a windfall in payments to wealthy lenders. Also, the Federal Reserve System, after President Carter's appointment in 1979 of Paul A. Volcker to head the board of governors, kept interest rates high to curb inflation by restraining borrowing by private individuals and businesses.

Global Income Redistribution

Not only did the 1980s witness a redistribution of income within the United States, but a marked redistribution occurred within the global economy. In this redistribution the Americans were losers, the Japanese and Germans winners. Hard economic statistics tell the story, but massive borrowing at home and abroad temporarily maintained a high level of consumerism in the United States. As one wag put it, "Americans wanted chocolate ice cream sundaes and eighteen inch waists at the same time."

The facts:

1. The United States went from having a $166 billion "trade account surplus" (covers trade in both merchandise and services) in 1980 to a $340 billion trade account deficit in 1987. To buy the foreign consumer goods Americans wanted, the nation borrowed to pay the trade deficit. Unlike the practices in the 1980s, Americans in the late nineteenth century borrowed foreign capital primarily to invest in railroads, manufacturing, mines, and other productive enterprises, not for consumer goods. As previously noted, in the 1980's the U.S. government also borrowed heavily abroad to pay the costs of the U.S. government that Reagan and the voters refused to pay by taxes.

2. Data from the *World Bank Atlas* in 1989 revealed that in two years between 1985 and 1987 the U.S. economy fell behind the Japanese in comparative national public and private assets (*wealth*, such as actual assets—land, production resources, housing, and inventories plus financial assets, such as stocks, bonds, insurance, deposits; *not income*). In 1985 the Americans held $30.6 trillion in assets, the Japanese $19.6; but by 1987 Japan had leapfrogged ahead with $43.7 trillion to the United States's $36.2. The United States also sold assets to gain capital. By 1988 foreigners owned a record 12 percent of all U.S. manufacturing assets compared to 3 percent in 1980. Total foreign investment in U.S. corporations and real estate grew from $83 billion in 1980 to $304 billion in 1988.

3. In 1980 the U.S. government and private interests led the world in net overseas investments with over $106 billion, but in 1985 Americans had become an international debtor. In 1986, the Japanese led in net

overseas investments with over $180 billion, and Germany was second with $113 billion.

Some changes reflect historic trends, such as the the development of the European economic community and the economic growth of the nations of the Pacific Rim, but many resulted from Washington's fiscal, monetary, trade, and industrial policies.

Economic Winners and Losers

Public policies helped to create definite economic winners and losers in the United States. By regions, in the 1980s, the farm belt, the "oil patch," the Midwestern "rust belt," and the Southwest joined the Southeast as losers. The major urban centers of the Atlantic and Pacific coasts were the big winners, what Representative David R. Obey (D., Wis.) called our "bicoastal economy." The two coasts led in the growing "service sector"—financial services, investors, lawyers, accountants, business consultants, importers, retailers, high tech entrepreneurs, and chief executive officers of large corporations. These well-educated, talented professionals, put in long hours at the right time in the right place and made a lot of money. The decade-long Reagan defense buildup also made defense industries obvious winners.

In the Reagan years many retirees benefited from solid pension plans, the government's anti-inflation policy, paid-up medical insurance, cost-of-living escalators in Social Security, rising interest rates, and increases in real estate and security values. In 1959 35 percent of those over 65 lived in poverty compared with 22.4 percent of the total population and 26.9 percent of those under 18. In 1987 the percentage of the elderly in poverty dropped to 12.2 percent, but in the 1980s over 20 percent of children under 18 were poor. *Forbes* reported in 1988 that the U.S. government spent $10 for each person over 65 compared to $1 for each child under 18. The Office of Management and Budget reported in 1986 that Americans over 65 made up 12.2 percent of the population but received 27.2 percent of the federal spending. Older people are well organized and have the vote; children are not and do not.

On the other hand, there were clear economic losers, notably high school drop-outs, female-headed households, children under 18, African Americans and Hispanics, young minority males without jobs, the working poor, the underclass, those in the rural backwaters, and the homeless. Family incomes stagnated after 1973. Families, in terms of 1987 dollars, did not recover their 1973 median family income of $30,820 until 1987 when it reached $30,853. Families headed by an adult under 30 saw their inflation-adjusted income collapse by one-fourth between 1973 and 1986. Few young families benefited from Social Security, but they paid higher Social Security taxes.

The United States in the 1980s also had the lowest percentage of workers in unions of any industrial society, in part because of the decline of the highly unionized manufacturing sector such as steel and automobiles, and in part because of government hostility to organized labor, as evidenced by President Reagan's firing of striking air controllers in 1981. One statistic indicates the growing distance from the work bench to the board room. In 1979 the average CEO made 29 ($406,104.40) times the annual income of the average manufacturing worker ($14,003.60). By 1988 *Business Week* reported the compensation of the average CEO ($2,570,241) had grown to 93 times the earnings of the average factory worker ($27,637).

In the years from 1975 to 1990 the U.S. economy lost its primacy. Most Americans knew that they lived in a far more interdependent and competitive world economy, and a lower standard of living appeared the future norm. In 1946, in part as a result of World War II, the United States was the world's top oil exporter, held a near monopoly on automobile production, and produced more electricity and steel than the rest of the world combined. U.S. workers received the highest wages and best health care. In the 1940s, Henry R. Luce, the founder and publisher of *Time*, *Life*, and *Fortune*, had called this century "the American Century." In some sense, Luce's American Century ended in the mid-1970s. But most Americans in the booming 1980s did not yet realize that the public policies of the Reagan administration had assisted the U.S. economic international demise and further skewed the distribution of income at home. A saving grace may be that Americans have been in similar situations before, in the 1890s and the 1920s, and bailed themselves out through imaginative politics and innovative public policies. The nation also had the good fortune in 1989 to watch the most perilous situation that ever had confronted humanity, the East–West ideological and nuclear cold war, come to an end. This historic change provided Americans an opportunity to focus on the troublesome aspects of the Reagan legacy.

THE ELECTION OF 1988

For the fifth time in six elections the Republicans won the White House in 1988. The Bush–Quayle ticket won 53.4 percent of the popular vote and 426 electoral votes to Dukakis–Bentsen's 45.6 percent and 111.

But troublesome overtones for U.S. democracy appeared in the Bush–Dukakis contest. The turnout of voters was the lowest percentage since 1924—50.2 percent of those of voting age. The candidates did not discuss the most important historical development of the era, the significance of the approaching end of nearly a half century of cold war. The campaign gave little notice of U.S. pressing economic concerns and did not seriously address the nation's needs.

The 1988 campaign also produced little in the way of specific policy proposals to deal with the growing number of homeless, the crack cocaine and AIDS epidemics, the increase of urban violence, the troubled state of the once-proud U.S. heritage of universal public education, the despoiling of the environment, corruption in the public service and greed in private life, and the people's loss of confidence in their country's future.

The Bush campaign had the cream of the nation's political strategists—28 had worked in 3 or more presidential campaigns—a sizable campaign war chest, and the power of incumbency in the popular Reagan administration. Bush had a lock on the nomination by March. An eastern establishment Republican, the son of a Wall Street banker and former Connecticut senator, George Bush was a New England prep school and Yale graduate who flew 58 missions as a teenage naval combat pilot in World War II. After the war, Bush moved to Texas, made a fortune in oil, won a seat in the House of Representatives, then lost a 1970 Senate race to Lloyd Bentsen. During the 1970s, Bush went on to serve in such appointed posts as chairman of the Republican National Committee, U.S. Ambassador to the United Nations, U.S. liason with the People's Republic of China prior to official diplomatic recognition, and director of the CIA. As Reagan's vice-president, Bush became a loyal foot soldier in the "Reagan Revolution." Bush, as a member of the National Security Council, had difficulty escaping some responsibilty for the Iran–Contra Affair, but during the election campaign he said he was not involved in Iran–Contra because he was "out of the loop." Yet, he also said that he conferred regularly with the president, especially on foreign policy matters, but he adamantly held that those talks were confidential.

Michael S. Dukakis, the best financed Democrat in a generation, outdistanced all his Democratic rivals in a marathon of primaries and caucuses to win his party's nomination. The son of Greek immigrants, a Harvard Law School graduate, and a long-time legislator, Dukakis served three terms as governor of Massachusetts. Many voters viewed him as intelligent, competent, and a model of public service and integrity, but they also saw him as aloof and lacking in passion, humor, and ordinary human feelings.

The Bush "Assault"

Republican strategists noted that early polls revealed voters had an unusually high, 40 percent, negative image of George Bush, and a Gallup poll in early June had Dukakis ahead of Bush 52 percent to 38 percent. In a blitz of negative TV campaign commercials, "30 second sound bites," Bush's managers launched a savage and relentless assault on Dukakis to knock down his positive image. Bush's campaign advisers discovered certain issues that made Dukakis vulnerable. For example, Republican TV spots blasted a Massachusetts prison furlough program, and pointed out that Willie Horton, a convicted murderer on a weekend furlough from a Massachusetts prison, raped a woman and pistol-whipped her husband in Maryland. The TV ad made clear that Horton was African American. At the Republican convention, Bush led the delegates in a TV performance of a pledge of allegiance to the flag and during the campaign he visited a factory that made flags. The Bush campaign relentlessly attacked Dukakis's 1977 veto of a flag-pledge bill for Massachusetts school children. The message pointed out that Dukakis was "soft on crime" and lacking in patriotism. Bush also pledged "read my lips—NO NEW TAXES." Bush attacked Dukakis as a liberal, dubbed "that L word."

Bush had won the image war by the end of August. Dukakis did not tell the people who or what he was; the Republicans did. Dukakis's talk about the "Massachusetts Miracle" and "good jobs at good pay" was not enough. He failed to play up his immigrant origins and the American Dream. And above all, he did not take advantage of voters' nervousness about the economy and the growing disparity between the rich and the poor. The Democratic party appeared second only to the Republicans as the world's most enthusiastic free enterprise supporters.

The Results

In November, with Bush's victory, the Republicans continued their stranglehold on the White House, but lost one seat in the House, remained as a 45–55 minority in the Senate, and lost one governorship and one state legislative house. Of House incumbents who ran for reelection, 98.3 percent won. Moreover, Congressional politics had become awash in special interest money from Political Action Committees (PACs). Contributions by PACs to congressional campaigns grew from $55.2 million in 1979–1980 to $147.9 million in 1987–1988. Even the presidential campaigns, though supposedly financed by public funds with $46 million for each ticket, saw abuses go unchecked as the major parties each raised over $60 million in additional funds for state parties to conduct voter registration drives and other activities not covered by the federal law.

THE BUSH ADMINISTRATION

Moderate or Conservative?

In his convention acceptance speech, Bush claimed to favor a "gentler and kinder" America, and in the campaign said he wanted to be known as the "education president" and the "environmental president." But, once in office, budget restraints and Bush's conservatism limited such initiatives, as well as actions to cope with the pressing needs in housing, health care, and urban assistance. By mid-term, Bush's allegiance to the Reagan Revolution seemed clear, as evidenced by his Supreme Court nominations, his 1990 civil rights veto, and his clear statements against abortion and for school prayer.

Deficit Reduction?

By June 1990, the problems of recession and inflation and the requirements of the Gramm–Rudman deficit reduction law of 1985 combined to demand action on the national budget. President Bush retracted his "Read my lips—no new taxes" pledge. He asked the congressional leadership to conduct negotiations to get significant deficit reductions. Once the president took the first step, Democrats, who had been beaten over the head by the Republicans in state tax revolts from California to Massachusetts and in the 1984 and 1988 presidential campaigns, seemed ready to support tax increases and budget cuts, especially on the military side, with SDI, major new weapons systems, and nuclear hardware at the top of the list. After a rousing political battle, a compromise increased taxes $120 billion over the next five years and reduced the deficit by $40 billion in fiscal 1991 and by a projected $500 billion over five years. The law also took the first step toward reducing the economic disparities of the 1980s tax laws with tax reductions on the poor, slight increases on the middle class, and the largest share of the tax increase, 6.4 percent, applied to those with incomes over $200,000. The law cut Medicare benefits and farm spending, but initiated the first national efforts at child care and Medicaid coverage to poor children to age 18.

The president's reversal on "no new taxes" produced a serious rift in the Republican party as conservatives denounced his "betrayal." But the Treasury Department soon reported more grim news in fiscal 1991, a record $287.6 billion deficit had followed the $220 billion deficit of fiscal 1990. By November 1991, the Congressional Budget Office predicted more red ink, another record defict of $362 billion in fiscal 1992.

Though the 1990 congressional session ended in a media circus over the budget, Congress compiled a significant legislative record. Congress passed, in fact strengthened, Bush's proposal for the first Clean Air Act since 1977, with an emphasis on curbing acid rain, toxic pollutants, automobile emissions, and urban smog. Congress approved a bailout of the savings and loan industry at an estimated cost of $500 billion over the next 30 years. Congress enacted the Americans With Disabilities Act; raised the minimum wage from $3.80 in 1990 to $4.25 in 1991, the first increase since 1981; expanded the number of immigrants allowed into the United States from 500,000 to 700,000 a year, with an emphasis on skilled workers; and passed the first significant housing legislation in a decade. Although Congress also passed a major civil rights bill and a mandatory leave bill for employees having a baby or needing to care for an ill family member, Bush successfully vetoed both bills. Congress failed, however, to act on campaign finance reform.

Two Wars Won in Two Years—Panama and the Persian Gulf

President Bush believed his most important public experiences had been in foreign affairs. He drew two major political lessons from Vietnam. First, if the United States is to act militarily it should use massive force to gain a quick victory and limit U.S. casualties in order to hold public support. Second, fearful of the division on the home front that followed news reports from Vietnam, the military should limit journalists' access to the war zone and control the information flowing to the U.S. people.

The president's first test came in Panama in December 1989 (see pp. 162–164), followed by a much larger operation in the Gulf Crisis in 1990–1991 (see pp. 164–169). During the 1991 Gulf War, Americans watched their TV sets spellbound as the new military technology produced a continuous display of extraordinary weapons exploding on targets with deadly precision. U.S. Patriot missiles intercepted and exploded Iraqi Scud missiles out of the sky. There were few pictures of the suffering and death that had been the nightly TV fare of the Vietnam War as the government tightly censored news from the front. Americans celebrated the rout of the battered Iraqis, made General Norman Schwarzkopf a U.S. hero, and gave President Bush an extraordinary 90 percent endorsement in the public opinion polls.

Positive Developments in Eastern Europe and the Middle East

In August 1991, Bush further benefited from the failed coup in the Soviet Union. He supported the victorious Russian President Boris Yeltsin and the democratic forces who stood up to the tanks in the streets of Moscow against the communist hard-liners. In the fall of 1991, the Bush administration's tireless efforts finally brought all the Arab parties together with Israel in a UN-sponsored conference in Madrid for an unprecedented peace parley between Israel and all its Arab neighbors. With the end of the cold war and major progress on the reduction of nuclear arms, could President Bush create the "New World Order" he envisioned? (See pp. 170–174.)

A BLEAK FORECAST

An October 1991 *New York Times*–CBS News poll revealed that 61 percent believed that the president was "more likely" to do a better job of handling foreign policy than any Democrat, whereas only 17 percent thought a Democrat would do a better job than Bush in foreign policy. In that poll, however,

Americans believed that a Democratic president would "do more to improve health care . . . race relations . . . education . . . and the economy" than George Bush. That poll also revealed that 60 percent believed that the country had "pretty seriously gotten off the track" and 79 percent of registered voters said that domestic issues would matter more in deciding how they vote in 1992. The same poll in November showed that President Bush dropped in his overall presidential approval rating from a peak 88 percent after the Gulf War to 51 percent, and only 25 percent approved Bush's handling of the economy. The change in opinion was attributed to a worsening recession and public anger over a perception that Bush focused more on foreign policy than on domestic issues of unemployment, health care, education, urban ills, and an aging infrastructure. Troubled banks and other financial institutions joined the savings and loans, real estate values continued to drop, retail and auto sales lagged, and many Americans viewed their national government with increasing cynicism or anger. The Democratic Congress and Republican president became caught in a legislative–executive gridlock of vetoes and partisan charges on bills dealing with energy, crime, banking reform, urban ills, family leave, repeal of the "gag rule" on abortion counseling in publicly financed clinics (p. 246). After much haggling, a $151 billion highway and mass transit construction bill, a resubmitted 1990 civil rights bill (p. 243), and a bill for the extension of unemployment benefits for the long-term unemployed became law in 1991. With the enormous national debt and record budget deficits, traditional Keynesian responses, such as tax cuts and increased spending, did not seem to be viable options. Even the Federal Reserve's six reductions of the discount rate from 6 percent to 4.5 percent in 1991 failed to stimulate investment or consumer spending. A fearful public hunkered down.

The administration also had setbacks in the 1991 off-year elections. A little known liberal Democrat, Harris Wofford, campaigning for national health insurance and strong national measures to revive the economy, defeated Bush's attorney general and popular two-term governor Richard Thornburgh for a Senate seat in Pennsylvania. The nation focused on ex-Nazi and former KKK Grand Wizard and "born-again Christian" David Duke's unsuccessful, but dramatic race as a anti-quota, anti-affirmative action, anti-welfare, anti-tax Republican candidate for the Louisiana governorship. Bush denounced and renounced Duke, but Duke's words were not very different from the Reagan–Bush political rhetoric of the previous decade. By year's end Bush appeared defensive, but he could take comfort in the fact that the public took an even dimmer view of the Democratic Congress and the national Democratic party seemed in disarray.

The serious domestic problems, unaddressed in the election of 1988, remained. What could be done about a national debt that reached $3.2 trillion in 1990, continuing trade imbalances, troubled key industries such as automobiles struggling to compete in the global economy, and a falling standard of living for the average American? Would there be effective proposals to reverse urban decline, insufficient and substandard housing, gang violence in the streets, the drugs and AIDS epidemics, continued family breakdown, and the staggering problems of the underclass and the homeless? Would there be serious public discussion of the decline of U.S. education, a troubled health care system and the 34 million Americans without health insurance, and rising racial and ethnic tensions? Were there the necessary resources and public will and imagination to bail out the savings and loans, reform and secure many unsteady major banks and insurance companies, and rebuild the nation's aging infrastructure? What would be the remedies for the deepening recession of 1990–1991? Would Americans' growing insecurities about the future and cynicism about politicians and the political process deepen, or would the 1992 presidential campaign come to grips with these issues and produce a civic renewal and effective public policies?

CHAPTER 1

Basic to the study of the foreign policies of the United States is the series published by the State Department, *The Foreign Relations of The United States.* Unfortunately, publication of this series, containing declassified government documents lags more than 30 years after the event. Moreover, several historians have recently accused the State Department of withholding, on the grounds of national security, documents that might embarrass some officials. Another indispensable primary source is the series *Public Papers of the Presidents of the United States,* an annual collection of public statements and executive documents. The Council on Foreign Relations publishes annually two important volumes, *The United States in World Affairs* and *Documents on American Foreign Relations.*

Historians have disagreed sharply in interpreting the cold war. The early orthodox or official position held that the policy of the United States was nothing more than a defensive move against Soviet expansion. This view is ably presented in John Spanier, *American Foreign Policy Since World War II** (1965); and Herbert Feis, *From Trust to Terror** (1965). William A. Williams's study, *The Tragedy of American Diplomacy** (1962) sparked a school of revisionist writing, often referred to as the New Left. Important revisionist works blaming the economic and strategic interests of the United States as the expansionist

---

Key: * Available in paperback
     # Out of print

force responsible for the cold war include: Dana L. Fleming, *The Cold War and Its Origins,* 2 vol. (1961); Gabriel Kolko, *The Roots of American Foreign Policy** (1963); Gar Alperovitz, *Atomic Diplomacy: Hiroshima and Potsdam* (1965); and Walter LeFeber, *America, Russia, and the Cold War, 1945-1975** (3rd. ed., 1976). Although acknowledging that U.S. policymakers failed to accept the reality that World War II had produced, postrevisionist writers have placed varying blame on both sides. Among these are: Louis Halle, *The Cold War as History** (1967); John L. Gaddis, *The United States and the Origins of the Cold War** (1972); Daniel Yergin, *Shattered Peace: The Origins of the Cold War and the National Security State* (1977); and Robert L. Messner, *The End of an Alliance: James F. Byrnes, Roosevelt, Truman, and the Origins of the Cold War* (1982). Useful collections of essays on the origins of the cold war include Thomas Hammond, ed., *Witnesses to the Origins of the Cold War* (1982) and Walter Isaacson and Evan Thomas, *The Wise Men* (1986).

Specialized studies of the Truman era include John Gimbel, *The Origins of the Marshall Plan* (1976); Bruce Kuklick, *American Policy and the Division of Germany* (1972); and Barton J. Bernstein, *Politics and Policies of the Truman Administration** (1970). Participants in the shaping of policies in Europe during the Truman administration, who have written personal accounts, include: Harry S Truman, *Memoirs,* 2 vol. (1955–1956); Robert Ferrell, ed., *Off the Record: The Private Papers of Harry S Truman* (1980); Clark Clifford, *Counsel to the President* (1991); Dean Acheson, *Present at the Creation* (1969); George F. Kennan, *Memoirs, 1925-1950* (1967); James F. Byrnes, *Speaking Frankly* (1947); Lucius D. Clay, *Decision in Germany* (1950); Charles E. Bohlen, *The Transformation of American Foreign Policy* (1969); and Arthur H. Vandenberg, Jr., ed., *The Private Papers of Senator Vandenberg* (1952). For a counterview consult Robert A. Taft, *A Foreign Policy for America* (1951).

Policies of the Eisenhower administration are treated somewhat critically in Herbert S. Parmet, *Eisenhower and the American Crusades* (1972); Norman Graebner, *The New Isolationism** (1956); and Townsend Hoopes, *The Devil and John Foster Dulles* (1973). More favorable interpretations of Republican policies appear in James Burnham, *Containment or Liberation* (1953); William H. Chamberlain, *Beyond Containment* (1953); Thomas K. Finletter, *Foreign Policy: The Next Phase* (1955), and Stephen Ambrose, *Eisenhower: The Presidency* (1984). Eisenhower wrote in his own account in *Mandate for Change* (1963) and *Waging Peace* (1965). In addition one should consult Robert H. Ferrell, ed., *The Eisenhower Diaries* (1981); Richard H. Immerman, ed., *John Foster Dulles and the Diplomacy of the Cold War* (1990); and Louis Galambos, ed., *The Papers of Dwight David Eisenhower,* vol. XII–XIII. The standard account of the U-2 incident is Thomas Ross and David Wise, *The U-2 Affair** (1962).

Close advisers of Kennedy have written accounts that must be used carefully (see references in Chapter 8). In addition are Roger Hilsman, *To Move a Nation* (1967) and Robert S. McNamara, *The Essence of Security* (1968). More critical are Richard J. Walton, *Cold War and Counter-Revolution: The Foreign Policy of John F. Kennedy** (1972) and Donald C. Lord, *John F. Kennedy, The Politics of Confrontation and Conciliation* (1977).

CHAPTER 2

In 1946 two correspondents of *Time,* Theodore H. White and Annalee Jacoby, wrote *Thunder Out of China,* a surprisingly frank treatment of both Chiang-Kai-shek and Patrick Hurley's mission. For the next two decades journalists, public officials, and historians debated in print the reasons for the communist triumph in China. Among the studies critical of U.S. policy toward China's civil war are: Tang Tsou, *America's Failure in China, 1941-1950** (1963) and Herbert Feis, *The China Tangle** (1953). In 1949 the State Department published *United States Relations With China, 1944-1949,* a white paper defending U.S. policies. Among the important works by participants in making and carrying out policy in China are: O. Edmund Clubb, *The Witness and I* (1974) and Karl Lott Rankin, *China Assignment* (1964). The role of the "China Lobby" in influencing policy is investigated in Ross Koen, *The China Lobby In American Politics* (1974) and S. D. Bachrack, *The Committee of One Million: "China Lobby" Politics, 1953-1971* (1976). One should also consult Russell Buhite, *Patrick J. Hurley and American Foreign Policy* (1973); Warren Cohen, *America's Response to China* (1971); and M. Schaller, *The American Occupation of Japan: The Origins of The Cold War in Asia* (1985). General Wedemeyer wrote his account of events in China in *Wedemeyer Reports* (1958).

The factors influencing Truman's decision to aid South Korea have been analyzed in T. R. Fehrenbach, *This Kind of War* (1963) and Glenn Paige, *The Korean Decision* (1968). Important works critical of the U.S. role in Korea include: I. F. Stone, *The Hidden History of the Korean War* (1952) and Joyce and Gabriel Kolko, *Limits of Power** (1972). General MacArthur wrote his views in *Reminiscences* (1964), while his chief aide, General Courtney Whitney made a strong defense in *MacArthur: His Rendezvous with Destiny* (1956). Allen Whiting, *China Crosses the Yalu* (1960) and David Rees, *Korea: The Limited War* (1964) offer different views. More critical voices appear in John W. Spanier, *The Truman–MacArthur Controversy** (1959); and William Manchester, *American Caesar: Douglas MacArthur, 1880-1964* (1978). Using new sources, Robert M. Blum wrote *Drawing the Line: Origin of American Containment Policy in East Asia* (1982).

One should also consult the primary sources listed in Chapter 1.

CHAPTER 3

There are few good surveys of the United States in the Third World. Useful studies include: Robert A. Packman, *Liberal America and the Third World** (1973) and James W. Howe, *The United States and the Developing World: Agenda for Action,* an annual beginning in 1973. Two accounts critical of U.S. policy are: Richard J. Barnet, *Intervention and Revolution, The United States in the Third World** (1968) and Melvin Gurtov, *The United States Against the Third World** (1974). George McGhee illuminates the problems in *Envoy to the Middle World* (1983). The role of the CIA is explained by Thomas Powers, *The Man Who Kept the Secrets: Richard Helms and the CIA* (1979).

An extensive literature treats the relations of the United States with Latin America. Samuel Baily, *The United States and the Development of South America, 1945-1975* (1977) and David Green, *The Containment of Latin America* (1971) offer differing views. For the role of the CIA in Guatemala consult David Wise and Thomas Ross, *The Invisible Government** (1964) and Stephen Schlesinger and Stephen Kinzer, *Bitter Fruit** (1982). Problems with Castro's Cuba are analyzed by Haynes Johnson, *The Bay of Pigs* (1964) and Peter Wyden, *Bay of Pigs** (1979). Robert F. Kennedy described the actions of ExCom in *Thirteen Days** (1969). Robert A. Devine compiled an excellent collection of essays in *The Cuban Missile Crisis** (1971). Intervention in the Dominican Republic is discussed by U.S. Ambassador John Bartlow Martin, *Overtaken By Events* (1966); Theodore Draper, *The Dominican Revolt: A Case Study in American Policy* (1968); and Jerome Slater, *Intervention and Negotiation: The United States and Dominican Revolution* (1970). For the Alliance for Progress see Jerome Levinson and Juan De Onis, *The Alliance that Lost Its Way* (1971).

The various crises in the Middle East are detailed in Walter Laquer, *Confrontation: The Middle East and World Politics* (1974); Robert W. Stookey, *America and the Arab States* (1975); J. C. Hurewitz, *Soviet-American Rivalry in the Middle East* (1969); and William B. Quandt, *Decade of Decision: American Policy Toward the Arab–Israeli Conflict, 1967–76* (1977). More specialized studies include Hugh Thomas, *The Suez Affair** (1966) and Edward R. F. Sheehan, *The Arabs, Israelis, and Kissinger* (1976). Kissinger's role is also the subject of John Stoessinger, *Henry Kissinger: The Anguish of Power* (1976); Matti Golan, *The Secret Conversations of Henry Kissinger** (1976); and Barry Ruskin, *Paved with Good Intentions: The American Experience and Iran* (1980). A balanced treatment is presented in Eugene V. Rostow, ed., *The Middle East: Critical Choices for the United States* (1976), whereas Stephen Green offers a sharp indictment of U.S. policy from 1948 to 1967 in *Taking Sides: America's Secret Relations with a Militant Israel* (1984). Jimmy Carter's *The Blood of*

Abraham (1985) offers an overview of conflicts in the Middle East and U.S. efforts as a mediator for peace.

Among the useful studies of U.S. policies in Africa are: Stephen Weissman, *American Foreign Policy in the Congo, 1960-1964* (1974); Anthony Lake, *The "Tar Baby" Option: American Policy toward Southern Rhodesia* (1976); and Barbara Rogers, *White Wealth and Black Poverty: American Investments in Southern Africa* (1976).

One should also consult works noted that cover the Truman, Eisenhower, and Kennedy administrations. An important interpretation of foreign policy in the Johnson administration is Philip Geyelin, *Lyndon Johnson and the World* (1966). Johnson wrote his own account in *The Vantage Point* (1971). Nixon offered his explanation in *RN: The Memoirs of Richard Nixon* (1976).

CHAPTER 4

The intense battle of words over the Vietnam War fought by journalists and historians, as well as by military and political leaders, poses many pitfalls for the unwary reader. Even such collections of documents as *The Pentagon Papers* in both the Senator Mike Gravel four-volume edition (1971) and in the *New York Times* single volume edition (1971) must be used carefully as partial records only. The Defense Department has published a more complete record in *U.S.—Vietnam Relations, 1945-1967*. Another useful primary source is U.S. Senate Committee on Foreign Relations, *The United States and Vietnam, 1944-1947* (1972).

The best study of the early phases of the war remains Bernard Fall, *The Two Vietnams: A Political and Military Analysis** (1963). George Kahin and John W. Lewis, *The United States in Vietnam** (1967) offers useful insights. For a survey see Peter Poole, *The United States and Indochina from FDR to Nixon* (1973).

For accounts critical of the Vietnam policies of the United States consult Theodore Draper, *Abuse of Power** (1967); Townsend Hoopes, *The Limits of Intervention** (1969); J. C. Goulden, *Truth Is the First Casualty: The Gulf of Tonkin Affair* (1969); David Halberstam, *The Best and the Brightest* (1972); Daniel Ellsberg, *Papers on the War* (1972); Frances Fitzgerald, *Fire in the Lake** (1972); and Neil Sheehan, *A Bright Shining Lie: John Paul Vann and America in Vietnam* (1988). Senator Fulbright wrote two criticisms of U.S. policies, *The Arrogance of Power** (1966) and *The Crippled Giant* (1972). For a defense of U.S. action in Vietnam see Guenter Lewy, *American in Vietnam* (1978). The My Lai incident is covered in Seymour Harsh, *My Lai 4* (1970). Two commanding generals of U.S. forces in Vietnam have written their accounts: Maxwell Taylor, *Responsibility and Response* (1967); William C. West-moreland, *Report on the War in Vietnam* (1969) and *A Soldier Reports* (1976). In his *Diplomacy for a Crowded World* (1983) George W. Ball sharply criticized Nixon's foreign policy. A more balanced treatment may be found in Robert J. Pranger, *Detente and Defense: A Reader* (1976).

For policy in Laos consult Bernard Fall, *Anatomy of a Crisis: The Laotian Crisis of 1960-1961* (1969). The Nixon doctrine is discussed by Virginia Bro-dine and Mark Selden, *Open Secret: The Kissinger–Nixon Doctrine in Asia* (1972).

One should also consult references listed in previous chapters on each administration.

CHAPTER 5

Many participants in the making of U.S. foreign policy during the period of détente and its collapse have written useful accounts. In addition to Nixon's *Memoirs*, noted in Chapter 3, one should consult Gerald Ford, *A Time To Heal* (1979); Jimmy Carter, *Keeping Faith: Memoirs of a President* (1982); and Ronald Reagan, *An American Life* (1990). Several cabinet members and presidential advisers have also published their versions of events. From the Nixon and Ford administrations we have Henry Kissinger's *The White House Years* (1979) and *Years of Upheaval* (1982). From the Carter administration there are Cyrus Vance, *Hard Choices* (1983) and Zbigniew Brzezinski, *Power and Principle: Memoirs of the National Security Adviser, 1977–1981* (1983). Reagan administration officials, who have written accounts, include Alexander Haig, *Caveat: Realism, Reagan and Foreign Policy* (1984); Jeane J. Kirkpatrick, *The Reagan Phenomenon—And Other Speeches on Foreign Policy* (1983); and Donald T. Regan, *For the Record* (1988).

The early stages of détente are described in C. Bell, *The Diplomacy of Détente: The Kissinger Era* (1977), whereas a broader period is covered by Raymond L. Garthoff, *Debate and Confrontation: American–Soviet Relations from Nixon to Reagan* (1985).

The literature on arms control and national security is both extensive and polemical. Insider accounts include those by Secretary of Defense Harold Brown's *Thinking About National Security* (1983) and by long-time National Security Council staff member William Hyland in his *Moral Rivals: Superpower Relations from Nixon to Reagan* (1987). Works critical of U.S. policies in the arms race include: Gerald C. Smith, *Doubletalk: The Story of Salt I* (1980); Peter Pringle and James Spigelman, *The Nuclear Barons* (1981); James Fallows, *National Defense** (1981); Jonathan Schell, *The Fate of the Earth** (1982); George F. Kennan, *Nuclear Delusion: Soviet–American Relations in the Atomic*

*Age** (rev. ed., 1983); Strobe Talbott, *Deadly Gambits: The Reagan Administration and the Stalemate in Nuclear Arms Control* (1984); Michael Parenti, *The Sword and the Dollar* (1989); and Nick Kotz, *Wild Blue Yonder—Money, Politics, and the B-1 Bomber* (1989). Less critical analyses may be found in Thomas H. Etzold, *Defense or Delusion: America's Military in the 1980's* (1982); Michael Krepon, *Strategic Stalemate, Nuclear Weapons, and Arms Control in American Politics* (1984); Michael Mandelbaum, *Reagan and Gorbachev* (1987); and Coit D. Blacker, *Reluctant Warriors: The United States, the Soviet Union, and Arms Control* (1987). One should also consult Gregory Hooks, *Forging the Military–Industrial Complex* (1991).

An overview of U.S. overt and covert aid to forces opposing communism in the Third World in the 1980s may be found in: Bob Woodward, *Veil: The Secret Wars of the CIA, 1981–1987* (1987); Steven Emerson, *Secret Warriors: Inside the Covert Military Operations of the Reagan Era* (1988); Peter J. Schrader, ed., *Intervention in the 1980's: U.S. Foreign Policy in the Third World* (1989); and D. K. Kyvig, ed., *Reagan and the World* (1990).

Studies of the U.S. role in the Middle East have proliferated as new crises arose. Useful surveys of U.S. policy in the early years of the 1980s include Seth P. Tillman, *The United States in the Middle East: Interests and Obstacles* (1982) and Gary Sick, *All Fall Down: America's Tragic Encounter with Iran* (1985). Efforts to deal with Mideast terrorists are discussed in D. C. Martin and J. Walcott, *Best Laid Plans: The Inside Story of America's War Against Terrorism* (1988). Insider accounts of the efforts of the Carter administration to obtain the release of U.S. hostages held by Iran include Pierre Salinger, *America Held Hostage* (1981) and Hamilton Jordan, *Crisis: The Last Year of the Carter Presidency* (1982). One should also consult Gary Sick's *October Surprise* (1991).

Among the flood of books on U.S. policy in Central America those critical of Washington's actions include: Walter La Feber, *Inevitable Revolutions: The United States in Central America* (1983); Raymond Bonner, *Weakness and Deceit: U.S. Policy and El Salvador* (1984); James Chace, *Endless War** (1984); E. Bradford Burns, *At War in Nicaragua: The Reagan Doctrine and the Politics of Nostalgia* (1987); Leslie Cockburn, *Out of Control* (1987); Thomas W. Walker, *Reagan Versus the Sandinistas* (1987); Roy Gutman, *Banana Diplomacy: The Making of American Policy in Nicaragua, 1981–1987* (1988); and Peter Kornbluh, *Nicaragua, The Price of Intervention* (1987). More supportive of recent U.S. policy in the area is *The Report of the President's National Bipartisan Commission on Central America** (1984). Helpful to the study of the Iran–Contra Affair are *The Tower Commission Report** (1987); Jonathan Marshall, *The Iran–Contra Connection* (1987); Oliver North, *Under Fire* (1991); Theodore Draper; *A Very Thin Line: The Iran–Contra Affair* (1991); and Thomas Carothers, *In the Name of Democracy* (1991).

CHAPTER 6

The events covered in this chapter happened so recently that literature dealing with them remains limited. The best primary sources are major newspapers and official government publications such as the *Congressional Record* and the *Department of State Bulletin*. Periodicals such as *Foreign Affairs* and *Foreign Policy* contain interpretive essays by scholars in international relations.

The following secondary accounts are noteworthy: F. Kempe, *Divorcing the Dictator: America's Bungled Affair with Noriega* (1990); J. Dinges, *Our Man in Panama* (1990); R. Jervis and S. Bialer, eds., *Soviet–American Relations after the Cold War* (1990); Robert S. McNamara, *Out of the Cold: New Thinking for American Foreign and Defense in 21st Century* (1989); Robert W. Tucker and David C. Hendrickson, *The Imperial Temptation: The New World Order & America's Purpose* (1992); Norman Friedman, *Desert Victory: The War for Kuwait** (1991); M. Mechizuki et al., *Japan and The United States: Troubled Partners in a Changing World** (1991); F. J. Macchiarola and R. B. Oxnan, eds., *The China Challenge: American Policies in East Asia** (1991); M. G. Bard, *The Water's Edge and Beyond: Defining the Limits to Domestic Influence on United States Middle East Policy* (1991); and D. E. Neuchterlein, *America Recommitted: United States National Interests in a Restructured World* (1991).

CHAPTER 7

There are two standard surveys of economics that contain thorough reviews of U.S. economic history and policy since 1945. Each includes a survey of classical, Keynesian, and post-Keynesian theory: Campbell R. McConnell and Stanley L. Brue, *Economics* (1992) and Paul A. Samuelson and William D. Nordhaus, *Economics* (1992). See also Gordon A. Fletcher, *The Keynesian Revolution and Its Critics* (1987).

Adolf A. Berle's classic, *The American Economic Republic** (1963), embodies the optimism and aims of welfare capitalism, linking the attitudes of New Deal reformers and the Great Society of the 1960s. On the age of affluence and the sociocultural assumptions of Americans from the late 1940s through the 1960s, see David Potter, *People of Plenty** (1954). Potter's book is invaluable in understanding public alarm and confusion since the 1970s about the limits of U.S. prosperity—and the continuing appeal of the U.S. economic system to people of other nations. John Kenneth Galbraith's *The Affluent Society** (1958) and *The New Industrial State** (1972) contain stinging critiques of consumer culture and private corporate power. On the "discovery" of poverty in the affluent society, see Michael Harrington, *The Other America* (1962).

Since 1945, critics, social scientists, journalists, and others have documented the human side of economic and cultural change. Influential commentaries on midcentury life include David Riesman et al., *The Lonely Crowd** (1953) and William H. Whyte, Jr., *The Organization Man** (1957). On the youth rebellion and radicalism of the 1960s, sympathetic studies include: Paul Goodman, *Growing Up Absurd** (1962), Theodore Roszak, *The Making of a Counter Culture*# (1969); Charles Reich, *The Greening of America*# (1970); Philip Slater, *The Pursuit of Loneliness** (1970). On the impact of the counterculture, and more critical: Robert Nisbet, *The Twilight of Authority** (1975); Daniel Bell, *The Cultural Contradictions of Capitalism** (1976); and Christopher Lasch, *The Culture of Narcissim** (1979). On the failed social and welfare policies of the 1960s consult James Q. Wilson, *Thinking about Crime** (1975); Charles Murray, *Losing Ground** (1984); and *In Pursuit of Happiness and Good Government** (1988).

On the environment see Rachel Carson, *Silent Spring** (1962). During the 1970s, whether economic growth was able to persist without catastrophic global consequences came into question: Three books—Richard A. Falk, *This Endangered Planet*# (1971), Club of Rome, *The Limits to Growth*# (1971), and Robert Heilbroner, *An Inquiry into the Human Prospect** (1974)—were widely read and discussed. Twenty years later, they seemed dated yet important documents of their time. Evironmental efforts and changes in the 1970s and 1980s are reported in an article by Greg Easterbrook and Evan Eisenberg, "The State of the Earth," *The New Republic*, April 30, 1990. On suburban and exurban growth, especially during the 1970s and 1980s, see Joel Garreau, *Edge City* (1991).

Deregulation and Republican economic views of the 1980s are covered by Milton Friedman, who started the free-market attack on welfare capitalism, public monopolies, and regulated enterprise, in *Capitalism and Freedom** (1963). Martin Feldstein, ed., *The American Economy in Transition** (1980) contains a number of post-Keynesian analyses and forecasts. Paul Blumberg, *Inequality in an Age of Decline** (1980), gives a different view of long-term economic trends.

On debt and the savings and loan disaster consult Alfred L. Malabre, Jr., *Beyond Our Means** (1987) and Thomas Paulette and Thomas E. Ricks, "Just What Happened to All that Money Savings and Loans Lost?", *The Wall Street Journal*, November 5, 1990. The financial excesses of the 1980s are covered by Myron Magnet, "The Money Society," *Fortune*, July 6, 1987; Edmund Faltermayer, "The Deal Decade: Verdict On The Eighties," *Fortune*, August 26, 1991; and James Stewart, *Den of Thieves* (1991).

CHAPTER 8

A strong introduction to constitutional history is Alfred H. Kelly, Winfred A. Harbison, and Herman Belz, *The American Constitution, Its Origins and Development** (6th ed., 1983) and the 7th edition by Kelly and Harbison (1990). A superb study of the role of the Supreme Court in U.S. history by a leading American Constitutional scholar and public servant is Archibald Cox's *The Court and the Constitution* (1987). Edward S. Corwin's *The Constitution and What It Means Today** (1974) is a standard. The best case books are Malcolm M. Feeley and Samuel Krislow, *Constitutional Law* (2nd ed., 1990) and Stanley I. Kutler, *The Supreme Court and the Constitution** (3rd ed., 1991). A most useable, well-written, and edited guide for teachers and students is Elder Witt's *The Supreme Court and Individual Rights** (1988), published by *Congressional Quarterly*. Pulitzer prize winning *Washington Post* reporter Bob Woodward, of Watergate fame, and Scott Armstrong, in their investigative journalistic style, pierced the solemnity and secret deliberations of the Court in *The Brethren: Inside the Supreme Court* (1979). An excellent survey of part of the post-World War II years is in the New American Nation Series, Paul L. Murphy's *The Constitution in Crisis Times, 1918–1969* (1972). The standard reference book on the Constitution, Court decisions, personalities, and legal terms and doctrines, published as part of the bicenntential and edited by Leonard W. Levy with the aid of many constitutional and legal historians, is the 4-volume, *Encyclopedia of the American Constitution* (1986). A reading of Alan F. Westin's documentary study of the Truman Steel Seizure Case in 1952, *The Anatomy of a Constitutional Law Case** (1967), is an excellent way to learn how the U.S. judicial system works.

The Warren Court, 1953 to 1969, dominated the judicial history of the post-World War II years. The leading legal scholars' assessments are Alexander Bickel's *Least Dangerous Branch, The Supreme Court at the Bar of Politics** (1962) and *The Supreme Court and the Idea of Progress** (1978); Archibald Cox's, *The Warren Court** (1968); Bernard Schwartz, *Super Chief, Earl Warren and His Supreme Court* (1983); and *Inside the Warren Court, 1953–1969* (1983) by Bernard Schwartz with Stephen Lesher.

Important issues faced by the Court are studied in Paul Simon's *The Antagonists* (1989), a revealing story of the conflicts between judicial activism and judicial restraint through two adversarial giants on the Court, Hugo Black and Felix Frankfurter; Milton R. Konvitz, *Expanding Liberties: Freedom's Gains in Post War America* (1976); Alan Barth, *The Price of Liberty* (1972); J. Harvie Wilkinson III, *From Brown to Bakke: The Supreme Court and School Integration, 1954–1978** (1979); Norman Dorsen et al., *Political and Civil Rights in the United States Today* (1980). Jake Bass's journalistic yet scholarly account of the key court in the civil rights struggles, the 5th U.S. Circuit Court of Appeals in New Orleans, *Unlikely Heroes* (1982), tells the story of the often heroic roles of southern federal judges. Derrick A. Bell, Jr., *Race, Racism and American Law*, (2nd ed., 1980) is an analysis of African Americans' attempts to achieve constitutional rights. Brilliantly written case studies are Anthony Lewis's *Gideon's Trumpet** (1964) on the right of counsel, and his study of the First Amendment rights of free speech and press in *Make No Law* (1991), a study of the key 1964 case, *The New York Times v. Sullivan*, on freedom of the press relative to government officials; Richard Kluger's *Simple Justice** (1977), the definitive work on the legal struggle of African Americans to bring desegregation, culminating in *Brown v. Board of Education of Topeka*; Peter Irons, *Justice at War* (1983), the story of the Japanese American World War II internment cases, and his book of essays on personal struggles for civil liberties, *The Courage of Their Convictions: Sixteen Americans Who Fought Their Way to the Supreme Court* (1988), which reveals "the live faces behind the masks of constitutional law"; and Bernard Schwartz's *Swann's Way: The School Busing Case and the Supreme Court* (1986). Fred W. Friendly and Martha J. H. Elliot's *The Constitution: That Delicate Balance** (1984) is a series of case studies that reveals personalities behind the judicial processes and doctrines, written in a lively style and accompanied by a series of excellent videocasettes.

The papers of Justices Warren, Douglas, Brennan, Frankfurter, and Harlan are available. Indispensable to the study of the Supreme Court are the decisions themselves in *United States Reports*. The articles published in law school *Law Reviews* are the most thoughtful commentaries. Also, The *New York Times* reporting of the Supreme Court in the post–World War II era is excellent.

CHAPTER 9

The study of race relations in the years after World War II should begin with Gunnar Myrdal's two-volume *An American Dilemma** (1975). For path-breaking African American scholarship see sociologist E. Franklin Frazier, *Black Bourgeoisie** (1965), *Negro Family in the United States** (1966), *E. Franklin Frazier on Race Relations** (1968); historian John Hope Franklin, with Alfred A. Moss, *From Slavery to Freedom** (1987); sociologists St. Clair Drake and Horace Cayton, *Black Metropolis*, 2 vol. (1945); and social psychologist Kenneth Clark *Dark Ghetto** (1965). Building on the research of Frazier and other pioneer social scientists is C. Eric Lincoln and Lawrence H. Maniya, *The Black Church in the Africa American Experience** (1990). Gordon Allport's *The Nature of Prejudice** (1958) broke new ground.

A clear, short history of the Civil Rights era is Harvard Sitkoff's *The Struggle for Black Equality: 1954–1980** (1981). The most up-to-date, thorough, and readable study of the civil rights movement is Taylor Branch's *Parting the Waters: America in the King Years, 1954–1963* (1988). Two 1991 books tell us much in riveting personal terms: Nicholas Lemann's *The Promised Land* is a study of the post-World War II migration of southern African American sharecroppers to the northern urban centers with its impact on African Americans, whites, and northern cities and the resulting public policy response, the

War on Poverty; and Alex Kotlowitz's *There Are No Children Here* is a study of two African American children in a Chicago public housing project. Social scientist Andrew Hacker, in the tradition of Myrdal, has produced a penetrating analysis of race relations in America, *Two Nations: Black and White, Separate, Hostile, Unequal* (1992).

Louis E. Lomax tells an important story in *When the Word is Given: Elijah Muhammad, Malcolm X and the Black Muslim World* (1979). Harold Cruse's *The Crisis of the Negro Intellectual** (1967) is a provocative work. Two psychi- atrists, William H. Grier and Price M. Cobbs in *Black Rage** (1980), helped explain the depths of African American anger and anguish.

To Secure These Rights* (1947)—Report of the President's Committee on Civil Rights; U.S. Commission on Civil Rights (1957 on)—annual and special reports; and the *Report of the National Advisory Commission on Civil Disor- ders** (1968) on the urban riots of 1967 are invaluable government studies.

The regular reports of the Bureaus of the Census and Labor Statistics help the serious student cut through the stereotypes and misinformation.

The role and actions of civil rights organizations in these years are analyzed in case studies by August Meier and Elliot Rudwick, *CORE: A Study in the Civil Rights Movement, 1942-1969** (1975) and Clayborn Carson, *In Struggle: SNCC and the Black Awakening of the 1960's** (1981). The best biographies of the leading African American figure are Stephen B. Oates, *Let the Trumpet Sound, The Life of Martin Luther King, Jr.** (1982) and David Garrow's *Bearing the Cross: Martin Luther King, Jr. and the Southern Christian Leader- ship Conference** (1964). James W. Silver's *Mississippi: The Closed Society* (1978) is trenchant on racial problems in the author's home state. Two journal articles stand out. August Meier wrote a brilliant essay, "On the Role of Martin Luther King," *New Politics*, Winter 1965, and Richard M. Scammon and Ben J. Wattenberg, "Black Progress and Liberal Rhetoric," *Commentary*, April 1973, provoked much thought and controversy. A report by the Center for the Study of Social Policy, *A Dream Deferred: The Economic Status of Black Americans** (1983) challenges the findings of Scammon and Wattenberg.

Case studies of landmark civil rights confrontations are Elizabeth Huckaby's *Crisis at Central High, Little Rock, 1957–1958* (1980); William H. Chafe's *On Civilities and Civil Rights* (1980) (on the Greensboro sit-in's); Doug McAdam's *Freedom Summer* (1988) (Mississippi Summer Project, 1964); David Garrow's *Protest at Selma** (1978); and J. Anthony Lukas, *Common Ground: A Turbulent Decade in Three American Families** (1985) (on busing and school desegrega- tion in Boston).

The most powerful and influential writings are autobiographical statements by participants in the racial cauldron of the 1950s and 1960s: Martin Luther King, Jr., *Stride Toward Freedom, The Montgomery Story** (1958), *Why We Can't Wait** (1964), *Where Do We Go From Here: Chaos or Community** (1968); *The Autobiography of Malcolm X** (1965); James Baldwin, *The Fire*

Next Time* (1962); John Howard Griffin, *Black Like Me** (1960); Claude Brown, *Manchild in the Promised Land** (1965); Stokely Carmichael and Charles V. Hamilton, *Black Power: The Politics of Liberation in America** (1967); Frantz Fanon, *The Wretched of the Earth** (1963); and Howell Raines, *My Soul Is Rested** (1983).

CHAPTER 10

Any study of the presidency would profit from an examination of *The Federalist Papers** (numbers 67 to 77). Political scientists Clinton Rossiter's *The American Presidency** (rev. ed., 1960) [rep. 1987]; Richard E. Neustadt's *Presidential Power and the Modern Presidents: The Politics of Leadership from Roosevelt to Reagan** (1989); Thomas E. Cronin, *The State of the Presidency** (1982); and Richard M. Pious, *Rethinking The Presidency** (1979), are particularly useful on the sources and uses of presidential power. James D. Barber combines political science and psychobiography to write a most thoughtful study of presidents since the first Roosevelt in *Presidential Character** (rev. ed., 1977). Arthur M. Schlesinger, Jr.'s historical account is a trenchant, though partisan study of the *Imperial Presidency** (1973) [rep. 1989].

The Coming to Power: Critical Presidential Elections in American History* (1981), ed. by Arthur M. Schlesinger, Jr. and Fred. L. Israel (1971) and Theodore H. White's four books on the *Making of the President, 1960*, 1964*, 1968, 1972* examine elections. Jules Whitcover analyzes the elections of 1976 in *Marathon, The Pursuit of the Presidency,* and Jules Whitcover and Jack W. Germond examine the elections of 1980, 1984, and 1988 in *Blue Smoke and Mirrors: How Reagan Won and Carter Lost the Election of 1980* (1981), *Wake Us Up When It's Over: Presidential Politics in 1984* (1985), and *Whose Broad Stripes and Bright Stars: The Trivial Pursuit of the Presidency, 1988* (1989). The most penetrating analysis of the politics of the 1980s has been provided by journalist Sidney Blumenthal, whose latest book sums up his work, *Pledging Allegiance; The Last Campaign of the Cold War* (1990), the story of the election of 1988. Joe McGinnes worked in the Nixon 1968 campaign and then wrote a scary but hilarious little book, *The Selling of the President, 1968** (1969). A reporter's view of the press coverage of the presidential campaign of 1972 is Timothy Crouse's *The Boys on the Bus** (1973).

The electorate is studied in the 1940s and 1950s by pollster-journalist Samuel Lubell, *The Future of American Politics** (1950); a generation later by two pollsters, Richard M. Scammon and Ben J. Wattenberg, *The Real Majority** (1970); and by Norman H. Nie, Sidney Verba, and John R. Petrocik, *The Changing American Voter** (1976).

Truman's *Memoirs,* 2 vol. (1955–1956) are the best by a twentieth-century president. Robert J. Donovan wrote the best Truman biography, really a history of the Truman years, with *Conflict and Crisis: The Presidency of Harry S. Truman, 1945-1948** (1977) and *Tumultuous Years: The Presidency of Harry S. Truman, 1949-1953** (1982).

The Eisenhower presidency is viewed by Emmet J. Hughes, a speechwriter for Ike, in *Ordeal of Power: Eisenhower Years* (1963). A perceptive, and appreciative political scientist's study is Fred I. Greenstein, *The Hidden-Hand Presidency, Eisenhower as Leader** (1982). Charles C. Alexander's *Holding the Line: The Eisenhower Era, 1952-1961** (1975), is a thorough work.

The Kennedy years are brilliantly and favorably told in Arthur M. Schlesinger, Jr.'s *A Thousand Days: John F. Kennedy* (1965) and critically examined in British journalist Henry Fairlie's *The Kennedy Promise** (1973). The best researched and written one-volume study is Herbert S. Parmet's *JFK: The Presidency of John F. Kennedy** (1983). The massive and controversial *Report of the Warren Commission* (1964) is the starting point for study of the assassination.

Doris Kearns wrote a fine piece of psychobiography in *Lyndon Johnson and the American Dream** (1976). *New York Times* reporter Tom Wicker's little book, *JFK and LBJ** (1968), tells much about both men and presidential decision making. Johnson's press secretary, George E. Reedy's *The Twilight of the Presidency** (1971), is insightful and critical of Johnson and of the modern presidency. Jim F. Heath's *Decade of Disillusionment: The Kennedy–Johnson Years** (1975), is a fine survey. Barry Goldwater's *Conscience of a Conservative** (1961) was the bible of the right-wing ideologues.

The best work on Richard Nixon, and much of post-World War II politics, remains Gary Wills, *Nixon Agonistes: The Crisis of the Self-made Man** (1970). Richard Nixon's *Six Crises** (1962) is most revealing. The Watergate literature is exhaustive, but the best contemporary study is Anthony Lukas's *Nightmare: The Underside of the Nixon Years* (1976). Jonathan Schell's *The Time of Illusion** (1976) is a most thoughtful interpretation of "Watergate." *The Washington Post's* Robert Woodward and Carl Bernstein's two books, *All The President's Men** (1974) and *The Final Days** (1976) are extraordinary examples of investigative reporting and lively writing. James Doyle, the press secretary for Cox and Jaworski, tells the story brilliantly from the Special Prosecutor's office in *Not Above the Law** (1977). John Dean, the man who accused the president and made it stick, tells all in *Blind Ambition** (1977). Judge John Sirica describes the Watergate story as he saw it from the bench in *To Set the Record Straight** (1979).

Stanley I. Kutler's *The Wars of Watergate: The Last Crisis of Richard Nixon* (1990) is an exhaustive new study by a top legal historian who argues that the constitutional and criminal justice system worked and the Watergate experience "elevated moral considerations of public officers . . . and public business." The report of the House Judiciary Committee, *Impeachment of*

*Richard M. Nixon, President of the United States** (1974), is most important. Harvard Law professor, Raoul Berger's two studies, *Impeachment* (1973) and *Executive Privilege* (1974), were timely and scholarly.

Betty Glad, *Jimmy Carter: In Search of the Great White House* (1980) is a critical analysis. A political scientist's views of the Carter administration is Erwin C. Hargrove's *Jimmy Carter as President: Leadership and the Politics of the Public Good* (1988). Gaddis Smith's study of Carter's foreign policy, *Morality, Reason and Power* (1986), reveals much about the man and his administration both at home and abroad. James L. Sundquist's *The Decline and Resurgence of Congress** (1981) is a classic on the role of Congress in the post–World War II years.

The Reagan literature is voluminous. The most revealing studies are Gary Wills's *Reagan's America** (1988); Lou Cannon's definitive biography, *President Reagan: The Role of a Lifetime* (1991); and Kevin Phillips's *The Rich and the Poor: Wealth and the American Electorate in the Reagan Aftermath* (1990). An inside view of Reaganomics by a reporter who had special access to the director of the Office of Management and Budget is William Greider's *The Education of David Stockman and Other Americans** (1982), and a critical analysis of Reagan's domestic policies is Frances F. Piven's and Richard A. Cloward's *The New Class War: Reagan's Attack on the Welfare State and Its Consequences* (1982). Studies of the electorate include Frances F. Piven and Richard A. Cloward, *Why Americans Don't Vote** (1988) and Richard Scammon, ed., *America Votes: A Handbook of Contemporary American Election Statistics*, 19 vols., 1956–1990.

INDEX

Abernathy, Ralph D., 270–271
Abortion, 218, 230–231, 245–248, 341
Acheson, Dean, 6, 13, 17–19, 35–37,
    40–41, 88–89, 298
Affirmative action, 216, 223, 230,
    233–234, 241–243, 261, 264, 274
"Affluent society," 190, 191, 260, 264
Afghanistan, 123–124, 133–134, 152,
    153, 161–162, 319
African Americans, 189, 195, 210,
    213–214, 219–223, 241, 249–282,
    285, 321. *See also* Civil rights
Agnew, Spiro T., 271, 305, 307–309,
    312
Agriculture, 198–199
AIDS, 277
Albania, 157
*Alexander v. Holmes County Board of
    Education*, 231
Algeria, 79–80, 175
Allende, Salvador, 66
Alliance for Progress, 60
American Medical Association,
    186–187, 189
Americans with Disabilities Act (1990),
    264
Andropov, Yuri, 127
Angola, 84–85, 134, 135, 160–161
Apartheid, 135
Apportionment, 216, 223–225

Arbenz Guzmán, Jacobo, 56–57
Assassination, 60, 100, 139, 259, 266,
    269–270, 301, 304
Atlantic Charter (1941), 52, 250
Attica prison riot (1971), 272
Australia, 47, 176
Austria, 10, 22
Automobiles, 177, 180, 184, 190,
    192–193, 196, 200, 336
Aviation and aerospace industries, 193

"Baby boom" generation, 194–196
Baghdad Pact (1955), 70, 72–73
Baker, James, 154, 156, 160, 165,
    168, 170, 172
Baker v. Carr, 224
Bakke, Allan P., 233
Bakker, Jim and Tammy Faye, 329
Balaguer, Joaquin, 65
Ball, George, 104
Bani-Sadr, 80
Banks, 203–207, 329, 339
Bao Dai, 89, 90, 95, 96
Barr, David, 34
Batista, Fulgencio, 58
Bay of Pigs, 25, 59–60, 99, 283, 300
Begin, Menachem, 78, 79, 318
Belgium, 81–82
Bell, Daniel, 197
Bennett, W. Tapley, 65

Bentsen, Lloyd, 337
Berger, Ralph, 228
Berger v. New York, 228–229
Berlin, 10–12, 20, 23–26, 154–155
Bernstein, Carl, 308, 311
Betts v. Brady, 226
Billingsley, Andrew, 277
Bipartisanship, 5, 29, 290
Birmingham, Alabama demonstrations
  (1963), 256–258, 259
Birth control, 217, 218
Black, Eugene, 71
Black, Hugo, 212, 216, 218, 226, 229
Blackmun, Harry A., 230, 245, 246,
  247
Black Muslims, 265–266
Black Panthers, 272
"Black Power," 268–269
"Bloody Sunday," 262, 272
Bob Jones University v. U.S.,
  232–233, 274
Boesky, Ivan, 329
Boland Amendments, 142–143, 148,
  149, 330
Bork, Robert H., 240, 247, 329
Bosch, Juan, 64–65
Bowers v. Hardwick, 244
Brandenburg v. Ohio, 218–219
Branzburg v. Hayes, 238
Brennan, William J., Jr., 234, 236,
  238, 240–241, 246, 247
Brezhnev, Leonid, 76–78, 120
Bridges, Styles, 29, 33, 35
Brown, H. Rap, 270
*Brown v. Board of Education of
  Topeka, Kansas*, 210, 219–223,
  252–253, 271–273
Brown II, 220–223
Brzezinski, Zbigniew, 122
Buckley, James, 131
Buckley, William, 138
Budget and Impoundment Control Act
  (1974), 315–316
Bugging, 228–229, 308–310, 312
Bulgaria, 154–155
Bullitt, William C., 33–34
Bundy, McGeorge, 103, 106
Burger, Warren E., 229–239
Burns, Arthur, 187
Bush, George, 247, 289
  and Afghanistan, 161–162
  and Angola, 160–161
  and Cambodia, 159–160

Central American policy, 157–159,
  162–164, 340
and civil rights, 236, 243
cold war, 153–157, 171–174, 340
and Communist China, 174–175
dissolution of USSR, 172–174, 340
economic policy, 339–341
and election of 1988, 153, 284–285,
  289, 314, 336–338
and Japan, 175–177, 202–203
Middle East policy, 164–171,
  340–341
power of the presidency, 338–342
Supreme Court appointees, 241,
  247–248
tax policy, 338, 339
as vice-president, 129, 320, 337
Busing, 213, 216, 233, 272
Byrd amendment, 84
Byrnes, James F., 3, 4, 31, 221

Cairo Declaration (1943), 37
Cambodia, 47, 88–90, 94, 106,
  111–113, 116–117, 134, 159–160,
  195, 297, 306, 314–315
Camp David accords, 78, 318
Canada, 157
Capitalism, 182–183, 185–190,
  196–198, 201, 208–209
Capital punishment, 230, 244
Caribbean Basin Initiative, 143
Carmichael, Stokely, 268, 269
Carson, Rachel, 207
Carswell, G. Harrold, 229, 309
Carter, Jimmy, 286, 318–321, 334
  and Afghanistan, 319
  Camp David Summit (1978), 78, 318
  and civil rights, 233, 272–273
  and détente, 121–124
  economic policy, 198, 200, 201
  and election of 1976, 272–273, 289,
    314, 316–317
  and election of 1980, 320–321
  and Iran, 79–80, 318–319
  Mideast Peace Agreement (1979), 79,
    122
  and Panama Canal Zone, 68
  and Rhodesia, 84
  and South Africa, 85
Casey, William J., 80, 128, 145, 147,
  315, 329–330
Castillo Armas, Carlos, 56–57
Castro, Fidel, 58–64, 85, 141

Central Intelligence Agency (CIA), 9,
40, 56–61, 66, 69, 82, 85, 91,
98, 101, 102, 106, 133–134, 138,
142, 143, 145, 147, 163, 310,
315, 329–330, 337
Chambers, Whittaker, 36
Chamorro, Violeta de, 158
Chamoun, Camille, 73–74
Chemical industry, 193–194
Chemical weapons, 150–151, 165
Cheney, Richard, 154, 156, 166
Chernobyl nuclear accident, 207
Chicago, 267–268, 270
"Chicago Seven," 270
Chile, 65–67
China, Nationalist, 27–36, 47–49, 87
China, People's Republic of, 35, 40,
42–43, 46, 48–50, 89, 117, 119,
122, 174–175, 308, 318
China Lobby, 31, 33, 35, 49
"Christmas bombings" (Vietnam), 115
Chrysler Corporation, 177, 190, 200
Church and state, 212–213, 217–218,
238–239, 246, 298
Churchill, Winston, 4, 37, 49, 91–92
Civil rights, 195, 196, 249–282,
301–302, 304, 306, 339, 341. *See
also under specific presidents*
affirmative action, 216, 223, 230,
233–234, 241–243
desegregation, 210, 213–214,
219–223, 230–233, 252–253,
258–260, 267, 271–272, 274
legislative apportionment, 216,
223–225
reverse discrimination, 233–234, 241,
261
women's rights, 234–237, 243, 248,
264, 286
Civil Rights Acts, 223, 230, 232,
234–236, 242, 243, 259, 260,
270, 271, 274–275, 285, 309
Clark, James G., 262
Clark, Tom C., 228–229
Clay, Lucius, 10–11
Clements, Earle, 92
Cocaine, 163–164, 277
Colby, William, 66
Cold war, 1–26, 51–85, 89–96,
118–130, 140–146, 152–162,
171–174, 251, 290–291, 295,
296–298, 331, 336
Colombia, 143, 163

Cominform (Communist Information
Bureau), 8
Commander-in-chief, president as, 295,
303
Committee for European Economic
Cooperation (CEEC), 8
Committee to Reelect the President
(CREEP), 307, 308, 310–311
Commonwealth of Independent States,
173–174
Communist China. *See* China, People's
Republic of
"Comparable worth," 236–237
Computers, 193
Congo, Republic of, 81–82
Connally, Tom, 13, 35, 40
Connett, William, 64–65
Connor, Eugene "Bull," 256–257
Consent decrees, 242–243
Construction industry, 191–192
Consumer Product Safety Commission,
321
Contadora, 143
Containment, 5–12, 37–50, 126, 153–155
Contras, 143, 145–149, 158, 330
Coolidge, Calvin, 332
Cooper v. Aaron, 222
Council of Economic Advisers, 182,
187, 188
Counterculture, 195–196
Cox, Archibald, 308, 312
"Crack" cocaine, 277
Criminal due process, 216, 225–229,
237–238, 243–244, 309
Cristiani, Alfred, 158–159
Cruzan v. Missouri, 244–245
Cuba, 25, 53, 58–64, 99, 122, 134,
141, 144, 160–161, 168, 283,
299–301
Czechoslovakia, 8, 10, 12, 56, 57, 69,
70, 154–155, 291–292

Daley, Richard J., 267–268
D'Amato, Alfonse, 166
Dean, John, 310–313
Death penalty, 230, 244
Deaver, Michael K., 329
"Deep Throat," 311
Defense budgets, 9, 124–126, 156, 173
Deficit finance, 180, 183, 187, 188,
197–198, 201, 203, 273, 321–324,
326, 329, 333–334, 339–341
DeLacy, Hugh, 29

Dennis v. United States, 212, 218
Détente, 118–124, 130
Dewey, Thomas E., 252, 290–293
Diem, Ngo Dinh, 95–100, 310
Dillon, Douglas, 92
Dinkins, David N., 246
Disabled persons, 264
Dobrynin, Anatoly, 120
Dodd Amendment, 141
Dole, Robert, 130
Dominican Republic, 64–65, 162, 303
Domino theory, 6, 92, 116
Douglas, William O., 212, 217
"Doves," 104–107, 111–114
Dred Scott v. Sanford, 245
Drexel Burnham Lambert, 204
Duarte, Jose Napoleon, 141–142, 158
DuBois, W. E. B., 252
Due process of law, 216, 225–229,
    237–238, 243–244, 309
Dukakis, Michael S., 289, 337–338
Duke, David, 341
Dulles, Allen W., 58–59, 91
Dulles, John Foster, 5, 19–21, 36,
    46–49, 56–58, 70–72, 92, 94, 96

Eagleton, Thomas F., 307–308
Eastland, James, 221
Economic Opportunity Act, 189
Economic policy. *See also under*
    specific presidents
    Keynesian, 182–183, 187, 188, 197
    supply side, 201, 320, 321–324
Economy, U.S., 179–209
Eden, Anthony, 71
Education, 281, 286
    church and state, 213–214, 217–218
    civil rights and, 210, 213–214,
        219–223, 230–233, 252–253,
        258–260, 267, 271–274
Egypt, 68–79, 122, 131, 170, 318
Ehrlichman, John D., 312, 313
Eisenhower, Dwight D., 130–131, 214,
    286, 289, 291
    and Africa, 80–81
    atoms for peace proposal, 20
    Berlin crisis (1958–1959), 23
    and Chile, 66
    and civil rights, 220–221, 222
    economic policy, 187, 192
    and election of 1952, 18–20, 46, 90,
        286, 289, 295–296

Formosa Resolution, 48–49
Geneva Conference (1955), 22
inauguration, 21
and Iran, 69
and Jordan, 73
Latin American policy, 56–58, 59
and Lebanon, 73–74
and McCarthy, 21–22
and Nationalist China, 47–48
and the New Look, 20–21
powers of the presidency, 295–298
and South Africa, 84
Southeast Asia Treaty Organization
    (SEATO), 47
Suez crisis (1954–1956), 70–72
and Union of Soviet Socialist
    Republics (USSR), 72–73, 74
Vietnam War, 86, 90–98
Elections, congressional
    of 1950, 17, 18
    of 1974, 314
    of 1982, 325
Elections, presidential
    of 1948, 13, 252, 288–289, 290–293
    of 1952, 18–20, 46, 90, 286, 289,
        295–296
    of 1956, 286, 296
    of 1960, 24, 289, 298–300
    of 1964, 102, 284, 286, 289, 302
    of 1968, 109, 229, 271, 289,
        304–306, 309
    of 1972, 286, 289, 307–308, 310
    of 1976, 272–273, 289, 314,
        316–317
    of 1980, 79–80, 123, 124, 200, 201,
        273, 285, 288, 289, 320–321
    of 1984, 129, 284, 286, 289,
        326–327, 328
    of 1988, 153, 284–285, 289, 314,
        336–338
Ellsberg, Daniel, 310
El Salvador, 140–143, 145, 158–159, 163
Employment Act (1946), 181–182,
    185–186
Endara, Guillermo, 163
Environmentalism, 207–208, 339
Environmental Protection Agency
    (EPA), 321, 325
Equal Employment Opportunities
    Commission (EEOC), 247–248,
    259
Equal Rights Amendment, 234

Ervin, Sam J., 308, 311, 312
Estonia, 2
Ethiopia, 122
Europe, Eastern, 154–157, 171. *See also specific countries*
Europe, Western, 4–7, 12–21, 156–157, 171. *See also specific countries*
European Community, 171
European Economic Community (EEC), 335
European Recovery Program (ERP), 9, 32
Executive privilege, 296–297, 312
Exxon Valdez oil spill, 207

Fair Deal, 186–187, 293
Faisal, King of Iraq, 73
Falwell, Jerry, 320
Family income, 276–278, 332–333, 335, 336
Faubus, Orval E., 222
Federal Bureau of Investigation (FBI), 294, 309–310
Federal Highway Act (1956), 192
Federal Reserve, 202–204, 206, 322, 334, 341
Ferraro, Geraldine A., 286, 326
Finland, 2
Firefighters v. Stotts, 234
Flag burning, 247
Florio, James J., 246
Ford, Gerald R., 289
  and détente, 120–121
  economic policy, 198
  and election of 1976, 272–273, 289, 314, 316–317
  and Rhodesia, 84
  Sinai Accord (1974), 78
  and South Africa, 85
  Supreme Court appointees, 230
  as vice-president, 312
  Vietnam War, 116
Ford Motors, 177, 190
Formosa (Taiwan), 34, 35, 40, 46, 47–49, 119, 122
Formosa Straits crisis, 47–48, 86
Forrestal, James V., 28, 32
Fortas, Abe, 226
France, 20, 22, 69–72, 88–96, 157, 167
Frankfurter, Felix, 223–224
Freedom of Information Act (1966), 297

"Freedom riders," 255
Free speech, 212, 218–219, 238, 246–247
Free Speech Movement, 195–196, 264
Fulbright, J. William, 59, 72, 87, 105
Fullilove v. Klutznick, 233–234
Furman v. Georgia, 230

Galbraith, John Kenneth, 190, 191, 260
Garner, John Nance, 301
In re Gault, 227
Gemayel, Amin, 325
General Motors, 177, 184, 190, 192
Geneva conferences, 22, 23, 91, 92–95, 127–130, 152
Germany, 4, 7–8, 154, 156, 179, 328, 333–335
Germany, East
  Berlin crisis, 10–12, 23, 24–26
  popular uprisings (1989), 154–155
Germany, West, 19, 157
  joins NATO, 16, 20
  missiles in, 128
Ghana, 80
Ghettos, 191–192, 265, 267–268, 270
Gideon v. Wainwright, 226, 237
Ginsberg, Douglas H., 240
Gizenga, Antoine, 81–82
"Glasnost," 152
Glaspie, April, 165
Goldwater, Barry, 82, 145, 230, 286, 289, 302, 304, 306, 319
Gorbachev, Mikhail, 129, 130, 140, 149, 168, 171–174, 328, 331
Gramm-Rudman Act (1985), 339
Grand Alliance, 1–3, 5–6
Great Britain, 3–4, 5–6, 10–12, 22, 47, 69–72, 82–84, 87, 128, 157, 167
Great Depression, 180–181, 195, 283, 321–322
Great Society, 101, 189–190, 208, 260, 272, 301–302, 304
Greece, 5–7, 16, 32, 33
Green Berets, 99, 303
Greene, Harold, 148
Greensboro, North Carolina sit-in, 255
Green v. New Kent County, 223, 232
Grenada, 144, 162, 325
Griggs v. Duke Power, 230, 242
Griswold v. Connecticut, 217

Gross national product (GNP), defined, 180
Grove City College v. Bell, 235–236, 274
Gruening, Ernest, 87
Guatemala, 56–57, 58
Gulf of Tonkin Resolution, 101, 103, 105, 113, 303, 306

Haig, Alexander M., Jr., 124, 141, 312
Haldeman, H. R., 311–313
Hallucinogenic drugs, 196
Harlan, John M., 216
Harriman, W. Averell, 3, 38
Harrington, Michael, 66, 188–189, 260
Harris v. McRae, 230–231
Hart, Gary, 326
Hasenfus, Eugene, 146–147
Hatfield, Mark, 113
"Hawks," 111, 305
Haynsworth, Clement F., 229, 309
Heller, Walter, 188, 197
Helms, Richard, 66
Helsinki Conference, 157
Highways, 192–193, 341
Hill, Anita F., 248
Hills, Carla A., 175, 176
Hispaniola, 64–65
Hiss, Alger, 19, 36–37, 298
Hitler, Adolf, 2, 166, 328
Ho Chi Minh, 88–89, 91, 94, 95, 303
Holmes, Oliver Wendell, 228
Homelessness, 208
Homosexuality, 218, 244
Honduras, 57, 142–143, 145, 158
Hong Kong, 47
Hoover, Herbert, 18, 35, 298
Hoover, J. Edgar, 310
Hopkins, Harry, 28
Hostages, in Iranian Revolution (1979), 79–80, 147, 149, 150, 318–319
House Un-American Activities Committee (HUAC), 36, 294, 298
Housing, 180, 186, 189, 208, 213–214, 258, 259–260, 264, 267, 268, 270, 339
Hughes, Charles Evans, 211
Human rights, 85, 121, 123, 140–141, 152, 174, 175, 250, 251, 318
Humphrey, George, 187
Humphrey, Hubert H., 48, 271, 289, 298, 304–307
Hungary, 154–155
Hunt, E. Howard, 283, 310, 311

Hurley, Patrick J., 27–29
Hussein, King of Jordan, 73, 136
Hussein, Saddam, 165–170, 177
Huston Plan, 309–310

Immigration, 261, 286–287, 339
Impeachment, 45, 78, 313–314
Independent voters, 286–287
India, 52
Indochina War. *See* Vietnam War
Indonesia, 116
Industrial policy, 109
Infant mortality, 276, 277, 281
Inflation, 55, 183–184, 197–201, 273, 318, 319, 322, 333–334
Inter-American Conferences, 55, 57, 60
Intermediate-range nuclear forces (INF), 127, 330–331
Internal Revenue Service, 232, 233, 293
Iran, 3–4, 69, 70, 72–73, 79–80, 123, 137–138, 146–151, 164–165, 175, 318–319, 329–330
Iran-Contra Affair, 146–149, 315, 328–330, 337
Iraq, 68, 70, 72–73, 137–138, 149–151, 164–169, 175
Iron Curtain, 4, 10, 20
Isolationism, 18
Israel, 68–78, 122, 131, 135–137, 151, 165, 166, 170, 199, 292, 318
Italy, 157

Jackson, Henry M., 121, 307
Jackson, Jesse, 273–274, 285, 326
Jacobsen, David, 147
Japan, 1, 27–28, 37, 38, 40, 88, 157, 175–177, 179, 202–203, 333–335
Jaworski, Leon, 308, 312, 313
Jefferson, Thomas, 238–240
Jenner, William, 42, 45
Jiang Jieshi (Chiang Kai-shek), 27–36, 42, 46, 49
Johnson, Louis, 35, 89
Johnson, Lyndon B., 60, 76, 286, 298
    and civil rights, 222, 259–263, 266–267, 301–302, 304
    and Congo civil war, 82
    and Dominican Republic, 64–65, 303
    economic policy, 188–190
    and election of 1964, 102, 284, 286, 289, 302

and election of 1968, 109, 229, 271, 289, 304–306, 309
Great Society, 101, 189–190, 208, 260, 272, 301–302, 304
and Panama, 67
powers of the presidency, 297, 303–306
and Rhodesia, 82–84
Six Day War (1967), 74–75
trip to Germany (1961), 26
Vietnam War, 86–87, 92, 99, 100–109, 197, 303–304
War on Poverty, 188–189, 259, 260, 265, 266, 271, 272, 275, 301–302, 304
Joint Chiefs of Staff (JCS), 9, 28–36, 38–39, 43–45, 47–48, 91, 92, 98, 105–106, 136
Jordan, 68, 73, 136, 170
Judd, Walter, 31, 32, 33
"Junk" bonds, 204, 205, 329

Kaifu, Toshiki, 176
Kasavubu, Joseph, 81–82
Katanga Province, 81–82
Keating, Kenneth, 62
Kelly, John H., 165
Kennan, George F., 7–9, 126, 331
Kennedy, Anthony M., 240, 241, 247
Kennedy, Edward M., 243, 309, 310, 318
Kennedy, Jacqueline, 301
Kennedy, John F.
  Alliance for Progress, 60
  assassination, 100, 259, 301
  Bay of Pigs, 25, 59–60, 99, 283, 300
  Berlin crisis (1961), 24–26
  and civil rights, 222, 258, 298
  and cold war, 298, 301
  and Congo civil war, 81–82
  Cuban missile crisis, 62–64, 301
  economic policy, 183, 188
  and election of 1960, 24, 289, 298–300
  and Nationalist China, 35
  New Frontier, 298, 300–301
  and South Africa, 84
  test-ban treaty, 64, 301
  Vietnam War, 92, 98–100, 301
Kennedy, Robert F., 60, 255, 304
Kent State University, 113, 195, 306
Kenya, 135

Kerner Commission, 266–267, 277–278
Kerry, John, 146
Keynesian economics, 182–183, 187, 188, 197
Khomeini, Ayatollah Ruhollah, 79, 137, 138, 150, 318–319
Khrushchev, Nikita, 22–26, 41, 52, 62–64, 301
Kim Il-Sung, 38, 41
King, Martin Luther, Jr., 249–250, 253–255, 256–258, 262–263, 267–270
Kirkpatrick, Jeane, 145
Kissinger, Henry, 65–67, 76–78, 109–111, 114–115, 118–121
Knowland, William, 35, 36, 40
Kohl, Helmut, 171
Korea, 19
  division, 37–39
  North (People's Democratic Republic), 39, 40–43, 175
  South (Republic of), 38–39, 40–43
Korean War, 20, 37–46, 90, 133, 162, 293–296, 303
Korry, Edward, 66
Kosygin, Aleksei, 74
Kurds, 151, 165, 169
Kuwait, 149–151, 164–169

Laos, 47, 88–90, 94, 98, 99, 106, 306
Latvia, 2
Lawn, Jack, 163
Lebanon, 68, 72–74, 86, 135–137, 170, 325
Left, 288–289
Legislative apportionment, 216, 223–225
Legislative veto, 327
LeMay, Curtis, 115
Leveraged buyouts (LBOs), 204, 205
Lewis, John L., 184
Liberia, 85
Libya, 139–140, 162, 328
Liddy, G. Gordon, 283, 310
Life expectancy, 281
Lithuania, 2, 156
Little, Malcolm (Malcolm X), 266, 272
Little Rock, Arkansas riots, 222
Lodge, Henry Cabot, 100
Luce, Clare Booth, 31
Luce, Henry R., 336
Lumumba, Patrice, 81

MacArthur, Douglas, 29, 38, 39–46
McCarran Internal Security Act, 18
McCarthy, Eugene, 304
McCarthy, Joseph, 18, 19, 37, 45, 90, 219, 293
McCarthyism, 17–18, 21–22, 37, 195, 264, 293, 296
McClesky v. Kemp, 244
McCloy, John J., 37
McCone, John, 102
McCord, James W., 283, 311
McFarlane, Robert C., 146–149, 329–330
McGhee, George, 80
McGovern, George S., 113, 114, 286, 289, 307–308
McNamara, Robert, 74, 86, 99, 101, 104, 106, 127
McNaughton, John, 104, 106–107
Madrid Conference (1991), 170, 340
Malaysia, 116
Malcolm X, 266, 272
Malenkov, Georgi, 21
Manchuria, 28, 30, 31, 32
Manila Conference (1954), 47
Mansfield, Mike, 101, 104–105, 114
Mao Zedong (Mao Tse-Tung), 27, 28, 31, 35, 46, 47, 49–50, 119
Mapp v. Ohio, 227–228, 238
Marijuana, 196, 240
Marshall, George C., 6–8, 10–11, 13, 29–34, 55–56, 68, 69, 89
Marshall, Thurgood, 232, 247, 248, 252–253
Marshall Plan, 7–8, 10, 290
Martin, Joseph, 44–45
Martin v. Wilks, 242, 243
"Massive retaliation," 21
Medical insurance, 186–187, 189–190
Medicare, 189–190, 332, 333, 339
Meese, Edwin, III, 147, 240, 329
Meritor Savings Bank v. Vinson, 235
Mexico, 143
Mideast Peace Agreement (1979), 79, 122
Military, U.S.
  Air Force, 29, 62, 91, 169
  Army, 21, 74, 222
  demobilization after World War II, 4–5
  Marines, 29, 31, 65, 73–74, 98, 135–137, 144, 325

National Guard, 25, 113, 222, 263, 269–270
  Navy, 21, 62, 150–151
Military-industrial complex, 130–133
Milken, Michael R., 204, 329, 332
Milliken v. Bradley, 231–232
Minority groups, 249–282. *See also* Civil rights
Miranda v. Arizona, 226–227, 237, 243–244
Mitchell, John, 230, 271, 309–311, 313
Miyazawe, Kiichi, 177
Mobutu, Joseph, 82, 135
Moi, Daniel arap, 135
Molotov, V. M., 8
Mondale, Walter F., 286, 326, 328
Money society, 203–205
Mongolia, 31
Montgomery, Alabama bus boycott, 249–250, 254–255, 264
"Moral Majority," 320
Morse, Wayne, 87
Moscow Summit (1991), 171
Mossadeq, Mohammed, 69
Moyers, William, 60
Mozambique, 84–85
Mueller v. Allen, 238–239
Mugabe, Robert, 84
Muhammad, Elijah, 265–266
Muskie, Edmund S., 307
Mutual Defense Assistance Act (1949), 16
My Lai massacre, 112
MX missile, 124, 129, 156

Nagasaki, 37
Namibia, 84, 85, 134, 160
Nasser, Gamal Abdel, 70–72, 74, 76
National Association for the Advancement of Colored People (NAACP), 213, 232, 247, 250–255
National Labor Relations Board (NLRB), 185
National Security Council (NSC), 9, 16–17, 33–36, 39–41, 62–63, 86, 89–91, 95, 96, 105–106, 146–149, 315, 328–330, 337
New Deal, 179–180, 182, 185, 186, 208, 211, 250, 288, 291–293, 301
"New equality," 261
"New Frontier," 298, 300–301

New York v. Quarles, 237
New York Times v. Sullivan, 218
New York Times v. United States, 238
New Zealand, 47
Nicaragua, 57, 141–149, 158, 163,
329–330
Nigeria, 85
Nixon, Donald, 309
Nixon, Richard M., 318
campaign for California governorship,
62
and Chile, 65–67
and civil rights, 231, 264, 271–272,
298, 306
and cold war, 298
crime control, 229
and Cuba, 59
and détente, 119–120
economic policy, 198, 199
and election of 1960, 298–300
and election of 1968, 109, 229, 271,
289, 304–306, 309
and election of 1972, 286, 289,
307–308, 310
Hiss case, 36
impeachment inquiry, 78, 313–314
Latin American trip (1958), 58
Nixon Doctrine, 111
pardon by Ford, 316
powers of the presidency, 297,
308–314
resignation, 78, 116, 314
and Rhodesia, 84
and South Africa, 84
and Soviet Union, 308
Supreme Court appointees, 229–231,
271, 309
trip to China, 122, 308
as vice-president, 19, 295–296, 298
Vietnam War, 105, 108–116, 197,
306
Watergate, 76, 78, 283, 307–314
Yom Kippur War (1973), 76–78, 199
Nkrumah, Kwame, 80
Nofziger, Lyn, 329
Noriega, Manuel, 162–164
North, Oliver L., 146–149, 315, 330
North Atlantic Treaty Organization
(NATO), 13–16, 20, 23, 154, 156,
157, 171, 290, 295, 297
Nuclear weapons, 1, 3, 11, 16–17,
20–23, 25, 37, 46, 49, 63–64, 78,

126, 127, 152–157, 169, 171–174,
294, 301, 326–328, 330–331, 340

Obey, David R., 335
Occupational Safety and Health
Administration (OSHA), 321, 325
O'Connor, Sandra Day, 230, 241–242
Office of Economic Opportunity
(OEO), 189, 260, 272, 302, 309
Office of Management and Budget
(OMB), 315–316, 335
Oil, 59, 69, 72, 76, 78, 79, 85, 123,
140, 143, 149–151, 164–169, 170,
176, 190, 193, 199, 200, 202,
207, 318, 336
Olympic Games, 124
Omnibus Trade and Competitiveness
Act (1988), 176
OPEC (Organization of Petroleum
Exporting Countries), 76, 199, 200
Open Door policy, 29
Oppenheimer, J. Robert, 294
Organization of American States (OAS),
55–57, 65, 142, 143, 149, 164
Organization of Petroleum Exporting
Countries (OPEC), 76, 199, 200
Ortega, Daniel, 158

Pahlavi, Shah Mohammed Reza, 79
Pakistan, 47, 70, 72–73, 123, 131,
162, 175
Palestine Liberation Organization (PLO),
78, 135–136
Panama, 143, 162–164, 340
Panama Canal, 53, 62, 67–68, 122, 318
Patronage, political, 286–287
Patterson, Robert P., 28, 32
"Peaceful coexistence," 21, 96–97
Pentagon. *See* U.S. Department of
Defense
Pentagon Papers Case, 230, 238, 309,
310
"Perestroika," 152, 155
Perifoy, John, 56
Perle, Richard, 156
Persian Gulf crisis (1987–1988),
149–151
Persian Gulf War (1991), 164–169,
175, 177–178
Pescadore Islands, 48
Philippines, 40, 47, 52, 88
Phillips, Howard, 153

Phillips, Kevin, 331
Plessy v. Ferguson, 219–220
Podgorny, Nikolai, 114
Poindexter, John M., 147–149,
    329–330
Poland, 2, 8, 154–155
Political action committees (PACs),
    314, 338
Pollution, 207–208
Pol Pot, 116, 134
Poor People's March, 269, 270–271
Portugal, 84
Potsdam Conference, 28
Potter, David, 190
Poverty, 191–192, 196, 208–209,
    230–231, 237, 260, 267–269,
    275–277, 279, 298, 301, 335
Powell, Lewis F., Jr., 230, 233, 240
Presidency, powers of, 289–314,
    316–342
Prisoners of war (POWs), 46, 115
Privacy, 217–218, 229, 230, 240,
    244–246, 248

Qaddafi, Muammar al-, 139–140,
    328

Racism. *See* Civil rights
Railroads, 184, 192, 251
Randolph, A. Philip, 251
"Rap" Brown Amendment, 270
Rayburn, Sam, 10
Reagan, Ronald, 67–68, 273, 285
    Africa policy, 134–135
    Caribbean policy, 143–144, 162, 325
    Central American policy, 140–146
    and civil rights, 233–236, 274–275
    cold war, 124–151, 153
    economic policy, 186, 201–202, 274,
        320–324, 333–336
    and election of 1976, 272–273, 289,
        314, 316–317
    and election of 1980, 79–80, 123,
        124, 200, 201, 273, 285, 288,
        289, 320–321
    and election of 1984, 129, 284, 286,
        289, 326–327, 328
    Iran-Contra Affair, 146–149, 315,
        328, 329–330, 337
    Middle East policy, 133–140,
        146–151, 325
    military-industrial complex under,
        130–133
    powers of the presidency, 320–331
    and Soviet Union, 326, 328,
        330–331
    Strategic Defense Initiative (SDI),
        328, 330–331
    Supreme Court appointees, 230,
        239–240, 248, 329
    tax policy, 332
Reaganomics, 274, 320–324, 333–336
Real estate, 202–207
Recessions, 199–202, 206–207
Red Scare, 264, 293
Reed v. Reed, 236
*Regents of the University of California
    v. Bakke*, 233
Rehabilitation Act (1973), 264
Rehnquist, William H., 230, 237,
    239–248
Republic of China (Taiwan), 119, 122.
    See also Taiwan (Formosa)
Reuther, Walter, 184
Reverse discrimination, 233–234, 241,
    261
Reynolds v. Sims, 224–225
Rhee, Syngman, 38, 39, 47
Rhodesia, 81–85
Richardson, Elliot L., 312
Ridgway, Matthew, 45–46, 48
Right, 288–289
Right to die, 218, 244–245
Rio Pact (1947), 55, 58, 144, 164
Riots (1965–1967), 267–268, 270
Rockefeller, Nelson A., 272, 302
Rodino, Peter W., 308, 312–313
Roe v. Wade, 230, 246
Rogers, William P., 76, 296–297
Romania, 154–155
Roosevelt, Eleanor, 251, 290
Roosevelt, Franklin D., 5, 27, 29, 31,
    37, 179–180, 182, 183, 185, 186,
    208, 211, 248, 250, 251,
    288–293, 301
Rostow, Eugene V., 126
Rostow, Walt W., 74–75, 99, 105–106
Roszak, Theodore, 195–196
Rusk, Dean, 63, 99, 100, 105

Sadat, Anwar al-, 76–79, 318
Salomon Brothers, 204
SALT (Strategic Arms Limitation
    Talks), 120–124, 130, 318
Sandinistas, 141–143, 149, 158
Satterthwaite, Joseph, 81

"Saturday Night Massacre," 312
Saudi Arabia, 72–73, 131, 137, 166, 170–171
Savimbi, Jonas, 85, 134, 160
Savings and loan crisis, 205–206, 329, 339
Scalia, Antonin, 239, 241, 247
Scammon, Richard M., 275
Schlesinger, Arthur M., Jr., 25
Schools. *See* Education
Schwarzkopf, Norman, 340
Secrecy, presidential, 296–297, 312
Segregation. *See* Civil rights
Segretti, Donald, 307, 311
Selma, Alabama demonstrations (1965), 262–263, 272
Service, John S., 27, 28, 29
Sexual harassment, 235, 248
Shriver, Sargent, 189, 308
Shultz, George, 139, 146, 151, 198
"Silent majority," 111, 304
Sinai Accord (1974), 78
Singapore, 116, 176
Sirica, John J., 308, 310–313
Sit-ins, 255, 256
Six Day War (1967), 74–75
Slavery, 261, 270
Smith, Al, 298
Smith, H. Alexander, 42
Smith Act (1940), 212, 217
Social security, 186, 189, 194, 203, 302, 332, 333, 335
Somalia, 122
Sorensen, Theodore, 63, 81
Souter, David H., 241
South Africa, Republic of, 81–82, 84–85, 134–135, 160
Southeast Asia Treaty Organization (SEATO), 47, 105, 121
Southern Christian Leadership Conference (SCLC), 255, 256, 264, 271
"Southern Manifesto," 221
Souvanna Phouma, 98
Soviet Union. *See* Union of Soviet Socialist Republics (USSR)
Spain, 16
Sputnik, 22
Stagflation, 201
Stalin, Joseph, 2–3, 21, 28, 37, 41
START (Strategic Arms Reduction Talks), 127–130, 154, 171
Statutory rape, 236

Steel industry, 179, 192, 200, 295, 336
Stevens, John Paul, 230
Stevenson, Adlai E., 49, 63, 287, 296, 298
Stock market, 206–207, 322, 329
Strategic Arms Limitation Talks (SALT I and SALT II), 120–124, 130, 318
Strategic Arms Reduction Talks (START), 127–130, 154, 171
Strategic Defense Initiative (SDI), 127, 129–130, 153–154, 156, 328, 330–331
Stuart, J. Leighton, 34
Student Nonviolent Coordinating Committee (SNCC), 255, 262, 264, 268
Students for a Democratic Society (SDS), 195
Suburban expansion, 191–192, 264
Suez crisis (1954–1956), 70–72
"Supply Side Economics," 201, 320, 321–324
Supreme Court, 210–248, 251–253, 255, 270, 274, 295, 313–314, 325, 327. *See also specific presidents*
Swann v. Charlotte-Mecklenburg Board of Education, 231
Symington, Stuart, 298
Syria, 68, 72–73, 75, 76, 170, 175

Taft, Robert A., 5, 9–10, 13, 18, 35, 36, 42, 289, 295, 325
Taft-Hartley Act, 184–185, 186, 292
Taiwan (Formosa), 34, 35, 40, 42, 48–49, 119, 122
Tax policy, 180, 183, 187, 188, 197, 201–203, 213, 223, 315–316, 320, 326, 329, 332, 338, 339
Tax Reform Act (1986), 203
Taylor, Maxwell, 99, 101, 102, 105–106
Telephones, 264
Television, 194, 287, 288, 299–300, 319, 326, 330
Teller, Edward, 127
Teng Hsiao-Ping (Deng Xiaoping), 117
Terrorism, 136–140, 141, 143, 150–151, 158–159, 249, 254, 255, 259
Terry v. Ohio, 229
Test Ban Treaty (1963), 64, 301
Tet Offensive, 107–108, 304

Thailand, 47, 98, 116
Thieu, Nguyen Van, 111, 114–115
Third World, 51–68, 157–162. *See
also specific countries*
Thomas, Clarence, 247–248
Thornburgh, Richard, 341
Three Mile Island incident, 207
Thurmond, J. Strom, 252, 273, 289,
291–293
Tiananmen Square massacre, 174
Tito, Josep Bros, 11
Tower, John, 147–149
Tower Commission, 330
Truman, Harry S., 228, 296, 297, 303,
318
 Berlin crisis (1948–1949), 11, 12
 bipartisanship, 5
 and civil rights, 251–252, 290, 292,
 293–294
 cold war, 1, 3
 economic policy, 182, 183–185,
 186–187, 189
 and election of 1948, 13, 34, 252,
 288–289, 290–293
 Fair Deal, 186–187, 293
 Hiss case, 19, 36–37, 298
 and Iran, 69
 Israeli independence, 68, 69
 Korean War, 37–46
 MacArthur controversy, 43–46
 and Nationalist China, 27–36
 and NATO, 13–16
 and People's Republic of China,
 35–36
 powers of the presidency, 290–295
 reorganization of national defense, 3,
 9
 and Third World, 52–56
 Truman Doctrine (1947), 5–7, 33,
 72–73, 290
 veto of McCarran Internal Security
 Act, 18
 Vietnam War, 89–90
Trump, Donald, 204
Tshombe, Moise, 81–82
Tuchman, Barbara, 128
Turkey, 5–7, 16, 32, 63, 70, 72–73,
157
Tydings, Millard, 18

U-2 incident (1960), 24
Ukraine, 173

Underclass, 208–209, 276–278. *See
also* Poverty
Unemployment, 55, 180–182, 187,
197–199, 201, 202, 260, 265,
267, 276, 277, 280, 318, 319,
321–322, 325, 341
Union of Soviet Socialist Republics
(USSR), 1–4, 8, 10–12, 16–17,
20–46, 52, 56–57, 59–60, 62–64,
69, 72–78, 84–85, 88–89, 97,
114, 117, 120–130, 133–134, 141,
152–157, 159, 161–162, 166,
168–169, 171–174, 177–179, 199,
308, 319, 326, 328, 330–331, 340
Unions, 121, 184–185, 200, 234, 251,
287, 292, 295, 336
United Arab Republic (UAR), 73–74
United Fruit Company, 56–57
United Nations, 3–4, 6, 12, 39–46,
50, 62–64, 67, 69, 81–84,
159–162, 166, 168–170, 174–175,
177–178, 340
U.S. Department of Defense, 170
 budget, 9, 16, 25, 124–133, 156,
 201, 320, 321–324, 333, 335
 establishment of, 9
 procurement scandals, 328–329
 and Vietnam, 102, 104, 106
U.S. Department of Health, Education,
and Welfare (HEW), 187
U.S. Department of State, 19, 28, 29,
31–34, 48–50, 88–90, 141
U.S. Strategic Air Command (SAC), 20
U.S. v. Leon, 238
U.S. v. Nixon, 313–314
University of California at Berkeley,
195, 264

Vance, Cyrus, 121–122
Vandenberg, Arthur H., 5, 6, 12, 17,
33, 34, 55, 290
Venezuela, 58, 143
Vietnam, 47, 91–95, 117, 156,
159–160
Vietnam War, 49, 86–117, 121, 133,
162, 168, 189, 195–198, 230,
266, 268, 301, 303–304, 306,
314–316
Vinson, Frederick M., 211–214
Violence, racial, 249–250, 259, 270,
272, 275. *See also* Terrorism
Volcker, Paul A., 334

"Voodoo economics," 320, 321–324
Voting, 195, 255, 262–264, 271,
 272–274, 283–289, 321. *See also
 entries beginning* "Elections"

Wallace, George C., 256, 262, 271,
 273, 304–305, 307
Wallace, Henry A., 5, 9, 13, 288–289,
 291–292
Walsh, Lawrence E., 148, 330
Wards Cove v. Atonio, 242, 243
War on Poverty, 188–189, 259, 260,
 265, 266, 271, 272, 275,
 301–302, 304
War Powers Act (1973), 136, 140, 144,
 315, 325, 327
Warren, Earl, 214–229, 240, 253
Warsaw Pact, 20, 154, 156, 157
Washington, Booker T., 250
Washington, D.C., marches on,
 258–259, 269–271
Watergate, 76, 78, 116, 283, 307–314
Wattenberg, Ben J., 275
Watts riots, 264, 265
*Webster v. Human Reproductive
 Services*, 245
Wedemeyer, Albert C., 28, 30, 32–33,
 36
Weinberger, Caspar, 128, 129
Welfare state, expansion of, 179–180,
 181–182, 185–190, 287, 293
Westmoreland, William C., 101,
 103–104, 106, 108

White, Byron R., 241, 242
Wilder, L. Douglas, 246, 273
Wilson, Edwin G., 5
Wilson, Woodrow, 5
Wiretapping, 228–229, 230, 240,
 308–310
Wofford, Harris, 341
Wolfe, Tom, 205
Women's rights, 234–237, 243, 248,
 264, 286
Woodward, Robert, 308, 311
World Court, 145–146
World War I, 182, 261
World War II, 1–5, 88, 181–185, 214,
 250–251
Wright, Jim, 147

Yalta Conference, 28, 29, 31, 36, 37,
 94
"Yankee imperialism," 58, 94
Yeltsin, Boris, 172–174, 340
Yemen, 166, 168
Yom Kippur War (1973), 76–78, 199
*Youngstown Sheet and Tube Co. v.
 Sawyer*, 295
Yu Daway (Yu Ta-wei), 30
Yugoslavia, 11
"Yuppies," 204

Zaire, 82, 85, 135
Zhou Enlai, 42
Zimbabwe, 82–84

ABOUT THE AUTHORS

Albert C. Ganley, a graduate of Williams and Cornell, has taught history at Williams College, Vestal (N.Y.) Central School, Manhasset (N.Y.) High School, La Jolla (Calif.) Country Day School, and in the Harvard-Newton program. A former John Hay Fellow at Harvard, he is former chair of the Phillips Exeter Academy history department and the Cowles Professor of the Humanities, Emeritus. He is author of *The Progressive Movement* and *Japan: A Short History.*

Thomas T. Lyons, a graduate of Harvard College and Graduate School of Education, taught U.S. history at Dartmouth College and Mt. Hermon School. Earlier a fellow at Wesleyan and Stanford, he is former chair of the history department at Phillips Academy, Andover. He is author of *Presidential Power in the New Deal, The Supreme Court and Individual Rights in Contemporary Society, Reconstruction and the Race Problem, Black Leadership in American History,* and other books. In addition, he was honored with a Distinguished Secondary School Teaching Award from Harvard University in 1966 and the New England History Teacher Association's Kidger Award in 1985. Presently he teaches U.S. history at Phillips Academy.

Gilbert T. Sewall is president of the Center for Education Studies and director of the American Textbook Council in New York City. A former instructor of history at Phillips Academy, Andover, and education editor at *Newsweek,* he is author of *Necessary Lessons: Decline and Renewal in American Schools.* His articles on education and other subjects have appeared in *Fortune,* the *New York Times,* the *Wall Street Journal,* and many other publications.